Florence Nightingale,
Feminist

ALSO BY JUDITH LISSAUER CROMWELL

*Dorothea Lieven: A Russian Princess in
London and Paris, 1785–1857* (McFarland, 2007)

Florence Nightingale, Feminist

JUDITH LISSAUER CROMWELL

McFarland & Company, Inc., Publishers
Jefferson, North Carolina, and London

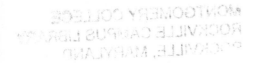
LIBRARY OF CONGRESS CATALOGUING-IN-PUBLICATION DATA

Cromwell, Judith Lissauer, 1935–
    Florence Nightingale, feminist / Judith Lissauer Cromwell.
      p.   cm.
    Includes bibliographical references and index.

    ISBN 978-0-7864-7092-1
    softcover : acid free paper ∞

    1. Nightingale, Florence, 1820–1910 — Biography.
2. Nursing — England — History. 3. Feminism —
History —19th century. 4. Sex role — History —19th century.
5. Women — England — History —19th century. I. Title.
RT37.N5C76 2013
610.73092 — dc23   2013002073
[B]

BRITISH LIBRARY CATALOGUING DATA ARE AVAILABLE

On the cover: Florence Nightingale, copied by Henry Hering,
Elliott & Fry, half-plate glass copy negative, 1858 (1950s)
(© National Portrait Gallery, London); background image
© 2013 Shutterstock

Manufactured in the United States of America

*McFarland & Company, Inc., Publishers
  Box 611, Jefferson, North Carolina 28640
  www.mcfarlandpub.com*

To my mother,
Charlotte Breuer Lissauer, M.D.

Liberty ... that everybody should have the power of developing himself, without hurting anybody else.—Florence Nightingale

Table of Contents

Preface

One of the world's most famous women has inspired much written material. But no one has so far examined Florence Nightingale's life from a post-feminist perspective. This unique viewpoint, combined with archival research, forms the basis of *Florence Nightingale, Feminist*. It is the first full-length, post-feminist account of this modern woman's life.

In-depth review of Nightingale's personal papers at the British Library, the Claydon House Archives, and the Wellcome Library sheds new light on Florence's fraught, life-shaping relationship with her mother, as well as on Nightingale's other key connections. Her deep ties to family and friends empowered Florence to develop into the renowned figure she would become.

Creator of modern hospital nursing and pioneer of public health, Nightingale, to contemporaries, personified the Victorian ideal of nurturing female. Hindsight allows us to appreciate how Florence's achievements superseded that stereotype. She established a profession that not only suited women but also proved acceptable for them within the context of her time. This trailblazing accomplishment anchors Nightingale among the founders of modern feminism.

Child of conventional, upper-class Victorian rearing, young Florence identified an evil in the world: the waste of female talent. She yearned for something "springing from a truer foundation than conventional life." Nightingale felt the need for a profession, a "necessary occupation," something to satisfy and make full use of her faculties.

Convinced of her singular destiny to serve God and humanity by helping the poor and sick, Florence resolved to dedicate her life to nursing. Appointed superintendent, during the Crimean War, of the British army's first female nursing establishment, Nightingale had to do "more than any other woman had to do before." Success in the face of desperate odds made her Great Britain's only heroic figure to emerge from that war. This experience clarified Florence's purpose in life and invigorated it with importance. She must shield her "children," the common soldiers, from another Crimean catastrophe: the needless death of thousands due to preventable causes.

Ensuing years devoted to army sanitation at home and in India made Nightingale the first woman to "direct the labors of" two government offices. Concomitantly, her eponymous, groundbreaking nurse training school raised the hospital nurse from despised, ignorant, inebriated domestic drudge to valued medical professional. Florence Nightingale thus provided women with a career and a path to financial independence.

Rebellion played no part in her success. In the straitlaced, rarefied Victorian society in which her family wealth and connections placed Florence, revolt would have meant cutting herself off from family and friends. Nightingale cared too deeply about these relationships to sever them. Rather, she insisted on her right to fulfill her dream.

Belief in her cause gave Florence the strength to renounce erotic love and marriage as incompatible with full-time nursing. But she did give full rein to her robust maternal streak. Debilitating illness forced a choice: either focus on her "children" or continue to enjoy "all that makes life pleasant." Florence opted for the former. From age 37 until her death, Nightingale refused to let weakness and pain affect the zeal and tenacity with which she introduced basic sanitation to army installations, thereby saving thousands of lives. At the same time, Florence attended to every detail of her school, including the personal and professional growth of each "daughter."

Florence Nightingale, Feminist owes a debt of gratitude to many. I particularly want to acknowledge the British Library Board and the Claydon House Trust, who have kindly allowed me to quote from their collections, as well as the Henry Bonham-Carter Will Trust and its administrator, Radcliffes-LeBrasseur, for generous permission to quote from the Florence Nightingale papers located in the Wellcome Library and elsewhere.

For gracious permission to quote from *Ever Yours, Florence Nightingale: Selected Letters*, my thanks to editor Martha Vicinus; my appreciation to the American Philosophical Society, publisher of *Florence Nightingale in Rome, Letters Written in the Winter of 1847–1848*, Mary Keele, ed.; my appreciation to the Wilfrid Laurier University Press, publisher of *Collected Works of Florence Nightingale*, Lynn McDonald, ed., for allowing me to use extracts from that work.

Every effort has been made to contact the copyright holders for material contained in Ida B. O'Malley's *Florence Nightingale, 1820–1856: A Study of Her Life Down to the End of the Crimean War*, Thornton Butterworth, Limited, London, 1931; likewise for Cecil B. F. G. Woodham-Smith's *Florence Nightingale*, Constable, London, 1950; and similarly for the owner/copyright holder of the William Edward Nightingale image. If, for any reason, proper acknowledgment has not been made, the copyright holders are invited to contact the author in care of the publisher.

I appreciate the consideration of those institutions that have let me use items in their holdings as illustrations: Claydon House Trust; Florence Nightingale Museum Trust; Hampshire Record Office; Institute of Our Lady of Mercy Archives; author Christine Freeman Jenking; National Portrait Gallery, London; and Photographic Survey, the Courtauld Institute of Art, London.

My recognition of their efforts on my behalf to librarians at Columbia University, the Costume Institute of New York's Metropolitan Museum of Art, and, particularly, the New York Public Library; librarians in the manuscript reading room of the British Library and the Wellcome Library; archivists at Claydon House and the Florence Nightingale Museum.

I am grateful for the patience and wisdom of medical advisors Myron Buchman, M.D., and Herman Steinberg, M.D.

And, finally, my thanks to my family and friends for their support and forbearance.

Introduction

Most people have heard of Florence Nightingale. Not all know why. And if they do, "nurse" or "Crimean War" can scarcely be expected to generate excitement. This book, the first full-length account of Nightingale's life to be written by a woman from a post-feminist perspective, will engage today's reader.

For decades biographers have shown Nightingale as manipulating a psychosomatic, possibly imagined, illness to force her will on family and friends. Modern scholarship proves otherwise. This turns her from a neurotic into a compelling woman who had a dream in the days when such dreams were taboo, and makes more poignant her epic struggle to succeed.

Now is the time to revisit Nightingale's narrative, for today we see a woman's position differently from prior generations. Yet, we are linked to those generations. When Florence came into the world (1820) railroads did not yet crisscross Great Britain. Females were held to be inferior to men. Marriage constituted the only career open to women. At the end of her life (1910) Nightingale talked on the telephone. Thanks to her, females had a respectable profession and a career path to financial independence. In the same year, my nine-year-old mother dreamed an incredible dream: to become a doctor. Today, no barriers exist to what my granddaughters may aspire to be. Our past shapes our present. That is why Florence Nightingale's story is timely.

Born into wealth and privilege, brought up in the cream of Victorian society, a precocious, fun-loving six-year-old longed to be useful — to nurse the indigent sick. "My daydreams were all of hospitals"; starting in her teens, Florence "visited them whenever I could."[1] But before she satisfied her longing to have "a profession, a trade, a necessary occupation, something to fill & employ my faculties,"[2] Florence had to free herself from "the prison called family." That meant hurting those she loved most — her parents and sister.

Coincidence pitchforked Nightingale into the Crimean War (1854–1856). Appointed chief of the first female nursing cadre to enter that most hidebound of male bastions — a British military hospital — she gave the world a dramatic example of what energy and resolve can achieve in a desperate situation. "Though I am unable to tell you who was responsible for leaving the sick in that wretched condition, I am able to tell you who rescued them from it."[3] Conditions propelled Nightingale into more than nursing. Her genius "lay in coming to hospitals miserably disorganized or rather unorganized, & in organizing them."[4]

Nightly, lantern in hand, Florence made her rounds through four miles of wards "thickly lined with beds laid on low trestles raised a few inches from the ground." A "dim light burned here and there." During this endless and "not easily forgotten" walk, she ministered to hundreds of patients. Nightingale's "manner to the men" was "so tender and kind."[5] They revered the Lady with the Lamp. And a grateful nation turned its only heroic figure to emerge from the Crimean carnage into an icon.

"I can never forget"[6] that fractured army of bloody, lice-infested skeletons. It flooded into Florence's hospitals during the first dreadful Crimean winter. Despite extreme physical debility due to a disease caught during the war that tied Nightingale to bed for 30 years, she devoted herself to curing conditions that triggered the Crimean calamity: the death of thousands due to easily avoidable causes.

As a female, Nightingale could not be the public face of reform. So she worked behind the scenes. And inspired others. Exuding charm and wit, vitality and fervor, Florence, no less than her goals, attracted politicians and professionals as crucial allies.

Consequently, the army introduced high sanitary standards to barracks and hospitals throughout the land. Thousands of soldiers owed their lives to Florence Nightingale.

Many served in Britain's premier colony. So Florence spearheaded sanitary reform for army installations on the Indian subcontinent. "You initiated the reform which initiated public opinion which made things possible, and now there is not a station in India where there is not something doing."[7] Nonetheless, Nightingale believed that "unless you improve the sanitary condition of the civil population you cannot insure immunity for the soldiers from epidemics."[8] True, thousands of Indians still died from typhoid and cholera. But thousands lived because a bedridden female who had never been to India taught civil, military, and medical officials what must be done to bring basic hygiene to the entire land and how to do it. No senior India official would dream of taking up his post without first visiting Miss Nightingale.

She did not invent modern hospital nursing. Florence prepared to become a nurse by studying medical institutions at home and abroad. She gained hands-on experience through nursing friends, family, and the poor on her father's estates. When the Crimean War gave Nightingale a chance to act, she organized practical ideas into a coherent whole, which she infused with humanity or what a close friend called Flo's Incredible Bonté.

By insisting that probationers at her pioneering Nightingale School for Nurse Training have sterling character and receive rigorous scientific and practical education, Florence raised nursing from despised drudgery into a respectable occupation. Zeal for sanitary reform, expertise in hospital organization, and commitment to statistics made her *the* formative influence on professional hospital nursing. And her resolve that nursing be a secular vocation gave it credibility. Within a decade, Nightingale's school effected the evolution of nursing into a career that empowered women with economic independence.

One of history's most well-known women has motivated many to examine her life story. Why, therefore, place another book on already crowded shelves?

The basic facts of Florence Nightingale's life are consistent. Interpretations differ.

All biographies derive from Sir Edward Cook's comprehensive *Life of Florence Nightingale* (1913), commissioned by her family shortly after Nightingale's death. The first to have unlimited access to her papers, Cook also interviewed those who knew her. Ida O'Malley's *Florence Nightingale* (1931) and Cecil Woodham-Smith's *Florence Nightingale* (1951) used family papers unavailable to Cook and later lost or destroyed.

Several collections of Nightingale's letters, plus her books and articles, have been published. Biographies usually focus on one or more facets of Florence's life, work, or personality. Many worship. Others belittle. Tomes by or on contemporaries abound. My full-length biography takes the foregoing into consideration and, with the help of archival research, adds new insights.

The reader will meet a lively, arresting young woman who attracted a wide circle of friends of both sexes, let alone eligible suitors; a brilliant scholar who read Hebrew, Greek, and Latin, not to mention Egyptian hieroglyphics; a skilled and compassionate nurse; an exceptional organizer; a witty conversationalist; and a faithful servant of God.

Shaped by the central conflict in her life — how to reconcile a desire to please her determined, conventional mother with a resolve to fulfill her dream — Florence Nightingale made an indelible and positive impact on women's issues at a time when females were viewed as the weaker and inferior sex and women's liberation had barely begun to enter the national dialogue.

1

The Child Is Mother of the Woman

Daughters, brought up in a conventional life, seldom wish for anything else. A few ... wish for something springing from a truer foundation than conventional life. It is for these sufferers to lead the way.[1]— Florence Nightingale

The first idea I can recollect when I was a child was a desire to nurse the sick. My daydreams were all of hospitals and I visited them whenever I could. I never communicated it to anyone — it would have been laughed at — but I thought God had called me to serve him in that way.[2]— Florence Nightingale

On a murky, rainswept November morning in 1854, a battered British steamer made its weary way past Constantinople's gleaming mosques and minarets, to anchor gratefully off the fabled Golden Horn. The ship carried a motley group of women. Great Britain's government had sent them to nurse the thousands of casualties crowding into its grossly inadequate army hospitals during the first dreadful weeks of the Crimean War.

No female had ever before nursed in a military medical facility. Florence Nightingale had been preparing for this moment all her life. The only "person in England ... capable of organizing such a scheme"[3] looked as "you would expect in any other well-bred woman who may have seen perhaps rather more than thirty years of life; her manner and countenance are prepossessing, and this without" having "positive beauty; it is a face not easily forgotten, pleasing in its smile, with an eye betokening great self-possession, and giving, when she wishes, a quiet look of firm determination to every feature."[4]

A respected family of prosperous, upper-middle-class manufacturers and bankers, liberal in politics and Unitarian[5] in religion, rooted in hilly Derbyshire, England's industrial heartland, nurtured Florence's father. A bachelor uncle left him property with the proviso that the boy take his uncle's surname. So William Edward Shore became William Edward Nightingale, known as WEN.

Under his uncle's will, if WEN had no son his property would pass to his only sibling, then her eldest son. But money generated by the discovery of lead on his land belonged to WEN absolutely. By his twenty-first birthday (1815) wise investment had made WEN rich.

Tall and slim with courteous mien and sterling character, educated at a top academy, then Edinburgh and Cambridge universities, the scholarly young man stretched his mind further with overseas travel. "Modest curiosity about everything, a surprised, innocent, incredulous smile as he listened intently,"[6] WEN indulged in his favorite activities — reading and conversation. A charming dilettante, if not dreamer, handsome and introspective, WEN spent his happiest hours in his library. But the financial acumen inherited from shrewd Derbyshire forbears made Florence Nightingale's father an astute custodian of his wealth.

—ɯ—

Florence's maternal grandfather, liberal Unitarian William Smith, amassed a mercantile fortune in the nation's capital. And used his seat in parliament to advocate better conditions for sweated workers, abolition of slavery, and rights for Dissenters and Jews. The Smiths were active in London's cultural scene as well, and entertained generously at their country house. They had ten handsome, energetic children. The most attractive, gregarious and elegant Frances, known as Fanny, loved life and pleasure.

She got engaged to a debonair but impecunious army officer, younger son of an earl and, thus, part of Britain's ruling elite. As his wife, ambitious Fanny would gain entrée into influential, upper-crust society. For the hereditary, land-owning aristocracy still dominated society and politics, which were closely knit. Upper-middle-class

William Edward Nightingale, 1794–1874. Known as WEN, Florence's wealthy and intellectual father, the first of her immediate family to come round to supporting Florence's nursing career, taught Florence "all I ever knew ... gave me all the ideas I ever had" (author photograph from image displayed [August 2009] at the Florence Nightingale Museum, London).

families like the merchant Smiths and manufacturing Shores might be wealthy, but even the richest among them could not match the landed magnates in money, prestige, and power.

Fanny's future parents-in-law frowned on the marriage of their nobly born son to a daughter of commerce, and a Unitarian to boot. So Fanny asked her father to find a well-paid army post for her beloved and to settle some money on them. William Smith failed to find a position for his prospective son-in-law; and he regretfully informed his daughter that recent financial reverses ruled out his support of her marriage.

Unwilling to count the world well lost for love, Fanny broke her engagement. A year later she accepted her brother's university friend, wealthy William Edward Nightingale.

Fanny's lively, close-knit family disapproved. Beautiful and worldly, kind and generous, Fanny could be extremely stubborn if thwarted. Quiet, pensive WEN, exceedingly intelligent but hardly ambitious, preferred his library.

WEN's family disliked the engagement, too. He did not need wealth, but WEN did need sons. Twenty-nine-year-old Fanny, six years WEN's senior, seemed old for childbearing. And in cohesive Unitarian society her former engagement did Fanny's reputation little good. Still, WEN had fallen deeply in love, so his parents gave in gracefully.

WEN knew he had not been Fanny's first choice but thought she valued his utter reliability and would grow to love him and make a good, if demanding, wife. She did.

—⟋⟍—

Three years before Florence Nightingale's parents married, the battle of Waterloo (1815) ended twenty years of war and heralded the heyday of Great Britain's global hegemony. She led the industrial revolution, owned the world's largest empire, and her navy ruled the seas. Travel had again become safe. So travel-loving WEN took his bride on an extensive Continental honeymoon. After a year Frances (after her mother) Parthenope (after the ancient Greek colony pre-dating Naples, city of her birth) came into the world with considerable difficulty.

Exhausted, the new mother failed to provide enough milk. Medical wisdom mandated only breast milk for at least the first nine months of life. Fanny took fright, more especially as her husband became ill. This did little to help the flow of Fanny's milk. Baby Parthe sickened, seemed near death. Willful Fanny gave in. She hired a wet nurse.

This experience convinced Fanny that her firstborn needed special protection. Mother and daughter formed a singular tie.

A year later (May 12, 1820), a second Nightingale infant greeted the world, this time in a large, elegant villa standing on the hill overlooking Florence's Duomo and Boboli Garden. Fanny and WEN also named this daughter for the city of her birth, but unlike her sister, the infant got only one name. Indeed, little Flo's birth rather disappointed her parents, for the Nightingale will left WEN's property to his sister if he had no son. Still, Fanny had conceived easily, so she and her husband felt confident of more babies.

They were wrong.

While balmy spring sunshine bathed the villa's beautiful park and filtered through the trees onto baby Flo's lace-trimmed bassinet, Fanny lay ill. Alarmed at her failure to provide enough milk for little Parthe barely a year before, Fanny made no attempt to breast-feed this time. Later she explained to Florence that she had been unable to nurse her, but the younger daughter faulted her mother for not, at least, having tried.

WEN would have been happy to wend his leisurely way around the Continent for many more months, but ambitious, energetic Fanny had other ideas. She sought social success, the only achievement possible for a Victorian female. So after three years the Nightingales with their two little girls and attendant servants crossed the choppy, gray-green Channel to England.

—⚏—

Before his marriage Florence's father bought land and designed a modern dwelling for it. WEN could well have afforded to build a baronial pile but instead used a local Derbyshire contractor and gray Derbyshire stone for his ascetic gentleman's residence.

Lea Hurst stood on a quiet country road. A simple wooden gate hanging between plain stone pillars indicated its driveway, which opened to a circular lawn with gravel path and flower beds. At the back, stone steps connected a succession of grassy sloping terraces, in spring and early summer full of wallflowers, pansies, forget-me-nots, and peonies; apple trellises and lavender bushes made a border.

The main rooms of the Elizabethan-style house with its clustered chimneys, peaked gables, and stone mullioned windows opened onto the garden. Full of light, they boasted a superb view. Buttercups, bluebells, and scented clover carpeted the wooded heights and soft green hills in early summer; later wild roses hung on hedgerows and white blossomed elder bushes studded the landscape. Below in the valley burbled the Derwent River. From the house, a long path with magnificent vistas wound to the top of the woods.

Yet, Florence's mother felt dissatisfied, not to mention lonely. True, WEN's family lived nearby, but Fanny missed London's lively cultural and political scene, missed her large, ebullient family, and missed the social status of daughter to a member of parliament. Raised in southern England, used to her father's urbane London house, still under the cosmopolitan sway of her Continental travels, Fanny felt cut off in Derbyshire. And its harsh winter brought a nasty shock. Biting winds blew; blizzards blocked the steep roads; Lea Hurst's stone floors froze Fanny's feet. But worst of all, her little girls got bronchitis.

Having developed fashionably delicate health after her return from the Continent, Fanny could, and did, go to the seaside to bathe in healing salt water. But it would be far better for her and for thin, fragile Parthe and Flo to live closer to the ocean. So Fanny convinced her husband that although Derbyshire would suffice for the summer, they needed a larger house in a warmer part of England for the rest of the year.

Concerned for his Fanny's well-being no less than their daughters' welfare, WEN searched for a year before he found what he knew would please his wife. Four-thousand-acre Embley Park stood within easy reach of the sea and of London. The estate boasted a majestic stand of oaks, beeches, and cedars of Lebanon opening onto fields of wildflowers, and lush gardens famed for azaleas and camellia trees. Rhododendron thickets lined the long road leading to the house, which commanded a vista of verdant Hampshire farmland. Several socially prominent families lived nearby; so did Fanny's wealthily married sisters. And unlike industrial Derbyshire, rural Hampshire had good shooting — a must for any female aspiring to be a successful hostess.

Embley provided Florence's charming, poised mother with a fitting stage for her social ambitions. Fanny invited the intellectuals and politicians she knew from her parents' liberal, Unitarian drawing room together with neighboring aristocrats. Unitarianism meant little to Fanny as a religion, so she dropped it in favor of the more fashionable Church of England. This did not signify lack of sincerity. Fanny Nightingale merely preferred a more socially acceptable milieu in which to practice her piety and raise her daughters.

Florence's mother ran her household faultlessly. Embley meant comfort, diversion, and good company. Within ten years, Fanny succeeded in elevating the Nightingales into England's elite. "My mother is a genius," Flo later wrote. "She has the genius of order, to make a place, to organize a parish, to form society. She has obtained by her own exertions the best society in England." She "has a genius for doing all that she wants to do."[7]

The Nightingales now spent their summers and October at Lea Hurst, the Season (spring) and September in London, and the rest of the year at Embley.

Victorians put mothers in charge of raising daughters. And a mother's main duty consisted of marrying her daughters well. Marriage to a man of character and means connoted success, indeed, a female's sole path to happiness and purpose in life. For members of the fragile and inferior sex needed the protection that only strong and superior males could provide. Fanny wanted the best for Flo and Parthe — the finest choice of husbands. That meant not only moving in the first social circles but also giving the girls a top-quality education.

Fanny valued her heritage of having grown up in a large family, so Parthe and Flo often stayed with cousins, or cousins visited them. Flo entered into all her cousins' lively games, like building a play house.

> We stick little sticks in the ground in our larder and interlace them with rushes, making a little enclosure in which we keep potatoes etc. We have made 2 sofas in our parlor; we have dragged up several boughs of laurel, and are going to make a bower with it in the dining-room, and have made a little tool-house in our larder, in which we keep, viz. 1 spade, 2 rakes, 2 hoes, 4 baskets. [We] banked up the kitchen door [and] made a new one. We have made a sofa of sand in the kitchen, covered with heather. Our moss-beds were so wet, we cannot sleep in them.

The children then made "a great addition to our provisions."[8] Florence listed and drew in neat columns the cones and acorns used as pretend fruits and vegetables.

A "child of much more character" than her sister, Flo turned out to be "a shrewd little creature with a clear head." It made "her thoroughly mistress of all attempts by dint of thorough & diligent application,"[9] Fanny told a prospective governess.

Flo's mother spent several weeks of the year away from home either on the social round or recruiting her strength at spas and seaside. Nonetheless, Fanny monitored her children through their daily accounts. Seven-year-old Flo wrote about spending much time on "figures, music ... making maps of Palestine (and such like about the Bible) & then we walk & play, & do my patchwork, & we have such fun."[10]

Daily the girls must find an object to draw, practice the piano, and do needlework. Flo and Parthe read the Bible, took notes on the Sunday sermon and, at their mother's insistence, wrote a summary when they got home. They learned poems by heart. Seven-year-old Flo wrote her father, in French, about a poem she had memorized. It began, "'Oh he is gone my good auld man. And I am left forlorn.' These lines make me think of you ... I would really like you to come back today."[11]

Fearing her slight, delicate daughters might die young, like too many contemporaries, Fanny mandated physical exercise. Regardless of rain, the girls must walk vigorously twice daily, but in truly terrible weather they played badminton indoors. And a London specialist created exercises to strengthen specific parts of each girl's anatomy.

Flo liked accompanying her mother on her frequent visits to the poor on WEN's estates, for Fanny took seriously her religious duties no less than those of a landowner's wife. Flo copied her mother by bringing jellies and puddings to sick villagers. As well she picked bluebells and wild roses to brighten the sickroom. And when her parents forbade entering a cottage lest she catch infection, Flo rode up to the door on her pony.

When she contrasted the poverty of villagers with the luxuries of home, Flo asked herself how she could be of more use to the poor. Perhaps through practice. So the eight-year-old tabulated how many grains of James' powder (a common remedy for sundry ailments) should be taken by people of different ages. She carefully recorded the illness and symptoms of each person she met, especially children, and what cured them. Flo nursed sick dolls but, unlike other little girls, did so on a different scale. Having mended her cousins' cast-offs, she nursed "18 dolls *all* ill in rows in bed."*[12]

More attractive than her sister, engaging little Flo favored her father in looks. Parthe turned out to be a plain version of her mother. But Flo's parents could not comprehend why their willful, mischievous child seemed less content than their "most happy" Parthe, whose "perfect disposition" mastered or adapted "itself at once and easily, not from reflection, but from natural and unsought power to the circumstances of its world."[13]

Sibling rivalry intensified. Fanny began to send lively, assertive Flo and compliant, passive Parthe on separate visits to their cousins. At home the girls fought so persistently that Fanny resorted to keeping them in different rooms except for meals and exercises. Still, her daughters did share a nursery. Flo recalled her long recovery from whooping cough at age six, as one of the happiest times of her childhood. Parthe had been sent to cousins to avoid contamination. Flo had the nursery, not to mention adult attention, to herself. And beloved Aunt Mai took care of her.

WEN's only sibling, Mary, called Mai, had adored Flo from infancy, and the child responded. Intellectual like her brother, and deeply pious, gentle Mai gave Flo love, lessons, and friendship; and they shared jokes. So Flo cried when Mai got engaged to Fanny's favorite brother, cheerful, practical Sam Smith, a Cambridge graduate and lawyer. Flo decided she no longer loved him. In church she sat between Mai and Sam to separate them. "On Wednesday aunt Mai was married to uncle Sam. I, Papa, uncle Sam,

---

*When six-year-old Flo "had the whooping cough her thirteen dolls had it too & were found with pieces of flannel round 13 necks." Parthenope, lady Verney, *Recollection*, undated but written soon after her marriage (1858), Claydon House Trust N39.

Pop,* and mr. Bagshaw [clergyman] went first. Mama and aunt Mai in the bride's carriage." When "they were married we were all kneeling on our knees except mr. Bagshaw. Papa took aunt Mai's hand and gave it to uncle Sam. We all cried except uncle Sam, mr. Bagshaw and Papa."[14]

At the lavish wedding breakfast Flo admitted to enjoying the festive mood, let alone the selection of feather-light angel cakes, the tarts, jellies, trifles, syllabubs (sweetened milk or cream and egg white beaten to a froth and flavored with vanilla or a little wine), coffee creams in cups of almond paste, and summer's lush peaches, raspberries, and grapes. Aunt Mai's wedding day figured as the happiest and unhappiest Flo had ever spent at her dearly loved Grandmother Shore's Derbyshire home.

—⚭—

"The most merry little grig," Flo inquired "into the why and wherefore of everything. 'How is it spelt Mama' when she heard a new word — 'how is it made' when she saw a new" object. "Everything with fun and spirits."[15] Yet, Flo's conduct failed to satisfy her mother. Fanny wanted to curb her ebullient, fun-filled seven-year-old. Flo's mental powers made her too hungry for knowledge; and she did not suffer fools gladly, which caused impudence to adults and offense to Parthe. A strict disciplinarian, Fanny believed children should be seen but not heard. Flo ought to be a quiet, good, happy little girl. Like Parthe. Who fitted perfectly into the pattern of Victorian childhood.

Fanny knew how much Flo wanted to please her. So she challenged the child "to be good." And to assure her regimen when away from home on the social circuit, Fanny engaged a young, vigorous, well-qualified governess of sterling moral character.

Clever, "just and well-intentioned,"[16] Miss Christie, even so, completely misread Flo. The governess "turned inward all the overflowing energy & busy child life."[17] She "brought me up most severely," Florence recalled. When naughty, she had "to sit still by miss Christie, till I had the spirit of obedience."[18] Miss Christie "did not understand children" and "used to shut me up for six weeks at a time. My sister, on the contrary, she spoilt."[19]

This regimen made Flo see herself as different, diminished. She had a

Opposite: Frances (Fanny) Smith, Mrs. William Nightingale, 1788–1880, and her daughters, Parthenope and Florence (sitting on her mother's lap). Nightingale's relationship with her resolute and society-conscious mother shaped her life. "You would have done nothing" if "you had not resisted me" (artist: Alfred E. Chalon [1824], Photographic Survey, The Courtauld Institute of Art, London, Private Collection).

*Another nickname for Parthenope Nightingale.

dreadful secret — she was a freak, a monster. "My greatest ambition," Flo later wrote, "was not to be remarked. I was always in mortal fear of doing something unlike other people, and I said 'If I were sure that nobody would remark me I should be quite happy.' I had a morbid terror of not using my knives and forks like other people."[20]

A morbid terror of attracting adult censure. No wonder Fanny's sister found Flo withdrawn when she visited her cousins, and given to daydreaming. But Aunt Mai thought "the more she [Flo] is thrown upon herself the better it is for her."[21]

Flo's mother as well as her governess sought to curb yet another undesirable practice: Flo's focus on an older female — like Aunt Mai. Fanny and Christie failed to recognize the sensitive child's awareness of her mother's disapproval, and her hunger for a female surrogate who would give unqualified maternal love.

—⚊—

Trying hard to please Fanny, nine-year-old Flo promised to

> run before breakfast to gate ... ½ an hour's walk before dinner, long walk after, or if cold and dark long walk before and ½ an hour's after, to do 20 arms [exercises] before I dress, 10 minutes before breakfast & ten after exercises. [If not done well enough,] 10 more, to practice one hour a day, if you like it, as I shall not have as much to do, 1¼ regularly; to draw ½ an hour regularly, not to lie in bed, to go to bed in proper time, to read the Bible and pray regularly before breakfast and at night, to visit the poor people and to take care of those who are sick, to take medicine when I want it, to go regularly after breakfast, on Sundays to church ... to read, write and do the Bible, to read any book you put out for me, [to] read this paper everyday, to write to you.[22]

Flo thought daydreaming her worst problem. Like many imaginative children she escaped into make-believe, inventing stories that featured herself as heroine. So engrossing were these daydreams that Flo forgot time and place. "When I was a child and was naughty," she recalled, "it always put an end to my dreaming for the time. I never could tell why. Was it because naughtiness was a more interesting state than the little motives which make man's peaceful civilized state, and occupied imagination for the time?"[23]

Christie taught her charges basic Latin, geography, and English history. As well, she gave daily lessons in singing, piano, and social arts like needlework, dancing, flower arranging, manners, and conversation — essential skills for a young lady to succeed in the marriage stakes. Flo copied texts to develop ladylike handwriting; she kept a diary in French to improve her writing and grammar. (Flo already spoke fluently through chatting with her mother's French maid.) She liked to write, to gather wildflowers on her walks with

Christie, to observe and catalogue each and describe exactly where she found it.

When new leaves burst into life, the family moved to London. Flo and Parthe learned calisthenics. They also saw the sights. A children's party at Vauxhall enchanted Flo. Lights gave the gardens and fountain a magical glow; the green, red, and white lamps looked like stars — they illuminated a castle with musicians inside. Fireworks ended a charmed evening that brought the Nightingales home by boat at eleven o'clock.

By age ten Flo judged herself "more good-natured and complying."[24] Aunt Mai agreed. Flo proved "very quiet and tractable"[25] when left to herself. Still, Flo thought she should become more patient. And she tried to be good, careful about small things, like nightly washing all over, including her feet. "Pray let us love one another more than we have done," Flo wrote Parthe. "Mama wishes it particularly, it is the will of God, and it will comfort us in our trials through life."[26]

Flo now conformed to the image of a Victorian child, raised to repress impulsive emotions, love God, her parents, and siblings; to treat the lower classes patiently and kindly; to be polite to neighbors and loving to relatives.

In forcing her younger daughter into this framework, Fanny ingrained in Flo a sense of not quite measuring up to Fanny's expectations, bred in the child a thirst to please her mother, to prove her love. And Fanny's tendency to defend her firstborn and criticize Flo increased the little girl's feeling of low self-worth.

Florence Nightingale's relationship with her mother shaped her. Flo loved Fanny, yearned for her approval, but thought Fanny failed to recognize the intensity of her feelings. They never forged that special mother-daughter bond so crucial to a girl's self-confidence.

—⚹—

After two years Christie left to get married. Her successor satisfied neither Fanny's social standards nor WEN's intellectual demands. So he "took his girls in hand, and taught them himself. He is a *very* superior man, full of great interests; took high honors at college."[27] Steeped in the arts, humanities, and sciences, Florence's father had time and inclination to share the knowledge that filled his brain and the books that filled his library.

Victorian sons were educated in the classics first at boarding school, then university. Daughters, taught at home under the maternal eye, rarely learned the classics. But WEN's liberal, Unitarian heritage bred in him the belief that women should be well educated so as to be superior companions for their husbands. Fanny failed to share WEN's scholarly interests, but did want her girls to have every advantage in the marriage mart, so she let him invade her turf.

WEN taught his daughters history, geography, grammar, composition, and philosophy. They built on their familiarity with French and basic Latin to became proficient in both, also Italian. Fanny's youngest sister, unmarried Julia, taught them German.

Flo admired pretty, vivacious Aunt Ju. She and her circle thought good works could give young ladies, even those not married, a purpose in life. Julia Smith helped her relatives where she could and tried to influence them to help others. Her married sisters found Ju useful when sickness struck but deplored her single status.

Under WEN's tutelage, Flo thrived on Greek, but Parthe balked. One year older, plainer, often poorly, and paling beside her charismatic sister, Parthe followed where Flo led. She adored Flo, felt possessive about her. Yet, jealousy lurked below the surface. For no matter how clever or talented — and Parthe qualified in every respect — she proved no match for brilliant, motivated Flo. In any case, Parthe preferred music and art, not to mention her mother's drawing room, so she conceded the classroom to Flo. Nevertheless, Parthe resented the camaraderie between her father and sister.

WEN encouraged his talented, thoughtful daughter to stretch her mind with reading. He tutored Flo in the great liberal issues of the day (1830s): parliamentary reform, abolition of the slave trade, poor-law relief, and Catholic emancipation. The child responded. "I had the most enormous desire of acquiring" knowledge. "For 7 years of my life I thought of little else but cultivating my intellect."[28] Stimulated by her father's exacting standards, Flo rose before dawn to study. Under his guidance her intellect bloomed. "To his remarkable power of speculative thought she added a mathematical precision which led her to follow out an idea into its logical consequences. Her mind was a curious compound of her practical mother & her speculative father."[29] Philosophical discussions with her father taught adolescent Florence to question, develop, and support her opinions. WEN's education instilled intellectual self-confidence in his favorite child.

As Parthe evolved smoothly into a young lady at ease in her mother's drawing room, Flo rode to hounds with her father. She became more shy and awkward, more pensive and insecure — not uncommon in a twelve-year-old. Besides, the lazy, female, drawing-room life of chatting, reading aloud, sketching, and singing bored Flo. She wanted to be useful, like Aunt Ju. So Flo made an effort to know the Old Ladies — Grandmother Shore and her spinster sister — and to look after them when they felt poorly.

—⚬⚬⚬—

After giving birth to three daughters, Flo's favorite aunt, Mai Smith, produced the long-awaited son who would eventually inherit WEN's entailed property. The Nightingales were thrilled, especially Flo. My Boy Shore came to stay at Lea Hurst while his worn-out mother and his aunt Fanny recruited their strength at a nearby spa. Shore's nurse fell ill. Twelve-year-old Flo took over — and got credit for keeping the frail, precious baby alive. Best of all, Fanny approved. Victorians associated self-sacrifice with femininity. So proof of her perplexing daughter's selflessness, what a close friend would later describe as Flo's Incredible Bonté, calmed Fanny's fears about Flo's so-called masculine intellect.

Shore and his sisters often stayed with the Nightingales, and when all four parents were absent Flo took charge. Looking after these little cousins gave Flo confidence; the children needed her and, like their mother, Mai, they loved her. Stronger, more dynamic, let alone more devoted and amusing than Parthe, Flo became surrogate mother to the small Smiths. They were the world's sweetest children, but My Boy Shore meant the most. Flo loved bathing, feeding, and putting him to bed. "I am very sorry to hear that your baby is still so poorly," she wrote her favorite cousin and dearest friend, Hilary.* "Our baby is much better for he has got two teeth through."[30] Flo loved babies for themselves, but babies also offered the chance to fulfill her greatest wish: to be of use.

—៣—

My Boy Shore, her father's approval, and intellectual stimulation gave Flo infinite satisfaction. So did the butterflies flitting around the rosebuds in Embley's scented garden and the nightingales throbbing their songs in the shrubbery. But what, Flo asked herself, did all that beauty mean? How did it connect with her need to do right and be good? For Flo's metaphysical discussions with her father, study of Greek philosophy and Latin logic, not to mention her mother's mandatory summary of the vicar's Sunday sermon, made the pensive teenager start to question her purpose in life.

Flo thought Parthe better at being useful — because of her happy-go-lucky nature. Flo still felt shy, ill at ease. Would she ever fit into the world of fashion where her beautiful, self-assured mother and now graceful, elegant Parthe moved so smoothly?

Flo tried. To please Fanny she learned to like a newfangled fashion in

---

*Hilary Bonham-Carter, eldest daughter of Fanny's sister Joanna, and Flo's closest friend through childhood and adolescence. One year apart in age, both had serious minds, but unlike her dynamic cousin, Hilary had a docile disposition. During her father's frequent absences from home on business and her mother's accompanying him or being pregnant, Hilary took increasing responsibility for managing the household with its large domestic staff, governesses and tutors. After her father's death, seventeen-year-old Hilary became second mother to her five younger siblings.

food: sandwiches; at night she wrapped her thick, auburn hair into curling papers so as to have modish ringlets; and she devoted her spare time to caring for a baby cousin. Flo shared her liking of art, music, and literature with Parthe, but their mother still preferred to keep the sisters apart. "Dear Pop," reproached Flo, "why don't you write? I should think you had plenty of time, and I write you such long letters, and you, but very seldom, write me 2 or 3 lines. I shall not write to you, if you don't write for me."[31]

WEN meanwhile, fulfilled his wife's social ambition by standing for parliament. Passage of the great parliamentary reform bill (1832) and abolition of the slave trade (1833) encouraged Flo's father to believe a more liberal day soon would dawn, might even bring poor-law reform, and legislation to regulate factory conditions.

Fourteen-year-old Flo feared that were WEN elected, "we shall not see half so much of dear Papa, and he will not be able to teach us as he did." Moreover, having to spend half the year in London would mean seeing "much less of Lea Hurst and Embley and the poor people." But "pray, pray no governess," Flo begged her mother. "We will do our lessons by ourselves if he will still be so good as to go on teaching us at intervals."[32]

Parthe welcomed WEN's decision. She identified with her mother's desire to have a house in London. For WEN promised that, if elected, he would accede to his wife's aspiration for a permanent residence in the capital.

WEN lost. He refused to follow the common practice of bribing voters. Disillusioned, WEN turned from politics to his library. As well, he improved his estates, took care of his health, and shared his dreams of better times with his favorite child.

Her husband's defeat dashed Fanny's hope of becoming a political hostess. WEN's renunciation of politics meant no London house. Embley must serve as the family's social center. But to fulfill Fanny's objective, the house needed to be enlarged, modernized, and fully redecorated. That challenged WEN's interest in architecture. And Fanny's idea that while alterations were underway the family should travel appealed to her husband, too. Continental living would be cheaper, the girls could finish their education abroad, their health might well improve, and they would profit from exposure to Continental polish.

As Fanny and WEN mulled over this notion, a hard and unusually long winter gripped England. Influenza swept through Embley and nearby Wellow village.

Flo had gone to cousins. Estate business took WEN from home. Parthe developed a persistent high fever and racking cough. Again, Fanny feared for the life of her precious firstborn. With help from her unmarried sister Julia, Fanny nursed Parthe herself. Parthe recovered. However, this illness confirmed Fanny's fears of Parthe's frailty and convinced the mother that she alone stood between her daughter and death.

One year later influenza again struck the Nightingale household. Parthe had prudently been sent to stay with cousins, but Fanny, WEN, and several mobcapped maids fell ill. "Dear Pop," Flo wrote her sister, "notwithstanding your ungracious silence towards me after the 2 propitiatory notes I had sent imploring forgiveness & the title of 'the book' I was to send, I write to tell you"[33] of the invalids.

Efficient Florence ran the household, nursed the sick, and rose at four each morning to study before her small Smith cousins woke to claim their favorite. This experience convinced Flo that she must somehow find a way to be of permanent use.

Concomitantly, bad harvests caused starvation and riots throughout the countryside. The misery she saw in the villages strengthened Flo's resolution.

To her parents, meanwhile, the Continent seemed extremely attractive. Besides, Fanny reasoned, foreign travel would wean Florence from her odd fixation on being useful, particularly to the poor and sick.

Amidst the bustle of preparation, friends and family filled Lea Hurst. Parthe practiced her Italian and her sketching, and dreamed of Continental grandeurs. Flo nursed her dreams in secret. She had lately been useful, tending to the sick at home and helping the poor. Going abroad meant leaving them, as well as Aunt Mai, My Boy Shore, cousin Hilary, and Flo's beloved range of interlaced Lea Hurst hills. But seeing new places and meeting new people might shed light on an absorbing question — what her life should be.

Because while teenaged Flo stood daydreaming on the carpeted corridor "outside Shore's door" she received confirmation of her ambition to be useful, the first of her "calls to work" (February 7, 1837). "Behold the handmaid of the Lord." He would show Florence "the way to do good."[34]

2

Seesaw

In making myself worthy to be God's servant the first temptation to be overcome is the desire to shine in society.[1]— Florence Nightingale

The Nightingales set sail for France in bright autumn (1837) sunshine. Once they were well into the Channel, however, drizzle turned sky and water gray. Too excited for sleep, Florence braved the weather to walk the lamp-lit decks and chat with the mate into early morning. Then she watched the dawn. And when seventeen-year-old Flo found the elegant bedroom she shared with Parthe at Le Havre's premier hotel to have neither windows nor washing facilities, she felt herself truly arrived in a foreign land.

Having traveled south on the river Seine, admired Rouen's cathedral and explored the city's medieval streets and bustling squares, the Nightingales entered their commodious, custom-built carriage. WEN had designed it to hold his family, their personal servants, and a year's worth of luggage. As the coachman galloped his spirited six-horse team along roads lined with tall, slender poplars, Flo and her father sat on the roof enjoying fresh air and an unobstructed vista of the splendid fall countryside.

Before the advent of the railway, Continental journeys could be troublesome and risky. Rutted roads caused carriages to overturn. Bandits menaced. Inns might — and usually did — have damp sheets or, worse, bedbugs, so the well-to-do brought their own linens, plus servants to launder them. Then again, the traveler had ample time to admire nature's beauty, or marvel at a distant cathedral looming dark in the purple dusk.

Moonlight playing on the spires of Chartres Cathedral mesmerized Flo. She tried to describe it, as well as nature's splendor, but mere words failed to suffice. Flo's diary did record with mathematical precision the distance between stops, the day and hour of arrival and leaving. Florence commented on the art and politics of places she passed through, tabulated statistics on their laws, land systems, and social conditions — particularly of the poor — how many beggars she saw, what the children were doing, how the houses looked. And wherever possible, Flo visited charitable institutions.

—ᴍ—

The Nightingale carriage traveled slowly south to Nice,

a charming place — bright blue [sky] and brilliant July sun, which gives us a second summer in December. Cactuses, aloes and sundry other plants quite unknown to the learned of England ramp about here wild and in the gardens you see orange trees covered with fruit and even flowers, palm trees with dates, and all sort of hothouse plants *now*. We have taken most beautiful rides all about Nice on magnificent donkeys.[2]

After clammy, bug-ridden inns, the family settled thankfully into a splendid suite at the comfortable Hôtel des Etrangères, situated in a scented orange grove. And since the English colony led a scintillating social life, soirées ousted cathedrals, moonlight, and scenery in Flo's diary. She danced every quadrille at the season's biggest ball, Flo wrote her favorite cousin and close friend, Hilary. Still, "the worst of traveling is that you leave people as soon as you have become intimate with them, often never to see them again."[3] So when their comfortable carriage conveyed the Nightingales to their next stop, Flo refused to admire the famous Corniche. Sitting inside on the cushioned seat, she cried.

The travelers arrived at one of Europe's richest and most splendid cities early in the new year (1838). Genoa la Superba's Baroque palaces, fountains and statues, its lush gardens, opera and theaters, seemed to Flo "an Arabian Nights dream come true."[4] She delighted in the opera, not to mention balls; at the season's most magnificent, Florence lost count of her partners. But the idleness and ignorance of Genoa's nobles, the poverty of its people, troubled her. And at a deaf and dumb institute Flo, to her dismay, saw seemingly intelligent inmates, sad and sickly, living in cold, grubby rooms.

After sealing their six-week stay at Genoa by giving a brilliant soirée, the Nightingales left for the semi-independent duchy of Florence. Thanks to the tolerant policy of its ruler, culture and fashion combined to make the city Italy's intellectual capital. There were parties aplenty for Fanny, conversaziones for WEN, and superb opportunities for the girls.

Italian masters taught them singing and piano. Flo loved the Italian opera, "so beautiful, so affecting, so enchanting: how could one ever wish for anything else if one were always looking at that"?[5] In her diary she tabulated data on score, libretto, and performance. And because Fanny and WEN moved in the crème de la crème of society, their daughters shared in a dazzling round of parties, picnics, and balls.

Concomitantly, Flo volunteered to nurse a sick English lady living at the same hotel. And Flo liked the way an infant school benefactor perceived the pupils as his children.

By late spring the Nightingales were exploring small, historic North Italian cities like Verona, with its well-preserved Roman amphitheater, and Ravenna, with its breathtaking Byzantine mosaics. In waning summer they lingered at Lakes Maggiore and Como, feasting their eyes on vistas of grape-laden vineyards set against the pink granite peaks of the Dolomites. Before early snow made the mountain passes treacherous, Florence and her family crossed the Alps to Geneva.

Its society meant privation and scholarship. Geneva overflowed with intellectuals. They had fled the harsh repression of Austria, which controlled North Italy. Forced into poverty after a life of ease, these exiles spoke eloquently of prison, torture, and separation from families brought on by their attempts to unify Italy under the flag of freedom. Men and women alike now sought to train themselves and succeeding generations to foster growth of a benign, liberal, and united Italy. Geneva's intelligentsia found in Florence Nightingale a rapt audience. Serious conversation replaced parties and balls.

—∞—

Clouds cloaked Mont Blanc as the Nightingale carriage turned towards Paris. On the Swiss side, farmers gathered their green and purple harvest. Grapes perfumed the ambient air; brimming bins and baskets stood in dim village doorways and cluttered the steep, narrow streets. But after the carriage "crossed the Jura mountains above lake Geneva and" made its way northwest "through the plains of France," Flo judged the journey "exceedingly uninteresting."[6]

Parisian society centered in salons. Uniquely French, grounded in the grand tradition of the eighteenth-century Enlightenment, salons were hubs of culture and politics. Conversation meant everything. No man could rise to repute without a salon setting, and women ruled them all. When the Nightingales arrived, Paris salons had evolved into meeting places for the post–Revolutionary aristocracy of merit — of brains, money, ability, and the fittest survivors of the Terror. Women still reigned. Fanny Nightingale's sister had given her an introduction to one of the most notable salons.

Mary Clarke (Clarkey), by birth half–Irish, half–Scottish, but fully French in education and inclination, received intellectual lights at her home every Friday evening.

"Quite unconscious of her appearance, she glides about, she runs, she stands, she exhibits herself amid" lovely faces "with serene self-satisfaction and imperturbable assurance that could not be surpassed if she had the head of Venus herself."[7] Clarkey's "childlike naturalness [she said whatever entered her head], her mercurial gayety, and her sparkling wit," her "audacious fun, combined with an originality amounting to eccentricity," spelled "death to ennui." She "might displease or exasperate,—she very often did both,—but she was incapable of boring anyone."[8]

When her widowed mother settled in Paris for her health, Clarkey determined on a salon.

> To what did the French literary man owe his exemption [from] the miseries of English writers, [she asked]. To whom should he give thanks that the rich, the ignorant, and the vulgar made no insolent jokes upon poor authors living in garrets. [To] the women who from the earliest days of literature gave them all the succor they could, bringing them into contact with the rich and the great, showing them off with every kind of ingenuity and tact. [Only] in France, do we find it a general rule and custom for women of all ranks to make common cause with the whole talent and genius of the nation.[9]

Mary Clarke Mohl (Clarkey) 1793–1883. Prominent Parisian salon hostess and believer in equality of the sexes. For more than 40 years Nightingale's close friend, confidante, and support (artists: Annan and Swan. © National Portrait Gallery, London).

The Nightingales were not the sort of people who normally appealed to Clarkey. Intellectual WEN might be able to hold his own in conversation with the habitués of her salon, but Clarkey had grave doubts about WEN's ladies. Not only did she consider England a cultural backwater, but Clarkey loathed its females. "Why don't they [mothers] talk about interesting things? Why don't they use their brains?" Daughters "have no manners. I can't abide them in my drawing-room. What with their shyness and their inability to hold their tongues, they ain't* fit for decent company."[10]

A successful salon hostess must keep boring people at bay. But Clarkey felt disinclined to offend Fanny's sister by rejecting her introduction. So Clarkey invited the Nightingales to her Saturday evening children's party.

---

*Upper-class English often used "ain't" instead of "isn't" or "aren't," and "don't" instead of "doesn't."

They entered a spacious, bright apartment, at the back overlooking gardens, in front the quiet, elegant rue du Bac. At one end of the large double drawing room a wood fire crackled merrily as two men, bent over the brass firedogs, earnestly tried to make the teakettle boil. They were Julius von Mohl, famed Oriental languages scholar, and Claude Fauriel, noted expert on medieval Provençal literature. In the middle of the room a small, frizzy-haired, cheery woman led a group of children in a boisterous game of Blind Man's Buff. Florence instantly joined them. That earned her Clarkey's approval.

Clarkey soon loved all the Nightingales — WEN for his aloof charm, Fanny for her beauty and kindness, Parthe for her elegance. And they loved Clarkey. Through her WEN met interesting people who could converse intelligently about world affairs. Conventional Fanny and Parthe found Clarkey a wise and amusing friend; like all Paris, they accepted her intimate yet platonic friendship with Fauriel, who esteemed Clarkey's intellect and treated her as an equal. But of the four Nightingales, it was Flo who stood closest to Clarkey, twenty-seven years her senior.

Clarkey hated the upper-class customs that constrained young ladies' lives. "If somebody asked me 'would you rather be a woman or a galley-slave?' how quickly I should cry out 'long live the galleys!'"[11] The sexes were intellectually equal in Clarkey's salon. She favored scholarly male company — especially Fauriel and Mohl — over women. Except for Flo. Clarkey admired her mind, appreciated Florence's dry humor, and applauded what she called Flo's Incredible Bonté.

Florence's new friend opened her eyes to a different way of life than the one Fanny Nightingale gave her girls. In Clarkey's world men and women could co-exist as equals. A single and far from wealthy female could create for herself an intellectually fascinating existence, while at the same time enjoying a close relationship with her mother.*

Clarkey did as she pleased, arranged her daily contact with Fauriel (much older, he failed to reciprocate her passion but valued her friendship) and Mohl as best suited them all. But when she visited her married sister in Scotland, Clarkey faced all the evils of being female. Upper-middle-class women sat in the drawing-room; men disdained their views on any topic other than domestic; mothers and wives had little power, often were left reliant on their children; brothers came before sisters; and society censured unmarried females.

Clarkey feared her new friends were doomed to the same fate, but while Flo and Parthe were in Paris she could at least expose them to clever people. Clarkey took the girls everywhere — to private parties, studios, galleries and

*Mrs. Clarke and her daughter shared the rue du Bac apartment.

concerts, to the opera and theater, receptions and balls. And in her salon they met the best political and intellectual society.

Florence reveled in Clarkey's Paris. Poise born of her scintillating social life in Italy had erased much of Flo's shyness. Association with reflective people like herself in Geneva honed Flo's conversational skills and added to her self-confidence. So did four months in Paris. Elegant and distinguished, if not beautiful, extremely well-read with a wide range of interests, articulate in five languages, the mischievous and engaging child had grown into a charming, witty young lady.

The Nightingales landed in England to find a new monarch sitting on the throne. Nineteen-year-old Florence made her much dreaded formal debut at Queen Victoria's drawing room. When the majordomo sonorously announced her, Florence, fashionably clad in a white, wasp-waisted Paris gown with full train, glided towards the young queen. Sinking into a deep curtsy, Florence kissed Victoria's hand, and gracefully backed herself and her train out of the room. This faultless presentation, to say nothing of her newfound assurance, made Flo eager to shine in her first London season. Pleased, Fanny Nightingale focused her pride and hope in her attractive and gifted, if still too fixated on serving humanity's unfortunate, younger daughter. "Elegant rather than beautiful," tall "and graceful of figure, her countenance mobile and expressive, her conversation most interesting,"[12] Flo had "rich brown hair" and a "very delicate complexion"; under fine, arched eyebrows "gray eyes, which are generally pensive and drooping, but when they choose can be the merriest eyes I ever saw; and perfect teeth, making her smile the sweetest I ever saw." Her "beautifully shaped head," and "long, white round throat" completed Flo's "perfect grace and lovely appearance."[13]

To her mother's exasperation, however, Flo failed to share Parthe's fondness for fashion. So when Fanny took her daughters to parties, she hounded Florence to pay attention to her clothes. *"Make* Flo wear her white silk frock to-night,"[14] echoed plain, pale Parthe. But in the lamp-lit dusk of late spring evenings, when powdered, liveried footmen handed the Nightingale ladies from their smart town carriage and ushered them into a fairy-tale world of light, music, and laughter, Flo felt exceedingly uneasy at the sight of emaciated people huddled on the pavement, hungry for a glimpse of the elegant men and women arriving for the ball.

Perhaps, Flo thought, music and personal relations might provide the key to life. She had "the strongest taste for music." Had Flo not eventually lost her voice to constant sore throats, "I should have wished for no other satisfaction." Singing "excited my imagination and my passionate nature so much."[15]

Since Florence's cousin and contemporary, beautiful, magnetic Marianne Nicholson* turned out to be "as music-mad as I am, we are reveling in music all day long. Schultz, who is a splendid player, and Crivelli, her singing master, give us lessons."[16]

Her popular cousin's friendship flattered Flo and increased her assurance. Besides, Marianne's favorite brother, Henry, who had loved Flo since they built playhouses together as children, now paid her gratifying attention. Pleasant and reliable, if not vivacious like his sister or brilliant like his inamorata, Henry, eldest son of an extremely rich man, enjoyed excellent prospects. And his personality promised that Henry would be a good husband and father. Both families approved, for Victorians accepted marriage of first cousins. But the Nightingales and Nicholsons agreed that since Flo and Henry were still young, they should take time to know one another better.

—⚏—

Having pleased her mother with a successful Season, Flo spent the summer at Lea Hurst helping entertain a steady stream of visitors including Henry and Clarkey. From then on, Clarkey spent three to four weeks of every summer with the Nightingales. She showed interest "in everything; reading all the new books" whilst "lying curled up in a great armchair, or in a corner of the sofa."[17]

Derbyshire's chilly autumn breezes drove the Nightingales south. They found WEN's alterations to have turned orange-brick Embley into an elegant neo–Jacobean mansion. Delighted, Fanny promptly invited all her relatives for Christmas and enlisted energetic, capable Florence to help organize the house. But Flo thought this life of "faddling, twaddling, and endless tweedling of nosegays in jugs"[18] (to quote Clarkey) lacked purpose. And she felt guilty for encouraging Henry. Flo did not love him, but she did want to fortify her friendship with his doting sister Marianne.

Furthermore, Flo felt exceedingly impatient. Why, after two years, had God not spoken? Because she had failed to prove herself ready for His instructions. Rather, Flo had yielded to worldly temptations like love of pleasure and desire to shine in society.

Mental challenge might distract from temptation. True, "our society consisted of clever intellectual men, all very good society — that I allow. They never talked gossip or foolishly but they took up all our time."[19] Being the daughter of an English country house meant being always amiable, eternally ready to entertain guests. Of course Flo could snatch a few hours alone, but

---

*Eldest daughter of a wealthy landowner and Fanny's sister Anne. The Nicholsons and Nightingales were staying at the same Regent Street hotel.

not enough for real action or rigorous thought. Maybe studying mathematics would test her mind. But how to win Fanny's consent?

Having fretted herself into fever, Flo confided in her beloved and supportive aunt. Deploying a cascade of tactful verbiage, Mai Smith convinced her sister-in-law Fanny that a little change would benefit Flo. Hence, as the new decade opened (1840), Flo's parents let her visit intellectual, droll Aunt Mai and jovial, no-nonsense Uncle Sam.

—ɷ—

Aunt and niece rose daily before dawn to study. Yet, Flo sought to tackle math more thoroughly. "I am much impressed with the idea that hard work is necessary to give zest to life in a character like hers, where there is great power of mind and a more than common inclination to apply. *So* I write," Mai ventured, "to ask you if you in any way object to a mathematical master."[20]

Fanny did object. Her daughter's destiny lay in marriage. Of what possible use could math be? Yes, Fanny's social set included math luminaries, three of them even women. But she feared the entry of a math tutor into her well-regulated home. Math tutors were usually very bright, very ambitious, and very poor. Letting a young man like that spend hours alone with charming, attractive Florence would surely mean trouble.

Gentle Mai persisted. WEN proposed history or philosophy as more fitting for a female. Education should equip her to be a pleasant, useful wife. A girl could learn masculine subjects like Greek and Latin to enhance her listening skills in male company, but WEN drew the line at math. Besides, Victorian medical wisdom, if wisdom one could call it, thought brainwork might endanger a girl's health, even impair her ability to bear children.

Florence insisted.

Mai turned a family crisis into compromise. Nearing the end of her seventh pregnancy, an aunt got news of her eldest son's death. She appealed to Fanny. Flo handled children so well; could she help? Yes. So when pink and white hyacinths perfumed the air, Flo went to her aunt and uncle. There she had regular lessons with a leading mathematician. Fanny wanted Flo at home after her aunt gave birth, but Flo felt happy to be doing good, more especially as her deeply religious aunt clung to her.

—ɷ—

Exuding vitality and intellect, twenty-year-old Florence returned home to delight her mother by entertaining a constant flow of guests. Teetering between heady social success and heavy qualms, nonetheless, Flo questioned how to become worthy of God's instructions other than tending the poor and ill on her father's estates and being useful to family members. "Ladies' work has always to be fitted in," Flo confided to friend and favorite cousin Hilary, but a man's "business is the law."[21]

To engage her mind and mitigate the triviality, not to say tedium, of her life, Florence rose while silvery moonbeams still skittered over Embley's velvet lawns. She delved further into math as well as Greek and philosophy, then astronomy.

Bored she might be in her parents' drawing room, even frustrated, but Florence learned a valuable lesson: how to deal with many different personality types. Hence, when the Nightingales spent Christmas and New Year (1841) at Waverley with their wealthy Nicholson relatives and Henry planned to entertain his parents' eighty guests with *The Merchant of Venice*, Flo got the hardest job: organizing and stage-managing the entire production. That included keeping the volatile cast up to the mark.

After their triumphant performance, the young people danced until five in the morning. Graceful dancing, enormous vitality, and impressive learning, coupled with the sparkling wit and excellent mimicry that lay behind a serious, modest mien, made society notice the younger Miss Nightingale. That pleased her mother. And it pleased Flo. But she believed it wrong to succumb to admiration and flattery. Rather, Florence thought she must defeat her desire to shine in society so that God would judge her ready for His commands.

Concomitantly, trade reverses, high bread prices (due to protectionist corn laws) and a business downturn caused unemployment and starvation. Thousands died in "the hungry '40s." Flo saw terrible suffering on her father's estates and in London streets. Hunger, sweated labor, ignorance, and filth filled the lives of those living outside her cocoon.

To her family's discomfort, Florence began pointing out the contrast between their lifestyle and the mounting misery of many Britons. And while sitting on the sturdy wooden bench encircling the thick trunk of a majestic tree Flo, stitching at her delicate embroidery, started to see splendid Embley with its shaved green lawns and lush, scented gardens as a lure to be held at arm's length. Her fate lay with the world's less fortunate.

Fanny sought "the usual conventional life for her daughter."[22] Flo pondered how to do more to show God her readiness to serve. Apparently cottage visiting and village schoolteaching did not suffice. Yet, how could she do more when social duties prevented regularity? Flo focused on the poor in Lea Hurst's village, but incessant demands for medicines, food, and clothes drew protests from her usually generous mother. And when Flo wanted to stay at Lea Hurst rather than remove with the rest of the family, Fanny refused. When she finally did get Flo to Embley, a family friend died in childbirth. Flo insisted on foregoing the fall season to care for the motherless newborn. No. Florence could not be forever gadding around to attend people in need. Flo worried herself into illness. Fanny let her go for a short time only — unsatisfying for all concerned.

Florence escaped to her childhood refuge — daydreaming — of how better to serve the earth's unfortunate. Her health suffered. When the Nightingales again went to Waverley for Christmas with the Nicholsons, one of Flo's heavy chest colds confined her to bed. Dreaming intensified. It frightened Florence. For in the Victorian climate of complete ignorance about mental health, Flo feared her dreaming might well lead to loss of control over her mind. And guilt about Waverley's heir exacerbated Flo's misery. Henry wanted to marry her. Flo did feel fond of him, but not to the point of being in love with Henry. Terrified of family furor if she refused him, Florence also dreaded losing the friendship of Henry's adoring sister Marianne.

Mr. Nicholson's pious unmarried sister stepped in. Hannah thought union with God through Christian compliance and simplicity would reconcile Flo to the life her family wanted for her. Flo and Hannah talked for hours about the soul's path to God.

> The fault of us young people is too much groping in our own minds, too much refining on our [feelings, owned Flo.] I only say this [to] show you that your kindness & your books, are, I hope, not entirely wasted upon me, [that] I have not neglected making the most of them. [How] grateful I am for your interest in me, [how] thankful, when the invisible sympathy takes a visible form & speaks [through] the mouth & life of a human creature.[23]

Hannah Nicholson's friendship inspired Florence to deepen her spiritual life. But unlike Hannah, she sought union with God not as an end in itself, but as preparation for action on God's behalf. So Flo confided neither her call nor her dreams to Hannah.

—m—

Having wooed his cousin for two years, Henry Nicholson proposed. Guilt engulfed Florence. To her, marriage meant overpowering love for a man, since marriage would mean giving up her goal to serve God. Besides, how could future life as chatelaine of Waverly differ from present life as dutiful daughter of Embley? Flo did not feel such intense love for Henry; indeed, she had encouraged him to fortify her friendship with Marianne. If passion meant delight in another's presence plus a longing to please that person, Flo felt passion for Marianne. "There *is* a passion of the Spirit."[24]

Flo's refusal devastated Henry and infuriated his family. Marianne cut off her friendship. "I was not a worthy friend for her," Flo blamed herself, "I was not true either to her or to myself in our friendship. I was afraid of her: that is the truth."[25]

Who has not blamed herself for the end of a friendship? In all justice, serious-minded Florence and social butterfly Marianne lacked any basis for friendship except Henry. Marianne failed to share her cousin's intellectual or philanthropic interests. She knew "so little of her aim in life or what her gifts are for but amusing herself and other people."[26]

Flo kept heartbreak to herself while she helped her mother entertain the cream of society at Embley. "I have walked up and down all these long summer evenings in the garden and could find no words but: My God, my God, why hast thou forsaken me?" Flo confided to cousin Hilary. *"Je ne comprends rien,*[27] only this: that there are strange punishments here for those that have made life consist of one idea and that one not God." Flo begged her pious cousin to "pray for me — not for" peace. "I can perform my duties as well at home without it, indeed, I am more use to my father and mother than I was five years ago — but for truth, truth, truth and a manifestation of God."[28]

3

"My little plan"

Mrs. Nightingale bothered and fretted because Florence did not faddle after the poor in her fashion.[1]— Mary Clarke (Clarkey) Mohl

Seven years after Florence Nightingale first heard God's call, the prominent American abolitionist and director of Boston's Perkins School for the Blind visited Embley (1844). "Having heard much of dr. Howe as a philanthropist," Florence "resolved to consult him upon a matter which she already had at heart."[2] When the gentlemen joined the ladies in Fanny Nightingale's paneled, pilastered drawing room after dinner, Flo walked gracefully across the custom-woven pale green carpet and disposed herself on a multi-colored tapestry chair beside the famous physician. Would, Florence asked, he meet her privately in the library the next day before breakfast?

Richly carved Gothic-style oak shelves adorned WEN's library; caryatids separated its sections, and antique busts sat on the top shelves. A benign breeze wafted summer sunshine into the room through tall, open windows. Wearing a tight-waisted gingham morning dress with round neck, three-quarter sleeves, and a double flounce around her ankles, Florence stood in front of the empty fireplace.

"Dr. Howe, if I should determine to study nursing, and to devote my life to that profession, do you think it would be a dreadful thing?"

"By no means," Howe replied. "It would be a very good thing."[3]

—⁂—

Flo "dug after my little plan in silence"[4] all summer. It energized her work among the cottagers. And friendship with the new vicar and his wife gave Florence the chance to partake in their plans to improve education at the village school.

Still, twenty-four-year-old Flo knew life "cannot be merely a gaining of experience — it is freedom, voluntary force, free-will, & therefore must be a hard fought battle."[5] To prepare for the opening skirmish — her secret ambition to train as a nurse in a large public hospital*— Florence began systematically to study books and pamphlets about medical institutions, nursing, and social conditions among the poor.

Her mother, meanwhile, had drawn distinguished Embley neighbors into the Nightingale circle. Dubbed Lord Cupid in his younger days, former Whig foreign secretary and future prime minister Lord Palmerston had recently married his longtime lover.† She turned her husband's home, stately, colonnaded Broadlands, into a center of fashion and society. There Florence met Lady Palmerston's handsome, curly-haired son-in-law, Lord Shaftesbury, one of Victorian England's most eminent humanitarians.

His successful conversion of religious values into social reform via political action inspired Flo. She listened avidly to Shaftesbury's description of his most recent parliamentary success. Passage of the mines act barred underground work for women, and children under the age of ten, as well as initiating accident prevention. Shaftesbury planned next to put his energies into a ten-hour act to limit the workday in textile mills. He and Florence discussed his Ragged schools. They offered free education to destitute children. Shaftesbury started to supply Florence with hard-to-get government blue books on public hospitals. And he introduced her to leading reformers.

Since social demands left Flo little time to herself, she rose before dawn to study at the small table set in front of her Lea Hurst bedroom window. Another small table, plain mirror, and simple bookshelves furnished the top-floor room, formerly the nursery, and a drab carpet partially covered the scrubbed wooden floor. Virginia creeper framed windows looking onto gardens linked by stone terraces and heaped with hollyhocks, dahlias, and geraniums. Beyond, a wooded meadow descended sharply to the rushing Derwent River, whose red rock banks stretched to heather-covered hills. But as pale light filtered through the pre-dawn darkness, Flo had eyes only for hospital material.

Her "calm dignity of deportment" without "shyness or presumption, and a few words indicating deep reflection, just views, and clear perceptions of life and its obligations, and the trifling acts showing forgetfulness of self, and devotedness to others"[6] drew society's notice. What, Florence asked the philanthropic Prussian ambassador, Baron von Bunsen, and his wealthy, well-connected English wife, could an individual do "towards lifting the load of suffering from the helpless and miserable?"[7] The Bunsens told her about Prus-

---

*Only the poor entered hospitals; family members nursed middle- and upper-class Victorians at home.

†Emily, formerly Lady Cowper. After a youthful marriage of convenience, widowhood left Emily free to follow her heart.

sia's Kaiserswerth institute. Founded by a Protestant pastor and his wife, the institute trained lay deaconesses[8] to nurse the sick poor.

The idea of going to Kaiserswerth struck Florence as a commendable, if faraway, goal. She sought immediate action.

—⁂—

Worry over how to achieve it caused Flo sleepless nights and loss of appetite. She became ill, too ill to join the family Christmas party at Waverley. At least she need not visit the Nicholsons when her relations with Henry and Marianne were so strained. Still, Flo felt somewhat sorry for herself as she sat alone at Embley watching forlorn snowflakes fall from a leaden sky, while Waverley guests enjoyed themselves at a great fancy-dress ball. Would she ever find her way from home to hospital, settle her friendship with Marianne, and prove herself fit to serve God?

Favorite cousin and closest friend Hilary Bonham-Carter kept Flo company during her convalescence. Hilary had been educated at a prominent Unitarian academy for young ladies. There the devout teenager had discovered in herself a talent for drawing. Hilary dreamed of an independent artist's life, but family responsibilities came first. Her father's early death and her sense of duty to mother and younger siblings made Hilary vow not to marry, a decision Mrs. Bonham-Carter greeted with relief, as she proved incapable of managing her large household. Clarkey begged her to let Hilary study at a Paris atelier. "Come NOW," Clarkey pleaded with Hilary, "*don't* undertake a hundred small things in England, which you *must* do." Give up "small things now and do them when you go back. Have character and sense enough to make a sacrifice of a small thing to a large one."[9] But to Clarkey — and Flo's — disgust, sweet and docile Hilary made the best of keeping house, teaching her sisters, arranging flowers and, when her mother judged that social engagements allowed it, attending a London atelier for ladies.

Hilary admired Flo, felt passionate about her much as Flo did about Marianne — a delight in her presence and strong desire to please. The cousins walked for hours through Embley's well-timbered woods as the weak winter sun shone on dead leaves and frozen twigs crackled underfoot. They talked of many things, especially a lady's right to work and relations between the sexes. For Clarkey had shown them that a man and a woman could much more easily be friends in France than in England.

When Hilary left, Flo's beloved double cousin My Boy Shore, son of WEN's sister, Mai, and Fanny's brother Sam, came to convalesce after measles. "A sickly child," when "he went to school, I prepared him. In the holidays I taught him. When he went later to college, I was his instructress." Flo had ambitions for Shore, but "he did not succeed in the way in which I wished."[10]

Nonetheless, they strolled Embley's graveled paths, admired early spring snow-drops and crocuses unfurling their petals, read aloud, discussed dogs, and talked earnestly about the importance of resisting worldly temptation.

Bronchitis then felled Flo. And she felt extremely frustrated. A year had passed since her conversation with Dr. Howe, eight since her call. Clarkey suggested writing as a remedy. "One's feelings waste themselves in words, they ought to be distilled into actions and into actions which bring results,"[11] Flo replied.

—∞—

Beloved Grandmother Shore took sick. Florence and her father hurried north. Flo stayed to nurse the old lady, made her comfortable, kept her company, and elevated her spirits with droll stories about her grandchildren. Free of Embley's perpetual flow of visitors, Grandmamma Shore's house proved a haven that soothed Flo's uneasy spirit.

She ceded her post to Aunt Mai when Shore arrived at Lea Hurst for his summer holidays. Flo's love for him made her feel God's love. "What a blessing to feel that nothing can separate between us and our God, nothing that we can do, that He wishes to be reconciled to us, not us to Him." Nothing "Shore can do can ever separate between him and me. When he is naughty it makes him dislike me, not me him."[12]

Flo's parents then let her minister to her old nurse, who "fought the fight out till overpowered by the material universe, like a good *man* and true." How "*unheimlich* [uncanny] it is coming out of the room where there is only her and God and me, to come back into the cold and false life of prejudices and hypocrisy and conventionalisms."[13]

Since their daughter proved a superb nurse, the Nightingales could scarcely object to her spending every spare moment in easing the sufferings of the sick in nearby Wellow village. But when she "saw a poor woman die before my eyes" because "there was no one but fools to sit up with her, who poisoned her as much as if they had given her arsenic,"[14] Flo reasoned that if her fate lay in helping the indigent sick, she must get training. In three months at Salisbury Hospital, the large public institution near Embley, Flo could acquire skills ample enough to triple her usefulness in the village. And she would gain enough knowledge to educate others. For Flo dreamed that during "those dreaded latter days" after her parents' deaths she might rent a small house at Wellow to start "something like a Protestant sisterhood, without vows, for women of educated feelings"[15] to nurse the poor.

—∞—

Salisbury Hospital's chief physician, Dr. Fowler, and his wife came, as they often did, to dine at Embley. After savoring their postprandial port, the gentlemen joined the ladies. A westering sun cast its gentle glow over Fanny Nightingale's high-ceilinged drawing room as Florence dropped her bomb-shell.

Fanny and WEN saw delivering soup, clean clothes, and soothing talk to cottagers as Christian duty, teaching in a village school as correct, and donating to charity as admirable. Nonetheless, in all fairness, they drew the line at nursing in the filthy, stinking wards of a cavernous public hospital.

Disgusting as these cold, crowded, gin-soaked institutions were in 1845, the thought of their attractive, gifted daughter associating with the wanton women who made up the nursing cadre — for profession one could hardly call it — struck the Nightingales with horror. Chronically drunk, hospital nurses not only had sex with male patients but also "obliged" the medical students. How could carefully raised, fastidious Flo want to desert her wealthy, socially prominent home to associate with such females, let alone scour out slops, take soiled and verminous rags off sickly bodies, and restrain screaming patients during surgery? Besides, her delicate health would never stand the strain. Dr. and Mrs. Fowler agreed.

—∭—

Quarrels rocked the Nightingale household.

Sympathetic to Florence's views on the sad state of the world outside Embley, zealous to discuss politics, religion, and social conditions, WEN failed to understand, much less condone, his favorite child's eagerness for action. A despised occupation like nursing certainly did not fit into his image of her brilliant future. Flo had let her father down.

Living in the shade of an attractive younger sister starting to win a name in society, plain, sickly Parthe felt frightened. By playing the adoring sister she could share in Flo's social success and growing status as an expert on hospitals and health care. But where would Parthe be if Flo decamped for sordid hospital life? And if she did indeed become a nurse, the scandal would kill Parthe's chances of marriage. No worthy man would want to unite with a family whose daughter had sullied herself by willingly associating with wanton women. Parthe dissolved into hysterics at the mere mention of nursing.

"Mama was terrified," Florence confided to favorite cousin Hilary, not about "the physically revolting parts of a hospital, but things about the surgeons and nurses which you may guess."[16]

Sex constituted a taboo subject to upper-class Victorian females like Fanny Nightingale. Because the Victorian ideal of The Perfect Lady trained females to believe they had no sex drive. Florence tells us mothers taught their daughters that "'women have no passions.' In the conventional society, which men have made for women, and women have accepted, they *must* have none, they *must* act the farce of hypocrisy, the lie that they are without passion — and therefore what else can they say to their daughters, without giving the lie to themselves?"[17]

Lack of libido justified the Victorian woman's claim to moral superiority over men. Nonetheless, although females were the stoutest supporters of this moral standard, they also agreed that their weaker natures made them inferior to males. So women promoted duty over passion, compliance over autonomy.

Fanny accused Flo of having "an attachment" she was "ashamed of,"[18] a secret love affair with some "low vulgar surgeon." How else to explain this sudden, abnormal desire to "disgrace"[19] herself?

Florence loved her mother, hungered for her approval. The wish to nurse had grown so precious that Fanny's contemptuous dismissal of "my little plan," her accusation of forbidden sexual desires, mortified Flo, sapped her self-confidence. Uneasy, Florence continued outwardly to conform to Fanny's social demands. Inwardly, however, Flo clung to her resolve to nurse.

—⁂—

"My poor little hope, requiescat in pace [rest in peace], no one can know its value to me, no one can tell how dear a child however infantine is to its mother, nor how precious an idea," Flo confided to Hilary. Consumed by guilt for having aroused her mother's disapproval, convinced of God's punishment for sinning although sure He had "something for me to do for Him — or he would have let me die some time ago," Flo hoped "to do it by living." But how? "I am dust & nothing — a curse to myself & others. This morning I felt as if my soul would pass away in tears — in utter loneliness."[20]

Faith in God helped Flo hide her feelings of isolation and disgrace. She read the latest books, heard the finest musicians, showed interest in math, economics, and science. Flo accompanied her father to British Association (for the advancement of social science) meetings.* She took up the suggestion of Clarkey's friend Julius Mohl and translated the *Theologica Germanica*. But none of these activities fully engaged Florence's mind. Nor did they calm her troubled spirit.

A new friendship did.

The Nightingales met Selina and Charles Bracebridge through Clarkey. Rich and childless, socially impeccable, they were noted travelers and ardent Hellenists.

---

*Founded in 1831, the British Association held annual meetings, which were a clearinghouse for scientific information. WEN, a founding member, attended regularly; Florence joined him when the Association began to admit women.

He "claimed descent from lady Godiva."*[21] Scion of a prominent Warwickshire family, Charles had, as a young man, joined the Greeks in their fight for independence against tyrannical Turkish rule (1828–1830). Fluent in several languages, shrewd in business and liberal in politics, "one of the best specimens of an English country gentleman of the old school," Charles bred Arab steeds on his ancestral acres and liked to wear wide-brimmed hats and flowing capes. Florence thought him "the best and noblest of men. All his life he was fighting battles against cruelty and oppression."[22]

Selina Bracebridge, 1799–1874. "More than mother" to Florence, Selina gave her "strength to do and dare everything." Nightingale reverend Selina as having true humility and with it "the most active heart and mind and buoyant soul" imaginable (photograph by J. G. short of Lyndhurst, date unknown. Hampshire Record Office 94M72/F6p7/4).

Poised, capable Selina, "a tall, stately, irresistible line of battle ship,"[23] an "accomplished gentlewoman, skillful alike with pencil and with needle," warm and sympathetic, had, besides, "much literary culture."[24] Florence, twenty years her junior, thought Selina a "thorough woman of the world" who, nonetheless, had never "had a worldly thought." Flo knew "many more intellectual, many more brilliant," but "I never knew such an union & harmony of opposite qualities." Selina had "the heart of a woman, the judgment of a man — she is practical & poetical — the habits of a man of business, the imagination of an artist — the hand of earth, the soul of heaven."[25]

"There is a woman in

*An eleventh-century Anglo-Saxon noblewoman who pestered her husband to reduce taxes on Warwickshire's Coventry citizens. He agreed — if Godiva would ride naked through Coventry's crowded marketplace. She did. But Godiva's long hair covered her entire body except her legs.

whom to trust."[26] Selina came to mean "eyes to the blind & feet to the lame — many a plan, which disappointment has thinned into a phantom in my mind, takes form & shape & fair reality when touched by her."[27]

Selina Bracebridge's friendship brought Florence caring, unconditional support, the complete sympathy she so wanted and that her mother failed to give.

— ᴍ —

As day dawned over Flo's much-loved Derbyshire hills, she meditated on the spiritual world, wrote letters, and studied material about medical institutions. After breakfast, household chores and Lea Hurst guests absorbed Florence's time. On July 7 — she always devoted the seventh of each month, the day Flo first heard God call, to self-examination — she guiltily noted neglect to study Greek with her father, read her friends' letters aloud to her mother, or chat with Parthe. But Flo did accompany WEN on his daily ride and read novels aloud to her mother and sister.

In her limited free time, Florence followed her favorite field path. It wound behind Lea Hurst, revealing a splendid vista of hills and valleys, to the gray stone cottages of Holloway village. "O happy, happy six weeks at the Hurst, where I had found my business in this world. My heart was filled. My soul was at home. I wanted no other heaven. May God be thanked as He never yet has been thanked for that glimpse of what it is to *live*."[28]

Charles Holte Bracebridge, 1799–1872. Wealthy, well-known traveler and Hellenist. Owner of Atherstone Hall. "More than earthly father" to Florence and, with his wife, Selina, "the creator" of Nightingale's life (artist and date unknown. Reproduced with permission from Christine Freeman Jenking's *Memories of Atherstone*).

Florence "rubbed mrs. Spence for a second" time.

I am such a creeping worm that if I have anything of the kind to do, I can do without marriage, or intellect, or social intercourse, or any of the things that people sigh after, [Flo wrote in her diary.] My imagination is so filled with the misery of the world, that the only thing worth trouble seems to me to be helping or sympathizing there — the only thing where labor brings any return.

It satisfies my soul; it supplies every want of my heart and soul and mind. It heals all my disease. It redeems my life from destruction. Everything else that I do, I always feel that I am not doing it well or that somebody else would do it better, or that I am not quite sure whether it is right, whether I am doing it for the sake of God and whether I had not better be doing something else.[29]

Another soul-satisfying activity: planning a course of study for women working in factories, farms, or at home who longed for the learning and delight only to be found in books. Florence taught the older, brighter girls, who, in turn, taught others. In this way she made the most her time and talent, while nurturing confidence in her students. But Flo hardly ever succeeded in getting to the village school except "by stealing out of the house unseen because I was sure to be stopped."[30]

Nursing and teaching villagers, learning about hospitals in the chill moonlit privacy of her little top-floor bedroom, lightened Flo's frustration. "I should be very glad if I could have been left here, when they went to London, as there is much to be done, but" Fanny refused. Nevertheless, in London "you can at least have the mornings to yourself." In the country, "how long do you think we have ever been alone? Not one fortnight." And forever "expected to be looking merry & saying something lively."[31]

Florence spent three mornings a week nursing patients at a private London institute for spinal diseases. As well, she taught at one of social reformer Lord Shaftesbury's Ragged schools for waifs. Flo loved to work at this filthy, disease-ridden place. One day she snuck some of her grubby, verminous pupils up to her bedroom for games and treats. Outraged, Fanny Nightingale insisted that her daughter no longer venture outside unless a footman went with her.

—⁂—

Bubbling with energy and intelligence, meanwhile, Florence pleased her parents. She graced their drawing room each evening, either reading aloud, accompanying herself on the piano while singing delightful Schubert lieder, or quietly embroidering. But while Flo bent her head over excruciatingly boring needlepoint, her mind busied itself with a new plan. "I have never felt inclined to say 'resign yourself,' but 'overcome.'"[32]

How, Florence cudgeled her brain, could she contrive to visit Kaiserswerth, the Rhineland institute founded by a Protestant pastor to teach lay deaconesses to nurse the poor? For Prussian ambassador von Bunsen had not forgotten Florence's asking what one person could do to help the sorrows of the world. He sent her reports on Kaiserswerth.

Really, Flo reasoned, a religious sisterhood dedicated to charitable works could scarcely be compared with the gin-soaked semi-prostitutes who "nursed" in British hospitals. Besides, Kaiserswerth had no medical students to raise Fanny's hackles. And how could she object to Flo going there when the impeccable Prussian ambassador and his aristocratic English wife provided Flo with a steady stream of information about the place?

But Fanny Nightingale had other plans. Confident of having squelched Flo's abnormal ambition to train as a hospital nurse, Fanny turned to another troubling issue — her daughter's close friendships with older females, like Clarkey, Aunt Mai, and Selina Bracebridge. Blind to the fact that these friendships signified Flo's thirst for sympathy, for unequivocal mother love, Fanny thought marriage the best antidote. So she increased pressure on Flo to take interest in one of the eligible men attracted to her.

4

"Idol of the man I adored"

"Marrying a man of high and good purpose, and following out that purpose with him is the happiest" lot. "The highest, the only true love is when two persons, a man and a woman, who have an attraction for one another unite together in some true purpose for mankind and God."[1]— Florence Nightingale

Throughout her twenties Florence Nightingale balanced on a tightrope between her nursing dreams and her duties to family. Concomitantly, her country changed from an agricultural nation into the world's premier industrial power. During this transition Victorians, especially members of the upper-middle class like Florence's parents, clung to conventional norms — and none more so than that of the female model.

Women were inferior to men, weaker and less rational; hence, they needed male protection. A daughter, considered a girl regardless of age until she married, lived in her father's house under her mother's eye. A father's financial position determined his daughter's status. Later, her husband's would.

Sexual naïveté and complete innocence constituted the standard for a carefully raised Victorian female. But Flo thought if young women like her,

who never commit a false step, whose justly earned reputations were never sullied even by the stain which the fruit of mere "knowledge of good and evil" leaves behind were to speak, and say what are their thoughts employed upon, their *thoughts*, which alone are free, what would they say? [...] That, with the phantom companion of their fancy, they talk [of] what interests them most; they seek a companion for their every thought; the companion they find not in reality they seek in fancy, or, if not that, if not absorbed in endless conversations, they see themselves engaged with him in stirring events, circumstances which call out the interest wanting to them. Yes, fathers and mothers, you who see your daughter proudly rejecting all semblance of flirtation, primly engaged in the duties of the breakfast table, you little think how her fancy compensates itself. [And] you say, "She is not susceptible. Women have no passion."[2]

Females nurtured. Their purpose in life consisted of marriage and children. But Flo "did not agree *at all* that a woman has no reason" for "not marrying a fond man who asked her, and I don't think Providence does either." God "clearly marked out some to be single women," others "to be wives," and "organized them accordingly for their vocation. I think some have every reason for not marrying." For "these, it is much better to educate the children who are already in the world and can't be got out of it, than to bring more into it."[3]

Men acted. Laws reinforced their superiority. A wife's money, property, children, even her body and soul belonged to her husband. In turn he revered The Angel in the House, the wife and mother. Femininity meant living for others, like family, and occasionally visiting the poor and sick.

Some wealthy women sought serious activity. Society approved of their turning to charity. But Florence Nightingale thought if such work were to be done, it should be done with instruction and knowledge. Hence her desire to train at Salisbury Hospital and, when parental opposition shattered that plan, to learn nursing at Germany's Kaiserswerth.

Females like Florence, who sought fulfillment outside the confines of Victorian womanhood, had to fight the idea that only conventional morality mattered, that society would censure any female who wanted freedom to fashion her life. And to make matters more difficult, Victorians stigmatized their unmarried sisters as odd, redundant. A bad sister (prostitute, adulteress, or divorcée) meant loss of prestige for the whole family. Fanny and Parthe, who identified fully with her mother, feared Flo's wish to break from the accepted norm, the Perfect Lady, would mark her as a bad sister and disgrace them.

One glorious summer morning Flo walked "before breakfast, everything in a

> blaze of beauty. [The] voice of the birds is like the angels calling me with their songs, and the fleecy clouds look like the white walls of our home. Nothing makes my heart thrill like the voice of the birds; but the living chorus so seldom finds a second voice in the starved and earthly soul, which, like the withered arm cannot stretch forth its hand till Christ bids it.[4]

Later that day she joined her family for the brief drive to Broadlands, to dine with prominent Whig politician Lord Palmerston and his warmhearted wife. Emily Palmerston constructed her parties with meticulous care. So when the company assembled in the Palmerstons' casual but elegant drawing room, Fanny Nightingale heard her hostess's deep, drawling voice introduce Florence to Richard Monckton Milnes.

They were immediately attracted to each other.

"A most bland-smiling, semi-quizzical, affectionate, highbred, Italianized little man of 5 feet, who has long olive-blond hair, a dimple next to no chin, and flings his arm around your neck when he addresses you in public society,"[5] Milnes favored a fashionably high and stiff shirt collar with satin stock and frilled shirtfront. Hair waved over his ears to a tall and wide coat collar; sidewhiskers framed his face with its straight nose, high forehead, and slightly protruding lower lip. Gray eyes surveyed the world under arched eyebrows.

Educated at home until he went to Cambridge, Richard found the strain of final exams too much for him. Hence, he left without a degree and, after studying in Germany, stayed on the Continent for several years during which time he wrote poetry. Lacking the means to live a literary life, Milnes then turned to politics. As a liberal member of parliament he focused on factory reform and introduced a bill to establish juvenile reformatories.

Eleven years Florence's senior, intelligent and extremely well-read, extroverted Richard had, by the time he met her, made a mark in society. "A social favorite, a poet, and a real poet, quite a troubadour, as well as a member of parliament; traveled, sweet tempered and good hearted, very amusing and very clever," wrote a future prime minister who, in a novel, fictionalized Milnes as Mr. Vavasour. He "saw something good in everybody and everything, which is certainly amiable, and perhaps just, but disqualifies a man in some degree for the business of life, which requires for its conduct a certain degree of prejudice."[6] Indeed, Milnes's fellow members of parliament judged him a political lightweight; and his mundane speeches routinely emptied the chamber.

Vavasour's breakfasts were renowned. Whatever your creed, class, or merit — one might almost add your

Richard Monckton Milnes, 1st Baron Houghton, 1809–1885. Socially conscious socialite and intellectual, the man Nightingale "adored," whose offer of marriage "tempted" her (artist: George Richmond [circa 1844]. © National Portrait Gallery, London).

character — you were a welcome guest at this matutinal meal, provided you were celebrated. [Vavasour] prided himself in figuring as the social medium by which rival reputations become acquainted, and paid each other in his presence the compliments which veiled their ineffable disgust. [He] liked to know everybody who was known, and to see everything which ought to be seen.[7]

Inheritance and shrewd investment had, meanwhile, significantly improved the Milnes family finances. So Richard took an extended tour to Constantinople and Egypt.* On his return, he accepted Fanny Nightingale's invitation to Embley.

—⟋⟍—

Drawn to Milnes, comfortable in his company, Florence admired Richard's intellect and knowledge, his poetic talent and linguistic fluency. She appreciated Richard's keen interest in all kinds of people. Generous, kind, and known as a good man to go to in trouble, Milnes "treated all his fellow mortals as if they were his brothers and sisters."[8]

Above all, Flo valued Richard's readiness to be of use. He supported education of factory workers, formation of penny savings banks for laborers, and abolition of capital punishment. Besides, Milnes could be serious about the right subjects — pity for the famine-stricken Irish, factory reform, and juvenile reformatories. Increasingly, Florence came to rely on his sympathy.

She may not have known that Richard's enthusiasm for boys' reformatories ranged side by side with a keen interest in flogging. Nor did his push to abolish the death penalty stop Milnes from collecting hangmen's autographs. Indeed, his early and intense curiosity about the more bizarre forms of crime and punishment foretold Richard's fascination with, but not practice of, sadomasochism. He amassed a comprehensive collection of erotica including every edition of the works by and hand-written notes of the Marquis de Sade.

Florence enchanted Richard. Her approval of his philanthropic goals delighted him. Their mutual attraction grew. Yet, it troubled Flo. Could she reconcile her feelings for Richard with her wish to nurse? Would he sympathize?

Is it surprising that there should be so little real marriage, when we think what the process is which leads to marriage. [The acquaintance starts] under the

*Milnes rented a small riverboat with one tiny cabin to cruise the Nile for several weeks. As companion he chose an "eccentric and muscular" young Englishman. "Gross and strong pleasures," Milnes wrote at the time, "seem by their very nature to destroy the power of enjoying the finer and simpler pleasures of delight." Milnes's official biographer, writing when (1949) homosexuality still counted as a crime in England, says Milnes first discovered his homosexual tendencies at Cambridge (Pope-Hennessy, *Monckton-Milnes*, vol. 1, p. 166).

eyes of an always present mother and sister. [It] is fed — upon what? — the gossip of art, musical and pictorial, the party politics of the day, the chit-chat of society, and people marry or sometimes they don't marry, discouraged by the impossibility of knowing any more of one another than this will furnish. [Parents] say "be prudent, be careful, try to know each other." But how are you to know each other? Unless a woman has lost all pride, how is it possible for her, under the eyes of all her family, to indulge in long exclusive conversations with a man? "Such a thing" must not take place till after her "engagement." And how is she to make an engagement, if "such a thing" has not taken place?[9]

—⁂—

Fanny Nightingale approved of Flo's suitor. A literary light and member of parliament, Richard had enough brains to satisfy finicky Flo. He would engage in her humanitarian concerns. She would be a fitting hostess for his famous London breakfasts and lavish country house parties, let alone hold her own among Richard's intellectual friends. True, the Milnes wealth fell short of the Nightingale fortune, but Richard had excellent connections and his father stood on the verge of receiving a peerage. By marrying Milnes, Florence would fulfill her mother's dearest wish — a desirable union for her daughter.

Besides, it behooved Flo to marry — to scotch her mother's recurring dread. Were WEN to die, Fanny and her daughters would not be penniless, but they would be homeless. The Nightingale entail in his bachelor uncle's will left WEN's landed property, Lea Hurst and Embley, to Mai Smith, then to her son, Shore. But as Mrs. Monkton Milnes, mistress of a country estate and a London house as well, Florence could provide her mother and sister with appropriate residence.

Although neither Richard's poetry nor his politics had lived up to their early promise, Fanny reasoned that as a member of parliament he had status — per se — as well in society, for politics and society were still closely interwoven. Fanny had compromised in marrying WEN, like Milnes a wealthy dilettante, and had settled down happily with him. Energy and ambition had got her the social success she sought. Flo could achieve likewise.

Her mother's common sense resonated with Florence. Susceptible to society's lure, she also felt strongly tied to family. Flo loved her parents, yearned to please them. Equally, Florence felt compelled to fulfill her dream of nursing.

—⁂—

She wavered. Marriage meant a modicum of freedom, but not much. It might, indeed, result in exchanging one golden cage for another. Yes, Milnes had more sympathy for her philanthropic ambitions than Fanny, but given the climate of Victorian England he could scarcely be expected to condone Florence's full-time commitment to nursing.

A handful of husbands did let their wives work for social causes, like Elizabeth Fry for prison reform, but these women still found domestic duties a barrier to public work.

> When shall we see a woman making a *study* of what she does? Married women cannot; for a man would think, if his wife undertook any great work with the intention of carrying it out,—of making anything but a sham of it—that she would "suckle his fools and chronicle his small beer" less well for it,—that he would not have so good a dinner—that she would destroy, as it is called, his domestic life.[10]

Conversely, "if there is any good in me," Richard told Florence, "it is that I would lay out my life in good service to others."[11] But, Flo asked herself, did she want to fulfill her dreams through her husband?

Then, too, Richard reveled in his social position. His ideal of life with Florence thus diverged from her model self-image. "If I might be utterly emptied of my self-love, so that I could think honestly and soberly of myself as a mere tool to do any work the Almighty might be pleased to appoint me. Oh! For this I would willingly sacrifice all hopes of success of any kind."[12] Yet, yet—"self-love" commanded a considerable amount of Flo's attention. And she thirsted for her mother's praise, which the scintillating social life of Mrs. Monckton Milnes would certainly warrant.

Florence's independent-minded "Clarkey darling," meanwhile, gave her further fruit for thought on marriage. After the death of her dear friend Fauriel, followed by that of her mother, Clarkey felt extremely lonely. Not only did the Channel separate her from her only living relative, her married sister, but an intellectual chasm divided them. So at age fifty-four Clarkey yielded to the persistent wooing of her close friend and junior by ten years, the distinguished German Orientalist Julius von Mohl. He had loved Clarkey for years.

To avoid inevitable gossip, they kept their intentions secret. One radiant summer morning Miss Mary Clarke donned her finest clothes and took a hansom cab to the church where two witnesses, sworn to secrecy, awaited. The new wife and husband then returned to their respective homes. Two days later the Mohls and their witnesses dined at the railway station restaurant. The newlyweds then departed for a Swiss honeymoon.

"To think that you are now two months' wife" and "I have never written to tell you" that your marriage "gave me more joy than I ever felt in all my life," Flo told her friend. "Why didn't I write before? Because I thought you would be rather let alone at first & that you were on your travels."[13]

To marry is no impersonal verb. [In] single life the stage of the present & the outward world is so filled with phantoms [of] vague remorse, fears, dwelling on the threshold of every thing we undertake alone. Dissatisfaction with what is, & restless yearnings for what is not, cravings after a world of wonder. [The] stage of actual life gets so filled with these that we are almost pushed off the boards & are conscious of only just holding on to the foot lights by our chins. Yet even in that very inconvenient position love still precedes joy. [Laying] to sleep these phantoms (by assuring us of a love so great that we may lay aside all care for our own happiness ... because it is of so much consequence to another), [love] gives that leisure frame to our mind, which opens at once to joy.[14]

—⁂—

Florence felt far from joyous. Richard's wish to marry had thrown her into an agony of indecision. Flo longed to nurse, but God had failed to speak again. That must mean she had not yet proved herself worthy to serve Him. Fanny failed to comprehend why Florence hesitated to accept Milnes's flattering offer. Life at home grew more difficult. The mental and emotional energy needed to crush her true desire and act the dutiful daughter, plus uncertainty over marriage and the problems it posed, sapped Flo's appetite and broke into her sleep. She lost weight, became listless. Migraines, then bronchitis, attacked.

Flo fled into daydreams. Yet, they terrified her — her mind might slip out of her control. As dreams lasted longer, grew more frequent and intense, Florence chastised herself. Daydreaming signified menace.

We fast mentally, scourge ourselves morally, use the intellectual hair-shirt, in order to subdue that perpetual day-dreaming, which is so dangerous! We resolve "this day month I will be free from it"; twice a day with prayer and written record of the times when we have indulged in it, we endeavor to combat it. Never, with the slightest [success.] It is the want of interest in our life which produces it; by filling up that want of interest in our life we can alone remedy it. [But] how obtain the interest which society declares *she* does not want, and *we* cannot want?[15]

Little did Flo realize that daydreams are a common, not to say normal occurrence. Daydreaming can foster creativity, help solve problems, and keep one focused on goals.

—⁂—

When brisk autumn breezes turned Derbyshire hills and dales to amber and gold, Florence took to her bed with another wheezing, racking cough. How could she possibly face three winter months at Embley? The benign Hampshire countryside would turn cold, the water-meadows would freeze, and the thatched cottage roofs would congeal with frost. Embley could thus count on seeing fewer guests. This meant more opportunity for family quarrels ranging Fanny and Parthe on one side, Flo on the other, while peace-loving WEN stood aloof.

Selina and Charles Bracebridge offered an escape.

5

A Taste of Freedom

Oh, how happy I was! I never enjoyed any time in my life as much as my time in Rome.[1]— Florence Nightingale

The Bracebridges invited their ailing young friend to join them on a journey to Rome. By exchanging England's bone-chilling winter (1847–1848) damp for an extended stay in that balmy, sun-soaked city, Selina and Charles hoped to recover their health. All "I want to do in life," Florence confided to close friend and favorite cousin Hilary, "depends on my health, which, I am told, a winter in Rome will establish forever."[2]

Selina Bracebridge's sound common sense, to say nothing of her stellar social connections, commended her to Fanny Nightingale, and Fanny trusted Selina to keep Flo from committing any social solecism having to do with nursing. Then again, ministering to the poorly Bracebridges would occupy Florence and satisfy her yearning to be useful. Fanny approved of her daughter nursing family, friends, even villagers. Flo's full-time commitment to nursing made Fanny frown.

Above all, Fanny and WEN agreed that this chance to go abroad with such kind and cultured friends, such experienced travelers, came at a favorable time. Congenial company plus exposure to classical antiquity and Renaissance treasures could well deflect their precious child from her stubborn pursuit of a nursing career, not to mention bring Flo to her senses about marriage to Richard Monckton Milnes.

WEN retired to his library to research and draw up a detailed sightseeing itinerary.

Parthe raised a ruckus at the idea of months-long parting from her younger sister. Feeling guilty over utterly failing to understand Flo's ambition to nurse, never mind giving it her sisterly support, Parthe also felt envious. Flo enjoyed seemingly easy social success, and she had attracted an eligible suitor. Parthe wanted to be part of Flo's life. But once her parents convinced their older daughter that Rome might well be the making of Flo, Parthe backed the plan. She helped Fanny shop for Flo's clothes. She collected introductions, and announced her sister's arrival to friends living in Rome. "God is very good to provide such a pleasant time and it will rest her mind," Parthe averred piously but without any true comprehension, "from wearing thoughts, that all men have at home when their duties weigh much on their consciences."[3]

Florence heaved a sigh of relief at the prospect of freedom from the fetters, boredom, and quarrels of home. And her spirits soared at the prospect of being with Selina, "the angel of my life."[4]

Of course Flo had qualms about leaving her family. These she eased by making sure to spend time with Parthe, and by promising to share her treat with sister and parents. In turn, they expected Rome to showcase Flo's writing talent. Nor were the Nightingales disappointed. "You may rejoice over your child's letters from the keen perception she has of every thing that is great and beautiful and her extraordinary power of apprehending what are the conceptions of other minds," Selina told Fanny. Flo's "observations deserve to be treasured up; and as her letters home contain the whole of these original and exquisite thoughts they must be *incomparable* like herself."[5]

—◊—

The ambient air held a hint of frost as Fanny and WEN stood on the quay waving farewell. Foam-flecked waves rendered the Channel crossing unusually rough. Seasickness at once felled Flo's French maid, but her mistress "adhered like a pancake to my back, screwed my eyes tight close," and focused on keeping her head still. "No tongue can tell the rapture with which you open your eyes at last and see"[6] land instead of heaving gray water. Selina fared less well, so the friends hurried to the comfort of Paris's elegant Hôtel Meurice, overlooking the autumn glories of the Tuileries Garden.

Flo found Selina's neuralgic headaches a distinct challenge to her nascent nursing skills. But once she felt able to leave her patient, Florence ventured out into the soft Parisian sunshine to cross the Seine. Ten years had gone by since she first visited Clarkey in her Left Bank apartment overlooking the rue du Bac. "Oh that I had an ink bottle a foot deep, and a year of time to describe" recently married Mrs. Mohl "and the dress and state I found her in," Flo told her family. When informally at home, Miss Clarke had often worn odd clothes, even kept her hair in curl papers. Now Mrs. Mohl "out–Clarked miss Clarke, but good kind god of hymen, how much thou hast done for her mentally — how happy she is."[7]

—◊—

Formerly, Flo had traveled slowly south through France in her father's custom-built carriage. Charles Bracebridge arranged to reach Rome with maximum speed.

So after Florence had gently massaged Selina's throbbing head, the Brace-bridge party left Paris in the diligence (commercial coach) bound for Châlons, a thirty-five-hour journey with two brief stops. Neuralgic headaches still laid Selina low, but Flo bubbled with vitality. She liked roughing it, and did very well on only two cups of coffee.

Eager to take advantage of autumn's benign weather, Charles let his ladies rest for only a day at Châlons before sailing south on the Saône River. "The entrée to Lyons is beautiful, quite beautiful. The city sits by her river shore under her crowned heights and stretches out her hand, spanning her stream with her white fingers like a queen whose broad brow is adorned, not weighed down, with her diadem," the Nightingales read. Action-oriented Flo thought a city "more affecting than any creation of nature — she seems to say, Look at me, with my busy veins boiling with joys and cares and anxieties, which you know nothing of, and my great brain full of thoughts and hopes and fears."[8]

The travelers next boarded a Rhône riverboat bound for Avignon. Driven indoors by fog, Selina and Flo sat in the main cabin "with a crowd of people talking Arabic, French, Irish, everything but English (as we deserted the ladies' cabin, because they were so cross there, and the miserable women did nothing but groan at the delay)." Giving her "dear people" details of her journey that she had no time to describe in her daily letter, Flo thought she "could not well be in any place more amusing."[9]

"The noble beautiful Rhône" at last "carried us like princes for 2 days — the ruined castles sitting like goats on pinnacles of rock which no other creature could climb — the towns like creations of nature, not of man, so cloudless and smokeless was their look." And "the glorious sky over all." Dusk saw the sun "glow like the pomegranate."[10]

Where possible, the friends journeyed from inland Avignon to the Mediterranean port city of Marseille by rail, otherwise diligence. Its coachman drove his horses over the rutted roads at "full gallop which was much better, as short and sharp is a mercy." Flo kept her "eyelids and lips *tight* shut, lest my eyes and teeth should jump out, and I not be able to find them in the dark."[11]

At Marseille the Bracebridge party boarded a snug Sardinian ship. After battling for their berths with an English peeress who tried to bully the captain into giving her and her screaming child the better cabin, Florence and her friends sailed from France's major Mediterranean seaport under clear blue skies. Flo rose daily at dawn to watch the sunrise. The travelers did some sightseeing when their ship stopped at Genoa and Leghorn and took a side excursion to Pisa before reaching Civita Vecchia, the port of Rome.

[Selina and Flo] always carried our sponges, soap and brushes every where [with] us in my green bag, and if ever we had half an hour or a room to ourselves, off with our clothes, a rush at the [washstand,] a covenant about the towel, mutual sacrifices, and a wash. At last we came to [think] we were wasting our time, and not attending to our improvement, if we ever saw a basin in a solitary place, without taking advantage — and it was meat and drink to us. If it was dinner v. wash, I always found it [better] to prefer the latter.[12]

—⁂—

On her first morning in Rome, Florence "scoured myself, and cleaned myself from the dust of many days, and as soon as" daylight dawned "almost ran till I came to St. Peter's. I would not look to the right or left." Nothing "in my life, except my death, can ever be greater than that first entrance into St. Peter's, the concentrated spirit of Christianity of so many years, the great image of our faith which is the worship of grief. I went in. I could not have gone there for the first time except alone." Florence "walked up to the dome" and knelt. "I have no art, and it was not an artistic effect it made on me — it was the effect of the presence of God."[13]

Mundane matters followed. Two days of a nonstop search for lodging. Florence admired Charles's Italian, "not only his accent, but his fingers, his gests, his jokes, his look out of his eyes are all first rate," so the "lodging house keepers adore him to the amount of many scudi [Italian currency]."[14] The friends settled on what Selina judged a "very tolerably comfortable" residence. Centrally located in a small street off the piazza di Spagna, the apartment consisted of nine rooms on the third floor of a "remarkable mansion." A "horrible, steep, half-lighted staircase," which "we all crawl up and down" with "utmost caution,"[15] constituted the only drawback.

Selina still felt poorly on moving-in day, so Florence went out to buy breakfast — Roman black bread and large, luscious, green Muscat grapes. She then searched the piazza Navonna for late autumn flowers, bringing back yellow and white margaritas, violet saffron crocuses, and scarlet carnations "to make us look a little pretty."[16] Flo then arranged her room. "My dressing box and everything which Parthe packed, all came out so beautifully."[17]

Having drawn up a budget, Florence and Charles sallied forth to the bank. "An imperial nobleman received us and treated me as if I had been the princess of Wales, and I had to sign my name about 42 times, and had a check book to bring home, and all for a poor little £100 — and we were both in such a fright, mr. B. because he had expected another imperial nobleman with the eye of fire upon him through the door," with whom he dealt at another bank, "for having forsaken it, and I because I did not know whether I was to make my mark, or sign a marriage contract with the Devil in red ink, and was afraid the emperor, who was so dreadfully gentlemanlike, would cheat me."[18]

Poor health kept both Bracebridges in bed well into the mornings and at home in the evenings during those first days in Rome. Nursing them — massaging Selina's headaches away and applying leeches to Charles — occupied much of Florence's time. Otherwise, she could do as she liked. "More than earthly father and mother to me,"[19] Selina and Charles understood their young friend's need for autonomy.

—⚏—

"Converts are always enthusiasts."[20] Once they felt better, the Bracebridges went into society. Free of Fanny's hectoring and Parthe's hysterics, not to mention her much-resented elder sister "governessing," Flo enjoyed society.

"How like a Roman I felt when I found myself sitting on a sofa in a pink gown, two kinds of cakes and a tablecloth,"[21] Flo wrote her family. After a Roman dinner party, she, Selina, and Charles heard instrumental music at the home of Americans, then attended a reception at the British embassy. They could easily "have gone to *five more* but we didn't — we shamefully turned tail and fled."[22]

Flo even felt able to afford levity on a fraught subject. "The moment I received your letter," she wrote Fanny, "I rushed out, and bought me *four* gowns! *three* of them to be worn all at once, viz, two skirts of white muslin, and one of petticoat, the fourth a black silk skirt, for the ceremonies,* which must all be attended in black. Now are you not pleased?"[23]

"You would be *content* if you could see dear Flo's improved looks from Roman air & Roman life," Selina wrote WEN. "You will readily believe that your precious child is the sun of our little circle. I cannot help telling you, though, how she is understood and valued by others. Sidney Herbert, for instance, *quite* appreciates her and talks of her forever."[24]

Everyone liked tall, handsome Sidney Herbert. Younger son of an earl, born and brought up at the hub of power and politics, Sidney had been educated at Harrow and Oxford. Always cheerful, with a "happy, joyous laugh" and "droll way of putting things,"[25] the charming, sweet-natured young man decided to dedicate his life to public service. Partly because he had been brought up to believe it the correct career, partly out of a sense of duty, but wholly without ego-driven purpose. Elected to parliament at age twenty-six,

*Audiences with the pope. In Florence Nightingale's day the pope ruled autocratically over Rome and the Papal States, which stretched across central Italy from coast to coast. The Church strangled every aspect of modernity, even prohibiting the railway and telegraph as works of the Devil. However, one year before Flo arrived in Rome, Pope Pius IX became pope. Decent and kindly, Pio Nono had read modern books exposing papal misgovernment and advocating a federated, united Italy, a concept dear to the hearts of those Italian exiles the Nightingales had met in Geneva ten years before. Pio Nono at once declared general amnesty for political offenders and granted freedom of the press and of speech. English liberals like the Nightingales and Bracebridges applauded Pio Nono's reforms. His audiences were highlights of Florence's stay in Rome.

Left: Elizabeth Herbert, Lady Herbert of Lea, 1822–1911. Gifted, well-born, and beautiful. Nightingale's intimate friend for more than 60 years. With her husband, Sidney, responsible for Florence's position in the Crimean War (artist: Richard James; after James Ronnie Swinton [1850]. © National Portrait Gallery, London). *Right:* Sidney Herbert, 1st Baron Herbert of Lea, 1808–1861. Aristocrat and parliamentarian. Nightingale's essential partner in army medical reform and ideal friend, "one who will and can join with you in work the sole purpose of which is to serve God. Two in one, and one in God" (artist: Sir Francis Grant [1847]. © National Portrait Gallery, London).

Herbert proved to have a talent for politics. Besides being a shrewd judge of people, he had a keen sense of backroom tactics. Herbert's refusal to indulge in partisanship earned him universal respect. Most recently, he had served in the cabinet.

Sidney put his wealth to work by paying private school fees for sons of poor gentlemen's widows, financing seaside holidays for impoverished clergymen. He planned to found a cottage hospital on his family estate. Historic Wilton belonged to Sidney's elder brother, the Earl of Pembroke, who resided abroad. Through mutual arrangement, Sidney lived at Wilton and managed the ancestral acres. His projected hospital would allow Wilton's village poor to recover from illness before returning to work. Herbert wanted to staff the hospital with German Protestant sisters, such as those trained at Kaiserswerth.

Sidney Herbert and his lovely, like-minded wife, Mary Elizabeth (Liz), were honeymooning in Rome. Fourteen years her husband's junior and two years younger than Flo, Liz also sheltered within Selina Bracebridge's maternal mantle. The Herberts and Florence were at once drawn to each other.

—⚏—

Liz, Selina, and Flo went to visit Santo Spirito Hospital.

On arrival, the three English ladies were met with a priest's admonition: they must ask the monsignor himself for permission to enter.

"Rather unwillingly we went up," Flo regaled her family. "To provide against all dangers, we made mrs. Herbert, who is accustomed to speak to live cardinals, go first."

At the third door, "I saw her curtseying on the threshold, lower and lower — I thought she was going to kneel down — we went in — an immense round table separated the sacred monsignore on one side and three impudent females on the other."

"Half rising, half ready to run round one side if we attempted to run at him by the other" the monsignor rapped out: What do you want? The hospital cannot be opened at any odd time.

"In a half scolding, half complaining voice" the monsignor then wanted to know whether the ladies were going to leave Rome soon.

"No one answered."

Flo concluded that "they meant me to tell the lie."

"*Very* soon," she said, "bowing to the earth."

"In that case," the monsignor replied, "when do you want to see the convent?"

"Tomorrow," flashed Flo.

"It's too soon," countered the monsignor. "We can't get it ready."

"Well then, Wednesday," Flo grudgingly conceded.

"Do you want to see the conservatoria *too*?" asked the monsignor in a pained voice.

"Of course," replied Flo.

"Again prostrating ourselves, we withdrew. I was laughing too much to make the least apology"; Liz Herbert went back to make it. Flo begged her family to tell no one this "truly impudent" story: "Inglesissimo, is the only adjective it deserves. However, we got what we wanted."[26]

Women who share an experience like that amidst daily and delightful contact over a period of several months are bound to bond for life. Liz, Selina, and Flo did.

—⚏—

Liz Herbert introduced Flo to several charitable institutions. At the Sacred Heart convent of the Villa Sante, nuns "bring up about 40 poor orphans entirely, till they are 18 or 19, when they find them places." After showing the English ladies the entire institution, the mother superior "offered us the best room in the villa for our retraite, if we would come. You know the women of the world in Rome all make retraites, generally once a year,"[27] Florence told her family. She forbore to say she would do likewise.

Drawn to Roman Catholicism, Flo studied its doctrine and ritual. But because she believed each individual to be responsible for her own mental and spiritual state, Florence distrusted dogma.

> The great merit of the *Catholic Church*: its assertion of the truth that God still inspires mankind as much as ever. Its great fault: its limiting this inspiration to itself. The great merit of *Protestantism*: its proclamation of freedom of conscience within the limits of the Scriptures. Its great fault: its erection of the Bible into a master of the soul.[28]

Rome showed Florence the practical good works of Catholic sisterhoods. Impressed, she got interested in the philanthropic work of Trinità dei Monti Convent, especially its large orphanage and girls' school. During her retraite Flo scrutinized the convent's organization, rules, and techniques, noting every detail that might be relevant to Embley's Wellow village school, and contrasted Trinità dei Monti's gentle atmosphere with the severity judged essential to control poor children in England.

Flo felt particularly connected to the convent's extremely efficient mother superior. Madre Santa Colomba wanted to turn the wild, dirty little urchins who came to her orphanage into People of God, apostles for His new kingdom on earth. So she engaged cheerful, caring teachers who held a positive view of their pupils.

Colomba believed in Florence's call to service. The two women talked long and earnestly. Flo recorded Colomba's wisdom. "It is no good separating yourself from people to try and do the will of God," the nun said. "That is not the way to gain his blessing. What does it matter even if we are with people who make us desperate? So long as we are doing God's will, it doesn't matter."[29]

—⚅—

In the happiest New Year she ever spent, Flo danced out 1847 and danced in 1848.

She followed WEN's meticulously researched sightseeing itinerary, feeling

> more and more every day my gratitude to that father, who taught me all I ever knew, who gave me all the ideas I ever had, who taught me interest in nations

as though they were personal existences, and showed me how to look upon all churches as but parts of the one great scheme, all opinion, political and religious, as but accidental developments of the one parent sap.[30]

Florence usually explored Rome with the Bracebridges and Herberts, but Charles's fall on the steep, ill-lit stairway leading to their apartment caused cancellation of an outing. Sensing Flo's disappointment, Selina suggested they go out alone. So after attending to Charles's cuts and bruises and settling him cozily in the library, the two women walked down a backstreet and took a ferry across the sluggish yellow Tiber.

Of "all my days in Rome this has been the most happy and glorious," Flo told her family. "Think of a day alone in the Sistine chapel with Selina, quite alone, without custode, without visitors, looking up into that heaven of angels and prophets." Flo seemed to see

> straight into Heaven itself, and that the faults of the representation and the blackening of the colors were the dimness of my own earthly vision, which would only allow me to see obscurely, indistinctly, what was there in all its glory. [Daniel] opening his windows and praying to the God of his fathers three times a day in defiance of fear. You see that young and noble head like an eagle's disdaining any danger, those glorious eyes undazzled by all the honors of Babylon. Then comes Isaiah, but he is so divine that there is nothing but his own 53rd chapter will describe him. [Rather startled at first to find] him so young, [Flo conceded that] M. Angelo knew him better; it is the perpetual youth of inspiration, the vigor and freshness, ever new, ever living, of that eternal spring of thought which is typed under that youthful face. Genius has no age.

Nobody could see "the Sistine without feeling that he has been very near to God, that he will understand some of His words better for ever after."[31]

Flo and Selina refreshed themselves with coffee and black bread at a small café in the sunny piazza, then bought roast chestnuts from an old woman. The friends juggled the steaming delicacies in their handkerchiefs as they peeled off the cracked brown skin and ate the sweet, soft, aromatic chestnut meat while walking up a winding road. At the top they admired a glorious view of the Campagna stretching away to the sea. Recalled to reality by the setting sun, Selina and Flo rushed down the hill to get to St. Peter's before it closed. They were rewarded by having the magnificent church to themselves.

Revisiting the Sistine early one morning in "splendid light, I looked almost for the first time at the Last Judgment. But I am afraid of it, and cannot look at it for more than 5 minutes at a time, when I return to the divine old prophets. How any *mortal* mind could have had such a conception as that Last Judgment is like a miracle — it so real, so living."[32]

—⚹—

Wrapped in Selina's mantle of maternal acceptance and sisterly support, delighted at her blossoming new friendship with sympathetic Liz and Sidney Herbert, thrilled with the cultural and political stimulation of Rome, and encouraged by Madre Santa Colomba's wisdom, Florence felt happy. No more daydreaming. She looked forward to home and reunion with her "dear people."

Meanwhile, political excitement gripped the Continent. In Rome, liberal Pio Nono's reforms were in full spate. To Florence and her friends' delight, he gave the Papal States a constitution and Rome secular government. The Milanese drove out hated Austrian troops, and Piedmont's king declared war on Austria. Sicily erupted. "The king of Naples had to cede to Sicily an amnesty for the rebels, freedom of the press, a constitution, assembly, self-government and the dissolution of Sicily's union with Naples. For all the people's cry was, We will have Pio Nono's reforms, nothing less, nothing else,"[33] Florence exulted.

The 1848 revolutions in Italy, France, the Austrian empire (central Europe and part of the Balkans), and the Germanies hampered the Bracebridge party's homebound journey. Flo, in any case, had "little interest in seeing other places." She preferred "to keep my vision of Rome as a purely distinct and undivided recollection of my life, a jewel for which no setting is wanted, for which no setting is sufficiently valuable." Florence favored going "home as we came out, without any other aim or object to divide our attention."[34]

They sailed from Leghorn to Marseille, then proceeded cautiously north through restless France. A brief stop in Paris to glimpse Clarkey, then home.

Frustration soon resurfaced. Flo bickered with Fanny and favored Parthe with sarcasm. Despite resolve, moreover, Florence, to her chagrin, experienced a revival of what she called vanity (wishing to impress people) and hypocrisy (erecting a façade of convention to please her family while pining to nurse). And although Flo applied to Wellow Village School the lessons she had learned with Madre Santa Colomba at Rome's Trinità dei Monti Convent school, she thirsted for more action.

The Herberts invited Florence to their country estate. At Wilton she met a group of socially impeccable, important people concerned with hospital reform. Not for nothing had Flo for years risen in the nippy pre-dawn to analyze and chart hospital statistics from Continental pamphlets collected for her by Clarkey and Julius Mohl, and by Prussian ambassador Bunsen and his wife, not to mention the government blue books that reformer Lord Shaftesbury sent. Florence Nightingale became known as an expert on hospitals.

Taking advantage of an enforced stay in London, she wheedled her father into letting her inspect London hospitals and help organize Ragged schools for destitute orphans. WEN deferred to his wife. Fanny demurred. But since other ladies helped with the schools and closer contact with hospitals might discourage Flo from visiting such disgusting dens of iniquity, Fanny grudgingly agreed. In this she deceived herself and underrated her daughter's determination. Florence went to as many hospitals as she possibly could, and worked at the Ragged schools using her notes on Madre Santa Colomba's institution as an example.

Shortly after, Flo accompanied her father to a British Association (for the advancement of social science) meeting at Oxford, the center "of loveliness and learning." Never "was anything so beautiful," either at home or abroad, "as this place is looking now," with "flowering acacias in the midst of its streets and palaces. I saunter about the churchyards and gardens by myself before breakfast, and wish I were a college man."

WEN and his favorite daughter worked "hard. Chapel at 8, to that glorious service at New college; such an anthem yesterday morning! And that quiet cloister where no one goes. I brought home a white rose to-day in remembrance. Sections from 11 to 3. Then colleges" until dinner. Next a "lecture at 8 in the Radcliffe library. And philosophical tea and muffins at somebody's afterwards." Ranged among "the great guns" who "occasionally are the philosophy"[35] stood Richard Monckton Milnes.

6

The Penultimate Battle

The thoughts & feelings that I have now I can remember since I was 6 years old. It was not I that made them. Oh God, how did they come? What are they? A profession, a trade, a necessary occupation, something to fill & employ my faculties, I have always felt essential to me, I have always longed for consciously or not. [The] first thought I can remember and the last was nursing work.[1]— Florence Nightingale

Richard Monckton Milnes visited Lea Hurst that summer (1848). The drawing room's tall French windows opened onto sunny, flower-scented lawns overlooking a splendid panorama of hilly Derbyshire countryside. Bees buzzed busily among gaudy crimson hollyhocks and delicate yellow dahlias. Wearing a high vee-necked, cotton chintz dress, scalloped at skirt and sleeves, patterned with pink-petaled and green-leafed flowers on a plain white background and tied at her slender waist with a sash in matching pattern, "the idol of the man I adored"[2] listened gravely to Richard's formal proposal.

Marriage "never tempted me. I hated the idea of being tied forever to the life of society, and only such a marriage could I have. I had never given up the idea of reaching at last a better life. But there came a marriage for me which fulfilled all my mother's ambition: intellect, position, connections, everything." Marriage to Richard "tempted"[3] Florence.

Richard understood her urge to serve the poor and sick. He might not be able to help Flo completely realize her goal, but as his wife she would have a better chance of at least some fulfillment. "I could be satisfied to spend a life with him in combining our different powers in some great object."[4]

Nevertheless, Milnes had status in society, and that status meant much to him. He would expect his wife to share it. Sympathetic, yes, but as a wealthy Victorian gentleman Richard could scarcely be expected to condone his wife committing herself fully to hospital nursing or, indeed, any other career. Besides, she would be far too busy with his famous London breakfasts. "Behind *his* destiny woman must annihilate herself, must be only his complement. A woman dedicates herself to the vocation of her husband; she fills up and performs the subordinate parts in it. But if she has any destiny, any vocation of her own, she must renounce it."[5]

Florence believed marriage must be founded on "a love so great ... we may lay aside all care for our own happiness ... because it is of so much consequence to another."[6] She did not have that kind of feeling for Richard. Indeed, overwhelming love left little, if any, room for reason. Flo had been applying logic to the question of marriage to Richard for months — furnishing her with further proof that she could not be enough in love with him. "I have an intellectual nature which requires satisfaction and that would find it in him. I have a passional nature which requires satisfaction, and that would find it in him. I have a moral, an active nature which requires satisfaction, and that would not find it in his" life. "I could not satisfy this nature by spending a life with him in making society and arranging domestic things."[7] Florence rejected Milnes.

Her parents' disappointment devastated Flo. Nor could she explain her decision, for Florence did "not understand myself— how can I hope to make anyone else understand my case?"[8] On her knees at church in deep reflection, however, Flo again heard one of God's "calls to service."[9] This conviction strengthened Florence's conscious rejection of erotic intimacy and deliberate suppression of the passional part of her personality. Faith also helped Flo come to terms with her choice.

"Oh God, no more love. No more marriage. O God."

Flo held firmly to her belief that "every woman cannot make herself into the complement of that particular man, which act is necessary to make of the two the one being almost divine which real married people *is*."[10]

Nonetheless, "the very thought" of seeing Milnes again "quite overcomes me."

> Not one day has passed without my thinking of him, that life is desolate to me to the last degree without his sympathy. And yet do I wish to marry him? I know that I could not bear his life. That to be nailed to a continuation & exaggeration of my present life without hope of another would be intolerable to me — voluntarily to put it out of my power ever to be able to seize the chance of forming for myself a true & rich life would seem like suicide. And yet present life is suicide.[11]

Some weeks later Parthe fell ill. This proved fortuitous. Parthe's doctor prescribed the water cure at Carlsbad, a fashionable spa in Germany's beautiful Black Forest near Frankfurt and, coincidentally, the Kaiserswerth institute.

Puzzling over a path to Kaiserswerth, Florence, while passing through Paris on her way to and from Rome, had enlisted close and sympathetic friend Clarkey's aid. Clarkey did not fully agree with Flo's ambition to nurse but did believe she should be free to pursue it. Clarkey and her husband, Julius Mohl, planned to visit his native Germany. They could easily arrange to be in Frankfurt while the Nightingales were at Carlsbad. Julius lured WEN with the offer of introductions to Frankfurt's intellectual elite. Without telling her mother and sister, Flo won her father's consent to visit Kaiserswerth while he indulged in erudite conversation and Fanny and Parthe recruited their health in grand style.

Alas, the revolutions rocking Europe reached Germany and settled in Frankfurt. So the Nightingales unpacked their trunks. Kaiserswerth seemed farther out of reach than ever.

"Marriage is the only chance (and it is but a chance) offered to women for escape from this death"[12] of family life. Flo had given up that chance — for what? No nurse training, no more sympathy from the man she adored. Daily more committed to dedicating her life to the poor and the sick, Florence felt desolate indeed.

The Bracebridges, von Bunsens, Herberts, other friends and social luminaries interested in improving conditions among the less fortunate encouraged Flo. But she wanted her mother's support. Florence loved Fanny too much to willingly cause suffering. She begged Fanny to let her nurse full-time. No.

Seeing her sins as boulders blocking the way, Florence resolved to cultivate patience with God's timing. She must become worthy of His commands — must resist society's lure, conquer her egotism, and overcome daydreaming.

—◊—

Wrapped in a woolen shawl against the pre-dawn cold, Florence filled notebooks with statistics from government reports on hospitals, sanitation, and municipal health that her friends and fellow reformers collected for her. She analyzed her data with arithmetic exactitude. As well, Flo delved into poetry, theology, and history in English, French, and German. This stretching of her mental powers stimulated independent thought, which, in turn, intensified Florence's sense of vocation. If she could not nurse now, "I desire for a considerable time only to lead a life of obscurity and toil," to let "whatever I may have received of God to ripen, and turning it some day to the glory of His name."[13]

Meanwhile, Flo seized every chance for lengthy visits — to Aunt Mai and Uncle Sam, who, together with cousin Hilary, supported her goals as well as her rejection of Milnes. Florence "had *no idea* of staying so long" with the

Herberts, "but Lizzie is poorly" — "in bed today, so I am really glad I stayed, as I teach in her school and do her jobs in the village, and she is in such a fidget if they are not done, because she says there is nobody in her family who *likes* doing it. Therefore she feels there is nobody whom she can ASK to do it."[14]

What "shall you say to me, if I profit by your kind permit, and stay till Tuesday?" Flo then asked her "dearest mother."[15] "You are very good in writing, & in writing such peaceful letters," Florence thanked Fanny. Nevertheless, "Parthe's letters *are my misery* & if you cannot stop her, I suppose I must come home."[16]

Despite Parthe's protestations, Flo spent as much time as possible with her beloved and revered friends the Bracebridges. What a difference Selina made "in my life. The very fact of there being one person" who did not judge Flo's thoughts "fit only for a dream not worth disputing," who did not view her "as a fanciful spoilt child who ought to take life as it is and enjoy it," that "fact changes the whole aspect of things." Since Flo had found "one person who does not think" society "*ought* to make one happy," she no longer experienced "that sinking of spirits at the thought of the three winter months of perpetual row."[17]

Perpetual row failed to stop Flo from nursing the sick poor on her father's estates. This Fanny reluctantly accepted, for by now (late 1840s) upper-class Victorian females had joined their country's growing interest in a gamut of medical, religious, and charitable activities centered on the indigent ill. Trained to be loving and emotional, but without sexuality, wealthy girls undertook altruistic work or devoted themselves to family, like Flo's docile cousin Hilary. Nonetheless, Victorians expected these daughters merely to dabble in charity, not commit fully.

Seeing her capable daughter chafe at idleness, realistic Fanny put Flo in charge of pantry, linen room, and stillroom — where jam and preserves were made from home-grown fruits and vegetables. "I am up to my chin in linen & glass," Flo told Clarkey. "In this highly educated, too little active age, it, at least, is a practical application of our theories to something." After making a detailed inventory, Flo inspected sheets, plates, silver, and crystal listing damages, replacements, and repairs. But amidst her "green lists, brown lists, red lists, all my instruments of the ornamental in culinary accomplishment, which I cannot even divine the use" of, "I cannot help asking in my head. Can reasonable people want all this?" And "why is woman considered by woman *herself* as more of furniture than man?"[18]

Despite Flo's effort to be a dutiful daughter, her commitment to nursing continued to provoke Fanny's rage and Parthe's hysterics. Torn between guilt at causing upset at home and faith in nursing as her vocation, Flo escaped into daydreaming about how to reach her goal. Lackluster appetite and loss of sleep, meanwhile, caused frequent fainting. And increased susceptibility to infection resulted in feverish colds.

—⁓—

"More than mother to me"[19] Selina Bracebridge and her husband, Charles, again provided escape. Planning to exchange England's winter (1849-1850) for a more benign climate, they invited Florence to join them on a leisurely Nile cruise.

Relieved at the thought of respite from the endless bickering between Flo and Fanny, ably abetted by Parthe, peace-loving WEN gladly gave permission. But Fanny balked. Poverty and disease prevailed in Egypt, Western women were harassed, and she knew of people who had died there. Besides, how could WEN justify rewarding Flo for being difficult — for staying with the Bracebridges, Herberts, or Sam Smiths for weeks on end and only with extreme reluctance returning home to help her mother entertain guests? And then, funding Florence on another foreign jaunt reflected so unfairly on Parthe.

WEN held firm. Dismayed at Flo's refusing Milnes, he thought his favorite, his brilliant Florence, could at least lead an intellectual life, which travel would stimulate. So WEN promised Fanny and Parthe a Continental fling as soon as revolutionary fever abated. They could stay at an elegant spa, move in exalted circles, and shop galore.

Stubbornly sticking to a conviction that her twenty-nine-year-old daughter would outgrow her abnormal desire to nurse, Fanny conceded that Egypt could succeed where Rome failed: turn Florence from sordid nursing into a life of cultured ease. Foiled in her ambition that Flo marry, Fanny seized on the literary career now open to women as a decent alternative. For Flo's letters from Rome proved talent. Parthe, eternally the elder sister certain she knew what would be best for Flo, agreed.

Flo hoped Egypt's climate would restore her health and the Nile cruise provide peace to settle her dilemma: follow the divine command or the call of family duty.

—⁓—

Appreciation of antiquity meant preparation.* Already familiar with ancient Hebrew, Greek, and Christian cultures, Flo now studied early Egypt-

---

*Forty years before Florence went to Egypt, Napoléon's invasion of the country (1798) gave birth to modern Egyptology. Nelson's naval defeat of France at Aboukir Bay (1798) ended Napoléon's North African ambitions, but the scholars he had taken with him continued their excavations and published their findings. After the Allied victory over France at Waterloo (1815), English and German scholars flooded Egypt. Their researches, as well as contemporary travel

ian civilization with her friend and noted Egyptologist Prussian ambassador von Bunsen. And Florence took private lessons on how to read hieroglyphics.

The Nightingales "equipped her *en princesse*,"[20] including a contraption, complete with mosquito netting, that could serve as sleeping bag or convert to a chair. Flo's luggage aroused "the admiration of all and I find all sorts of conveniences in my writing box. You labored so hard for my outfit which is indeed a splendid one. I don't believe there is anything I *can* want."

"Goodbye dearest people, thanks for all more than I can say, bless you more than I can bless you. I hope I shall come back to be more of a comfort to you than ever I have been. Thank you all a thousand times, ever dear Mum your loving child."[21]

After crossing the heaving, slate-colored Channel, Flo and her friends sped south to Marseille in chilly fall weather, reaching Egypt after an eight-day sail eastward across the Mediterranean. Disembarked at Alexandria, they asked their "janissary, Alee, who walks before us, and is the most gentle, yet most dignified being I ever saw (I am quite afraid to speak to him), to show us the way to the baths." A long walk took them "to a gateway, and through an avenue of date-palms, bananas, and petunias trellised overhead, to a long, low building with Pompeian baths in red and green, and blue squares, and low archways (against the heat), leading from one to the other." Selina, Flo, and Charles each got a twist of palm stems for washing themselves, with a lump of "beautiful"[22] Egyptian soap in the middle. Flo thought all European appliances paled in comparison to that nest of palm stems.

Since Alexandria offered few sights, Florence spent all her free time observing the hardworking sisters of St. Vincent de Paul.[23] She also inspected their excellent schools for poor children, and their hospital for the indigent sick.

A "delightful week in Cairo" made Flo wish they could stay longer. She loved riding in the streets, their "latticed windows meeting overhead, the pearls of Moorish architecture at every corner, the looking up to the blue sky and golden sunlight from the wells of streets and in the bazaars." But "you cannot conceive the painfulness of the impression made upon one by the" abject poverty of the people. Flo could almost believe "this *is* the kingdom of the devil" and "shudder under this glorious sun."[24]

accounts, provided Flo with further reading. Still, her journey predated the mature study of Egyptian archaeology, let alone the era of modern tourism. People and animals still lived among the antiquities, and few Europeans had traveled the Nile.

Victorians considered Egypt, entry to the exotic East, as the land of the Arabian Nights. A Nile cruise connoted romantic adventure. Although the river did boast a few steamboats, by far the most delightful and relaxing way to travel, not to mention the most costly, consisted of a *dahabieh*, a long, light-draft houseboat. Charles Bracebridge hired one originally built for a nobleman's harem. It had never carried Europeans, which, of course, enhanced its appeal.

Egyptian authorities required that passenger vessels not only register under both owner and renter names but also fly a personal flag. Flo, Selina, and Charles named their dahabieh in Parthe's honor. Flo made the swallow-tailed pennant. She sewed a red Latin cross on the blue flag, and white tape to mark "Parthenope" in Greek letters. "It has taken all my tape, and a vast amount of stitches, but it will be the finest pennant on the river, and my petticoats will joyfully acknowledge the tribute to sisterly affection, for affection in tape in lower" Egypt "is worth having."[25]

The *Parthenope* afforded space and privacy. Charles and Selina slept in the larger cabin, Flo in the smaller. Their attractive little sitting area had green-painted panels and a divan encircling its walls. Taking a midnight walk at the first stop, Flo gathered a bouquet of wild pink and white roses to brighten their quarters.

> Our store-room and pantry stand before us in the shape of two large chests on deck, which separate our domain from the crew's; our larder hangs overhead in the shape of a basket full of bread, and two cages full of oranges and meat; our kitchen is immediately beyond — another box, about six feet by four, and behind it is our water goullel; [filter] kitchen, scullery, still room, larder, safe, and pantry, all in a nutshell, or at least in a walnut. Ah! Would that you could keep house in England so, my dearest mother.[26]

Sailing in a large vessel that needed rowing or towing when the wind dropped took time. So to fight dejection and dreaming during her abundant leisure, Florence pored over the weighty tomes that filled her trunks. She charted ancient Egyptian dynasties, copied temple plans, and analyzed erudite opinions on Egyptian mythology. Flo read aloud to her friends, nursed poorly Charles, and wrote lively, detailed letters home. Besides, she delved into the Greco-Latin *Hermetica* (early Egyptian philosophy and theology). Like ancient Christian scriptures blending elements of Judaism, Christianity, and earlier traditions, the *Hermetica* stressed self-knowledge as a means to know God.

"They call me 'the wild ass of the wilderness, snuffing up the wind,' because I am so fond of getting away."[27] When the dahabieh moored, Flo walked in the moonlit desert. She longed to ramble alone, explore villages where people and animals lived in the same mud hut, talk to anyone who struck her fancy. But either Selina, Charles, an Egyptian attendant, or her personal maid always accompanied Florence.

By chance one evening, the *Parthenope* anchored next to a village at war with another on the opposite shore; its sheikh did not welcome the distraction of a dahabieh in his waters. Charles invited the sheikh to coffee onboard. Flo and Selina were charming. The sheikh shed his doubts. So much so that he gave the English party "three guards, and two cats, which we wanted almost as much, for the rats in my cabin are so fierce and bold, that I am obliged to get up at night to defend my dear boots. You cannot keep clear of rats with all your care, when you are anchored near grain-boats sometimes all night."[28]

Charles and his ladies had decided to head straight south to Abu Simbel. There they would turn north, allowing themselves ample time to explore antiquities.

"We shall never enjoy another place like" Abu Simbel, the "greatest point of our voyage — greatest" in every respect; "the absolute solitude of it — the absence of" that "horrible Egyptian present." Flo and the Bracebridges explored the massive temple of Ramses II by candlelight. Every inch "is covered with sculptures, perfectly uninjured except for the coloring, which is gone." Flo felt as if she "had never seen sculpture before."[29]

As the dahabieh approached Philae,* Florence kept watch on deck. "Moon light walk on the island. Sitting on Philae by the temple of Isis with the roar of the cataract I thought I should see *Him*. *His* shadow in the moonlight."[30]

"I have never *loved* a place so much — never felt a place so homey: thank God for all we have felt and thought here. Every moment of that precious week, from before sunrise" until well into night Flo "spent upon the sacred island, most of it in Osiris' chamber." She could not describe "the feeling at Philae. The myths of Osiris are so typical of our Savior that it seemed to me as if I were coming to a place where He had lived."[31]

Florence spoiled that happy, happy week with daydreaming, she noted in her diary. "Disappointed with myself & the effect of Egypt on me — Rome was better."[32]

Rome's familiar Christian images, plus Madre Santa Colomba's spiritual support, calmed Flo. Ancient Egypt caused stress by raising questions on the nature of God and the reason for one's existence. Modern Egypt's poverty intensified Florence's belief that she had been placed on earth to help the less

---

*An island in the Nile sacred to Isis, faithful wife to the beneficent king Osiris. In a parallel to the Passion of Christ, Isis resurrected Osiris after his brother killed him.

fortunate. And the need to suppress her feelings in cheerful letters home increased inner turmoil.

—⚭—

The sightseeing day began with eight o'clock breakfast. A small dinghy then took the friends

> to western Thebes; the asses rush into the water to meet us, or the crew carry us ashore; we mount the asses, and with a great multitude — for in Egypt every attendant has his ass, and every ass his attendant — we repair (preceded by a tall man with a spear, his wild turban coming undone in the wind) like a small army, to a tomb; the tomb instantly fills — we suffocate for two or three hours, the guides having, besides, lighted fires and torches therein. When nature can sustain no more, we rush [out.] Goullels, bread and dates are laid upon a stone. Those who have strength then begin again until till dark brings the delightful ride home, the quiet, the silence (except that no Arab is ever silent — the donkey men and the guides talk without one moment's pause). [The] sunset tints, the goats coming home, the women spinning at the head, the gamous (the great Nile buffalo) crossing the little branches of the Nile in large herds, [two] little children perhaps riding the neck of the largest. [The] evening picture is all beautiful.

Having dined, "we are all hung up by the tails, like the chameleons, pretending to be dead, and waiting for half-past seven, or at latest eight, to bury us, lo! a dreadful splash of oars." The courier "puts in his head, with an abominable grin at our mute misery, and says 'The Hungarian count!' or 'the German professor!'" Charles cravenly retires and "is generally heard to snore." His ladies "unwillingly, but nobly, sacrifice ourselves to our duty, sit up (in the brown Holland dressing-gowns we are sure to have on, having been much too tired to dress), and talk; but we never give one drop of tea, which has greatly limited these visitations." Do not, Flo begged her family, "think us grown ... savage or uncivilized. It is very hard to be all day by the deathbed of the greatest of your race, and to come home and talk about quails or London. What do people come to Egypt for?"[33]

—⚭—

Florence refrained from mentioning her infected throat. It and intense daydreaming sapped her energy for days.

"Luxor before breakfast. Long morning" alone, Flo recorded in her diary. "Sat on the steps of the portico, moving with the shadow of the sun, and looking at the (to me) priceless view. God spoke to me again."[34]

Ten days later Florence felt too ill to get out of bed. "God called me in the morning and asked me would I do good for Him, for Him alone without reputation."[35]

She thought "much about this question — my madre [Rome's Santa Colomba] said to me, '*Can you hesitate between the God of the whole earth & your little reputation?*'"[36]

Flo "tried to bring my will one with God's all the way" while she and Charles rode into Cairo for their mail. As she "sat in the large dull room waiting for the letters, God told me what a privilege he has reserved for me, what a preparation for Kaiserswerth in choosing me to be with" Charles "during his time of ill health & how I had neglected it — & had been blind to it. If I were never thinking of the reputation, how I should be better able to see what God intends for me."[37]

Instead of fulfilling the Nightingales' wish that Egypt would divert their Flo from nursing, her exposure to "the greatest of your race"[38] intensified Florence's faith, clarified her purpose in life, and deepened her dialogue with God. He had called her "to work," to "throw my body in the breach."[39]

Florence thought the mosques of Cairo the loveliest, "most gorgeous," finest in the world, she wrote her family. They belied description. The "great drawback is that as you must have a firman [permit] and a pasha's janissary, and pistols, and whips, and I don't know what besides, to visit them, you must not loiter, you cannot go again, and they remain in one's mind, quite ineffaceable, but still one great dream of confused magnificence."[40]

On her final day in Egypt Flo revisited Alexandria's St. Vincent de Paul Hospital. She and Selina were also invited to a pasha's harem. "If heaven and hell exist on this earth it is in" those "two worlds."[41]

The Bracebridge party then sailed northwest across the Mediterranean to Athens, where Charles owned property. Their unexpectedly protracted voyage[42] exhausted Florence, in any case a poor sailor but now suffering a low-grade fever.

After Egypt's grandeurs the Acropolis, which Flo could see from her bedroom window, seemed small and all of Athens "like a cork model, like an antiquarian's plaything." So Florence abandoned antiquity to spend all her spare time with an American missionary and his wife. The Hills ran a "perfect" school for girls. To "their greatest glory" these Americans had not "converted, in twenty years, one single soul," Flo told Parthe. The Hills wanted "each girl to revere the doctrines of her own church."[43]

On her thirtieth birthday (May 12, 1850), "the age Xt began his mission," Flo vowed no "more childish things, no more vain things, no more love, no more marriage." "Lord, let me only think of Thy will, what Thou willest me to do. O, Lord, Thy will, Thy will."[44]

That day Flo told Fanny she had "no regrets for the departure of a youth" she had "misspent, a life" she "disliked. But I am full of hope for the life which is set before me and for the occupations of which I hope I shall find myself better prepared than I have been for those of a life which is set behind me." Convinced her mother opposed full-time nursing from a sincere, if faulty, belief that she acted in Flo's best interest, the daughter felt truly "sorry for all the trouble I have given you, my dear Mother," but "I hope being now no longer a youth, I shall do so no more."[45] Florence's contrition notwithstanding, her letter could scarcely be expected to instill much comfort in Fanny's heart. Worse would follow.

—⟶⟶—

Despondent and enervated, Flo "let all the glorious sunrises, the gorgeous sunsets, the lovely moon lights pass by" while she sailed north on the Adriatic from Athens to Trieste. "I longed but for sleep. My enemy [dreaming] is too strong for me — everything has been tried." Rome, mental distraction, "the beauty of the East — all, all is in vain."[46]

Florence "never opened my heart" to Selina, "never *told* her I was wretched." Selina "never told me my life was fair and my share of its blessings great and that I *ought* to be happy. She did not know that I was miserable but she felt it."[47]

"To me wings, the pure heroic soul who lifted me out of the baser perplexities of life, or gave me strength to do and dare everything,"[48] Selina convinced Charles to brave their friend Fanny Nightingale's fury. In any case, planning to travel overland from Trieste to Le Havre, the Bracebridges thus decided on a route through Germany. They would stay in Düsseldorf for two weeks so that Florence could visit nearby Kaiserswerth.

"On the brink of accomplishing my greatest wish," with Selena "positively planning for me," Flo felt "unfit, unmanned for it." Guilt at causing the Bracebridges to betray Fanny's trust made Kaiserswerth seem "not to be the calling for *me*."[49]

Without her mother's sanction, Flo's self-doubt and fear of failure persisted despite magnificent mountain scenery, not to mention the cultural attractions of Vienna, Prague, and Dresden, where Flo fell under the spell of a Raphael Madonna. But she perked up in Berlin.

Thanks to introductions from her friend Prussian ambassadress von Bunsen, Florence met founders of charitable institutions, wealthy women acting on their principles. The city "pleases me wonderfully," its life "so much richer than that of London. People are so" busy with "great things." Of course, "political life is wanting but politics will not make up a woman's life," Flo wrote her family. "If an Englishwoman is not married and has no children, she has no profession, no career, no absorbing and compulsory vocation but a class in a Sunday school. And what's a class in a Sunday school to occupy all the mind and heart and imagination that God has given her? I shall meet with no réponse in this. So I abstain."[50]

Florence spent hours with the aristocratic matron of a new model hospital. "Beautiful as a statue," the "humility, fun, simplicity and dignity of the creature were what struck me the most. She has got deaconesses from all classes." The "hospital is like a palace, the deaconesses' rooms are just like ours at Embley." The matron had "her two rooms with books and prints and flowers, just as I think the intellectual and practical life ought to be always combined."

Her new friend introduced Florence to a women's hospital where another aristocrat had been matron for twenty years. She lived in "two rooms, exactly like my lady's drawing rooms in London. *This* is what I call the social freedom of Berlin. This is the *profession* of their women." Furthermore, Florence found "no more question about immorality" than "in private families in England and the licentiousness of the medical class is as much put a stop to as in our homes."[51] Scarcely words to set Fanny Nightingale's mind at ease.

Flo made no mention of Kaiserswerth. But this letter put her family on notice.

—⧉—

On a sunny summer evening Florence Nightingale first saw the ancient town of Kaiserswerth. It sat on the shore of the busy river "Rhine — dearer to me than the Nile."[52]

Pastor and Mrs. Fliedner had started with a small elementary school and a hospital to train volunteer deaconesses to nurse. Twenty years later the Kaiserswerth institute had grown to include a penitentiary, orphan asylum, and teacher training school. Basic education, care of the sick, and district nursing skills were taught. Cleanliness, neatness, and simplicity ruled.

"I never did my own hair till I came here."[53] Having left her personal maid with the Bracebridges, Florence, on her "first night in my own little room" at the deaconesses institute, "felt queer, but the courage which falls into my shoes in a London drawing room rises on an occasion like this. I felt so sure it was God's work."[54]

She went to church with the deaconesses and dined with the Fliedners. Florence participated in the novice nurses' Bible lesson, helped a sister gather vegetables from the garden, and accompanied another to sessions with the orphans where, Flo noted approvingly, teachers loved their pupils and promoted a positive outlook.

After strolling through the twilit garden with Pastor and Mrs. Fliedner, Florence sat with the apothecary sister. Hourly they toured the spotless wards — no smells; no revolting sights; male nurses for men patients; no male doctors in residence — even Fanny Nightingale could find no fault.

"Left Kaiserswerth feeling so brave as if nothing could ever vex me again & found my dear people at Düsseldorf."[55] (Note: Florence Nightingale referred only to her immediate family as "my dear people" — except, in this case, the Bracebridges.)

No more daydreams, no more illness. Exuding energy and euphoria, Florence took less than a week to write *The Institution of Kaiserswerth on the Rhine*. Selina and Charles postponed going home until she finished. Charles then edited the manuscript and sent it to London to be published anonymously. Aiming to inspire others, let alone justify her return, Florence's pamphlet told English ladies kept in what she called busy idleness but yearning for meaningful occupation about Kaiserswerth's work, joy, and camaraderie.

"One quiet autumn evening, after an absence of ten months" and another stormy Channel passage, Florence walked up "the steep hill which led to her mountain home, came up through the garden, softly, softly, and in at the steps of the drawing-room window"[56] to surprise "my dear people sitting in the drawing room & not thinking of me."[57]

7

The Prison Called Family

These persevering earnest desires of our Flo to walk in a different path from what they had hoped to see her take, cost them much struggle and unrest." They failed to "understand that she *cannot* be satisfied without following that which her soul longs for.[1]— Hilary Bonham-Carter

The prison which is called a family, will its rules ever be relaxed, its doors ever be opened? [The] iron chain is drawn tight round the family, fettering those together who are not joined to one another by any sympathy or common pursuit.[2]— Florence Nightingale

The Nightingales' delight at having their Flo with them for golden autumn (1850) days at Lea Hurst proved fleeting. Fanny's anger over Kaiserswerth shattered her daughter's happiness. Parthe greeted the news with hysterics, let alone refusal to speak to her errant sister. WEN took offense at his favorite child having allowed Charles Bracebridge to edit and arrange publication — even if anonymous — of her Kaiserswerth pamphlet.

Flo fled to Aunt Mai, currently caring for her ailing mother. "You are very good to let me stay here, *very*," Flo wrote Fanny from Grandmother Shore's nearby house. Mai's "devil of a conscience" failed to trouble her for keeping Flo, since it gave "the old last *happiness*.... And if the old people did but know what a haven of rest their shadow of death gives to the living young ones, they would be glad to live and not die."[3]

Peace of mind and Mai's unconditional support eased the sting of maternal and sisterly ire. Then Flo's first suitor, cousin Henry Nicholson, drowned in a sailing accident. His distraught family asked for Henry's beloved. After the funeral, Florence took Henry's mother and his sister Marianne to London to sort Henry's belongings, a chore the devastated ladies refused to face without Flo's comforting presence. They begged her to return to Waverly with them. Fanny refused permission.

Frustrated, Florence rounded on her family. WEN had "never known what struggle is." He had "good impulse" but felt sadly unfulfilled, for he had "not enough to do."[4] Although a true "father to his places ... people and cottages which he so loved & cared for: never pampering by indulgence: wise & careful: always helping them to help themselves,"[5] WEN would still have been happier with "a factory under his superintendence — with the interests of 2 or 300 men to look after."[6] Taking for granted the wealth WEN husbanded so wisely, Flo failed to acknowledge his skill in steering the family fortune through Britain's recent financial woes.

She bickered incessantly with Fanny, who stuck like a burr to her goal of a brilliant life for her gifted child. Florence must, of course, marry well, but if she preferred to stay single, why not become a literary light? Proud of Flo's letters from Rome and Egypt, let alone her scholarly status, Fanny completely failed to see why her capable, energetic daughter could not be satisfied with refining her God-given talents in her lovely, cultured home.

"You don't think with my 'talents' and my 'European reputation' & my 'beautiful letters' & all that I'm going to stay dangling about my mother's drawing room all my life," Flo imagined herself telling Fanny. "I shall go & look for" work. "You must look upon me as your son, your vagabond son without his" money. "I should have cost you a great deal more if I had married or been a" son. "You were willing to part with me to be married."[7]

> FANNY: You are a wretched, ungrateful girl. After all the money we've spent on your foreign flings, it's high time you accepted your family responsibilities.
> FLO: What more can I do? It seems as if nothing I've done is enough to satisfy you.
> FANNY: If you want so badly to nurse, abstain for six months "from doing *anything*" distressing to your poor sister, and "give up that time entirely to her."[8]

Flo had lately found teaching at an adult evening school for factory girls "the most satisfying thing I ever did."[9] Perceiving this harmless activity as a new threat, possessive Parthe reacted with a series of panic-stricken outbursts. Protective of her sickly firstborn, Fanny insisted Florence conform at least for Parthe's sake. Peace-loving WEN kept quiet to evade conflict. Flo unjustly accused him of "utter indifference." He "never cared *what I was* or what *I might become*."[10]

In the end, Flo agreed to commit "this act of insanity."[11] Because the "strongest character is generally the most submissive," since the "affections are also in proportionate strength. And by these it is led."[12]

Florence's wish to please her mother proved paramount. "When I feel her disappointment in me, it is as if I was becoming insane. When she has organized the nicest society in England for us, & I cannot take it as she wishes."[13]

—〰—

The sisters sketched and made music together, strolled Embley's graveled paths, talked of Parthe's favorite topics — art and literature. A "bird of paradise" floating "over this world without touching it, or sullying its bright feathers," Parthe seemed to Flo a "most difficult" character to describe because of her "simplicity." One could call Parthe "remarkably frank," but she "had nothing more to" say to her sister than to "her fortnight's acquaintance. Parthe talked as openly" to "one as the other." With "the widest sympathies" and "fewest friendships," Parthe liked everyone and "cared for scarcely" anyone. Although "she had this happy disposition," Flo thought her sister "happy much more from duty, than people gave her credit for."

"Unselfishness" constituted Parthe's "characteristic" and "enjoyment of the present" her "charm." Parthe represented "the true type of woman. She" had "not the smallest ambition."[14]

But she loved being a hostess. "And a very good vocation it is." Parthe needed "no other religion, no other occupation, no other training"; she "is in unison with her age, her position, her country. She has never had a difficulty, except with me. She is a child playing in God's garden & delighting in the happiness of all His works, knowing nothing of human life but the English drawing room." What "a murderer I am to disturb this happiness."[15]

Florence rued their disparate personalities; if only the sisters had been more alike, Flo could have done Parthe more good. Flo tried "to be tender & gentle"[16] but could "hardly open my mouth without" vexing "my dear Parthe."[17] And despite all that "intellect and kind intention could do," Parthe found Flo "a shocking nurse."[18]

Bitter about her bondage, Flo's nursing lacked her typically Incredible Bonté.

She wanted "to die. There is not a night that I do not lie down in my bed, wishing that I may leave it no more." Flo stayed "in bed as late as I can, for what have I to wake for? I am perishing for want of food — & what prospect have I of better?" She daydreamed about "situations which will afford me food," rued the "years I have watched that drawing-room clock & thought it never would reach the ten." As for the next twenty years, "it is not the misery, the unhappiness that I feel so insupportable, but to feel this habit, this disease gaining power upon me — & no hope, no help. This is the sting of death."[19]

Florence focused her limited private time on soaking up information about hospitals. And poured her frustration into writing *Cassandra*.* It

*Trojan princess Cassandra rejected the amatory advances of the god Apollo. To avenge this insult, Apollo put a curse on Cassandra: she would prophesy accurately, but no one would believe her. Victorian women interpreted this to mean that social censure would doom females who rejected marriage (and sexuality, which they equated) to silence or insanity.

condemned Victorian society for confining upper-class females to the prison called family. "Daughters come into the world without their own consent. The law gives them nothing. God gives them their time and faculties. May they not have these"? And if the life their parents and siblings "lead, does not interest them," or "exercise those faculties and employ satisfactorily that time, may they not use them elsewhere than at home?"[20]

Cassandra bewailed the boredom and pettiness caused by limits on female life and protested the waste of female energy and talent. "The time is come" for women to "do something more than the 'domestic hearth,' which means nursing the infants, keeping a pretty house, having a good dinner and an entertaining party."[21]

Most females were unaware of this evil — a woman's lack of power over her life, submission to husband and family, loss of identity except through her father or spouse. "One alone, awake and prematurely alive to it, must wander out in silence and solitude — such an one has awakened too early ... sees the evil they do not see" yet "has not power to discover the remedy for it."[22]

—⚏—

Once free of enslavement to Parthe, Flo went on a long visit to Sidney and Liz Herbert. At their country estate, Wilton, Flo met America's first female physician, finishing her medical training at an eminent London hospital. Common background and interests, to say nothing of mutual commitment to work, meant instant sympathy between Elizabeth Blackwell and Florence Nightingale.

They spent hours discussing "the problems of the present and hopes of the future."[23] "Do you know," Florence asked Elizabeth as later they stood in the shade of two magnificent cedars of Lebanon that were opposite Embley's drawing room, "what I always think when I look at that row of windows? I think I should turn it into a hospital, and just how I should place the beds."[24]

Blackwell tried to convince Flo's mother to let her nurse full-time. But an accident during Elizabeth's medical training had caused her to lose an eye. That robbed Blackwell's cogent reasoning of any resonance it might otherwise have had with Fanny Nightingale.

Her mother's adamant attitude increased Flo's thirst for sympathy. But when she bumped into Monckton Milnes at a party "he would hardly speak." Miserable, Florence

> wanted to find him longing to talk to me, willing to give me another opportunity to keep open another decision; or perhaps I only wanted his sympathy without looking any further. He was not ready with it. He did not show

indifference, but avoidance. No familiar friendship. No confidence such as I felt towards him.[25]

No wonder. Milnes got married soon after.*

That and Fanny's obstinacy forced Flo to face facts. She could "expect no sympathy or help from" her family. "I must *take* some things, as few as I can, to enable me to live."[26]

Serving God must mean reducing her misery as well as pleasing her family. So Flo resolved to "spend one hour a day at least at the school" for factory girls. "Without this, I" cannot "preserve my being" and "shall be more capable of doing what they want the rest of the day." She would keep "my hour & a half steady thinking before breakfast. Without this, I am utterly lost," whether "thinking" meant writing to aunt Mai Smith about spiritual matters "or writing for myself." Above all, Flo must put "contact with these 3," her parents and sister, "on a true footing." Now "vibrating between irritation & indignation at" her "state of suffering" and "remorse & agony at the absence of enjoyment I promote in them," Flo wanted to die. "This is childish."

Her parents and Parthe's "most earnest desire is for my happiness." Flo must fulfill "their desire by taking as much" happiness "as I can."

"I have so long been treated as a child" and have so long let "myself to be treated as a child that I can hardly assert this even to myself," and then only "with the greatest effort."

"I have so long craved for their sympathy ... *struggled* to make myself understood," that "I can hardly reconcile myself to this."[27]

—⁓—

Were Florence to take practical steps towards freedom, freedom to focus her life on nursing, she needed training. Kaiserswerth beckoned.

Upper-class Victorians had become interested in hospitals since Flo's abortive effort to train at Salisbury Infirmary six years before. And Fanny could hardly cavil at Kaiserswerth's piety and cleanliness. Located in the country, far from urban filth and moral menace, moreover, Kaiserswerth would not expose her delicate daughter to the drunkenness and sexual debauchery of nurses in an English metropolitan hospital.

Florence lobbied her father. He respected Flo's nursing of his mother and bringing comfort to the Nicholsons when Henry died. Besides, eye trouble had lately given WEN personal appreciation of Flo's care. Meanwhile, poorly

*A year later Florence and Richard remet. Both had moved beyond her refusal. He felt happy with his compliant, adoring spouse; Florence stood on the brink of fulfillment. They met as, and remained, friends. Flo befriended Richard's wife; Richard joined in Flo's causes; she stood godmother to his son; he named a daughter Florence.

Parthe blamed her ills on worry over Flo's mad resolve to nurse. Fanny agreed. Parthe's doctors again advised the water cure at Carlsbad. WEN had promised Fanny and Parthe a Continental jaunt once the political situation stabilized. It had. So WEN supported Flo's return to Kaiserswerth while Parthe and Fanny basked in the amenities of Carlsbad.

Valued family friends like the Bracebridges, Bunsens, and Herberts, let alone favorite relatives like the Sam Smiths and Bonham-Carters, urged Fanny to let Flo go to Kaiserswerth. Sensitive to Flo's feelings, willing to conciliate, ready to relieve her daughter's misery, Fanny, nevertheless, had difficulty in dropping her bred-in-the-bone belief that she knew best for her child. Still, Florence's mother did yield — albeit with bad grace.

Parthe refused to be reconciled. On the evening before Florence entered Kaiserswerth, her sister "threw my bracelets which I offered her to wear, in my face and the scene which followed was so violent that I fainted."[28]

—m—

Neat in her blue print deaconess uniform, thirty-one-year-old Florence found Kaiserswerth full of

> interest & strengthens me body & mind.... We have ten minutes for each [meal,] of which we have four. We get up at 5 — breakfast at ¼ before 6 — the patients dine at 11 the sisters at 12 — we drink tea, (i.e. a drink made of ground rye) between 2 & 3 — & sup at 7. We have two ryes & two broths — i.e. ryes at 6 & 3 — broths at 12 & 7. breads at the former, vegetables at 12. Several evenings [per] week we collect in the great hall for a bible lesson [or] account of missions etc.
>
> This is Life. Now I know what is to love and to love life, and really I should be sorry now to leave life. I know you will be glad to hear this, dearest Mum.[29]

No response.

Her reading and observation had, meanwhile, made Florence realize that her ultimate goal in committing to nursing consisted of becoming superintendent of nurses in a major hospital, mainly because that would allow her to educate other women to nurse. Since Kaiserswerth's structure gave the superintendent (matron) full charge of all deaconesses, Florence, for future reference, carefully noted how Kaiserswerth's deaconesses were trained to obey their superintendent. They must regularly give an "account of their office & have to take her counsel thereupon — & to be appointed by her." The superintendent's duties included acting as "mother of the house," having in mind "at least the welfare of every member &" caring "for it with zeal & love & power. She should help every sister find her heart, & seek" each probationer's "confidence to make their abode in the house as pleasant as possible & make them love their chosen vocation & become capable of it."[30]

Busy, happy, no more dreaming. Florence felt the lack of only one salient factor.

I sh'd be happy here as the day is long, [and] wish I could hope that I had your smile, your blessing, your sympathy [without] which I cannot be quite happy. My beloved people, I cannot bear to grieve you. Life & everything in it that charms you you would sacrifice for me — but unknown to you is my thirst, unseen by you are waters which would save me. ... Trust me. Help me, I feel within me that I could gladden your loving hearts which now I wound. Say to me "follow the dictates of that spirit within thee." Oh my beloved people, that spirit shall never lead me to say things unworthy of me who is yours in love — Give me your blessing.[31]

"Flo is on her zenith," WEN wrote Fanny. "You & I & all of us ought to thank her stars for satisfying her mind so thoroughly — in truth I often wonder how I and any can thwart a soul like hers." If "she fills her mind with her occupations whatever they may be peace is made and rebel I dare not — but your will is not mine."[32]

"Believe me," Fanny wrote Flo, "we will do our best to have faith as you ask.... We are not arrogating to ourselves a monopoly of wisdom only the anxious look out of affection.

"Let us hope ... happiness and better things" await "you at home, even tho' our opinions may differ with yours as to what the right always is as well as the way of doing it."

"I cannot write long on such matters. It is like the dividing soul and body with me," admitted the mother, struggling to come to terms not only with an alien concept, but one that defied her basic maternal instinct. "I will do my best I will indeed to think you right ... you must be merciful & not lay upon us more than we are able to bear."[33] There is no proof that Fanny Nightingale sent this letter.

—⚮—

Hostilities resumed when the Nightingale ladies reached home.

PARTHE (In tears): The Carlsbad cure proved useless because your stay at Kaiserswerth worried me so much.

FANNY (Scolding): No more talk of nursing. It is ruining your sister's health.

FLO (Cajoling): May I inspect Irish hospitals? Your friend Dr. Fowler did not want me to train at the Salisbury infirmary, but he and his wife would chaperone me in Ireland.

FANNY: Very well. But I forbid you to observe Sisters of Charity working amongst the poor of Paris. Only think how shocking to associate yourself with a Roman Catholic community; besides, such behavior would ruin your chance to marry well.

FLO: Don't forget I've decided not to marry.
FANNY: Your conduct will ruin Parthe's chances.

That made Flo pause.

Concomitantly, WEN's doctors, treating him for eye trouble and acute constipation, advised taking a cold-water cure at Umberslade Park, near Malvern, England's most elegant spa. Florence characterized the water cure as "a highly popular amusement within the last few years amongst athletic individuals who have felt the *tedium vitae* [boredom of life] and have indefinite diseases which a large income and unbounded leisure are so well calculated to produce."[34] Treatment involved a "horrible instrument of torture." On entering the shower building "'you hear a series of little yells and squeals proceeding from the victims along the line and sometimes a prolonged howl. You go into your own den and descend into a deep well. Above are three pipes of 2", 3", 4" bore, about ten feet above your head, and there you stand stark, staring *naked*" as the pipes rain 'little hailstones' 'onto the small of your back.'"[35]

Flo's father refused to go to Umberslade without her. "I know nothing like the petty grinding tyranny of a good English family. And the only alleviation is that the tyrannized submits with a heart full of affection."[36]

Besides daily water therapy, the cure included a healthy diet (WEN's doctor ordered a liberal dose of roughage instead of the usual quinine), leisure, mental activity, and vigorous walks. So father and daughter climbed Malvern's hilly streets and admired the splendid Norman church with its noted collection of ancient tiles and stained glass. They strode the Malvern hills, a humpback ridge crisscrossed with footpaths, to explore pre-historic sights, survey rolling pastures and ancient woodland dotted with castles. When rain confined them indoors, WEN and Flo played "battledore and shuttlecock like two fools."[37]

Florence felt glad her "youth is past," rejoiced "that it never can return." She hoped to "live, a thing which I have not often been able to say, because I think I have learnt something which it would be a pity to waste — & I am ever yours dear father in struggle as in peace with thanks for all your kind care."[38]

Flo now proceeded to horrify her mother anew. While undertaking to clarify her religious belief, Florence strengthened her friendship with a prominent Catholic convert. She had met Henry Manning* in Rome, through her

---

*A model cleric ministering to the spiritual and physical needs of his flock, Manning rose to become an Anglican archdeacon before converting to Roman Catholicism. Well-connected, cultured, and extremely efficient, he eventually became a cardinal and head of England's Catholic church.

friend Liz Herbert. Manning had been Liz's spiritual advisor before his conversion. She would have followed him into Catholicism had conversion not meant death to her husband's political career, let alone rupture with family and friends.

Catholicism appealed to Florence because its nursing orders offered women structured training. Yet, the Church insisted "peremptorily upon my believing what I cannot believe."[39] Familiarity with religious history and biblical criticism, not to mention Flo's belief in individual thought and action, made her too skeptical to accept Catholic doctrine despite long, earnest talks with Manning. Anglicanism gave Florence no work, but she still considered it her spiritual home and felt the tie of family too strongly to break it. Flo wanted to be free of family fetters, but not irrevocably to estrange herself.

Trying to define her relationship to a God she felt impelled to serve at a time when contemporaries held single women to be redundant, Florence wrote *Suggestions for Thought to the Searchers After Truth Among the Artisans of England*. Its first volume presented religious beliefs meant to battle atheism and justify God's laws to thousands turning from organized religion. The second volume explored religious psychology and included *Cassandra*, Flo's attack on a woman's lot. Her third volume focused on divine law and moral right.

"I believe in a perfect being, whom you call God."[40]

What is the character of God? Not to create a world to forgive it — or to damn it — or to save it by a church or by the sacraments or by atonement or by prayer, [but] to create a world according to a certain, definite plan by which each and every one of us is on the way to progress toward perfection, i.e. happiness.[41]

"*To be religious means to do good deeds on this earth.*"[42]

"It is surprising that *what God is* is a question which interests no one. They take, without inquiry, what is set down in a book." Hence, "one must lay aside inquiry, adopt an active life, and try to improve one's being."[43]

Besides addressing weighty issues like belief in God and the nature of morality, *Suggestions for Thought* articulated Flo's need to reconcile her religious belief with her urge to act, to justify her decision to take happiness. As well, the discipline of writing and therapy of self-expression helped Flo overcome despair and clarify what she must do.[44]

—◊◊◊—

Distraught at Florence's long absences from home, meanwhile (most recently to inspect hospitals in Ireland under the chaperonage of family friends the Fowlers) thirty-three-year-old Parthe fretted over her future. With her sister pursuing an independent path, what would become of Parthe, a redundant single female, when her parents died? Parthe blamed Flo. She owed

Parthe sisterly support. Flo eschewed marriage, but she could at least create openings for Parthe among the eligible men seeking her company. Then again, Parthe blamed Flo's erudition for putting off other men. And of course an eligible suitor would hesitate to marry into a family whose daughter's eccentricity threatened disgrace.

Flo's conduct would kill her, pain would kill her, Parthe wept in daily dramas. Desperate, the Nightingales turned to a friend, the eminent physician Sir James Clark, who counted Queen Victoria among his patients.

"After the fullest examination & consultation," Clark told WEN that "imbecility or permanent aberration is the inevitable" result unless Parthe were "placed under a firm & wise hand" away from home. Flo's presence aggravated "the disease," which yielding to Parthe would intensify. Opposition would perpetually increase "her nervous excite-

Parthenope Frances Nightingale, Lady Verney, 1819–1890. Florence believed that if she and her only sibling had not had such divergent personalities, they would have gotten along better (artist: Sir William Richmond [1869]. Photographic Survey, The Courtauld Institute of Art, London, private collection].

ment" and foster "the monomania about me," Flo confided to her friend Henry Manning. She felt that everyone at home blamed her "for seeking duty away from the sphere in which it has pleased God to place me."[45]

Clark persuaded Parthe's parents to let her visit him at his home, Birk Hall, in the bracing Scottish highlands. Parthe's complaint (neurasthenia* due to excess leisure), common among well-to-do women, could be treated under the aegis of a kind yet firm stranger. Pampering must stop. Parthe should have vigorous exercise and plain food away from her doting mother and anxious father. If neurasthenia turned into hysteria — which the medical men connected directly to the reproductive system — Parthe might need surgery.

Clark's regimen resulted in delusions, anger, and total inability to leave

---

*A condition characterized by mental and physical lassitude, usually due to worry, even depression, and often accompanied by headache, gastro-intestinal, and circulatory disorders.

her bed. Frantic, Fanny insisted Flo instantly stop touring Irish hospitals and hasten to Scotland to succor her sister. The day after Florence arrived, "we* came *downstairs*" and "established ourselves in the drawing room without difficulty," Flo informed Fanny, "had jelly & grouse for our dinner — & were downstairs as early as 11 o'clock."[46] A few days later Flo reported "that we have made our first walk this beautiful day & we come downstairs now at 10 o'clock — we sleep well and eat well."[47]

Parthe's about-face convinced Clark that her illness had no physical basis. His patient would never believe herself healthy, however, if the sisters lived in the same house.

Florence's Roman Catholic friend Manning had, in the interim, arranged for her to train in a Paris hospital run by the Sisters of Charity; the nurses were nuns.[48] Parthe reacted to this news with a fresh outburst of uncontrolled crying. Fanny insisted that Flo must under no circumstances jeopardize her sister's health.

Flo's beloved aunt Mai Smith, favorite cousin and confidante Hilary Bonham-Carter, and sympathetic friend Selena Bracebridge rallied support. Socially prominent friends like the von Bunsens, Herberts, and Shaftesburys backed them. Fanny vacillated — but not for long.

About to welcome eminent guests to Embley, Fanny appealed to WEN. She needed Flo to help entertain the company. WEN agreed. Florence could hardly distress her mother and hurl her sister into hysterics at such a time.

Flo vacillated. Then hurried to Derbyshire when her grandmother's dearly loved sister died. Florence shouldered all the distressing details death leaves in its wake, to say nothing of comforting her dearest Grandmamma Shore. Shaken, Flo again experienced God calling her "to the perfection of" His "service (to be a savior)."[49]

"I am so glad this year is over; nevertheless it has not been wasted," Florence wrote as 1852 ended. Having "remodeled my whole religious belief from beginning to" end (*Suggestions for Thought*), "I have learned to know God."

"Two terrible lessons I have learnt in Ireland [disenchantment with its Catholic hospitals] and in Scotland [Parthe must learn to live without her sister]: this last tore open my eyes as nothing else could have done."

"My life has been decided thereby. It has been a baptism of fire this year."[50]

—⚭—

Confident in her practical nursing skills no less than her knowledge of medical institutions, Florence set her sights firmly on becoming matron at a

---

*Jocular use of the first person plural to connote Parthe.

large public hospital. And since she stopped taking the trouble to mask her misery at having to grace Embley's drawing room, Fanny agreed to let Flo get what training she could with the Sisters of Charity in Paris.

Ostensibly, Florence would be visiting Clarkey and Julius Mohl. Actually, she would be "free to do her own foolishness," for although Clarkey failed to agree with all of Flo's social causes, she firmly believed Florence should have the autonomy to pursue them. If Flo wanted "to go to some wicked place the folk in England will" assume "she is still with me, and I will keep it snug."[51]

So Flo crossed the wind-whipped winter Channel together with cousin Hilary, at last allowed to study art under Clarkey's chaperonage at a distinguished atelier. Fighting a rear-guard action, Fanny made Hilary promise to make sure Flo bought some truly fashionable clothes.

Thanks to Julius Mohl, Florence had permission to visit every major medical institution in the French capital. She watched famous surgeons at work, toured wards, and charted organizational statistics. In the evenings, far from Fanny's strictures and, in Flo's words, Parthe's eternal governessing, Florence donned her new finery and informed her "dearest mother" that she had "already been to *two* balls, one concert at the conservatory, have one invitation to dinner, one to the opera, and two to evening parties, all to be consummated within the first week of my arrival at Paris."[52]

Barely had Florence finished packing a few basics for her stay with the Sisters when an urgent summons arrived. WEN's mother, Flo's adored Grandmamma Shore, lay dying. "I shall never be thankful enough," Florence wrote Hilary from Derbyshire, "that I came. I was able to make her be moved and changed" to relieve the old lady's terrible bedsores. Furthermore, Flo did "other little things" like ease her grandmother's labored breathing and bring spiritual comfort, "which perhaps smoothed the awful passage, and which perhaps would not have been done as well without me."[53]

Florence Nightingale had earned a reputation for strong character and unusual abilities. Her friends kept their ears open for a suitable position.

Charitable society ladies interested themselves in what they called decayed gentlewomen, many of them indigent governesses. Liz Herbert and Selina Bracebridge sat on the ladies' committee that supervised an Institution for the Care of Sick Gentlewomen in Distressed Circumstances. About to reorganize and relocate, the institution sought an enthusiastic, experienced superintendent. Mrs. Bracebridge and Mrs. Herbert recommended Miss Nightingale.

8

Harley Street

I have never repented nor looked back, not for one moment.[1]— Florence Nightingale

Bottle-green rhododendron leaves cupped bright blue flower clusters, azaleas bloomed in a profusion of pink and purple, when thirty-three-year-old Florence Nightingale left Embley for London. As her train steamed slowly into the station, Liz Herbert waited on the platform. The two ladies then entered the elegant Herbert town carriage and were driven to a private house in the best part of town. Here the ladies' committee that supervised the Institution for the Care of Sick Gentlewomen in Distressed Circumstances had assembled to interview Miss Nightingale. Mrs. Herbert made the formal introduction.

> THE COMMITTEE CHAIRWOMAN: What do you recommend for our institution at its new location in Harley Street?
> NIGHTINGALE: "The nurse should *never* be obliged to quit her 'floor,' except for her own dinner & supper & her patients' dinner & supper (& even the latter may be avoided by" using a pulley.)

The nurse, Florence continued with quiet confidence, should "have hot & cold water upon her own floor," sleep on "her own floor — in her own bedroom, she ought to have the requisites for making poultices, barley-water, warming all her medicines, dressings &c" on "the *same* floor as her patients." Without "a system of this kind, the nurse is converted into a pair of legs for running up & down stairs."

"The bells of the patients should all ring in the passage outside the *nurse's* own door, *on that story*, & should have a valve, which flies open when its bell rings, & *remains* open, in order that the nurse may see who has rung."

"The carrying of hot water all over the house is desirable. The cheapest way" would be "a boiler at the top of the house with a small fire to heat it," and "pipes bringing the hot water to each story." But "there might be a small boiler on *each* story."[2]

Impressive! Nonetheless, some committee members thought Florence seemed too young for such responsibility. Others worried about her social status; could a true lady take orders from other ladies; should she nurse non-ladies? What about Florence's readiness to leave home, her interest in surgical and medical matters, her visits to Catholic nursing orders? And the inevitable question: parental approval.

Why not ask that delightful Mrs. Douglas Galton (née Marianne Nicholson)? one lady suggested. Eager to prevent Flo's odd ambition from bringing disgrace on the entire family, cousin Marianne enlarged in dramatic fashion on her aunt and uncle's need to have Florence at home. Shocked, the committee considered withdrawing its offer.* Committee members Liz Herbert and Selina Bracebridge alerted Florence. She appealed to her father.

—m—

WEN did not fully agree with Flo that the world needed reform, still less with her zeal to act; but he did believe individuals should be free to satisfy their ambitions. Flo's father had come to accept her wish to nurse. Besides, WEN hated the nonstop bickering between Flo, her mother, and Parthe. His sister Mai Smith impressed on him how Kaiserswerth had improved Flo's nursing skills, how competently she had eased their mother's last days. This resonated. WEN, too, had benefited from Flo's care both at home and at Umberslade Park. Those whose views he respected, like brother-in-law Sam Smith and friends Selina and Charles Bracebridge, urged WEN to give Florence her freedom.

WEN supported his daughter by giving her a generous annual allowance.† And despite Fanny's exasperation at this liberal gesture, WEN promised Florence her mother's consent that she take the position of superintendent at the institution.

Although no medical students or improper patients would sully the institution's new location in exceedingly suitable Harley Street, Florence's mother greeted the news of her husband's promise by collapsing with an attack of spasms. And had to be revived with medicated cordials. Guilt at not giving Flo sisterly support caused Parthe to compensate by casting herself in the role of protector. She must preserve her errant junior from the ruin that would surely result from going to the Harley Street institution. So Parthe deployed her most potent weapon: hysterics. Cousin Marianne and her parents fueled

*Upper-class Victorians considered an unmarried female to be a girl regardless of age. Girls belonged under the parental roof. Society frowned on a single woman living apart from her family, particularly without her parents' sanction.
†Five hundred pounds. About $52,000 today.

the fire by telling everyone Florence had solicited the position, instead of the committee having offered it — meaning Flo would be doing the unthinkable for a woman of her class: going into service, hiring herself out for wages. This slur on their social status galvanized the Nightingales.

Fanny backed her husband. She feared losing Flo altogether; for if balked, Flo might move overseas, join a Catholic sisterhood, or do something equally likely to cut family ties. Here her mother misjudged Florence. Hunger for parental approval, especially from Fanny, meant Flo would never break with family. She could not be "quite happy" without her mother's "smile, your blessing, your sympathy."[3] Far from rejecting family, Flo clung to it — in her fashion but, like many adult children, on her terms.

WEN wrote to the ladies' committee officially consenting to his daughter's acceptance of their offer. And his financial support enabled Florence to go to Harley Street without pay, thus avoiding the social stigma of being in service. Her allowance also armed Florence against the accusation of youth. She engaged, at her expense, a respectable housekeeper who could also act as chaperone.

—⚞⚟—

Since "the thing is yet to be organized, I cannot lay a plan either before you or my people," Flo told close friend Clarkey. "And that rather perplexes them, as they want to make conditions that I shan't do this or that." Regardless, Flo "*must* live at the place, if I don't it will be a half and half measure which will satisfy no one."

"If you can do a little quacking for me, the same will be thankfully received."

In any case, "unless I am left a free agent and am to organize the thing myself and not they [the ladies' committee], I will have nothing to do with it."[4]

Elaborate negotiations ensued.

> [The ladies] refused me to take in *Catholic* patients — whereupon I wished them good morning, unless I might take in Jews and their rabbis to attend them. So now it is settled, and *in print*, that we are to take in all denominations whatsoever, and allow them to be visited by their respective priests and muftis, provided *I* will receive (in any case *whatsoever* that is *not* of the Church of England) the obnoxious animal at the door, take him upstairs myself, remain while he is conferring with his patient, make myself *responsible* that he does not speak to, or look at, *any one else*, and bring him downstairs again in a noose, and out onto the street![5]

Meanwhile, construction workers still hammered in Harley Street. So Florence decided to resume her aborted stay with the Sisters of Charity in

Paris. Extremely upset, Fanny and Parthe begged their Flo to spend her last weeks of what they called freedom at home. Clarkey backed them. But Florence refused.

—⁓—

After a few days in Paris, Flo had the "dirtiest and queerest" of her "many and queer" adventures — "measles in the cell of a Soeur de la Charité," she wrote Clarkey, at the time in England on her annual visit. The sisters "were very kind" and Clarkey's husband, "dear" Julius Mohl, inquired daily, besides sending Florence her favorite beverage — tea — which the sisters withheld. "Lastly, in his paternity," Julius came to collect Flo. He installed her in the Mohls' "back drawing-room, to my infinite horror.... It is the most impertinent, the most inopportune thing I have ever done — me established in a lady's house in her absence to be ill."[6] Mohl came "often to see me and talk, which I suppose is very improper, but I can't help it,"[7] Florence lamented to Clarkey in mock dismay.

Contractors' dust still covered the Harley Street building when Florence returned to London, but instead of yielding to Fanny's wish that she stay with the family, Flo preserved her independence. She got Aunt Mai to help her find a pied-à-terre. Florence planned to keep it even after moving into Harley Street. She intended to invite select friends to tea and have Sundays to herself.

> I have not taken this step, Clarkey dear, without years of anxious considera-
> tion, [of experience, of] fullest and deepest thought; it has not been done
> without advice, and it is a step, which, being the growth of so long, is
> [unlikely to be repented] or reconsidered. I mean the step of leaving them. I
> do not wish to talk about it — and this is the last time I shall ever do so, but
> as you asked me a plain [question,] I will give you a plain answer. I *have*
> talked matters over [with] Parthe, *not once but thousands of times*.

Therefore, "with the deepest consideration and with the fullest advice," Florence Nightingale took "the step of leaving home, and it is a *fait accompli*."[8]

—⁓—

London sweltered and the trodden grass in its dusty parks turned brown as Florence Nightingale embarked on her formal nursing career. Sixteen years after her first call from God, nine years after her failed attempt to train as a nurse at Salisbury Hospital, she took full charge at Harley Street.*

---

*"God said to me...I entered thee at Harley street August 12, 1853" (BL ADD. 45844, ff.4–6, May 7, 1867, private note, FN).

Nightingale instantly infused the institution with practical expressions of what Clarkey called her Incredible Bonté. Childhood desire to nurse, adolescent identification of nursing as her means to serve God, years of hospital self-training, and Kaiserswerth experience coalesced in a perfect plan for the three-floor, twenty-seven-bed hospital.

"Fear of dirt is the beginning of good nursing."[9] First, the Harley Street building must be scrubbed from top to bottom. Its furnishings were filthy and tattered, bed linen and new blankets moldy, and vermin ran "tame in all directions."[10] So Florence's housekeeper hired extra hands to help sew new household linens from scratch, to salvage old ones for dusters and dishrags.

Clean beds and good food meant better nursing than fussing over a patient dying from bedsores and scurvy. Instead of the local grocer continuing to make small, daily deliveries, Florence got bids from the best firms and negotiated wholesale prices. Having invested in a superior kitchen stove, she decided, "for the sake of securing economy and wholesome bread," to "bake at home, both bread, biscuits & gingerbread."[11]

Kitchen cupboards were devoid of cleaning equipment but crammed with jars of costly store-bought jam. Florence instructed the cook to make jam — a sizeable saving. And she supervised coal deliveries to assure that the institution got its due.

Her patients gave the new superintendent "joy & consolation." They were much "easier to manage than I expected" and "always to be cheered, tho' not always cheerful."[12] Assisting at a breast cancer operation, Florence observed the surgeon anesthetizing his patient with a new method: chloroform. She nursed the elderly governess back to health.

"Light is essential for growth, health and recovery from sickness — not only daylight, but sunlight," including "color, pleasant and pretty sights for the patient's eyes to rest on — variety of objects, flowers, pictures."[13] So Florence happily accepted her mother's generous weekly hampers. "More flowers, more game, more grapes — thankfully received I wd say many thanks for what we've got, but am afraid you wd say la reconnaissance est un vif sentiment des bienfaits futures."*[14]

Florence "rubbed cold feet perpetually" at night. One "old lady jumped out of bed and stood with her feet on the hearthstone in order to have them rubbed."[15]

Patients praised the unwearied and loving attention of their good, dear, and true friend, like a darling mother. Florence's sympathy for the poor, careworn women entered each detail of their lives. She understood their loneliness and fiscal worries. She helped former patients financially, got her family and

---

*"Gratitude is strong expectation of future favors."

friends to find convalescent homes or jobs, and continued to advise via correspondence.

Nightingale missed nothing. She attended doctors' visits to assure correct execution of orders, "experience having proved the impossibility of conducting this or any other institution where such attendance is not rigidly adhered to."[16] The "chemists sent me a bottle labeled Spirits of Nitre which, if I had not smelt it, I should certainly have administered it and we should have had an enquiry into poisoning."[17] So the superintendent personally reviewed delivery of all medicines.

Her institution clamored for a balanced budget based on strict accounting. "We have not funds to have an accountant and if we had he would be off with the money,"[18] Flo wrote Fanny. So the energetic new superintendent took over.

"I am now in the heyday of my power." Per patient cost dropped by half. Florence's "greatest enemy" on the committee trumpeted her "fame thro' London. And all because I have reduced their expenditure."

She initially vowed that whatever occurred "I *never* would intrigue among the com'tee." But experience caused Florence to conduct all "business by intrigue." She suggested privately "to A, B or C the resolution I think A, B or C most capable of carrying in com'tee & then leave it to them — & I always win."

Florence presented five of her proposals to the committee as coming from the doctors. The proposals were "carried in com'tee, without telling them that they came from me & not from the medical men — & then & not till then, I showed them to the medical men without telling *them* that they were already passed *in com'tee*."[19]

Within six months Nightingale had her hospital humming in perfect harmony.

—m—

Word of Florence's achievement spread. Society showered her with invitations. Florence accepted some. She asked special friends to tea in her pied-à-terre. And decided to take a short holiday with her family.

In his role as a county magistrate WEN concerned himself with management of the local hospital. Hence he took interest in Flo's work — and felt proud of her success. But Fanny clung to lifetime precepts about a proper young lady's conduct, not to mention maternal concern for Flo's health. Fanny refused to condone Flo wearing herself out on Harley Street. So Florence's friends flooded Fanny with tales of how the fashionable ladies on Flo's committee sang her praises throughout London.

When Flo was about the age of fifteen, her family "often missed her in the evening," Fanny regaled a friend. Consequently, Flo's mother "would take a lantern and" walk to the village to find her daughter "sitting by the bedside of someone who was ill, and saying she could not sit down to a grand seven o'clock dinner while this was going on."[20]

Flo "takes up one thing at a time, & bends her whole soul to that," Parthe chimed in. Once music, then mathematics, later "the truth as disguised in the myths & hieroglyphics of the old Egyptian religion, as the root of other religions." Now "all this is swept away." No more reading. First, because "she has not time for it"; second, "she says life is so vivid that books seem poor."[21]

Rather than face the reality of having stymied her sister's career, Parthe presented herself as facilitator. "To set F. at liberty to do her great work, Parthe has annihilated herself, her own tastes, her own wishes," to "take up all the little duties of home, to parents, to poor, to society, to servants — all the small things that fritter away time and life, *all* these Parthe does, for fear if anything was neglected people might blame F."[22]

With tears in her eyes, Fanny described her family to her friend as "ducks," who "have hatched a wild swan."[23]

Appreciation for her mother's attempt to come to terms with an alien concept, even manage to concede some satisfaction in Flo's success, combined with Flo's newfound security in winning freedom to fulfill her destiny. Consequently, the fraught mother-daughter relationship eased somewhat.

"Oh my boots! My boots! Dearer to me than the best French-polished." Where "are ye, my boots! I shall ne'er see your pretty faces more," Florence lamented to Fanny. "Chollocombes must, alas! make me a *new* pair. He has my measure."

"Thank you for Duolon's direction. I will have a pair of quilted bottines [high half boots] made there by & bye."

"I wish you would kindly send me the direction of a 'blanchisseuse de fin.'* It is quite the cheapest plan to go to the best, because they keep clean so much longer."

"I consent to have the £12 book-case *if* it does not come to more, & *if* you will kindly order it, (as Index Expurgatorius can go in) I will get a little cheap 3 shelver to hang against the wall besides."[24]

Flo believed Fanny's resistance to her full-time nursing derived from a well-intended wish to promote her daughter's best interest. Conscious of causing Fanny distress by not marrying, indeed, thwarting Fanny's basic maternal duty to settle her daughter well in life, Flo clung all the more to her mother's affection.

---

*Laundress for delicate clothing.

Nothing that you can say can ever hurt me [and] if I am ever hurt, it is not by words of yours but of my poor Pop's. I confess she often pained me [but] *never, never* you. I am sure the time will come when we shall love and sympathize more together instead of less, my dearest Mother — I dwell upon the thought of this love and sympathy with you as among my pleasantest thoughts, since I have always the feeling of your perfect love and kindness towards me.[25]

—⬩—

Meanwhile, cholera broke out in the capital. Harley Street stayed immune. Public hospitals were swamped. At Lea Hurst Florence had "toothache, and an abscess in her mouth." Fanny felt "*very* anxious about her, as she was evidently not strong."

FLORENCE: I'm leaving tomorrow.
FANNY: You can't. You're still poorly.
FLORENCE: I must. I've already made arrangements that depend on my presence.

"She is so excessively soft and gentle in voice, manner, and movement that one never feels the unbendableness of her character when one is near her."[26]

Turning necessity into virtue, the Nightingales yielded gracefully.

Doctors and nurses deserted Middlesex Hospital during the cholera epidemic, but Florence worked round the clock with female patients, most from the slums. Practical experience and systematic study caused her to judge cholera not infectious — i.e., passed from person to person. In fact, it is spread by ingesting contaminated food or water. Once the epidemic subsided, Florence returned to Harley Street.

Happily living her daydreams, Florence had, however, from the outset, seen Harley Street as a stepping-stone. "My difficulties here are certainly an excellent training for me; and then I shall attempt the real task" — nursing superintendent "in a public hospital."[27] Harley Street signified a major step beyond the busy idleness of home life, but the institution's limited size and scope curbed Nightingale's ability to admit all sorts of patients, particularly the poor. And Harley Street did little, if anything, to further her goal of educating other women to nurse.

—⬩—

While Florence Nightingale nurtured her nascent nursing career, Great Britain's cabinet, now including her friend Sidney Herbert and the Nightingale family's neighbor Lord Palmerston, took the country to war.*

*In Florence Nightingale's day the Ottoman Turks ruled a vast empire: the Middle East, much of the Balkans, and North Africa. For centuries Russia had sought to extend its power eastward

The Crimean War (1854–1856) differed from past wars. Men had always suffered horribly in battle, but those at home were only dimly aware of details. Now the advent of the telegraph allowed reports from Russia's Crimea to reach London in a few hours instead of ten days. So the editor of Britain's most influential daily newspaper adopted a novel (and sure to be lucrative) approach to war reporting. Rather than wait for government-issued war news, the *Times* sent a special correspondent with Britain's army.

Intent on invading the Crimea to smash Russia's powerful naval fortress at Sevastopol, thirty thousand superbly armed men, representing the world's leading industrial and financial power, sailed off to war (mid–1854) in the world's strongest navy. Smugly secure in their maritime supremacy and the invincibility of their army after its glorious victories over Napoléon, Britons forgot that the battle of Waterloo took place forty years before and that peacetime budgetary cheese-paring must leave its mark.

The first British troops to fight a major war since Waterloo landed on the Black Sea coast. Within weeks, cholera ran rampant through the camp and ships anchored offshore.

Concomitantly, Florence Nightingale interrupted her Lea Hurst holiday to nurse cholera victims at London's Middlesex Hospital. Study and experience showed her that control of cholera required rigorous disinfection of the area around the sick, destruction of dirty clothing, and sterilization of drinking water. But those in charge at the army camp were lethargic in the torrid Turkish summer. They ignored basic rules of hygiene. Vast numbers of sick men swamped inadequate medical facilities. Amoebic dysentery broke out.

Crammed into one decrepit hospital, a pestilential pit from which, soldiers said, no one emerged alive, or squashed onto ships and sent across the Bosporus to another squalid hospital, the sick had little chance. Doctors were overwhelmed, nurses nonexistent. Old or ignorant orderlies, often drunk from the extra rum rations given to ward off cholera, proved totally incapable of tending to their sick comrades.

---

into the Mediterranean at Ottoman expense via control of the Turkish capital, Constantinople. (Istanbul today). It commanded the Bosporus and Dardanelles, which link the Black Sea to the Mediterranean. Britain opposed. Russia's ambition threatened her naval supremacy and Mediterranean commerce, not to mention the route to India and Empire. An autocrat ruled Russia. English liberals, like the Nightingales, detested Tsar Nicholas I. He had been instrumental in suppressing the liberal revolutions that erupted all over the Continent (1848), including those in Italy that Florence had so enthusiastically supported during her stay in Rome. Now the Tsar's attempt to meddle in Turkey roused alarm in British breasts. The autocrat must be stopped. Britain would break Russian power in the Black Sea by capturing her mighty Crimean naval base at Sevastopol. Concomitantly, France's newly crowned emperor, Napoléon III, sought to ground his dynasty in military glory. He joined Britain. Turkey welcomed them as allies. Palmerston had for years distrusted Russian designs. He led the war party, ably abetted by the press, which had long vilified the Tsar as murderer of liberty and constitutions. Most Britons agreed.

Before the firing of a single shot, one in every five British soldiers had been hospitalized with cholera or intestinal disease. Almost a thousand died. And cholera wreaked havoc on medical supplies, at best meant merely to cover a brief summer campaign.

—⚏—

Harley Street's chief physician, meanwhile, thought Nightingale's talents wasted at the little institution. A major London medical facility, the rebuilt and reorganized King's College hospital, sought a nursing superintendent. He told Florence he could get her the position. Other doctors, as well as friends, endorsed the idea. She started to plan.

Nightingale's dream of training other women to nurse remained, she had already informed her ladies' committee, the major reason for her commitment to hospital work. The Harley Street "institution has been brought into as good a state as its capabilities admit." Nonetheless, admission of patients "not always proper objects for medical & surgical" treatment blocked Florence's goal of educating nurses.

> I therefore wish, at the close of the year for which I promised my services, to intimate that,—having as I believe, done the work *as far as it can be done*,—it is probable that I may retire, *if*, in pursuance of my design & the allegiance which I hold to it, I meet with a sphere which is more analogous to the formation of a nursing school.[28]

At the same time, Britain, and her allies France and Turkey, engaged Russia at the Crimea's river Alma.

Planning her next move in the service of God and humanity, Florence Nightingale sat down to breakfast in her private parlor at Harley Street, savoring her first sip of freshly brewed, piping hot coffee. Like thousands of her compatriots, Florence opened her copy of Britain's largest-circulation daily newspaper to relish the details of her country's glorious victory. Instead, the *Times* delivered a bombshell.

9

"There is but one person in England"

Though I am unable to tell you who was responsible for leaving the sick in that wretched condition, I am able to tell you who rescued them from it.[1]—
Sir John McNeill, M.D., government commissioner, Crimea

Hundreds of badly wounded British soldiers waited up to two days on the battlefield for basic medical attention. Overworked surgeons operated with sullied instruments, without chloroform, on tables caked with the blood and detritus of previous patients. Soiled, discarded clothing served for bandages. Neither splints nor morphine existed. Post-operative patients lay on the bare earth or on straw mixed with manure. They were then crammed into ships together with cholera victims for a four-day voyage across the turbulent Black Sea to Great Britain's main medical facility—the Barrack hospital at Scutari.* More than one in four men died.

"Can it be said that the battle of the Alma" (September 20, 1854) took "the world by surprise?" wrote the *Times* special correspondent from Constantinople. "Has not the expedition to the Crimea been the talk of the last four months? And when the Turks gave" Britain a "vast barracks to form a hospital did that not occur because English casualties were expected to be considerable?" Yet, "not only are the men kept" sometimes for days without "a medical man coming near their wounds — not only are they left to expire in agony, unheeded and shaken off," feebly snatching "at the surgeon whenever he makes his rounds through the fetid," congested ships, "but now, when" put "in the spacious building where we were led to believe" everything stood ready to "ease their pain and facilitate their recovery," we find "the commonest appliances of a workhouse sick ward"[2] wanting.

Such scenes were not new in army annals. Such scenes *were* new to the public.

---

*Opposite the Ottoman capital, Constantinople, on the Asian side of the Bosporus.

"It is impossible for anyone to see the melancholy sights of the last few days without feelings of surprise and indignation at the deficiencies of our medical system."[3] Britain did not even have "dressers or nurses" to carry "out the surgeons' directions" or attend the sick. But Britain's current ally (and ancient rival) France had Sisters of Charity, the *Times* special correspondent pointed out. These "devoted women are excellent nurses."[4]

That galled national pride and galvanized public anger.

The *Times* appealed to its readers. Donations poured in for a Fund to buy comforts for casualties. Men and women, including Florence Nightingale, volunteered their services.

—⚶—

Nightingale planned to lead four nurses — three funded by a philanthropic friend, one by herself. Florence's Harley Street housekeeper-chaperone offered to join them. Practical Sam Smith, Flo's steadfast support and Fanny's best-loved brother, hastened to Embley to get the Nightingales' consent. Florence won the backing of family friend and now cabinet minister Lord Palmerston. She must have assent from her Harley Street committee — which Liz Herbert could arrange — and secretary-at-war Sidney Herbert's sanction, too. Without it the Scutari medical authorities, standing shoulder to shoulder in staunch denial of any need for help, would bar her from the Barrack hospital.

Florence took a hackney cab across London to the Herberts' town house in elegant Belgrave Square. They had gone away for the weekend. So Florence hastened back to Harley Street. Shutting herself into her private parlor, Flo smoothed a crackling sheet of paper, sharpened her quill pen and, dipping it into the inkwell, wrote Liz about her plans.

Sidney, however, had an altogether different idea. For some time, he had been trying to introduce female nurses into military hospitals, but fierce resistance from army diehards forced retreat. Current conditions not only changed the equation but also justified daring action.

As cabinet secretary-*at*-war, Herbert controlled military finances. Conduct of the war per se fell to Herbert's colleague (and friend) the secretary-*for*-war, now swamped. Hence, Herbert first assumed unofficial responsibility for military hospitals, which his hard-pressed co-secretary welcomed. Herbert then proposed to bring in female nurses.

Already drenched by a shower of blame for the abysmal state of army hospitals, the government, in which Herbert figured as a stalwart member, could ill afford another debacle — like failure of the experiment to initiate female nursing. Herbert knew that to succeed within the strict disciplinary structure of a military hospital nurses must work under an authorized chief answerable both to hospital medical officers and to the government. Herbert also knew Nightingale. Not only were they close and like-minded friends, but Herbert had seen how quickly, at Harley Street, Florence had turned chaos into order.

—ɷ—

Before the postman delivered Flo's letter to Liz Herbert, her husband took up his pen. Well-meaning ladies were flooding him with offers of help. Because they had no idea of what a hospital meant, these women would either "recoil from the work, or be entirely useless"; nor would they "understand the necessity, especially in a military hospital, of strict obedience to rule."[5]

The "difficulty of finding women equal to a task" full "of horrors and requiring besides knowledge and good will, great energy and great courage will be great. The task of ruling them and introducing system among them is great; and not the least will be the difficulty of making the whole work smoothly with the medical and military authorities."

"There is but one person in England ... capable of organizing such a scheme."

Herbert promised Nightingale "plenary authority over the" nurses and "fullest assistance and co-operation from the medical staff." Florence would, furthermore, have "unlimited power" to draw "on the government for whatever" she thought "requisite for the success of your mission."

Her personal qualities, administrative experience, and "rank and position in society give you" unparalleled "advantages in such a work."[6]

Certainly Flo had spurned Fanny's social ambition for her. Nevertheless, she could scarcely cavil at the benefit Fanny's social success brought.

Would, Herbert asked, Florence's parents let her take on "this great work"? After all, a cavernous, all-male military hospital in a far-off, foreign land could hardly be compared to the genteel precincts of Harley Street. Still, "the work would be so national," requested by "the government who represent the nation," and, at "such a moment, that I do not despair of their consent." With "authority from the government, your position would" command universal respect, "especially in a service where official rank carries so much weight." Nightingale's status would assure "you every attention and comfort" en route and in Turkey and full "submission to your orders. I know these things are a matter of indifference to you except as they may further the great objects you have in view; but they are of importance in themselves and of every importance to those who have a right to take an interest in your personal position and comfort."[7]

"God guide you right in your decision," Liz added. "If you refuse, you will have lost the most noble" chance "of doing the greatest possible amount of good, & just *the* sort of good which *you* alone can do. There will be no"[8] difficulty about Harley Street.

—⟶⟶—

Florence instantly agreed. Flattered by the compliment paid their daughter, the Nightingales agreed as well.

When Florence again called at the Herbert town house, Sidney greeted her in his book-lined library. Blue and crimson velvet curtains festooned its tall windows and fell in graceful folds, tied back with cords from which hung huge silk tassels. A handsome, custom-woven carpet covered the floor, and a bowl of bronze chrysanthemums stood on Sidney's desk. In the grate a wood fire glowed as he and Florence discussed her mission.

Its salient points, codified in Herbert's official instructions, would later haunt them both. "Everything relating" to "distribution of the nurses" is "in your hands, subject, of course, to the sanction" of the chief medical officer; but choice of nurses is "solely under your control," also "power of discharge."

Florence must make each nurse understand the need for strict "attention to" hospital rules and "subordination which is indispensable in every military establishment."[9] Given, moreover, the contentious state of religion in Great Britain,[10] Sidney relied on Florence's

> discretion and vigilance carefully to guard against any attempt being made among those under your authority, selected as they are with a view to fitness and without any reference to religious creed, to make use of their position in the hospitals to tamper with or disturb the religious opinions of the patients of any denomination whatever, and at once to check any such tendency and take, if necessary, severe measures to prevent its repetition.[11]

A good hospital nurse, Herbert then wrote the editor of a popular daily newspaper, needed "great skill as well as strength and courage especially" in surgical cases, most of them gunshot wounds. Inexpert women would be useless. Eager and kind ladies were "little aware of the hardships they would" face, the horrors they would see. "Nor, even if capable in other respects, would" these ladies, used themselves to commanding servants, "always be ready to" implicitly obey orders "so necessary" in "a military hospital." To "rid themselves of the troublesome and inefficient," army doctors might thus be "compelled to exclude all the female nurses, good and bad."

The government had therefore decided to appoint "one person on whose energy, experience, and discretion" it could depend. She "should be the one authority to select," superintend, "and direct" the entire female nursing staff, "herself acting under" order "of the medical authorities."

Miss Nightingale had "greater practical experience of administration and treatment than any other lady in this country." She "will act in the strictest subordination to the chief medical officer of the hospital; and the nurses who accompany, or who follow her, will" be fully "under her authority." No more "nurses will be sent," Herbert emphatically stated, until Nightingale "shall have written home from Scutari" that "they are required."[12]

Herbert's instructions went to all departments. A Nightingale family friend arranged liaison with the *Times* business manager, about to depart for Scutari to administer the newspaper's Fund. Flo asked Liz Herbert to contact her friend, wife of Britain's ambassador at Constantinople, "to say, 'this is not a lady but a real hospital nurse,' of me. 'And she has had experience.'"[13] Sidney Herbert, fully aware of what the Bracebridges' presence would mean to Florence, not to mention her parents, invited them to accompany her. Charles Bracebridge immediately took charge of finances and travel arrangements.

—ɯɯ—

Amid the flurry of preparation and glare of attention, Florence's calm astonished everyone. Of course she radiated calm. Florence had dreamed of this moment, or something similar, all her life.

Nightingale wanted the most competent women, those she could shape into an efficient nursing staff. They must earn the respect of the doubting, not to say resentful, doctors. They must ground the viability of female nursing in military hospitals. And through these women Florence intended to start to raise nursing standards.

Hence, she planned to take a small, easily managed group of women, about twenty in all. But at Sidney Herbert's insistence, Nightingale ended up with almost twice that many.

Applications flooded into her headquarters at the Herbert town house. She asked Liz, Selina Bracebridge, and Mary Stanley, a socially conscious friend Flo had met in Rome, to interview the mostly unappealing and illiterate volunteers. Used to drinking, smoking opium, and offering sex to every male in sight, few, if any, understood the need for nurses to obey the strict rules of a military hospital. Only one "expressed a wish to go from good motive." As for the rest, "money was the only inducement."[14] Small wonder. The government paid almost twice the salary at a London hospital, plus all expenses. Suspecting these females of freeloading at government cost in hope of finding a husband, Liz and her ladies immediately eliminated the young or good-looking.*

Religious orders were a reliable source of skilled nurses, but several refused to place their members under Nightingale's authority. She, Herbert, and the army's head chaplain, however, convinced two Anglican sisterhoods that mil-

*Competent, confident Selina walked along the line of applicants pointing "you" or "not you."

itary discipline mandated Florence having sole command of nurses. With extreme reluctance the Roman Catholic leadership agreed to put ten nurses under her: five from an orphanage, five from the Sisters of Mercy convent in London's Bermondsey slum.[15]

Capable Reverend Mother Mary Clare Moore led her nuns. Six years Nightingale's senior, born in Dublin of Protestant parents, Moore converted to Catholicism with her widowed mother as a child and joined a Sisters of Mercy convent in her teens. The order soon appointed the efficient young woman founding superior of its Cork branch. At age twenty-five she transferred to Bermondsey in the same capacity. Moore's intellect, no less than her serenity, and ability to handle people at once appealed to Nightingale. From esteemed colleagues the two women grew into caring friends.

Composition of the nursing cadre raised an instant ruckus. Diverse groups grumbled at so many Anglican sisters and Catholic nuns. The Catholics especially were suspected of intending to proselytize despite government strictures. But Florence wanted nuns. They had some nursing skills. And she would not lose them to marriage.

Mary Clare Moore, 1814–1874. Superior in Bermondsey Convent of Mercy. Nightingale's esteemed colleague at the Barrack hospital, Scutari, and lifelong, cherished friend, the most truly religious mind Florence ever knew (artist and date unknown, courtesy Institute of Our Lady of Mercy Archives).

—⁂—

Each nurse must sign a government contract.* Nightingale

*Important to note in light of the subsequent flouting of Nightingale's authority. The official contract put her in charge of all nurses "required for the sick and wounded of the British army serving in the East" at the Scutari hospitals "or any future hospital that may be appointed for the sick and wounded of the said army." Each nurse agreed to serve "under the directions and to the satisfaction of the said miss Nightingale, the whole of whose orders she undertakes to obey, until discharged by the said miss Nightingale" (Frances Margaret Taylor, *Eastern Hospitals*

insisted that rules include instant dismissal for socializing with a soldier; no wearing colored ribbons or flowers; no going out singly, in pairs, or without consent; a small amount of liquor only with meals. "From the first moment I felt an impulse to love, trust, and respect her," an Anglican sister wrote. "Her appearance and manner impressed me with a sense of goodness and wisdom, of high mental powers highly cultivated and devoted to the highest ends."[16]

To underline cohesion, Florence had the thirty-eight nurses eat the same food, live in the same lodgings, and wear a uniform. (Nuns and sisters could continue to wear their habits.) Designed in haste, the hideous uniform consisted of a loose, dark gray tweed dress, matching jacket and short cape, plain white linen collar and cap.

"I came out, ma'am, prepared to submit to everything, to be put upon in every way," one nurse would inform Nightingale. "But there are some things, ma'am, one can't submit to. There is the caps, ma'am, that suits one face, and some that suits another. And if I'd known, ma'am, about the caps, great as was my desire to come out to nurse at Scutari, I wouldn't have come, ma'am."[17] She stayed. And proved an excellent nurse.

Outdoors, each nurse wore a brown straw bonnet with veil and brown scarf with "Scutari Hospital" embroidered in bright red. It provided vital identification in the rough milieu of an immense military camp bursting with bars, brothels, and men. One soldier grabbed at a nurse. His buddy recognized her uniform. "Leave the woman alone," he growled. "Can't you tell she's one of Miss Nightingale's?"

—w—

Her appointment caused a sensation. No female had ever been so honored.

Who *was* this mysterious *Mrs.* Nightingale! The press soon printed a biography. It revealed a young, attractive, rich, and popular *miss* who had left her lovely home, not to mention the lures of London society, to care for the poor and sick. Nightingale had offered to go to Scutari "at the risk of her" life, "at the pang of separation from all her friends and family, and at the certainty of" meeting "hardship, dangers, toils, and the constantly renewing scene of human suffering, amid all the worst horrors of war. There are few who would not recoil from such realities," but Nightingale immediately agreed "to form and control the entire nursing establishment for all sick and wounded

and English Nurses—a Narrative of Twelve Months' Experience in the Hospitals of Koulali and Scutari by a Lady Volunteer, vol. 1, pp. 13–14). The Anglicans and Catholics signed a separate section pledging not to proselytize.

soldiers and sailors." Not "one of England's proudest and purest daughters" stood "on so high a pinnacle."[18]

Of course this excitement affected Flo's family. How did her father like it? Britain's commander in chief later asked. "My father is not as other men are," Florence replied.

> He thinks that daughters should serve their country as well as sons he brought me up to think so — he has no sons — & therefore he has sacrificed me to my country — & told me to come home with my shield or upon it. He does not think, (as I once heard a father & a very good & clever father say,) "The girls are all I could wish — very happy, very attentive to me, & very amusing." He thinks that God sent women, as well as men, into the world to be something more than "happy," "attentive, and amusing." Happy & *dull*, religion is said to make us — happy & *amusing social life* is supposed to make us — but my father's religious & social ethics make us strive to be the pioneers of the human race.[19]

No "one else" is "fitted to do this work," Parthe proclaimed. The way "all things have tended to and fitted" Flo "for this is so very remarkable." Setting aside her adamant, not to say hysterical, hindrance of Flo's nursing ambition, Parthe convinced herself that she always wanted her sister to succeed. "One cannot but believe she was intended for it. None of her previous life has been wasted, her experience all tells."[20]

Parthe hurried to London to share in the buzz surrounding her sister. Eagerness made Parthe forget to feed Flo's little pet owl, Athena. Her death caused Florence to shed many bitter tears.*

Fanny, too, had read the *Times* articles describing the horrors of Scutari Hospital. The notion of her carefully nurtured daughter catapulted into such an inferno confirmed Fanny's worst fears about Flo's craze to nurse. An immense, crowded, all-male military hospital stood far from the rarefied climate of Harley Street. Yet, Fanny's aristocratic friends had for months been praising Florence. Now the entire nation joined in.

"God speed," Fanny wrote, "on your errand of mercy, my own dearest child. I know He will, for He has given you such loving friends [who] will be always at your side to help in [all] difficulties. They came just when I felt … you must fail for want of strength, and more mercies will come in your hour of need. They are so wise and good, they will be to you what no one else could. They will write to us, and save you in that and in all ways."[21]

---

*"Poor little beastie, it was odd how much I loved you." Strolling on the Acropolis one morning during her stay in Athens, Flo had seen "a little ball of fluff tormented by a group of children." She bought the baby owl for less than a penny. "It was very pretty to see" Athena sitting on Flo's "finger to receive her one daily meal, opening her wings wide as she swallowed each piece of meat" (Verney, *Life of Athena*, passim).

Flo's mother showed no support of her mission per se, no concession to Flo's pleas from Kaiserswerth three years before for her mother's "smile, your blessing, your sympathy," no affirmation that Flo gladdened her mother's "loving heart."[22] Rather, Fanny took refuge in a visceral maternal reaction: concern for her child's welfare, a concern she now delegated to Selina and Charles Bracebridge.

Nevertheless, Fanny had given in, even if reluctantly, despite Flo having persisted in flouting her authority. First Fanny had conceded Kaiserswerth, then Harley Street, now Scutari. So although her mother invoked God's rather than her own, blessing, Florence treasured Fanny's letter for the rest of her life.

—ɯ—

Nine days after reading that first shocking article in the *Times*, a week after writing Liz Herbert, five days after meeting with Sidney, Florence and her group left London.

They received an enthusiastic welcome on landing at Boulogne. Fisherwomen seized the suitcases and, refusing payment, hefted them to the hotel. Its manager invited his guests to order what they pleased for dinner — on the house. It was the least he and his compatriots could do for their English allies.

A huge crowd greeted the nurses in Paris, cheering them all the way to the hotel where Julius Mohl had reserved rooms. After dining with Florence, the Bracebridges, Sam Smith,* and the nurses, Clarkey observed that, unlike the nuns and sisters, those

Florence Nightingale, 1820–1910. Shortly before she left for Scutari (artists: Hilary Bonham-Carter drawing; lithograph by P. & D. Calnaghi [1854], courtesy Florence Nightingale Museum Trust, London).

*Florence asked Uncle Sam to accompany her as far as Marseille, for although Florence thought the newspapers exaggerated hospital conditions, she also mistrusted government assurances of adequate supplies. So before embarking at Marseille, Flo planned to buy provisions. Charles Bracebridge already had his hands full; resourceful Sam would be of great help.

nurses who came from hospitals had no religion unless one counted the worship of Bacchus.[23]

Nightingale had no time to admire nature's beauty during this journey south on the Rhône. Keeping her nurses "in good humor; arranging the rooms of 5 different sects each night, before sitting down to supper, took a long time; then calling all to be down at 6 ready to start. She bears all wonderfully," Sam wrote the Nightingales, "so calm, winning everybody, French and English."[24]

By the time they reached Marseille, Sam lacked adequate words to describe Selina's

> devotion to Flo, [or] Flo's to the cause. Neither sat down but for a hurried meal. Shopkeepers, visitors, nurses, servants, every single instant. [Flo] received in her little bedroom (not at bedtime) [local dignitaries and] shopkeepers with the same serenity as if in a drawing-room quite désoeuvrée (idle). She had superb influence on all. The rough hospital nurses, on the third day after breakfasting and dining with us [daily and getting all her attention,] were quite humanized and civilized, their very manners at table softened. "We never had so much care taken of our comforts before; it is not people's way with *us*; we had no notion miss N. would slave herself so for us." She looked so calm and noble in it all, whether waiting on the nurses at dinner, [no one else would] or carrying parcels, or receiving [officials.] The Bracebridges are fuller than ever of admiration of her, as I am.[25]

Clarkey thought those who loved Flo should be forever beholden to the Bracebridges for going with her. They might barely bring her back alive.

—m—

The setting sun streaked clear Mediterranean skies with tints of rose and purple, sailors on a nearby British battleship cheered, as Nightingale's party boarded the steamer *Vectis* for their eastward voyage. Built as a mail boat, infested with mammoth cockroaches, and so infamous for discomfort that the government had a hard time staffing her, the *Vectis* soon rendered Florence, a bad sailor at best of times, extremely seasick. Then a storm struck. Stewards' cabin and galleys were washed overboard; guns had to be ditched. By the time the *Vectis* limped into Malta Harbor, Florence felt too weak to move.

Conditions failed to get better. Almost all passengers were seasick, but a few hardy Anglican sisters sat down to dinner with Selina Bracebridge. Impressed with her strength and kindness, the exhausted and anxious sisters listened avidly to Selina's tales of "past travels, voyages, and perils by land and water in Syria, Greece, and the Mediterranean."[26]

The "blustering, creaking, shrieking" *Vectis* entered the Dardanelles at dawn in "wind and rain." Florence "staggered on deck" to "look at the plains of Troy, the tomb of Achilles." Trojan ghosts answered her "cordial hail" in "a dense mist"; it failed to diminish Flo's "enthusiasm for the heroes." Having "rushed on her way," the battered ship then rode at anchor off Constantinople's Seraglio Point in "thick and heavy rain." It made the fabled "Sophia, Sulieman, the Seven Towers, the walls, and Golden Horn" look "like a bad daguerreotype washed out."

Awaiting word "whether we can disembark direct into the hospital, which, with our heterogeneous mass, we should prefer,"[27] Florence Nightingale thought that even in her most intense daydreams she could never have imagined such a scene.

10

"The kingdom of hell"

What the horrors of war are, no one can imagine. They are not wounds, and blood, and fever, spotted and low, and dysentery, chronic and acute, and cold and heat and famine. They are intoxication, drunken brutality, demoralization and disorder on the part of the inferior; jealousies, meanness, indifference, selfish brutality on the part of the superior.[1] — Florence Nightingale

Florence in the hospital makes intelligible to me the saints of the middle ages. If the soldiers were told that the roof had opened, and she had ascended palpably to heaven, they would not be the least surprised.[2] — Augustus Stafford, member of the special parliamentary commission inspecting British army hospitals, Scutari

On November 5, 1854, a young English officer lay severely wounded in Scutari's Barrack hospital. From his cot in a crowded corridor he could see the hospital's central courtyard, a scene forever etched in his memory. Amputated limbs flew from the operating-room window, opposite, onto a heap in the courtyard. Our officer tried to sleep, to forget the bloody and maimed objects dropping onto that grisly pile.

"Look," cried his neighbor. "I believe that English nurse has come."

With an effort our officer lifted his head. He saw a mule cart hauling away the putrid heap of human flesh.

Florence Nightingale and her nurses had landed the previous afternoon.

The mountaintop near Scutari town revealed "a panorama of surpassing beauty": the "Turkish capital, with its mosques and minarets, its magnificent harbor, in which the huge man of war and the tiny kayak are alike secure, and the blue waters of the Bosporus," its banks studded with villages. The Black Sea lay to the north; to the south, the Sea of Marmara. "Poet or painter could hardly do justice to the landscape."[3]

Britain's main medical facility, the imposing Barrack hospital, stood on a hill south of Scutari. Built in a hollow square with towers on each corner, one side unusable due to fire, its center courtyard heaped with garbage, the structure sat atop huge, ill-constructed sewers. They disgorged foul air that rose through the pipes of open privies into corridors and wards packed with casualties. Blocked toilets, rotting floors, filth galore, rats, fleas, and other free-ranging vermin contributed to the chaos that characterized the hospital.

No ventilation, no bedrooms, no fuel, no cleaning or kitchen equipment existed, and far too few beds. Sheets consisted of canvas so coarse that men begged to remain wrapped in their bloody, sweat-soaked blankets. The huge hospital even lacked basic medical material like bandages and medicines. Cholera and typhus flourished.

Nonetheless, a few days before Nightingale arrived, Scutari's chief medical officer, anxious to avoid offending his superiors, reported that "as far as the present wants extend, we are satisfactorily supplied." The "sick and wounded" get "every care and attention."[4]

—◊◊◊—

"It is difficult to conceive a landing place" for "everything animate and inanimate" so "utterly inconvenient, and inadequate for the purpose," as Scutari's "so called pier."[5] In addition, a nauseating stench instantly assaulted the nostrils. It came from "buoyant cats, dogs, birds, straw, sticks, in fact of all sorts of abominable flotsam and jetsam floating in the stagnant water."[6] The sight of mangy, feral dogs salivating over a dead horse slowly drifting towards shore greeted the Nightingale group.

Florence calmly led her party up the steep, rutted causeway to the hospital where senior medical staff were assembled to extend a gracious welcome. These doctors met a woman "rather high in stature, fair in complexion, and slim in person," her thick brown hair "worn quite plain; her" face most "pleasing; her eyes, of a bluish tint," spoke "volumes" and sparkled "with intelligence." In "serious matters, a gentle smile" crossed her face, "proving her even"[7] temper.

She would need it.

Quarters for Nightingale, thirty-eight nurses, housekeeper Clarke, the Bracebridges, and their courier consisted of six dank, dirty rooms. Florence gave one big room to the nurses and Clarke, another "to the ten nuns, a small room or rather closet she kept for herself," and "a larger room she used as" an office. Charles Bracebridge and the courier slept in it. Selina shared Flo's "closet." Narrow dark stairs between it and the nuns' room led to the tower, "a fine airy room with windows on three sides, commanding splendid views."[8] This Florence assigned to the Anglican sisters. Forty-one women and two men housed in a space usually allotted to three doctors and their servants.

All rooms were bare. Except one. It contained the rotting corpse of a

Russian general, his white hairs mingling with the malodorous filth on the floor.

Fortunately, Florence had the foresight to bring iron bedsteads and other basics from Marseille. But she found the Barrack hospital bereft of cleaning equipment. Since the *Times* business manager, Bence MacDonald, sailed with her from Marseille to administer the Fund that Britons had donated for soldiers' comforts, Nightingale immediately asked him to buy two hundred sturdy scrubbing brushes, ample soap, and sacking to wash the floors.

—⚶—

Florence's patients consisted of two thousand sick and injured soldiers packed into the Barrack hospital; several hundred severely wounded filled the nearby General hospital. All were filthy, many near death "with dysentery or with open sores, who had not had a change of linen for months."[9] The wards reeked. There were no basins for washing the wounded, no towels, no drinking cups. Florence offered nurses and supplies. "No thank you, not needed," chorused the doctors.

They had orders to admit her but no orders to use her services. Understaffed and overworked they might be, but medical officers saw the intrusion of women into their jealously guarded male bastion as a menace. How could the government foist on them a young, do-gooding society miss and a bunch of feckless nurses? They had to tolerate enough irritating intruders, like those nosy *Times* correspondents. Hospital conditions would surely hound Nightingale and her staff back to England, said the medical men. They were wrong.

Florence resolved to win the doctors' goodwill. She would prove her professionalism. She would stick to the rules of a military hospital, obey those in authority, and make her nurses obey.

So for the time being Nightingale kept them busy making basic comforts like pillows and stump rests from the supplies she brought with her. This tedious task, plus cramped quarters, sparse eating facilities, the ubiquitous stench, and hordes of aggressive fleas, sorely tried the nurses as their first days at Scutari dragged slowly by. "We did not come for this," they grumbled.

—⚶—

Barred from nursing, Florence tackled two issues indisputably considered women's work: hygiene and food.

The Barrack hospital's filthy walls and floors aggravated the stench emanating from the rotten sewers below the building. And because they had amassed detritus from men with gangrene, typhoid fever, and diarrhea, the divans (low wooden platforms lining the walls of each ward) crawled with fleas, lice, maggots, and other vermin; dead rats lay beneath.

Besides being personally fastidious, let alone brought up to consider cleanliness basic to a lady's life, Nightingale believed good nursing began with "fear of dirt."[10] Once floors had been scrubbed with the brushes and soap, which the *Times'* MacDonald bought for her, walls and divans lime-washed, Florence tackled the huge, open, excrement-filled tubs. These stood in each ward to serve sanitary purposes for up to fifty men with dysentery or diarrhea, and only two or three chamber pots among them.

Florence asked Macdonald and Bracebridge to cross the Bosporus to Constantinople. There they could buy chamber pots in the city's teeming bazaar, for Scutari's meager shops had next to nothing of use. She asked orderlies to empty the tubs several times a day. They balked. Never raising her voice, never rebuking, Nightingale stood by each reeking tub, often for an hour at a time, until she charmed every orderly into emptying the tub regularly. Despite this extra work, no orderly ever employed "one word nor one look which a gentleman would not have used."[11]

> Your mind seems sorely troubled about chloride of lime,* [Flo wrote her mother.] Can you suppose that such a scavenger as I am have not a sack of [it] at the corner of every corridor & do not myself see to the fatigue parties cleansing out the places which require it? Alas! I am purveyor [supplier], scavenger, everything to these colossal calamities, as the hospitals of Scutari will come to be called in history.[12]

Appalled at the filthy, verminous state of her patients, who often wore "rags, or shirts saturated with blood,"[13] Florence asked Macdonald to buy enough shirts and sheets for regular changes. To her horror, however, the so-called laundry washed a grand total of six shirts per thousand patients monthly and washed bedding in cold water. Of course the sheets came back crawling with lice. Nightingale ordered them burned. She then rented a house in Scutari town, had boilers installed, and hired soldiers' wives to do laundry.

"In these hospitals, the purveyor considers washing both of linen & of the men a minor 'detail,'" Florence wrote her friend secretary-at-war Sidney Herbert in the first of many letters urging radical reform of the army medical administration.† "No washing whatever has been performed for the men either

---

*Bleaching powder, used as a disinfectant and deodorant.

†Army organization, if such one could call it, consisted of seven semi-autonomous sections, thus causing complications, confusion, duplication, turf wars, and convoluted systems of supply and control.

Three different departments administered army health and hospitals: commissariat, purveyor, and medical. In the forty years of peace following Waterloo, governments pared these departments to the bone. Besides, class-conscious Britain gave them no status — their members were not gentlemen. Ill-paid, despised, and painfully anxious about promotion, these civil servants were terrified of their superiors, especially the aristocratic army officers.

Herbert had charge of most army finances and transactions with *continued on page 114*

of body-linen or of bed-linen except by ourselves." Neither "basin, towel nor soap" existed "in the wards" when Nightingale arrived, "nor any means of personal cleanliness for the wounded." Naturally, "fever, cholera, gangrene, lice, bugs, fleas — & may be erysipelas — from the using of one sponge among many wounds" proliferated.

Fault lay "not with the medical officers, but in the separation of the department which affords every necessary supply, except medicines, to them."

"The cheese-paring system, which sounds unmusical to British ears, is here identified with you by the officers who carry it out," Florence bluntly told Sidney.

"The requirements are, unity of action & personal responsibility."

"Two or three hundred stump pillows, ditto arm slings, ditto *paddings* for splints — besides other medical appliances are being" manufactured "by us — & no provision appeared to have been made for these things before."

"All the above is written in obedience to your PRIVATE* instructions. Do not let me appear a govt. spy here which would destroy all my usefulness."[14]

—m—

Thirteen huge copper vats squatted at one end of the Barrack hospital. They cooked all food but had never met a scrubbing brush. Furthermore, their water rarely boiled because army cooks used green wood for fuel.

An orderly got the food ration (meat, including bone and gristle) for his ward. Having marked the meat, usually with a dirty rag or old nail, he dropped it in the vat. At his convenience the orderly then carried the so-called cooked meat through three or four miles of corridors to his ward and, using his bed as countertop, allotted the underdone, or overdone, but certainly cold, meat. Since no utensils existed, the patient ate with his fingers. If he could not, the food congealed at his bedside. Men on a liquid diet got greasy lukewarm water from the cooking vat. If a doctor ordered wine, the orderly drank it. Those sleeping or too ill to eat went without.

This disgusting food caused agony for those suffering from cholera or dysentery and not much comfort for anyone else. Bureaucratic infighting and official inertia precluded preparation of extra diets.

Using the provisions and portable stoves she brought with her, Nightingale created an extra diet kitchen in her quarters. Competent Reverend Mother

civilian contractors but no responsibility for the army's size and cost. He financed the mainly freestanding medical department; the purveyors department, a quasi subsidiary of the commissariat (under the treasury department), supplied it with some but not all needs — clothing, for example, came under the aegis of yet another department.

*Herbert had asked Nightingale to keep him frankly but confidentially informed about hospital conditions.

Moore from the Bermondsey Sisters of Mercy convent and resourceful house-keeper Clarke from Harley Street supervised preparation of nourishing potions made from wine, thin cereal, and arrowroot; soups, beef tea, and jellies made from meat and fresh produce. Bracebridge and McDonald took a boat across the Bosporus to replenish ingredients, which they bought in Constantinople's crowded bazaar. While dishing out delicacies, Clarke informed orderlies that the soldiers should consider themselves extremely fortunate to have Miss Nightingale come and look after them.

Within ten days of her arrival, "we have all the sick cookery now to do — & have got in 4 men for the purpose, for the prophet Mahomet does not allow us a female."[15]

Nightingale's extra diet kitchen provoked a problem. It involved hospital politics. The doctor selected his patient's diet. The commissariat and the purveyor had authority to provide extras — which usually proved to be Out of Stock. Hence, whoever could deliver extras became exceptionally popular, not to mention powerful, in the wards. That threatened Florence's strategy of cooperation with the medical officers. So she ruled that no food could leave her kitchen without a doctor's signed requisition plus the purveyor's signed form certifying unavailability.

—⚭—

Nightingale reached Scutari one day before the bloody Anglo-French victory at Inkerman (November 5, 1854). It followed the fiercely fought but indecisive engagement at Balaklava (October 25). Russian strength surprised the British and French generals. They confidently expected to take Sevastopol, Russia's mighty Black Sea naval base, by at least year end. Then the weather changed.

> It is now pouring rain — the skies are as black as ink — the wind is howling over the staggering tents — the trenches are turned into dykes — in the tents the water is sometimes a foot deep — our men have not either warm or water-proof clothing. [They] are plunged into the inevitable miseries of a winter campaign — and not a soul seems to care for their comfort.[16]

Troops belonging to the world's superpower lacked fuel to fight the frigid winds and cruel sleet that announced the start of a Russian winter. Men slept in mud, ate raw salt meat and stony dried peas, as they prepared to besiege Sevastopol. "The people of England" must "know that the wretched beggar who wanders about the streets of" London "leads the life of a prince compared with the British soldiers who are fighting out here for their country,"[17] boomed the *Times*.

Thousands suffering from exposure, dysentery, and severe battle wounds converged on the Crimea's inadequate medical facilities. Harassed doctors lacking equipment gave, at best, cursory remedies before shipping the men to Scutari. Their arrival caused a crisis in the already overcrowded hospitals. The medical officers turned to Nightingale. Would she "prepare for 510 wounded on our side of the hospital, who are arriving from the dreadful affair"[18] at Balaklava?

They descended from Sevastopol's rocky heights. One man had "raw flesh and skin hanging from his fingers, the naked bones of which protruded into the cold, undressed and uncovered."[19] Another, already dead, sat strapped, upright, on his mule, legs hanging stiffly, staring eyes wide open, teeth clamped on protruding tongue, head and body bobbing in dreadful derision of life as the animal stumbled over the steep, rutted track. "There's one poor fellow out of pain, anyway!" his comrades commiserated.

Small boats brought new amputees, men sick with fever, scurvy or frostbite, dying of cholera and dysentery, over Balaclava Harbor's cold, choppy water to overcrowded, ill-prepared ships. Bare decks and airless holds reeked of rotting flesh, excrement, and vomit. Flies and roaches infested the meager food supply. Fat white maggots feasted on festering wounds. A few surgeons moved gingerly around the close-packed piles of sick and wounded. Sailors tied up the dead, hoisted them overboard, then took on more casualties. After waiting two weeks to load the maximum number, the ship sailed for Scutari. Bad weather on the Black Sea often quadrupled the usual four-day journey.

At the Scutari pier the men "could, even when helped, scarcely crawl over this rough, hard, steep road." Eyes "closed, open mouths in ghastly gaunt faces, a slender stream of breath suspended in the frosty air alone showed life for an excessive number were specters; they did in reality more belong to the dead than to the living, for death was stamped indelibly upon them."[20] Other gaunt men clothed in bloody, tattered gray uniform coats lay "helpless (and very often senseless)" on stretchers "borne by noisy, careless Turks"[21] who seemed oblivious to the soldiers' sufferings.

Nightingale waited to receive them. With "half an hour's notice before they began landing the wounded"[22] and wards already crammed, she decided to make do with a damp, cold corridor. The purveyor proved unable, not to say unwilling, to outfit this improvised ward, so Florence had her nurses stuff straw into the sackcloth bags they had been grumpily sewing for several days. Hardly were these makeshift mattresses placed in two neat rows on each side of the corridor, "alas! only upon matting on the floor,"[23] when in staggered the ashen, bloody men, caked in filth and crawling with vermin.

Hardly one could undress without help. Usually "delicate in their conduct, refusing even assistance they needed if it seemed to involve any immodesty," the soldiers now suffered too much "to allow of much consideration of this sort; the one object on their side and on ours was to get them undressed and to bed as quickly as possible, so little nuns were seen hastily but gently pulling off jackets and trousers and unbinding ghastly and revolting wounds which had not been dressed for"[24] days.

"It seemed a hard rough place to lie down in, this noisy, windy passage, on a bundle of straw laid on the cold pavement, but to the poor men these hardships seemed luxuries, and they all expressed gratitude and delight." Some "shed silent tears, which all their trials, wounds, and hardships had not had power to bring."[25]

Nightingale had her skilled nurses deploy basins of water and clean rags. But rather than continuing the previous parsimonious practice of using one sponge to cleanse several men, Florence insisted that her nurses wash each patient with a fresh cloth.

When "all were settled quietly in bed," the less-experienced nurses "brought in and administered"[26] the soup and arrowroot cooked in Florence's extra diet kitchen.

Within eight hours every man had been washed, fed, and put in a clean bed.

—⁂—

Set in a vast military camp sitting on the fringes of a fabled foreign city, Nightingale's hospitals were fraught with temptation, especially for women of little education and less experience. They spanned a spectrum of skills and dedication. Six women who previously worked in hospitals soon renounced nursing for marriage. Florence sent home others who failed to meet the demands of the job. Four Anglican sisters had such "flibberty-gibbet" manners that they "do not command the respect imperatively necessary where forty women are turned loose among three thousand men. They do not keep the rules which I have made to ensure female decorum, but run scampering over the wards by themselves at night, feeding the men without medical orders. Their dressing of wounds are careless & slovenly." Nightingale asked their superior to recall these sisters, which Florence preferred "should arise thus, because you want them rather than because I don't."[27]

The five Bermondsey nuns followed their disciplined, serene Reverend Mother Moore in serving under Nightingale and accepting all her rules, even against proselytizing. To Florence these dedicated, positive, and able women embodied nursing virtues.

Nonetheless, Nightingale instructed all nurses "only to attend to patients in the wards of those surgeons who wished for our services, and she charged us never to do anything for the patients without the leave of the doctors."[28] As well, Florence banned all nurses from any ward with halfway well men, and from every ward after 8 P.M.

"I take rank in the army as brigadier-general, because 40 British females, whom I have with me, are more difficult to manage than 4000 men."[29]

—‍ᴍ‍—

Patients poured in for three weeks. Nightingale spent hours on her knees soaking bloody, filthy bandages off wounds dressed days before. "Ever watchful over her charge," Selina Bracebridge proved "most useful"; indeed, "without such a motherly friend, I cannot see how she could have got through many of the trials of her position."*[30]

Nightingale's calm assurance, let alone access to the *Times* Fund, "avoided a state of things too disastrous to" imagine, wrote a volunteer military chaplain. "Article after article of absolute necessity, as part of hospital stores," either did not exist or happened to be "so stored as to defy access to it." The Barrack and General hospitals "were absolutely without the commonest provision for the exigencies they had to meet." Indeed, "the whole business" showed an "utter want of that accord amongst the authorities in each department, which alone could secure any really vigorous effort to meet the demands"[31] of war.

"Any complaints?" asked the orderly officer as he made his round of the wards.

> NURSES: "We have three tiny spoons to feed fifty men their arrowroot diet."
> ORDERLY OFFICER: Each soldier has spoon, knife, fork, comb, razor, etc., in his knapsack.
> NURSES: Where can we find the knapsacks?
> ORDERLY OFFICER: I have not charge of them.

Since a soldier "carried insensible off the field" could scarcely be expected "to bring away his knapsack," the nurses applied to Nightingale.

You must ask the doctor to requisition the spoons, she said, having promised the chief physician not to send anything into the wards without a doctor's written request.

Doctor to nurse: Thank you for drawing my attention to the problem. "I will first write a requisition upon the commissariat, and then, should the articles not be forthcoming, give you a paper for miss Nightingale."

She "sent to Constantinople the same afternoon and bought the spoons."†[32]

---

*Selina called herself Boots because she took care of all the small tasks for which Flo had no time. (In the servant hierarchy of a wealthy Victorian household, the person who cleaned shoes also did odd jobs.)

†The Crimean War laid bare the flaws in Britain's army medical system, if system one could call it. In a military hospital, commissariat (contractors for all supplies — i.e., food, transportation, and stores), purveyor (supplier, through the commissariat, of equipment and food), and

—꿈—

The battles of Balaclava and Inkerman challenged hospital organization. And if lack of medical supplies or failure to handle the filth were not enough, mismanagement of resources beat everything. "Through all the departments there was a kind of paralysis, a fear of incurring any responsibility, and a fear of going beyond their instructions."[33] Nightingale found herself the only person with will, authority, and money to act. But rather than achieving a string of ad hoc successes at Scutari, she used basics like hygiene and food to introduce system into hospital administration.

People at home "could scarcely realize without personally seeing it the heartfelt gratitude of the soldiers, or the amount of misery which"[34] Nightingale and her nurses relieved. "She works them wonderfully, and they are so useful."[35]

"Comfort yourselves," Charles Bracebridge wrote his friends the Nightingales, "the good Flo has done and is doing is priceless, and is felt to be so by the medical men — the cleanliness of the wounds, which were horribly dirty, the general order and arrangement."[36]

Clad in a modest, but stylish, plain black dress of velvet-trimmed merino, spotless white linen apron, collar, cuffs, and fitted white cap, concealed under her sleeve a slender snakeskin bracelet containing plaited strands of hair from those she loved most — parents and sister — Florence, alone each night, walked "lamp in hand" along four miles of beds. "How many lives" she saved "by calling medical aid," or administering small "alleviations, is fully known only to herself, and" the Almighty. "Peculiarly skilled in the art of soothing, her gentle, sympathizing voice and manner always appeared to refresh the sufferer."[37]

> What a comfort [to] see her pass even, [a soldier wrote home.] She would speak to one and to another and nod and smile to a many more; but she couldn't do it all, you know, for we lay there by hundreds, but we could kiss her shadow as it fell, and lay our heads on the pillow again, content.[38]

Mother! a seventeen-year-old soldier cried out in pain.

Let me kiss you for your mother, said a soft voice. Nightingale bent to "kiss the spot." Is that better? her gentle voice asked. But the boy, comforted, had drifted off to sleep.

---

medical department were jointly responsible for army health. But purveyor and commissariat duties were blurred, cutbacks had decimated staff, and leadership too often proved inept. A doctor ordered requisitions; two others (one a senior official drowning in paperwork) must countersign them. The requisitions went to the purveyor; if the item proved Not in Store the requisition landed in the wastebasket. No one followed up. Purveyor and commissariat could supply only warranted items. So when soldiers entered the hospital without their packs, the purveyor refused them unwarranted articles like forks, knives, and shirts.

11

"These gigantic hospitals"

Without us, nothing would have been done here — & I am satisfied.[1] — Florence Nightingale

"The mere magnitude of the field, and its peculiarly horrible nature" made it impossible "to measure the real difficulties of the work miss Nightingale has done, and is doing. Every day brought some new complication of misery, to be somehow unraveled." Each "day had its peculiar trial to one who had taken such a load of responsibility, in an untried field, and with a staff of her own sex, all new to it."

"Courage ... diplomacy ... endurance ... cheerful compassion" are needed. She "fills that post, and" is "the one individual, who in this whole unhappy war, has shown more than any other, what real energy guided by good sense can do."[2] — Sydney Godolphin Osborne, volunteer military chaplain, Scutari hospitals

Ten days after Florence Nightingale reached Scutari and nine days after the carnage at Inkerman, the worst hurricane in memory hit Russia's Crimea (November 14, 1854). British ships anchored in Balaklava Harbor, waiting to unload their cargo of warm winter clothing and sturdy huts for soldiers besieging Sevastopol, were hurled helplessly against the rocks, and sank. Troops manned flooded trenches in threadbare uniforms. Tattered tents lacked floors. Stinging sleet, then snow swept over them. The men made do with scanty rations; no fresh meat, or produce, or bread; no means of making a fire to warm their food or themselves. Cold, wet, hungry soldiers fell easy prey to illness.

Commander in chief Lord Raglan informed the Barrack hospital that eight hundred sick and wounded soldiers had already sailed for Scutari. Not one free bed existed.

The hospital did have some empty rooms. But only because their abysmal condition caused Scutari officials to condemn them as useless.

NIGHTINGALE: Let us renovate those rooms.

OFFICIALS: We cannot take responsibility for authorizing the money. Much better to refer the entire issue to London.

Nightingale hired a common method of transportation, a caique, or small Turkish rowboat. The "carved and graceful" vessel, propelled by "picturesque-looking rowers sitting on benches," while passengers sat "on cushions on the bottom,"[3] conveyed Florence across the Bosporus to Constantinople. There she called on the one person who could approve spending. British ambassador Lord Stratford de Redcliffe yielded to Nightingale's urgent request with extreme reluctance. Barely had renovation begun when the Turkish workmen went on strike. Stratford backed out. Florence used her own money to hire new workers.* Wards for several hundred men "in the last stages of exhaustion" were finished on time. Florence supplied "utensils, including knives and forks, spoons, cans, towels, etc."[4]

"It don't matter being wounded *now*,"[5] said soldiers stoically manning the trenches before Sevastopol. Once they were with The Good Lady, all would be well. Nightingale and her nurses would receive them with clean linen and hot food. "We felt we were in heaven."[6]

—⁂—

Doctors began to rely on Florence's innate awareness about the hospital, her ability to appear when least likely and most wanted. Coping with frightful conditions during the 1854-1855 winter, often working for twenty hours on end to carry out God's work, work she had so long yearned to do, Nightingale missed nothing.

Always "full of life and fun when she talked to" soldiers, "especially if a man" felt "a bit down-hearted,"[7] Florence assigned beds, distributed stores, directed her staff, dressed wounds, and assisted at operations.

Surgery took place "in a ward, amongst the other patients, on a door or something like it, laid on two trestles."[8] Nightingale installed screens to shield the operating area. She "gave efficient aid"[9] during complicated procedures, surprising "the surgeons by her skill and presence of mind. After amputating a limb, they pass on to another, leaving her to take up the artery and do what is necessary."[10] During a "frightful amputation," Florence stood "with spirits, instruments, and lint in hand," six nurses "behind her, holding basins, towels, and other things the surgeons might want. A harrowing groan from the patient suddenly put them all to flight." Turning calmly, Nightingale called, "'Come back! Shame on you as women!' They returned holding each other's trembling hands."[11]

Five casualties arrived "in such a state of exhaustion the drs. gave them up." Florence "undertook them, washed their wounds, fed them, watched them through the night & brought them round. The three head medical officers write in the strongest terms of what she has done."[12]

*The war office eventually reimbursed Nightingale. At the same time it commended her action.

Florence Nightingale, 1820–1910. *The Lady with the Lamp.* Statue at the Crimean War Memorial, erected 1914. London's first statue of a woman, other than royalty (author photograph).

A volunteer military chaplain and his wife arrived at the Barrack hospital. Lady Alicia Blackwood asked Nightingale how she could help.

"Do you mean what you say?" Florence replied after a few seconds of silence, her "peculiar expression" making "an indelible impression."

"Yes, certainly, why do you ask?"

"Because I have had several such applications before, and when I have suggested work, I found it could not be done, or some excuse was made; it was not exactly the sort of thing intended, it required special suitability, etc."

"I am in earnest," Blackwood said.

"Very well, then, you really can help me if you will. In this Barrack hospital are located now some two hundred poor women in the most abject misery," in "rags; and covered with vermin. My heart bleeds for them; but my work is with the soldiers, not with their wives. Now, will you undertake to look after them?"[13]

Yes.

Alicia Blackwood put some women to work in the laundry. And with Selina Bracebridge's help, she started a lying-in hospital. The two ladies also organized a school for soldiers' wives and children. Charles Bracebridge raised the money. And he arranged distribution of tea and flannel petticoats, which daily brought twenty-six clamoring mothers and as many infants to his door. The Turks called them Bracebridge's Harem.* Nightingale disparaged their din as The Scourge of the Hospital.

—ɯ—

Her nightly rounds impressed a visitor as "endless" and "not easily forgotten." Corridors were "thickly lined with beds laid on low trestles raised a few inches from the ground." Wards with divans around the walls held "straw beds, and the sufferers on them." As "we slowly passed along, the silence was profound; very seldom did a moan or a cry from those multitudes of deeply suffering ones fill our ears. A dim light burned here and there." Florence put down her lamp before seeing to "any of the patients. I much admired" her "manner to the men — it was so tender and kind."[14]

Nightingale refused to let any man die alone. "Her slight form would be seen bending over him, administering to his ease in every way in her power, and seldom quitting his side till death released him."[15]

The hour had advanced "far into the night before" the Lady with the Lamp "reached her quarters."[16] But not to sleep.

---

*"Bracebridge was active everywhere, and from his acquaintance with the East, his persevering good humored attempts to help everybody about everything, was of infinite service" (Osborne, *Scutari and Its Hospitals*, p. 29).

Seated at a plain wooden table in her chilly little room where the roof leaked buckets in heavy rain, the woman who hated cold could see her breath in the glowing lamplight. Mice scrabbled in the walls as she ploughed through a pile of official correspondence before describing the dire conditions surrounding her in confidential reports to secretary-at-war Sidney Herbert. Florence wrote frankly about people, for she and Sidney agreed that good orders were futile unless energetic men effected them. Florence wrote angrily, for she saw few such men. Florence wrote fiercely "because of the non-success of your unwearied efforts for the good of these poor hospitals."[17] And she filled pages with proposals supported by statistics, critiques, and complex calculations. Living every hardship of a broken system, Nightingale urged radical reform.

Only when ghostly gray dawn diffused the star-scattered sky did Florence lay down her pen, flex her stiff fingers, and snatch a few hours of sleep. Selina Bracebridge often found her in the morning, collapsed and fully clothed, fast asleep on her narrow camp bed.

"Could you but see me, you would not wonder that I have no time to write — when my heart yearns to do so," read the Nightingales as they sat cozily around a cheerful fire in Embley's drawing room. "Could anyone but know the difficulties & heart-sinkings of *command*, the constant temptation to throw it up, they would not write" about "praying for grace that I may bear the praise lavished upon me." Would, Florence wondered, her mother ever understand? "Praise, good God! He knows what a situation He has put upon me." For "His sake I will bear it willingly, but not for the sake of praise."[18]

Parthe did value the praise now associated with her family's name. Praise enhanced Parthe's recently created role of sisterly support. She collected everything Flo needed. Most of Florence's requests were, of course, for her patients, but Parthe packed one dress anyway. "Barbarous woman," Flo replied, "there is a black *lace* bonnet & a black *silk* gown come & not my bear's grease"! Should "this savor of vanity, *let* me tell you you don't know what this climate is & as the natives oil themselves, so must I bear grease myself. I have been obliged to cold cream my hair. So let me have my bear's grease or I die. I left your castor oil grease behind on the mirror table like an honest woman."[19]

Each of the letters pouring in from soldiers' loved ones got a personal answer. "Your son" stayed conscious, Nightingale wrote, "till the very last. He prayed aloud so beautifully that, as the nurse in charge said, 'It was like a sermon to hear him.'" He "expressed himself to me as entirely resigned to die" and "was decently interred."*[20]

---

*Nightingale had badgered her government into persuading the Sultan of Turkey to give his British allies some land for a military cemetery. It lay near the Barrack hospital.

"Are you really going to do that unkind thing — to teach children to write?" Florence sighed in mock dismay when Alicia Blackwood and Selina Bracebridge shared their plans to start a school for soldiers' wives and children. "I am so tired of writing, I sometimes wish I could not write"![21]

—m—

Florence's Incredible Bonté and ladylike mien humanized the harsh ambiance of the huge army hospital. At its core pulsed her cramped quarters. Here Nightingale stored and allocated the provisions she brought from Marseille, plus what the *Times* Fund's Macdonald bought at her behest in the amply stocked bazaar across the Bosporus at Constantinople. Florence called her supply center The Caravanserai; the nurses, the Tower of Babel.

A "practical lesson in the working of true common sense benevolence,"[22] the caravanserai issued extras like arrowroot, rice pudding, jelly, beef-tea and lemonade, as well as linens and utensils only at a doctor's written request, and the purveyor's written confirmation that he lacked the item. Orderlies waited "at the door with requisitions"; a nun "saw they were signed and countersigned."

> [At midday] everything and everybody seemed to be there: boxes, parcels, bundles of sheets, shirts, and old linen and flannels, tubs of butter, sugar, bread, kettles, saucepans, heaps of books, and all kinds of rubbish, besides the diets which were being dispensed, [plus] nuns, nurses, orderlies, Turks, Greeks, French and Italian servants, officers and others waiting to see miss Nightingale; all passing to and fro, all intent upon their own business, and all speaking their own language.[23]

In the center stood "a large kitchen table; bustling about this, might be seen the caravanserai's high priestess," former Harley Street housekeeper Clarke. She "received the various matters from the kitchen and stores," which "sisters and nurses were ever ready to take to the sick in any and every part of these gigantic hospitals."[24]

A surprising source of provisions soon surfaced. Craving to share the dangers of her troops, agonizing in suspense during the campaign, puffing up with pride at her army's bravery, Queen Victoria envied Nightingale her opportunity to tend to those noble heroes. As well, the Queen admired Florence's self-sacrifice. So Victoria asked Liz Herbert to send her Nightingale's reports of the men and, through Sidney, learned what comforts they most needed. These the Queen sent for Florence to distribute "as you may think fit."[25]

Nightingale then suggested the Queen send something "the man will feel as a daily extra comfort which he would not have had without" her generosity — like "woolen material" to "cut up into comforters for the neck when the man begins to get out of bed" or "a brush & comb for each man? Or a razor."

"As the Queen is sending out soap, a most acceptable present, a zinc or tin basin (say 2000) & toweling would be appropriate."

"As to eau de Cologne, a little gin & water would do better."[26]

In what way, Victoria asked Florence, could she show esteem for her troops' courage? If a soldier fell ill on duty, Nightingale replied, his hospital stipend should equal that of a wounded man. Done — retroactive to the Alma, first battle of the war.

"It is as if the whole of England had thought of nothing but Scutari," Florence noted as the country emulated its Queen. "Not any one of these contributions is worth its freight; but the smaller the value, of course, the more importance contributors attach to it."[27]

So Nightingale scrupulously recorded and acknowledged each Free Gift. These were stored in a shed outside the hospital. Stately Selina Bracebridge, snugly wrapped in fur cloak, fur boots and hat, took charge. A one-legged convalescent assisted. He hung edibles on hoops suspended from the ceiling to foil vermin. And ingenious locks, frequently changed, guarded the store from ever-present thieves.

It would have been easiest for Florence to disburse all supplies at her discretion. Instead, she kept her main goal in focus: winning the doctors' trust. Without it, female nursing in military hospitals would fail. And that failure would kill her goal to raise nursing standards. So Nightingale insisted that nurses could not assign stores at will. Nurses must obey doctors in all patient matters.

Her ability to enforce the discipline essential in an army hospital impressed medical officers. So, too, did Florence's administrative talent and nursing skills.

—⁘—

She stood so near to success that Nightingale could stretch out her hand and almost touch it. Within six weeks she had repaired derelict space to house eight hundred casualties ("this I regard as the most important"), created an efficient extra diet kitchen, supplied cleaning apparatus for regular use in wards, combs to delouse patients' heads and beards, and two thousand cotton shirts and organized a laundry to wash them. Under her auspices Alicia Blackwood and Selina Bracebridge had established a lying-in hospital for solders' wives, "which the pressure of the misery of these poor women had compelled us to begin"; other wives, and widows, had been "relieved & attended to." Doctors trusted Florence's best nurses with compound fractures and daily dressings. And senior medical officers agreed with her "supervision & stirring-up of the whole machinery generally."[28]

This satisfaction proved short-lived.

Nightingale had won the doctors' trust by making sure her nurses obeyed hospital rules. Sister Elizabeth demanded extra portions for her patients. Not without the doctor's signed requisition, Florence insisted. Unpleasant scenes ensued. Elizabeth wrote home. A relative sent her tirade to the *Times*. The newspaper used Elizabeth's letter as fuel for its anti-government campaign.[29] Public reaction provoked an official investigation. Parthe Nightingale lobbied officials in her sister's defense and leaked selected sections of her letters to the press. Florence and Elizabeth testified in writing. The latter's story contained factual errors. Britain's government asked Sister Elizabeth to resign.

Her rebellion could be counted as mild in comparison to what came next.

—⁂—

Constant personal supervision constituted a crucial component of Nightingale's success in having forged her disparate cadre of females into an efficient nursing staff. Florence's full control over all nurses, which secretary-at-war Sidney Herbert avowed publicly (in the press) and officially (in his instructions), proved equally vital. Herbert had also vowed that no new "nurses will be sent" until Nightingale "shall have written home from Scutari" that "they are required."[30]

Not one of Florence's frequent and comprehensive letters asked Herbert for additional nurses. But as Russia's harsh winter set in at Sevastopol, hundreds more patients flooded into the hospitals. Britons saw Nightingale's success as the one bright spot in an abysmal war. Public and press clamored for extra nurses. Burdened by the war's many demands, misreading a letter from Bracebridge casually mentioning how Flo could use more help to indicate a need for added staff, Herbert acquiesced.

The praise cascading over Nightingale's mission had already caused applications to surge. In anticipation of Flo's probable need for more nurses Liz Herbert, Florence's socially conscious friend Mary Stanley, and their cohorts continued to screen candidates. But despite knowledge of Florence's selection criteria, the interviewers chose a large and heterogeneous party: twenty inexpert, gin-sodden nurses; thirteen ladies* who dreamed of tending to handsome young officers while supervising others at menial work; and fifteen Irish nuns who had some nursing ability. But one significant factor offset this advantage: the nuns recognized only the authority of their mother superior.

Upper-class Reverend Mother Frances Bridgeman of Kinsale frowned on the nuns in Nightingale's original group for their promise to follow her

---

*Mary Stanley et al. knew Nightingale had ruled out ladies; their social status would cause confusion in her and the military hospitals' command structure.

orders. "Ardent, high-tempered," and "rather difficult"[31] according to Britain's most prominent Roman Catholic convert, Henry Manning, Bridgeman refused to budge on her exclusive control over her nuns, not to mention insistence that she reported only to her bishop in Ireland. Moreover, Bridgeman openly declared her intent to minister to the spiritual needs of Catholic soldiers, a mission the government explicitly forbade.

To complicate matters further, Mary Stanley led the group. Although daughter of an Anglican bishop, Mary had strong Catholic leanings; indeed, the sole factor that kept her from converting consisted of fear at alienating the influential Stanley family. Now Mary, with help from her friend Henry Manning (Florence's and Liz Herbert's friend as well), sought to further the Catholic cause by spreading over Catholics the mantle of honor enfolding Scutari nurses. Furthermore, Mary coveted a share of her friend Flo's fame.

Stanley and Manning negotiated with the harassed secretary-at-war, Sidney Herbert. Rather than coming under Nightingale's direct authority, Bridgeman and her fifteen Irish nuns would report, instead, to Scutari's senior medical officer. That gave Bridgeman leeway to obey the orders of her bishop in Ireland, let alone giving her the quasi autonomy she would not have under Florence. And because Bridgeman and her nuns were in Stanley's nominal charge, Mary could claim to stand on equal footing with Flo.

This despite Herbert's official dictum that Nightingale had sole authority over all of the army's female nurses. Still, in all fairness, when Herbert addressed the new nurses on the eve of their departure he "told them to obey FN." Liz Herbert then reminded her husband about Mary Stanley. So Herbert added that Stanley would function "as miss N.'s representative till she could direct them."[32]

Anxious to assure the Nightingales that Mary's arrival would not threaten Flo's mission, Mary's mother told them her daughter had not wanted to take charge of the group. But because well-traveled Mary had the kind of *"good head"*[33] needed to unify and lead, the Herberts had asked her, and Mary reluctantly assented. She intended to stay only for a few days of sightseeing. But Mary's family knew better. She "has reached the height of her ambition," wrote one aunt to another. "Such nonsense" to "say she did not *wish* to go."[34]

Mrs. Stanley notwithstanding, Mary's leadership qualities consisted of traveling in grand style and squandering the money raised for her group on luxuries for the ladies. That angered the nurses. So a squabbling, penniless party arrived at Scutari.

—ᨠ—

"The 46 have fallen on us like a cloud of locusts," Charles Bracebridge wrote to Florence's uncle Sam Smith. "Where to house them, feed them, place them is difficult; how to care for them, not to be imagined."[35]

Preoccupied with thousands of severely sick and wounded soldiers, Florence heard of the Stanley party's pending arrival when Liz Herbert mentioned it casually in a letter to Selina Bracebridge. Nightingale at once conferred with her chief, Scutari's senior medical officer. A "rough, old, reddish-grey Scott,"[36] Dr. Cumming thought the hospitals had enough nurses. More would destroy order.

"I have toiled my way into the confidence of the medical men," Nightingale wrote Herbert. "I have, by incessant vigilance, day & night, introduced something like system into the disorderly operations of these women. And the plan may be said to have succeeded in some measure, *as it stands*." But while "expressing themselves satisfied with things as they are," the medical officers reiterate "that more women cannot be usefully employed or properly governed. And in this opinion I entirely agree."[37]

"More quarters cannot be assigned to us. The sick are laid up to our door." Flo and Selina had ceded their tiny room. The Bracebridges slept in the sitting room, Flo in a small space behind a screen in the caravanserai. Extra nurses could not live, unsupervised, in Scutari town — even were a house available. Filthy, rough and rowdy, chock-full of bars and brothels, the town could scarcely be compared to an English village. Besides, "the difficulties of transport are what no one in England would believe."

"I am willing to bear the evil of governing (& preventing from doing mischief) the non-efficient, which is my great difficulty & most wearing-out labor — because I acknowledge the moral effect produced." But "I am not willing to encounter the crowding greater numbers to exhaust our powers & make us useless & incapable — by wasting our time & nervous energy in governing that which cannot be governed."[38]

Well aware of the enmity existing among war-office diehards, not to mention many army officers, against females nursing in military hospitals, conscious that a minute mistake could be exaggerated to attack her entire mission, Florence opposed having more nurses than she herself could oversee.

—m—

At first Nightingale saw Mary Stanley as a nuisance and her Irish nuns as part of a scheme to bring Catholicism into the hospitals. But when she learned of Mary's accreditation to Chief Medical Officer Cumming, Florence feared her advent would imperil the success of the whole nursing venture. Because it rested on a clear line of authority: all nurses reporting to Nightingale, she reporting to the chief medical officer. Once this line was breached, other autonomous groups would come to Scutari. The consequence: chaos — with blame falling on Florence. By diluting her authority Herbert had destabilized her position and betrayed their plan.

On arrival, Stanley instantly announced herself to Cumming. Mary thus underlined her claim to stand on equal footing with Florence.

Dr. Cumming declined Mary Stanley's services.

Charles Bracebridge advised Nightingale to tread warily. So when Stanley's two male escorts formally announced the party to her, Florence asked Charles to be witness. Frostily, Nightingale declined any responsibility for the new nurses. She had not requested them, could provide neither accommodation nor work. They were assigned to Cumming. Bracebridge wrote a précis of the discussion and, to avert future confusion, asked the two men to sign it. They did, but blamed Nightingale for insulting them.

The Stanley party retreated to the British embassy. Its ambassadress arranged quarters in the sultan's luxurious summer palace. Nuns, nurses, and ladies still squabbled.

Meanwhile, Mary appealed to her friend Flo for funds. Without official sanction Florence thought she should not use government money to resolve financial problems caused by Mary's laxity. Nor could she use private donations, for Nightingale and Bracebridge accounted for every such penny. Besides, Mary reported to Cumming. She must apply to him. Cumming refused public funds. So Flo dipped into her own purse.

"What *do* you think happened last night," Mary whispered to Selina Bracebridge. "Now then for a hunt," one nurse said to another. "*Can you imagine*" what happened next? The nurse "actually found *something* on her gown! — actually *something*"! and "began diligently to capture the little lively inhabitants of her dress."

"We have ceased to think about" fleas and cockroaches, Selina calmly replied. "They are everywhere; it is very dreadful, but it can't be helped; and really the best thing is not to mind it. We shall get rid of them by and by."[39]

—⚉—

"You have sacrificed the cause so near my heart. You have sacrificed me — a matter of small importance now — you have sacrificed your own written word to a popular cry," Nightingale reproached Herbert. "Where conditions are imposed on me which render the object for which I am employed unattainable," the secretary-at-war must expect her to resign. Florence asked Sidney to "appoint a superintendent in my place."[40]

Astounded, remorseful, Herbert instantly refused. Nightingale must send the Stanley party back at his expense. But Florence realized that religion alone ruled that out. The government would hardly welcome an eruption of Irish wrath were Reverend Mother Bridgeman publicly rebuffed. Besides, it would be impolitic to return nurses while patients poured into the hospitals. And above all, the fuss would harm her cause.

So Nightingale suggested putting five nuns in the Barrack hospital to replace five ineffective ones (from the orphanage) in her group. Bridgeman refused. She must be at the Barrack hospital with all her fifteen nuns. That convinced Florence of Bridgeman's ulterior motive: to proselytize. "Our little society" of Bermondsey nuns, "the truest Christians I ever met"—"invaluable in their work—devoted heart and head, to serve God and mankind—not to intrigue for their Church,"[41] plus Protestant sisters and nurses all working as a team under Nightingale's watchful eye must not "become a hotbed of R. C. intriguettes."[42] Florence could not accommodate sixteen more females at the Barrack hospital. Medical chief Cumming agreed. Consequently, Bridgeman considered herself absolved of any duty to recognize Nightingale's authority in hospital matters.

"*Our* rev'd mother" Moore of the Bermondsey convent, "heart & hand with us," did "her best to stop"[43] the religious wrangling that so distressed Florence, to say nothing of distracting her from hospital matters. Moore crossed the snow-blown Bosporus in an open caique to broker a compromise: pending her Irish bishop's clarification of orders, Bridgeman and four nuns would nurse at the Barrack hospital reporting to Moore (under Nightingale).

This uneasy truce did not live for long. Some weeks later a new hospital opened at nearby Koulali. Bridgeman removed herself to it, nursing under Mary Stanley nominally reporting to Nightingale.

Florence's handling of the Stanley issue fed ammunition to her enemies: war-office bureaucrats opposed to female nurses in army hospitals; grumblers against her rules; accusers of egoism and power hunger who had no clue about either the nature of Nightingale's work or its challenges. These included intense pressure from the daily demands of her job; awareness of how much work remained; controlling a disparate group of women breaking barriers in an all-male military institution located in an exotic land far from home; and always, always, Florence's deep-seated fear of failure due to years of coping with her mother's disapproval. No wonder she did not welcome the irruption of a large number of unsolicited, unproven women who did not report directly to her. Yet, critics faulted Nightingale; she should at least have been more gracious.

Far from the saint of popular iconography but a woman toiling under terrific physical and mental strain, Florence lost her temper. To her, the issue centered on saving lives, not on who got praise. Certainly she could have been more gracious. But that would not alter *the* salient fact: Mary Stanley's accreditation to Scutari chief medical officer Cumming. Stanley's challenge to Nightingale's authority jeopardized the mission.

"It is impossible for me to ride through all these difficulties," Florence wrote Sidney Herbert as her first two months at Scutari closed. "My caique is upset — but I am sticking on the bottom still."[44]

12

Unparalleled Calamity

"There is a far greater question to be agitated before the country than that of these eighty-four miserable women — eighty-five, including me. This is whether the system or no-system which is found adequate in time of peace but wholly inadequate" in "time of war is to be left as it is — *or* patched up temporarily ... *or* made equal to the" growing needs "of a time of awful pressure."[1] — Florence Nightingale

The state of things gets worse the numbers of sick arriving daily is deplorable, and in such a state of dirt and nudity as wants to make you shudder. Flo has to do everything, clothe the men, find all that is missing in short her work is more than any other woman had to do before.[2] — Selina Bracebridge

As 1855 opened, British troops besieged Sevastopol in sub-zero weather. Whipping arctic winds caused six-foot snowdrifts. "Many of our men have been crippled by the cold," hobbling "about in the trenches" and "camps barefooted, and yet ankle-deep in snow. They could not get their frozen boots and shoes on their swollen feet,"[3] the *Times* special correspondent reported from the front.

Hundreds of casualties stumbled down the rough track leading from Sevastopol's heights to Balaclava Harbor, crossed the tossing Black Sea to the bleak Scutari pier, and staggered up the steep, rutted causeway to the Barrack hospital. Its two thousand plus patients lay "close to each other on each side of the corridors, leaving merely room to pass between."[4]

On her feet twenty hours at a time, often on her knees dressing wounds for eight, always nursing the most critical cases herself, Florence Nightingale, each evening, walked "miles along sick and dying men."[5] She would not allow any soldier to die alone. Florence saw two thousand deaths during the Crimean Calamity (her first six months at Scutari.)*

---

*Sixty-four of every hundred men who left England for the Crimea in spring of 1854 were by year end in medical treatment; of those, ten out of a hundred died and thirty-two out of a hundred were invalided home.

—ɯ—

"Flo has been working herself to death, never sits down to breakfast or dinner without interruption; often never dines," Charles Bracebridge wrote his friend secretary-at-war Sidney Herbert. The "attempt to do more will kill" her. "Today 200 sick landed looking worse than any others yet."[6]

They needed clothing, eating utensils, and bedpans.

PURVEYOR: There are none in store.
NIGHTINGALE: Are they expected from England?
PURVEYOR: No.
NIGHTINGALE: Can you get them from Constantinople?
PURVEYOR: No.
NIGHTINGALE: Are they even available there?
PURVEYOR: "If they are, I don't know how to get them."[7]

Nightingale did know.

No one familiar with her could expect Florence to stop caring for the sick, but by leaving the purveying of the huge Barrack and General hospitals to her Bracebridge — and several others at Scutari — thought the government imposed an unfair burden.

Herbert must be brought abreast of the situation. But because he would "never hear the whole truth, troublesome as it is, except from one independent of promotion," Nightingale broke her rule of reporting only what came within the confines of her responsibility. With detail and precision, she described the complete state of the hospitals, as well as the supplies that doctors asked her to provide since purveyor and commissariat could not. Florence's shattering letter did not result from "an indefinite feeling of feminine compassion." The "best men here" begged her to tell Herbert the truth.

Casualties arrived "without resuming their kits, also half-naked besides. And when discharged," they "carry off, small blame to them! even my knives & forks — shirts, of course, & hospital clothing." To "purvey this hospital is like pouring water into a sieve."[8]

[An ill or injured man must] cease to be a soldier & become a patient from the moment he cross the hospital doors; [leave] his clothes, blanket & kit behind in the store-room; [have] a warm bath after which he has a clean shirt & hospital suit given him & goes up to his bed or is carried upon a stretcher with *clean* blankets. That, when the patient leaves the hospital, he leaves every article used in the hospital behind & becomes a soldier again.

The hospitals needed strong, able stewards, cleaners, and orderlies; they must all be well paid, fed, and housed. A manager should be put in charge of daily matters like cooking, washing, and cleaning the wards. Now the purveyor performed or, rather, did not perform this daily routine. "I am really cook, housekeeper, & scavenger, (I go about making the orderlies empty huge tubs,) washerwoman, general dealer, store-keeper."[9]

"We need: an effective staff of purveyors out from England — but beyond this — a *head*, some one with *authority* to mash up the departments into uniform and rapid action."

"As your official servant, you will" say "I ought to have reported these things before. But I did not wish to be made a spy. I thought it better if the remedy could be brought quietly — & I thought the commission"* would "bring it. But matters are worse than they were two months ago & will be worse two months hence than they are now."[10]

"The truth is fearful," Herbert replied, "but it is the truth, and I will do my utmost to meet your"[11] needs. Nine moths later, Nightingale's improvements were in place.

—⁂—

Buried under war materiel bound for Balaclava, hospital supplies often by passed Scutari. When provisions did arrive, they either sat in the Turkish customs house, otherwise known as the Bottomless Pit, or languished in the purveyor's depot until a committee met to sign their release.

NIGHTINGALE: Please open these boxes.
FLUMMOXED DEPOT OFFICIALS: What will our superiors say?

She stood next to the boxes until they were opened.

"It is absolutely necessary," Nightingale wrote Herbert, to have "a government store house" to at once receive "stores for the British, from whatever ships."[12] Done.

Formation of a much-needed medical school would be easy and inexpensive, the unstoppable Florence then told Sidney. Her hospitals had neither operating nor dissecting rooms; postmortem examinations were rare. No statistics existed on age of death, method of treatment, the corpse's condition — i.e., "all the innumerable & most important points which contribute to making therapeutics a means of saving life."

Young doctors were "first-rate anatomists" but poor pathologists. None practiced "the science of healing." Nightingale asked that three lecturers — one each on physiology, pathology, and anatomy — be sent from England. If junior physicians "could thus be interested in their profession (let alone humanity) much vice would be checked, besides saving, in future, many hundreds of lives."[13]

---

*The government had sent a three-man commission to ascertain the state of both hospitals and patients. It had no executive powers.

The government built and equipped a state-of-the-art dissecting room.

Meanwhile, the *Times* continued to print damning reports from its correspondents in the field. Mounting public fury blamed the government. It fell. Nightingale family friend Lord Palmerston became prime minister (January 1855). He combined the duties of secretary of state *for* and *at* war. Palmerston appointed Lord Panmure war secretary.

Sidney Herbert no longer sat in the cabinet. But from his seat in parliament, Sidney continued to deploy his political skills in the interest of improving conditions for the soldiers. He asked Florence to continue sending him confidential reports. And Herbert continued to forward Nightingale's letters to the Queen.

—⁊⁊⁊—

Florence systematically organized and bettered her hospitals by introducing basic hygiene and special diets; by initiating proficient nursing; by spreading an atmosphere of kindness and calm; and by braving official inertia. But without weighty assistance she could do little about the stench coming from the sewers below the building, or the blocked toilets, let alone the vermin who "might, if they had but 'unity of purpose' carry off the four miles of beds on their backs, and march with them into the war office."[14]

As Nightingale walked across the garbage-strewn muck to inspect the General hospital, she asked herself why, despite a declining mortality rate, too many soldiers still died. Because, Florence concluded, the army failed to protect these once strong young men against disease and, when they fell ill, to cure them. If a healthy man inhaled fetid air, drank tainted water, and could not stay clean, he got sick — and infected his comrades.

Nonsense, scoffed Scutari's medical officers. But Florence knew about the latest sanitary advances from her reading in Lea Hurst's pre-dawn light and from talking with reformers like Lord Shaftesbury in London drawing rooms. So she lobbied for a full evaluation of the Barrack hospital's sorry sanitary state. And since the first government commission sent to Scutari proved a letdown because it had no teeth, Nightingale pressed for the next commission to have executive powers.

Her quiet persistence coincided with a peak in public outrage at government misconduct of the war. So the new Palmerston administration decided on two commissions.

Having read Nightingale's letters to Herbert, Lord Shaftesbury influenced creation of the sanitary commission. It must ascertain why the Barrack hospital's death rate failed to decline further and examine the method of moving casualties from Sevastopol to Scutari and the state of both Balaclava Harbor and Crimean army camps. Shaftesbury convinced Prime Minister Palmerston, his father-in-law, to grant this commission full power to make immediate and systemic upgrades. War secretary Panmure put an extremely able and zealous sanitary expert in charge.

Already a teenager committed to medicine when Florence entered the world, John Sutherland, Scottish by birth and education, had traveled widely before opening his practice in England's leading industrial port city of Liverpool. He at once took an active part in public health. Erudite and resolute, eccentric and with a keen sense of humor, the cultured and considerate doctor whose gentle expression seemed on the verge of a whimsical smile formed an instant alliance with Nightingale.

Sutherland's engineers soon ascertained that Scutari's hospitals sat on huge, rotting sewers filled with festering carcasses and rat colonies nested in the Turkish divans lining the walls of every ward. Within two weeks sew-

John Sutherland, M.D., 1808–1891. Sanitary and public health expert. Nightingale's close friend and colleague for more than 30 years (author photograph of image in Ida B. O'Malley's *Florence Nightingale, 1820–1856: A Study of Her Life Down to the End of the Crimean War* [Thornton Butterworth, Limited, London, 1931]).

ers were cleaned, a clear air passage created, and sewage directed to flow into the sea. The stench from the drain thus stopped backing up into the toilets and, from them, into the wards. Divans were thrown out. Sutherland agreed with Nightingale that hospital walls should be regularly whitewashed, wards and corridors refloored, windows repaired so that they could be opened to admit fresh air and light. Mortality fell from four in every ten cases to twenty-two per thousand.

War minister Panmure charged his second commission* to examine and improve the structure and management of the commissariat department, responsible for food, hospital supplies, clothing, and transportation. Panmure put James McNeill in charge.

---

*The McNeill-Tulloch commission to inquire into provision of supplies for the army in the Crimea. This commission stemmed from a parliamentary inquiry (the Roebuck committee) into the state of the army before Sevastopol. Roebuck's inquiry had exposed the breakdown of Britain's military supply system.

Tall, dignified, and extremely good-looking, McNeill had entered the service of the British East India Company as a physician while Florence toddled around Lea Hurst. Charming and competent, witty and urbane, McNeill then turned to diplomacy. He served in Persia for twenty years before returning to his native Edinburgh. There McNeill won universal respect for his administration of Scotland's poor law.

Since their business lay at Balaclava, McNeill and his fellow commissioner, Colonel Alexander Tulloch,[15] spent little time at Scutari. But they made sure to speak with Nightingale. Having unparalleled power and a resolve to succeed, they were willing to listen to someone — even if a woman — more familiar with the issues than themselves. McNeill "never heard a vain or thoughtless proposal" from this lady of "strong practical sense."[16]

Florence liked McNeill "best of all who have come." He soon had filthy, clogged Balaclava Harbor cleared and its facilities working. Streets were rid of rotting flesh. The rutted, mucky track leading to Sevastopol got paved. Hence, ample supplies moved easily up the steep slopes to provision the troops with warm clothes and decent food. McNeill "dragged the commissary general out of the mud. He has done wonders. Everybody now has their fresh meat 3 times a week, their fresh bread from Constantinople about as often."[17] Consequently, fewer soldiers came into Nightingale's hospitals and those who did were not living skeletons.

—m—

An unexpected, not to say unusual, ally then knocked at Florence's door. His "dress corresponded with the bent of his mind," in "all things devoted to his profession; he clothed himself completely in white, excepting only his large, wide cap, "made of dark-blue cloth edged with gold binding."[18]

After reading the *Times* reports from the front, the famous French chef of an exclusive London club volunteered to go to the war zone and teach soldiers how to cook plain, nourishing food. Alexis Soyer traveled at his own expense with four assistants and a secretary. Florence remembered how, in the Hungry '40s, Soyer taught concerned ladies like her aunt Julia to make healthy, low-cost soup for the starving poor.

So a "quiet and rather reserved" lady with a "lively sense of the ridiculous," but serious "on matters of business," welcomed Soyer. Her "mind disciplined to restrain" every feeling that would hinder "the action of the moment," Nightingale had "trained herself to command, and" by now "learned the value of conciliation towards others and constraint over herself." A "strict disciplinarian," she knew "how much success must depend upon literal obedience to her every order."[19]

Happily for Soyer, Florence had long sought to change the preparation of her patients' rations, especially meat. Callous army cooks stewed it in huge vats, then threw out the nutritious liquid. Soyer convinced them to keep the liquid, as well as add salt and pepper to the meat while it cooked, to improve the taste. He concocted appetizing, healthy meals from army rations. He devised ovens to bake breads and biscuits. And Soyer insisted that soldiers be permanently assigned to the kitchens for training as cooks.

Soyer also tackled the method of making that most refreshing, sustaining, and necessary of British beverages. Tea used to be tied up in a dirty rag, then immersed in a copper vat of boiling water recently emptied of stewed meat and, of course, not scoured. Soyer invented the Scutari Teapot, a large kettle with a filter to hold the tea.

One problem remained: how to keep dinners hot until they reached the wards — far away from the kitchens. Nightingale "submitted a very excellent" plan. "We introduced double cases in which to carry boiling water, thus keeping" the food "hot much longer."[20]

—⁂—

In Victorian Britain men joined the army to escape joblessness and crime or for want of a better alternative. Few had military ambition. Many deserted. Most drowned their miseries in drink. Their officers despised them as inebriated oafs, albeit brave in battle.

The military mind viewed war as a game of intricate rituals played by specific, set rules. Any disruption represented a nuisance. Among the worst nuisances were soldiers who fell ill or got wounded — to say nothing of those who tried to help them.

Florence cared for the common soldier as she had for the elderly governesses at Harley Street. She saw him realistically — "what has he done with the £1 — drank it up I suppose." "He asks us to find a post for his wife," Nightingale scrawled on another note, "he had better say which wife."[21] But she did much to change public perception of the soldier from sodden boor to compatriot with human feelings.

Finding that the men drank their pay because they disliked the official method of sending money home, Florence offered an option. Once per week any patient seeking to send money home could entrust it to her. She sent the money to her uncle Sam Smith, who bought postal orders, which he forwarded to the designated addressees.

The men drank less, began to save their pay, and on rejoining their regiments clamored to continue using Nightingale's plan. She offered it to the authorities. No. So in a letter to Herbert intended for Queen Victoria, Florence described the causes and cures for intoxication in the army and the hardship of sending money home. Victoria passed Nightingale's letter to Prime

Minister Palmerston. Impressed, he gave it to war secretary Panmure — who growled that her letter showed Florence's ignorance of the British soldier.

Nonetheless, the war office did open several offices based on Nightingale's model. Within six months, soldiers were regularly sending large sums of money home.

Recognizing the relationship between mental attitude and physical recovery, Florence then prevailed against stiff resistance to open a small reading room for ambulatory convalescents. She personally paid for reading and writing materials. The Inkerman café would, sneered officers, spoil their brutish men, let alone destroy discipline. It did neither.

"The army used to be divided into gentlemen and blackguards," wrote Chief Sanitary Commissioner Sutherland. Florence Nightingale "taught officers and officials to treat the soldiers with respect as Christians."[22]

When convalescents began to outnumber the ill, Florence enlarged her café. And Parthe, eager to participate in Flo's fame, headed a group of volunteers who got compatriots — from royalty to the humblest servant — to respond to Florence's request for equipment. "Please, my dear, acknowledge a print which the Queen sends you,"[23] Parthe prompted.

Nightingale next convinced Scutari's new military chief to have the bars thriving around the Barrack hospital shut and the streets patrolled after dark. She then got General Sir Henry Storks to buy a pleasant building near the Bosporus and midway between her hospitals, equip it for recreation, and hire teachers from England. Men crowded in for lectures and singing classes. They organized amateur theatricals. Women were excluded.

> I have never been able to join in the popular cry about the recklessness, sensuality, helplessness of [the soldier.] I should say (& no woman perhaps has ever seen more of the manufacturing & agricultural classes of England than I have — before I came out here) that I have never seen so teachable & helpful a class as the army. [...] Give them opportunity promptly & securely to send money home — & they will use it. [...] Give them a school & a lecture & they will come to it. [...] Give them a book & a game & a magic lanthorn & they will leave off drinking. [...] Give them suffering & they will bear it. [...] Give them work & they will do it. [...] I had rather have to do with the army generally than with any other class I have ever attempted to serve.[24]

—⁓∞⁓—

Meanwhile, the Mary Stanley issue festered. Mary had by now taken it upon herself to present Florence with a written statement. It declared that she held her consignment to Scutari's chief medical officer, Cumming, to mean that neither she nor her nurses (including the fifteen nuns who reported only to their reverend mother, Bridgeman) were under Nightingale's authority.

At the same time British officials converted Turkish barracks at Koulali, located a few miles from Scutari, into a hospital. It came under Florence's jurisdiction.

Built between mountains and sea, overlooking "one of the loveliest turns of the Bosporus,"[25] Koulali hospital caught cooling sea breezes. But heating, ventilation, hygiene, and kitchens left much to be desired although ample supplies and superior furnishings were provided by the British ambassador's wife, Lady Stratford. Since Nightingale's earlier exasperated remarks about Lady Stratford's cavalier attitude towards Barrack hospital problems had found their way back to ambassadorial ears, Lady Stratford wanted to grease the wheels for her friend Mary Stanley.

For the ambassadress had encouraged Mary to move her bickering group of ladies, nuns, and nurses to Koulali. Once there, Stanley announced her intention of managing the hospital. Nightingale knew personal supervision of the Stanley nurses would mean endless trouble and futile worry. Hence, she gave in with good grace.

Mary at once proclaimed her intent to use the Stanley nursing system. Florence resented Mary's "inexplicable conduct." She had "intrigued with the embassy & set up an opposition, (why opposition?) hospl. at Koulali, of which I remain nominal head,"[26] Flo wrote her mother. Nonetheless, Florence judged it distracting, enervating, and pointless to argue, let alone meddle, with Mary.

Stanley failed to establish extra diet kitchens or laundries. She proved incapable of controlling her staff. The ladies' garb of white fur coats and straw hats rather than uniforms resulted in "spiritual flirtation," which got "nothing done."[27] With "little other idea" than "riding out with the chaplains & officers & none at all of the work,"[28] the ladies' "helplessness" amused the doctors, who liked having them "for the sake of a little female society, which is natural but not our object,"*[29] Nightingale noted. The Stanley nurses "promise to do, but can't and don't perform,"[30] said one disgusted doctor. Mary let Reverend Mother Bridgeman and her "inefficient, somber, and disliked by all"[31] nuns openly proselytize. And Stanley continued explicitly to reject Nightingale's nominal authority.

Fever cases soon swamped wards already crammed with wounded. Ward

---

Punch satirized "Nurses of quality for the Crimea": "Miss Flouncester" thought it would "be so pretty, too, as well as so right, to go out as nurses to the poor fellows. Miss Nightingale had given a *ton* to the thing: and on one's return one would be quite *distinguée*." Miss Waltzingham agreed. "An evening party gave her no pleasure when she thought of the balls flying about at Sebastopol." And Miss Polker advised that they should take "stuff to rub in for bruises: for how bad must be a bruise from a great cannon ball!" (November 1854).

conditions worsened. To enter them made Mary ill. She stopped going into the wards altogether. No one knew how to keep accounts, so Florence's original personal loan of ninety pounds, then another four hundred pounds vanished. The nurses drank, flirted (or more) with every male in sight, and served as maids to the ladies — who made lemonade and flitted around ineffectually taking notes. Confusion reigned. Stores disappeared. Mortality rose. Chief Medical Officer Cumming came to inspect. And left in disgust.

Ambassadress Lady Stratford confided to Scutari's chief military chaplain that Nightingale's envy of Stanley caused the problems at Koulali.

The chaplain then told the ambassadress how Catholic nuns openly prose-lytized at Koulali. Their spiritual advisor, who had come with them despite strict government prohibition, helped the nuns. And did Lady Stratford know that this priest had secretly converted Mary Stanley?

Horrified, Lady Stratford dropped Stanley, for her lord's strict Protestant beliefs were well-known. Mary's position thus became untenable. Conse-quently, she put nursing under the nominal command of a Protestant lady as cover for what, basically, would be Reverend Mother Bridgeman's regimen. Stanley then decamped.

Since Nightingale had no wish, let alone time, to manage the squabbling Koulali nurses with their large contingent of recalcitrant nuns, she had already arranged with the war office to resign authority over that hospital. However, Florence delayed her official resignation until after Mary left. She would not give Stanley a chance to claim that she had managed a military hospital inde-pendent of Nightingale's control.

Blaming Florence for the Koulali debacle, Mary vowed revenge. She pre-sented herself to London society as a ministering angel betrayed by a beloved friend. "I would work under you if I could, but I do not understand your system," Mary wrote Flo. Having hidden her conversion so as not to alienate her powerful family, Mary offered to work under Florence if Flo would accept her conversion and let Mary use her own system. "You can scarcely tell what it would be to me if we could end this labor together."[32]

"I have no Mary Stanley and to her whom I once thought my Mary Stanley I have nothing to write," Florence replied. She cared little for Mary's conversion so long as it did not hinder the work. But by putting her ego before the cause Mary had committed an unforgivable crime. She "injured my work." Further, Mary "damped my courage to pursue it by the grievous blow of finding want of faith in her whom I so loved and trusted."[33]

—◊—

Six months after she arrived at Scutari, Nightingale could feel some sat-isfaction.

The Barrack and General hospitals had grown into model medical institutions. "Nothing could exceed the cleanly comfortable appearance of the wards." Wooden screens kept out "the cold and draught, and none of the wards were full." They had "new floors and windows; patients got hospital-dress and clean linen regularly." Each bed boasted a "plate, spoon, fork, cup, &c."[34] The newly paved corridors no longer held beds. Volunteer civilian doctors augmented the medical officers. Medicines were plentiful, as were "necessary instruments for scientific examinations," and devices to relieve "suffering, such as air-cushions, water-beds, warming-bottles, baths &c. Much had" been "done towards draining the building which" no longer stank. Repairs had started "in the kitchen, and the food improved; nurses attending the sickest patients got" comforts "from Nightingale's kitchen."[35] Convalescents read books and newspapers, played chess, dominoes, and other games sent from home at Nightingale's request.

Truly, God "entered thee at Scutari ... to be a savior."[36]

13

Balaclava Spring

If I ever live to see England again, the western breezes of my hill-top home
will be my first longing — though Olympus, with its snowy cap, looks fair
over our blue eastern sea.[1]— Florence Nightingale

Brightly colored flowers covered the crags above Balaclava when British
tactics changed from besieging Sevastopol to attack (1855). Casualties would
enter Crimean hospitals to spare them the rough Black Sea voyage to Scutari.
So with her Scutari hospitals in excellent order, Florence felt she could safely
leave them in the capable hands of Selina Bracebridge and Reverend Mother
Moore while she coped with her Crimean responsibilities.

These consisted of the Castle hospital, huts built on the Balaclava heights,
and Balaclava General hospital.* Both had female nurses serving under superintendents answering to Nightingale. She wanted to organize the nurses, introduce the washing and cooking innovations so successful at Scutari, and initiate
a new system that would assure allocation of supplies with minimum paperwork.

The war office notified commander in chief Lord Raglan, ambassador
Lord Stratford, and chief medical officer Dr. Hall of Nightingale's status,
orders, and the help to be given her. A ruinous war absorbed Raglan; diplomacy engrossed Stratford; malice consumed Hall.

The Crimean War's chief medical officer considered Nightingale a dangerous intruder. Her letters to Herbert reflected poorly on him. Her wealth,
powerful connections, and unlimited stores did him untold damage. Hall
thought comforts like toothbrushes, combs, jams, and jellies unnecessary,
indeed, totally unsuitable for army hospitals. He denied doctors chloroform
for operations because "however barbarous it may appear, the smart of the
knife is a powerful stimulant; and it is better to hear a man bawl lustily, than
to see him sink silently into the grave."[2] Having inspected Scutari's hospitals

---

*Henceforth referred to as Balaclava hospital to avoid confusion with the General hospital, Scu-
tari.

shortly before Florence arrived, he reported that "the whole hospital establishment" stood "on a very creditable footing."[3] None of Hall's subordinates dared contradict him.

A skilled political infighter* with over forty years in the army medical department, Hall liked a nurse who saw only what doctors chose to tell her. He belittled Nightingale's work. And resolved to bar her from Crimean hospitals. Claiming that because Herbert's instructions gave Florence authority over all nurses at British military hospitals in Turkey, she had no control in the Crimea. It belonged to Russia.[†]

—m—

Nightingale set sail in dazzling spring sunshine. With her went chef Alexis Soyer to help launch extra diet kitchens in the hospitals and teach troops to make nourishing soup; Charles Bracebridge to manage finances and keep a fatherly eye on Flo; Mrs. Roberts,[‡] Florence's best nurse, as quasichaperone and assistant on nursing issues; and teenaged Robert Robinson. Energetic and droll, he deserted his drums to proudly take the position of Miss Nightingale's Man.[§]

As the ship backed away from the Scutari pier "a most delightful view of the European and Asiatic shores"[4] appeared. So Soyer prodded Bracebridge to pry Nightingale away from work and come on deck to admire scenery she

---

*At the nadir of the 1854–1855 winter a regimental officer, visiting a ship about to carry wounded to Scutari, reported its hellish conditions to Raglan. Aghast, Raglan ordered instant action. An official inquiry ensued. Severely censured, Balaclava's chief medical officer, Lawson, had to resign and Raglan officially rebuked Hall, Lawson's superior. Then the senior medical position at the Barrack hospital became vacant. Hall replied to Raglan's meddling in his fiefdom by appointing Lawson. This stark reminder of Hall's power caused a wave of terror to wash over Scutari's medical staff, let alone horrify Nightingale. Doctors who had cooperated with her now feared to do so.

†In the haste of preparations for Nightingale's departure, the cabinet officially confirmed her "Superintendent of the Female Nursing Establishment of the English General Hospitals in Turkey." The subsequent official government contract signed by each nurse put Nightingale in charge of all nurses "required for the sick and wounded of the British army serving in the East." See also the footnote on p. 104.

‡Reliable and dedicated Elizabeth Roberts had over twenty years' experience as a surgical sister at London's prestigious St. Thomas's Hospital. Nightingale valued her nursing skills and work ethic.

§Not until he had reached his fifteenth birthday could Robinson convince his widowed mother to let him join the army. It, at once, sent him to the Crimea, where he succumbed to sickness and ended in the Barrack hospital. Clever and cheerful, Robinson attracted Bracebridge's attention; hence, in early 1855, he gave up being a drummer boy to become Florence's messenger. Robinson rarely left her side, escorting Nightingale in the evening when she crossed the muddy track between the two hospitals and trimming her lamp when she walked the wards at night. After the war, Florence sent Robinson to school and agricultural college, then arranged his employment on a large estate in Scotland. They stayed in touch throughout their lives.

had hardly had time to notice thus far. Constantinople's gilded minarets glittered in a golden haze, small caiques skimmed over calm blue water, and brightly dressed oarsmen propelled the Sultan and his suite in a flotilla of splendid boats hung with colorful brocaded silk.

"Poor old Flo steaming up the Bosporus & across the Black" Sea in "the *Robert Lowe* or *Robert Slow* (for an uncommon slow coach she is) taking back 420 of her" convalescents, "to be shot at again."

"What suggestions do the above ideas make to you in Embley drawing-room? Stranger ones perhaps than to me — who, on the 5th May, year of disgrace 1855, year of my age 35, having been at Scutari" six months "in sympathy with God, fulfilling the purpose I came into the world for.

"What the disappointments of the conclusion of these six months are, no one can tell. But I am" alive, although "to live for six months" at the Barrack hospital "has been death." With "more & more reason to believe that this is the kingdom of hell," Flo equally believed "it is to be made the kingdom of heaven."[5]

On Sunday, "day of rest and delightful weather," Soyer had his "first and best opportunity" to realize Florence's "amiable character and interesting powers of conversation." When "wit or pleasantry prevails," a "happy, good-natured smile" pervades "her face, and you recognize only the charming woman." They spoke of "her duty, not of what she had already done, but of what she was about to do."[6]

Soon after entering the Black Sea, Nightingale and the captain went below to visit the soldiers. One refused his medicine.

> FLORENCE: Why won't you take it?
> SOLDIER: Because I took some of that medicine once and it made me sick, so I've avoided medicine since.
> FLORENCE: [With a smile:] If I give it to you myself, you will take it, won't you?
> SOLDIER: Sure enough, ma'am, but it will make me sick just the same.

He took his medicine and, as Florence chatted with him about the battles he had fought in, the soldier forgot to feel sick.

—m—

Agog to glimpse the famous lady superintendent, a huge crowd greeted the *Robert Lowe*. Balaclava lacked house, hut, or even tent for hire, so Nightingale kept her quarters on the ship. Officials crowded on board to pay their respects.

She and Soyer squelched through muddy, rutted streets next morning to inspect Balaclava hospital, which boasted a well-deserved name for dirt and disorganization. Since it came under Chief Medical Officer Hall's direct control, the visitors were less than enthusiastically received.

Nightingale and Soyer then scaled "a narrow and almost perpendicular road cut out of the rock" to reach the Castle hospital. "In consequence of the ups and downs, it took us full three-quarters of an hour to accomplish the distance, and very uncomfortably too, the roads being so dirty."[7] As if to compensate, yellow jasmine bushes and small, brightly flowered shrubs bunched on both sides of the steep hill and the view proved "transcendentally beautiful and refreshing," the "harbor beneath filled with ships, the chain of rocky mountains, distant view of the" British and French camps, and "the traffic of thousands below, busily running to and fro."

The Castle hospital consisted of long "rows of huts, erected on the crest of the lofty mountain facing the sea, commanding a beautiful view of the bay."[8] Soyer and Nightingale received a cordial welcome from the chief physician and from nursing superintendent Jane Shaw Stewart. Unmarried sister of a duchess, singular among the Stanley ladies for hospital experience, Stewart had left the bickering Stanley cadre to nurse at Balaclava hospital. The authorities made her superintendent when the original left, then promoted Stewart to the newly opened Castle hospital. Her refusal to rest (Stewart caught a few hours' sleep fully clothed) made some think her mad. Florence expressed "relief to come to something which is above, entirely above, all that is mean & petty & selfish & frivolous & low into a higher & purer atmosphere, into truth & generosity."[9]

Nightingale inspected meticulously. She had "a kind word for all, and many a conversation with those who had been severely wounded."[10] For a long time, Florence sat at the bedside of a young officer suffering from an extreme case of typhoid fever.

As she and Soyer walked back to Balaclava, he asked about the young officer.

"Poor young man," Nightingale replied. "I very much fear for his life."

SOYER: "You were unwise to stay with such an infectious patient for so long."
NIGHTINGALE: "I am used to that. [I] have been very fortunate through my Scutari campaign, and I hope to be as fortunate in the Crimea."[11]

—⁓—

Early the next day a distinguished cavalcade assembled. It included Bracebridge, Soyer, sanitary expert Sutherland, several officers, and Nightingale in a fashionable riding habit, mounted on a frisky, golden-colored mare. The party made its slow way through a press of people, a "Babel of tongues" making "deafening noise," hundreds "of mules, horses, donkeys, artillery wagons, cannon, shot and shell, oxen and horses kicking each other, wagons upset in deep mud-holes, infantry and cavalry coming and going." By "way of enjoying the fun," the horses pranced and kicked "in all directions, particularly our fair lady's palfrey." Many women would have quailed. Florence, used to daily rides with her father, let alone riding to hounds with him, rose "above such weakness," even taking "considerable interest in this her first introduction to the turmoil of war."[12]

She intended to return Commander in Chief Raglan's courtesy call but found him away from headquarters. The officers suggested a visit to the front instead. Eagerly, Nightingale agreed.

> [Considering] what the work has been this winter, what the hardships, I am surprised — not that the army has suffered so much but — that there is any army left at all, not that we have had so many through our hands at Scutari, but that we have not had all.... Fancy working 5 nights out of 7 in the trenches. Fancy being 36 hours in them at a stretch — as they were, all December — lying down or half lying down often 48 hours without food but *raw* salt pork sprinkled with sugar — & their rum & biscuit — nothing hot — because the *exhausted* soldier *could not* collect his own fuel, as he was expected, to cook his own ration. And fancy, thro' all this, the army preserving their courage & patience [and] now eager (the old ones more than the young ones) to be led even into the trenches. There was something sublime in the spectacle.[13]

Seeing the soldiers at war strengthened the bond Nightingale had formed with them while they were her patients.

The troops gaped at the singular sight of a lady riding among them. Then they recognized Florence Nightingale. Tents emptied. The men gave The Good Lady of Scutari a rousing Three Times Three — which frightened Florence's golden mare more than all the drums of war.

> There was nothing empty in that cheer nor in the heart which received it. I took it as a true expression of true sympathy — the sweetest I have ever had. I took it as a full reward of all I have gone through. I promised my God that I would not die of disgust or disappointment, if he would let me go through this. In all that has been said against & for me, no one soul has appreciated what I was really doing, none but the honest cheer of the brave 39th.[14]

What a contrast "looking down upon Sevastopol — the shell whizzing right and left" — with "the most flowery place you can imagine — a beautiful little red which I don't know, yellow" jasmine, wild iris, lilies and orchids, mignonette, and forget-me-not. "A serj't of the 97th picked me a nosegay. I once saved the serj't's life by finding him at 12 o'clock at night lying — wounds undressed — in our hosp'l with a bullet in his eye & a fractured skull. And I pulled a stray surgeon out of bed to take the bullet out."[15]

—⁂—

Besides "reorganizing the two hospitals under our care, which were terribly 'seedy' — nurses all in confusion,"[16] Florence spent the next days inspecting regimental hospitals.[17] They were outside her bailiwick, but Nightingale wanted to broaden her knowledge of military medical institutions. "We saw a lady and three gentlemen [Chef Soyer, his secretary, and Sanitary Commissioner Sutherland] ride up to" our hospital, wrote its director. "An orderly came to say miss Nightingale sent her compliments to know if I had any objection to her going over my hospital. Of course, I had none so I joined the party." A "most pleasing person, *refined* and *delicate*, just fitted for the very trying position she fills," Nightingale expressed delight "with all she saw." Soyer fell into "raptures with my kitchen," interrupting Florence and the doctor's conversation to take her "to see the establishment and his *delight* at the grate made of Turkoman gun barrels."[18]

The bright May weather, meanwhile, turned. Nightingale slogged through chill, driving rain and cloying mud to the hospitals. As well, she dealt with the pressing business concerns of her many callers. Some remarked that Florence looked poorly. She admitted feeling tired — surely due to the unfamiliar exercise and fresh air.

Never robust, her whole life cushioned in comfort, finicky about cleanliness, Nightingale had, for six months, slaved amidst vermin and stench, cold and damp, snatching a few hours sleep in her camp bed set behind a screen in the caravanserai — in which constricted space she also had to take care of personal hygiene. "How long she will be able to keep up without serious illness one troubles to think," Selina Bracebridge had written the Nightingales. "She is very thin & very much exhausted but no illness yet thank God."[19]

Now, suddenly, "fever of an alarming kind"[20] seized Florence. Severe vomiting and diarrhea wracked her. Hastily summoned, senior medical staff diagnosed an acute case of Crimean Fever. Modern medicine diagnoses Nightingale's condition as brucellosis, a serious disease unknown in her day.*

Workers were still clearing Balaclava Harbor of rotting carcasses, so doctors ordered Florence's instant removal to the clean air of the Castle hospital. Carefully, soldiers carried her stretcher amidst a hushed escort of troops. Nurse

---

*Florence first thought she had typhoid or typhus, but her symptoms were typical of brucellosis: fever, extreme fatigue, delirium, inability to walk or eat, and prolonged gastric irritation. Although seldom fatal, the duration, debility, extended convalescence, and especially recurrence — all of which Nightingale experienced — make brucellosis a grave illness. In her day, no cure existed. Today, brucellosis is treated with antibiotics. Brucellosis is caused by ingesting contaminated or unpasteurized cow, goat, or sheep's milk or dairy products. Incubation is ten to thirty days, so Florence contracted it at Scutari, where a high incidence of Crimean fever existed. Having rejected the Barrack hospital's impure water, Nightingale refused to drink only wine, beer or liquor like most of the doctors and nurses and may have felt safer drinking milk (B. Dossey, "Florence Nightingale; Her Crimean Fever and Chronic Illness," *Journal of Holistic Nursing*, 1998; D. A. Young, "Florence Nightingale's Fever," *British Medical Journal*, 1995; E. J. Young, "An Overview of Human Brucellosis," *Clinical Infectious Diseases*, 1995).

Roberts held a white umbrella over her patient as protection against the watery sun. "It was a solemn procession."[21]

News of Nightingale's illness cast a pall over the army. At Scutari hospitals, men turned their faces to the wall and wept. All England prayed.

She hovered between life and death for days,* in her delirium writing distractedly, for only with pen and paper in hand would Florence lie still. Roberts shut her patient's door to all but doctors and nurses. And in keeping with contemporary medical wisdom, she cut off all Florence's rich brown hair to help fight the fever.

"Dearest, ever dearest, more than mother"[22] Selina Bracebridge rushed to Flo's side. The sight of her beloved face did Flo more good than all the doctors' ministrations, she later wrote Fanny. One can only wonder what effect the sight of Fanny might have had. But Florence's mother made no move to nurse her, as she had nursed the extremely ill Parthe during an influenza outbreak some years before. Fanny Nightingale had already, in her letter to Flo before she left for Scutari, delegated maternal responsibility to Selina.

Deep down, Fanny resented Flo's defiance in not marrying, in denying her mother's ambition, never mind her fundamental maternal duty — to achieve a brilliant marriage for her gifted, charismatic daughter. Flo could at least have had the selflessness to secure her mother and sister's future should WEN die and, thanks to the Nightingale entail, leave them homeless. Yet, Fanny gloried in the reflected glow of Florence's fame, especially now that the London season had begun. Indeed, the Nightingales were "tenderly treated and affectionately welcomed by one and all of all classes and opinions for"[23] Flo's sake.

Concomitantly, Florence chafed at confinement to her Castle hospital hut. The bed afforded no view except for knots in the wooden walls; only one small window showed a glimpse of sky. But when Selina brought a bunch of brightly colored Crimean flowers Florence began to feel better.

She recovered slowly, too feeble to feed herself or speak above a whisper.

On a wet and windy day two horsemen, wrapped in waterproof cloaks, cantered up the hill to the Castle hospital. One held the horses as the other hammered at the door of Florence's hut.

NURSE ROBERTS: Stop making that racket at once. How dare you disturb Miss
    Nightingale.
HORSEMAN: I want to see her.

*Robert Robinson's diary tells us Nightingale had an alarmingly high fever for two weeks. He spent the time bringing bulletins to Bracebridge, biting his nails at Balaclava, for Charles took extremely seriously his responsibility to take care of his friend WEN's cherished child.

ROBERTS: And pray, who are you?

HORSEMAN: Only a soldier, but one she knows well. I've come a long way and must see her.

"Mrs. Roberts, Mrs. Roberts!," whispered a weak voice from inside. "It is Lord Raglan. Tell him I'm infectious with fever; it's too dangerous for him to come in."

"I'm not afraid of fever," scoffed the commander in chief, pulling up a stool to Nightingale's bedside. He thanked her personally and in the name of his troops for all she had done. The soldiers prayed for her recovery; they wanted Florence to resume work.

The redoubtable Roberts had to admit Raglan's visit did her patient a world of good.

—m—

Florence wanted to convalesce at Balaclava, the better to finish her Crimean work. Crimean doctors demurred. They advised complete rest, then recuperation in England. Selina Bracebridge thought the long sea voyage would kill such a poor sailor. But physicians insisted that Nightingale would not get well unless she at least returned to the Bosporus; besides, the change of air would do her good.

Florence agreed to sail on the first ship stopping at Scutari. Sanitarian Dr. Sutherland, the Bracebridges, Soyer, Roberts, and Robinson escorted her stretcher down to the harbor. "When we reached the *Jura*, tackles were attached to the four corners of the stretcher" and pulleys slung Florence on deck. Although by far the easiest way for her to board, this maneuver "would try" the "courage of many who think themselves bold."[24]

A foul odor instantly greeted Nightingale's party; the stench even permeated her comfortably appointed cabin. That morning the *Jura* had landed four hundred horses. Someone still extremely poorly, who suffered from chronic seasickness, let alone insisted on fresh air, could scarcely be expected to benefit from traveling on a ship that, that day, had disgorged an army of horses.

Florence fainted. Sutherland ordered instant removal. Stretcher bearers took her to a nearby French ship until a British vessel became available. Meanwhile, Soyer approached his patron, traveling privately in a steam yacht. Lord Ward immediately offered it.

Nightingale believed her nemesis, Dr. Hall, and his underlings chose "the *Jura*, which was NOT going to stop at Scutari, *because* it was *not* going to stop at Scutari — and put me on board of her for England." Bracebridge "and Ward took me out, at the risk of my life — to save my going to England, though unconscious at the time that it was *intended*."[25]

—ᴍ—

The luxurious private yacht sailed out of Balaclava Harbor on a peaceful, sunny afternoon. But before long the Black Sea, "dancing mountains high" in heavy fog and pelting rain, made Florence extremely ill. As the boat entered the Bosporus "a shower of pearls, which gathered in millions upon the rigging and deck," signaled calmer weather. Slowly fading clouds disclosed a unique vista. Nightingale enjoyed it from her cabin, "the beautiful saloon upon deck, where she had a good view." Florence spoke to Soyer about improvements in her extra diet kitchen, and many "other matters of importance connected with the hospitals. I required her to keep her mind quiet, and to depend upon me."[26]

At Scutari, a big barge drew alongside. Its roof nearly reached the yacht's bulwarks, so sailors easily lowered Nightingale's stretcher onto it. Relays of four soldiers each then took the stretcher; twelve others shared the honor of carrying Florence's luggage, although two would have sufficed. Scutari's commander, staff, and chief physician, "followed by an immense procession," silent, with many weeping, escorted her. "Every soldier seemed anxious to show his regard, and acknowledge his debt of gratitude."[27]

Nightingale wanted to convalesce in the Barrack hospital, but Bracebridge installed her in a quietly situated, small house with airy, high-ceilinged rooms. One end of the drawing room faced the Bosporus; the other overlooked a lush private garden. From her bedroom Florence could see the cypress-shrouded British cemetery, where "five thousand & odd brave hearts" slept — "three thousand, alas! dead in Jan. & Feb. alone."[28] The house lacked only one amenity: a kitchen. So Robert Robinson brought all meals from the Barrack hospital, where Soyer concocted temptations for Nightingale's apathetic appetite.

She felt unwell for weeks. The Herberts sent a terrier, "the most engaging of all animals,"[29] to amuse Flo. Soldiers brought an owl, to take her pet Athena's place. Parthe wrote and illustrated *The Life and Death of Athena, an Owlet*, "to try and make Flo and mrs. Bracebridge laugh when Flo was recovering from her fever."[30] When Selina read Parthe's oeuvre aloud, Flo laughed and cried together. And while doing hospital laundry, a sergeant's wife put her baby in a wooden pen that Florence could see from her bed. A small pet or a baby was an excellent companion for the convalescent, Nightingale later wrote in her best-selling *Notes on Nursing*.

Florence's illness raised Britain's public passion to fever pitch. Soldiers' letters had familiarized homes throughout the land with Florence Nightingale. Biographies filled broadsheets and newspapers. Mothers called their baby girls Florence; so did racehorse owners. Because the Nightingales refused to furnish pictures, enterprising manufacturers invented images; hence, The Lady with the Lamp graced mugs, stationery, even ships. And at reunions veterans sang: "Forward, my lads, may your hearts never fail, you are cheer'd by the presence of a sweet Nightingale."[31]

—⚏—

As Florence began to feel better, Selina took her for long walks up and down the gently lapping Bosporus shore each evening, when breezes wafted off the water to cool the torrid days of Turkish summer. Nightingale's favorite doctor, sanitary expert Sutherland, said the fever saved her life. It forced Florence to rest. Sutherland begged her to do less work. But his patient complained that idleness caused her to suffer "from a compound fracture of the intellect."

"This comes, dearest people, to inform you that I think much & often of" you. "You may fancy what it cost me to leave Balaclava."

"I wish you would write your thanks to mrs. Roberts who nursed me to her own injury as if I had been her only child."[32]

Fanny Nightingale's reply contained the wish that her daughter would, "among the numerous lessons which your life has been spent in learning, be able to perfect the most difficult one of standing and waiting."[33]

Instead, claiming that her handwriting did the doctors credit, Florence used her three-month recuperation to catch up on correspondence. Each letter from a dead soldier's family received a reply. And Fanny got a special gift.

[T]he life's work of a poor Turkish widow. [Flo hoped Fanny would wear the gold robe] "for my sake. It will just suit you, & it is all *good Turkish*" wool. As I never go over to the bazaars & as it was a mere chance her offering me this for sale, I snatched at it, thinking it a fitting garment for you. [It] is not at all too fine by candlelight. And you have the only one in the world — if that is a recommendation.... They call me the Sultana of the Bosporus &, if I am, I think I have a right to insist upon the mother of the Sultana wearing a very fine gown.[34]

—⚏—

Meanwhile, a dreaded event loomed. The Bracebridges were leaving.

"For nine months she has been the moving power by which these hospitals were made to go at all — & no one can tell what she has been to me — more than my Egeria — almost my Holy Ghost." He figured as "the only man of senses & feeling & the only man but one of business in these miserable hospitals,"[35] the only man who would voluntarily lead such a pigging life without the interest and challenge it held for Florence.

Charles and Selina originally meant to stay for two months, certain Flo would have the hospitals organized by that time. They reckoned without the realities of Scutari. Flo's illness had already caused her friends to postpone their departure. Believing they needed a change, Flo encouraged the Bracebridges to go.*

Selina worried about leaving her. The doctors still wanted Florence to return home, but besides the tiring journey, Selina feared Fanny and Parthe would make Flo miserable by dragging her into society, not to mention making every attempt to foil her return to Scutari. So Selina consulted Flo's favorite physician. Sutherland suggested she recuperate with the Bracebridges in Switzerland.

"The idea is too pleasant — it is too good for me." How "can I? If miss N." goes, "says my troop, she will never come back & all my best, revd. mother & her crew, Roberts," other nurses, said they would leave "if I go. This is not so selfish as it first appears. With so many jarring elements, without a central authority, they wd. not be able to do any good."[36]

—⁂—

Mary Shore Smith, 1798–1890. Sole sibling of Florence's father, wife of her mother's brother Sam Smith. From Nightingale's earliest childhood to old age, beloved Aunt Mai figured as support, "spiritual mother," and "dearest friend" (author photograph of image in Ida B. O'Malley's *Florence Nightingale, 1820–1856: A Study of Her Life Down to the End of the Crimean War* [Thornton Butterworth, Limited, London, 1931]).

Florence would manage on her own. But the Nightingales thought she needed more support than a Catholic nun (Reverend Mother Moore) and a professional nurse (Mrs. Roberts). Flo also needed a chaperone. Many would rejoice to see her stumble: Mary Stanley, Reverend Mother Bridgeman, Dr. Hall, war-office anti-reformers, and officers who resented Nightingale's meddling in the exclusively male mili-

*Nightingale recognized the Bracebridges as "my more than earthly father and mother, without whom Scutari or my life could not have been, and to whom nothing that I could ever say or do would in the least express my thankfulness" (Piers Compton, *Colonel's Lady and Camp Follower: The Story of Women in the Crimean War*, p. 192).

tary. Indeed, as she was a single female interacting mostly with men, Florence's reputation did stand at risk, especially with the amount of press attention she attracted. So, shortly after the Bracebridges set sail loyal uncle Sam Smith arrived to assess Flo's situation, bringing his son, Shore, with him.

As a result, Shore's mother and Sam's wife offered to keep her cherished niece company. At first Flo demurred at taking Aunt Mai away from her family. Still, "if you can come, you only know what a support it will be to me." No "one gives me strength & courage & keeps me up like you."[37]

Flo's gaunt appearance shocked gentle Mai to tears. And the web of petty intrigue entangling her niece horrified Mai, who had never, in her sheltered life, met the privations and plots that signified Scutari. Several doctors warned new colleagues to avoid Nightingale. One physician admitted privately that Nurse Roberts dressed compound fractures and looked after surgical cases better then any of his assistants, but did not dare to say so to his superior officers. Indeed, many medical officers, mindful of their chief, Dr. Hall, chose to consider Nightingale superfluous now that the hospitals ran smoothly.

But Florence would never give in, never leave her post if even one soldier needed her. Besides, unfinished business beckoned from Balaclava. "Persistency, as you know," Mai wrote the Nightingales, "has always been a great part of her character."[38]

14

Contest for the Crimea

"The experiment of sending nurses to the East has been eminently successful," and "supplying trained instruments to the hands of the medical officers has saved much valuable life and remedied many deficiencies."[1]— Florence Nightingale

"Such questions as food, rest, temperature never interfere with her during her work; I suppose she has gained some advantage over other people in her entire absence of thought about these things; that is, her mind over tasked with great things has not these little questions to entertain. She is extremely quick and clear too," can "turn from one thing or one person to another, when in the midst of business, in the most extraordinary manner. She has attained" a "wonderful calm and presence of mind."[2]— Mai Smith

Constantinople baked under a blazing summer sun and clouds of flies buzzed over the Bosporus when Florence Nightingale returned to battle on behalf of her patients (1855). Thanks to her, Scutari hospitals were in perfect order. Crimean hospitals were not — yet.

Mismanaged and filthy Balaclava hospital must be rid of its inept and wayward matron, Miss Wear. So Nightingale suggested to Crimean war chief medical officer Dr. John Hall that Balaclava nurses transfer to the Castle hospital, there to serve under loyal, capable Jane Shaw Stewart. As well, Florence asked Hall not to consider nurses for the new Monastery hospital without first consulting her.

Incensed at this female meddling in his fiefdom, Hall harshly denied any intent to send nurses to the Monastery. But he did need at least two nurses at Balaclava. Hall offered to recruit them himself. Nightingale, concerned to keep control in the Crimea, could scarcely be expected to concur. She offered to have Matron Wear and one nurse stay, as long as they were assigned only simple tasks.

This exchange marked the opening barrage of a bitterly fought campaign.

—〰—

Britain and France's capture of Sevastopol, Russia's mighty naval fortress, failed to end the Crimean War. Hence, Hall opened new hospitals. And, neatly bypassing Nightingale, he sent convalescents home. She visited some when their ship stopped at Scutari. The soldiers' squalor so shocked Florence that she ignored the lingering frailty of illness and got ready to go to Balaclava. Ostensibly, Nightingale sought to secure nursing standards at the Balaclava and Castle hospitals; actually, she meant to confront Hall's resolve to shut her out of the Crimea.

At Koulali hospital, near Scutari but no longer Florence's responsibility meanwhile, the Stanley nurses under Reverend Mother Bridgeman's de facto leadership disregarded hygiene and dispensed extra diets at will. Costs escalated; so did mortality. Doctors insisted on Nightingale's system: scrupulous cleanliness and extras diets only on a physician's written order. Bridgeman refused. Medical officers took over. Lady nurses went home. Bridgeman's Irish bishop insisted on her remaining in the war zone.

"I would not undertake again to *work with miss Nightingale*, as I learned while I was at the Barrack hospital Scutari, *how very DIFFERENT from ours,* are miss Nightingale's views of nursing, hospital arrangements etc. etc.,"[3] Bridgeman wrote Hall.

A gift from heaven! Referring to Florence's letter suggesting removal of nurses from Balaclava hospital, Hall, breathing not one word about Bridgeman, invited Nightingale to recall Wear and her single nurse from Balaclava. Florence promptly consented.

Hall then invited Bridgeman and her Koulali nuns to Balaclava. She agreed at once. Bridgeman ordered her four nuns still under Nightingale at the Barrack hospital to join her. Removing nurses from her staff, Florence said, flouted all rules. Bridgeman stood firm.

Nightingale had nothing against sending nuns to Balaclava hospital, especially as most new army recruits were Irish and Catholic. Nonetheless, she insisted the planning go through and not around her. Senior officials, including Ambassador Stratford and Scutari's commander in chief, agreed. So General Storks advised Florence to escort the four nuns to Balaclava, thereby keeping a façade of control. But by going to the Crimea without consulting Hall, to say nothing of bringing other nurses from her Scutari staff with her, Nightingale alienated him further.

—〰—

Continuing to insist that Nightingale had no authority in the Crimea, Hall encouraged nurses and nuns to defy her. And he got his not unwilling chief purveyor, David Fitzgerald, to deny Florence supplies; as well, Fitzgerald refused to cash Nightingale's checks drawing on government funds. Fortunately, Nightingale brought ample provisions, which she supplemented on the spot by using her own money.

Having assured Florence that he did not want nurses at the Monastery hospital, Hall now assigned it to Balaclava hospital's former matron, the recalcitrant and inefficient Wear. "Dr. Hall is so clever, it is almost a pleasure to contemplate such cleverness, even at one's own expense,"[4] Flo wrote Aunt Mai, holding the fort with capable, completely trustworthy Reverend Mother Moore at the Barrack hospital.

The combatants, meanwhile, kept a facade of cordiality until the *Times*[5] featured Charles Bracebridge's speech to a packed and appreciative audience. Graphically describing the Barrack hospital's horrors, he told how Florence transformed the place in days. Charles further ignored Flo's express wishes by criticizing army authorities, attacking doctors' ignorance and rigidity, and citing instances of individual cruelty. And he committed a cardinal sin: Charles named Scutari's inept purveyor. Other papers reprinted the speech. Florence's enemies seized it as proof of her egocentric resolve to wage war on the army medical department.

Nightingale deplored Bracebridge's speech "*first*, because it is not our" business, "*secondly*, it justifies all the attacks made against us for unwarrantable" meddling "and criticism, and *thirdly*, because I believe" it "utterly unfair."[6] Florence thought Hall able in many ways, even if hide-bound in others. Conversely, he vowed to show this upstart, do-gooding society miss, young enough to be his daughter, that he — and he alone — had charge of medical matters in this war.

—॰॰—

"The extraordinary exertions" Nightingale "imposed upon herself" during days spent at the Castle hospital supervising installation of her system would "have been perfectly incredible, if not witnessed by many." Standing "for hours at the top of a bleak rocky mountain near the hospital," she gave nurses her directions in the swirling snow of a Russian October. Return trips were especially risky as "the road led across very uneven country."[7] One cold, wet, and pitch-dark evening, Florence's little donkey cart ran over a rock, landing at an upward tilt. After jumping five feet to safety, she helped extricate two badly injured nurses caught under the cart. The next day an officer gave Nightingale a sturdy covered carriage drawn by two hefty mules.

Searing stabs of sciatica, typical of recurrent brucellosis,* soon forced

---

*The Crimean Fever Nightingale suffered in May. Unknown to Victorian medicine, brucellosis, if untreated, recurs.

Florence into a Castle hospital hut for three weeks. Mrs. Roberts and superintendent Jane Shaw Stewart nursed her. "I wish you could see me in the most poetic spot in the world," Flo wrote her "'dearest mother ... looking out upon the old Genoese castle — upon peak upon peak in the cold moonlight or in the red glow of the autumnal sunset — for the nights are hard frost & listening to the everlasting roll of the sea at the foot of the steep cliff &,' thinking of God's 'everlasting patience.'"[8]

She had need of it. Sciatica crippled Florence, but it did not cripple her fingers. So from her bed, Nightingale fired the first salvo in her fight for official sanction of nursing control in the Crimea.

Since she had taken on the Castle hospital in May, Flo wrote Liz Herbert, "we have cooked *all* the extra diets for 500–600 patients & the *whole* diets for all the wounded officers by ourselves in a shed — & till I came up this time, (tho' I sent up a French man-cook, to whom I gave £100 pr ann., in July) I could not get an extra diet kitchen built promised me in May, till I came to do it myself."

In the interim, Shaw Stewart and Nightingale used their private means to provide "every egg, every bit of butter, jelly, ale & eau de Cologne," for sick officers. "On Nov 4, I opened my extra diet kitchen — but, for 24 hours, I would not bake the officers' toast" because "it disconcerted the extra diets for 550 patients. In those 24 hours, the officers" complained "to head quarters of our 'ill treatment' re toast."

Hall responded by reprimanding a couple of kitchen menials. With great politeness, Shaw Stewart asked that, in the interest of assuring compliance with his reprimands, Hall convey them to her. Hall used this as a pretext to tell his staff that Castle hospital nurses meant to stop obeying doctors. He also reminded Stewart of "his duty to care for the officers as well as for the men — his paternal care," Flo emphasized to Liz, "having begun for their toast & them on Nov 7, while" ignoring them since spring.

"These things are nothing," Florence noted, except that "they thwart the work." So if Sidney Herbert agreed, a "'private letter from some high authority to the commander-in-chief' saying, 'this work is not a silly display of feminine sensibilities but an authorized set of tools provided to the hand of the medical officers to supply extra diets, cleanliness, clean linen and hospital comforts to the patients, might greatly further these objects.'"[9]

While this letter traveled to London and Nightingale's sciatica subsided, cholera struck at Scutari. So the steady stream of instructions to Aunt Mai stopped. Florence rushed back to the Barrack hospital. Her status in the Crimea must wait.

A surprise awaited Nightingale at Scutari. "You are ... well aware of the high esteem I" have for your "Christian devotion" during "this great and bloody war," Queen Victoria's letter read, "how warm my admiration is for your services, which are fully equal to those of my dear and brave soldiers, whose sufferings you have had the *privilege* of alleviating." The Queen wanted to show her "feelings in a manner which I trust will be agreeable to you." She sent "a brooch,* the form and emblems of which commemorate your great and blessed work, and which I hope you will wear as a mark of the high approbation of your sovereign"![10]

"I hope," Florence's eternally governessing elder sister coached, "you will wear your Star to please the soldiers on Sundays and holidays." For "it will be such a pleasure to them to know that the Queen has done her best to do you honor."[11]

—⚉—

The first royal tribute given a woman for public service, plus Nightingale's illness, slow recovery, and continued devotion to the soldiers, heightened public admiration. Florence's friends thought Britons should have a chance to express their esteem in concrete fashion — and concomitantly send a forceful message to her enemies.

Nightingale would shudder at the usual honor, such as an inscribed bracelet or silver tea service, but would accept recognition that allowed advancement of her cause. Flo's friends thus agreed to raise funds for her to create nurse training. His Royal Highness the Duke of Cambridge, Queen Victoria's cousin and army commander in chief, chaired the organizing committee. Sidney Herbert served as honorary secretary.

To express "a general feeling that the services of miss Nightingale in the hospitals of the East demand the grateful recognition of the British people,"[12] the committee opened its first meeting to the public. Never, averred the *Times*, had London seen a more dazzling, eager, and united assembly.

"The abilities" she has shown "cannot be allowed to slumber," Herbert addressed the packed meeting. "The diamond has shown itself and must not be allowed to return to the mine."[13] He then read excerpts from soldiers' letters. "Before she came, there was cussin' and swearin', and after it was holy as a church."[14] It can't be done, another recalled doctors saying as they walked past his bed. It *must* be done, Nightingale calmly insisted.

More admiring and moving speeches followed, but Parthe thought Richard Monckton Milnes's the most true. In seconding the resolution to establish the Nightingale Fund, Flo's former suitor said "too much had been

---

*Designed by Prince Albert, the brooch had a red enamel St. George's cross and the royal cipher in diamonds. "Blessed are the merciful" encircled the whole, which also had the word "Crimea." The inscription on the back: "To Miss Florence Nightingale as a mark of esteem and gratitude for her devotion towards the Queen's brave soldiers — From Victoria R., 1855."

made of" her "sacrifice of position and luxury." The "luxury of one good action must to a mind such as hers be more than equivalent for the loss of all the pomps and vanities of life."[15]

Actually, the Nightingales were not present. Fanny savored the social triumph of having England's elite gather to honor her daughter, but she and Parthe quailed before the emotional impact. WEN feared that he might be called on to speak. So the family gave a reception afterwards.

> The most interesting day of thy mother's life. It is very late, my child, but I cannot go to bed without telling you that your meeting has been a glorious [one.] You will be more indifferent than any of us to your fame, but be glad that we feel this is a proud day for us; for the like has never happened before, but will, I trust, from your example gladden the hearts of many future mothers.[16]

At last! Fame brought Flo her mother's approval, approval she had so ardently sought all her life. Florence had proved to Fanny that by following her grail she would make her family proud, would, indeed, "gladden" her mother's "loving heart."[17]

"If my name and my having done what I could for God and mankind has given you pleasure, that is real pleasure to me. My reputation has not been a boon in my work," replied Flo, discouraged over battles with Hall, "but if you have been pleased, that is enough. I shall love my name now, and shall feel that it is the greatest return that you can find satisfaction in hearing your child named, and in feeling that her work draws sympathies together — some return for what you have done for me. Life is sweet after all."[18]

"Voluntary individual offerings" from the Crimea totaled four thousand pounds in the Fund's first week. Troops eventually gave five thousand more.* Their commander in chief said these impressive sums showed his soldiers' "universal feeling of gratitude" for "the care bestowed" on "themselves and their comrades" by Florence Nightingale's "constant personal attention."[19]

Bracebridge, Herbert, and Milnes among others, traveled the country to raise money. "I am sending you a Manchester newspaper and just a few lines to say *how* well the meeting went off yesterday," a family friend wrote Parthe. "At 12, when some of the mills 'loose' their workpeople, plenty of grimy hands came in, all ready to cheer and applaud *their* heroine — for they feel her as theirs, their brother's nurse, their dead friend's friend."[20]

Donations eventually came to forty-five thousand pounds.†

---

*Hall asked doctors not to contribute.

†Almost $4 million today.

Nightingale valued the "abiding support" of "such sympathy and such appreciation" in "the midst of labor and difficulties all but overpowering,"[21] she formally wrote Herbert. However, her present position precluded providing "a cut & dried prospectus of my plans, when I cannot look forward a month, much less a year." Impossible, too, "to find time in the midst of one overpowering work to digest & concoct another."[22] Florence "would never desert" her current post, so she asked Sidney to convey to the Fund committee "that I accept their proposal [to create nurse training], provided I may do so on their understanding of this great uncertainty as to when it will be possible for me to carry it out."[23]

Britons must continue to trust her — as their generosity proved they did. Nightingale then appointed a nine-man council[24] to manage the Fund until her return. Five members, including Bracebridge, Herbert, and Milnes were responsible for investing the money.

—ɷ—

"'Well, there's my little Flo sitting opposite me reading the subscriptions to the Nightingale Fund," Mai Smith wrote. "Who ever would have thought I should have got her to do that! She has such a nice little child's face like what she had at three, without a bit of curl or braid or anything, but the nice little hairs growing gradually and a little white muslin cap, a gray cloth gown sent by mrs. Herbert. The dear looks very handsome."[25]

Flo and Mai rarely finished "our little dinner (after it has been put off one, two or three hours on account of her visitors), without her being called away."

"'Do go to bed,'" Mai told her exhausted niece.

"'How can I; I have all those letters to write.'"

"'Write them tomorrow.'"

"'Tomorrow will bring its own work.'"[26]

Mai relieved Flo of writing letters to soldiers' loved ones. That allowed Florence, "driven by over-work more than usually of late from the sudden death (by cholera) of my excellent matron," and "from the illness of my assistant at the same time," to focus on nursing matters.

Nurses in a civilian hospital signed a contract that would not do for a military one, Nightingale wrote the government's official nursing recruiter. Used to directing women, the civilian hospital's head doctor "may be trusted with it — in military hosp'ls not. Bind the *superintendent* by every tie of signed agreement & of honor to strict obedience to her medical chief," but "let all his orders to the nurses go through" her. "I have never had the slightest difficulty about" this but "would never have undertaken the superintendency" had the nurses thought "themselves 'under the direction of the principal medical officer.' *I* am under his direction. *They* are under mine."[27]

If not closely supervised, nurses got drunk. If they failed to respond to discipline, Nightingale sent them home. And asked for new ones. "I am very anxious that mrs. Bracebridge" should "approve the nurses" and "that none should come without her approbation — because she knows so exactly what we want."[28]

—m—

Selina had engaged an assistant to administer the store containing free gifts (comforts for the soldiers that Queen Victoria and other donors sent) during Florence's first trip to the Crimea. A charming lady who arrived at Scutari with excellent references, Charlotte Salisbury took full charge when the Bracebridges left, on "written understanding that nothing" would "be given out of that store" except by Nightingale's "written order." Florence kept "account of every article given — which account could be, at any time, made known to the public — my responsibility being to the people of England."[29]

Nightingale marked Salisbury's greater responsibility by augmenting the army's meager pay out of her private purse. As well, Florence asked Salisbury to become housekeeper at the pleasant, airy house where she had convalesced, which she had kept for nurses needing a change from the hospitals. For this added work, Nightingale paid Salisbury a separate salary from her own funds. Salisbury brought a Maltese couple into the house to help there as well as in the hospital's extra diet kitchen. At the same time she wrote home disparaging Florence's hospital management in general, her disregard of patients and mis-use of free gifts in particular.

Items started to disappear — from the extra diet kitchen and from the free gifts store. Although reluctant to mistrust a lady living in her house, Nightingale could not condone abuse of free gifts. She began to ask questions.

Nurses staying at the house showed her bundles. One held linens, some marked "Barrack Hospital," others "FN." As Florence turned to leave, Salisbury entered. Oh, Miss Nightingale! she exclaimed, What a wet night, I'm soaked through. Florence got halfway to the hospital before she realized that a full moon shone in the clear, cobalt sky.

Nightingale conferred with General Storks, Scutari's military commander. They agreed that because only breach of trust could be proved, it would be best to dismiss Salisbury at once, with no more said. How could she leave at such short notice? wept the culprit. Florence let Salisbury continue to live at the house until she made arrangements. That night, nurses staying in the house heard strange sounds emanating from the basement where the Maltese couple lived.

Meanwhile, Nightingale inventoried all stores for which only she and

Salisbury had keys. The number of missing items mandated that Florence notify Storks. He sent an official to search the Maltese's rooms. They bulged with items belonging to the government or to Nightingale. General Storks formally interviewed Salisbury and witnesses. Facts revealed systematic fraud.

Florence feared scandal. It would damage her mission. Storks agreed. So Nightingale again promised Salisbury not to prosecute. And had her army salary deposited in a London bank so Salisbury could return home like others, rather than in disgrace.

Salisbury departed in a flood of tears. Loss of still more government property came to light. Storks advised Nightingale to open letters addressed to Salisbury and review the papers she left behind. This distasteful duty exposed Salisbury as having, from the start, vented her hatred of the Brace-bridges and vicious, totally unfounded suspicions of Nightingale to her friends in England, prominent among them Mary Stanley.

—m—

London buzzed over the Salisbury business. Stanley urged her to file a formal complaint against Nightingale for dismissal and against Storks for offensive conduct. As proof of innocence, Salisbury pointed to Storks not having penalized her. As justification, she falsely accused Selina Bracebridge of giving her discretionary power to distribute stores.

Hall pushed war-office anti-reformers to get secretary Lord Panmure to request a formal explanation from Nightingale and Storks. Florence could easily have refused, for she, not the government, had hired Salisbury. But that would mean deserting Storks, who might suffer professionally without her account. Besides, Nightingale saw herself as a war-office employee honor bound to obey orders.

"Flo has worked like a tiger and nearly finished her report,"[30] Mai told the Nightingales at year (1855) end. "The wind roars, the rain patters; I don't think" she "is conscious of the bluster, I never saw mind so continuously concentrated on her work."[31]

Put "in a new and arduous and responsible position,* I am overwhelmed with difficulties which officials at home can perhaps hardly appreciate," Florence concluded her closely written pages of tightly argued testimony.

> If my overloaded time and strength are to be taken up in answering [unproven accounts] of my dismissed servants, it would be [fitting] to know for what purpose. For I did and do expect to be supported in the discharge of my

---

*With the recent closing of Koulali hospital, Storks asked Nightingale to take its patients into the Barrack and General hospitals. She agreed, on condition that officers (who had their own servants and thus usually fared better than common soldiers) be treated on an equal footing with soldiers as regards nursing and the rules she had put in place.

proper duty, I did and do expect to be considered competent to decide upon the unfitness of persons employed by me as servants, and whom I discharge for proved breach of trust, without being thus called upon to answer their absurd accusations.[32]

A four-man commission fully exonerated Storks and Nightingale.

—∞—

Flo and Mai often joked about how falsely WEN and Fanny pictured "our lives when you talk of a comfortable tea" together.

MRS. ROBERTS: Are you ready for your tea?
FLO: [Without looking up from her writing.] Yes.

Roberts brought "two cups of tea and a plate of toast." She put "Flo's tea and toast on a chair beside her" large table piled high with papers, Mai's "tea on the little table where" she sat back-to-back with Florence, taking care of correspondence. Flo did "not leave off for a moment her writing but" took "a mouthful from time to time."[33]

Utter silence reigned.

Mai could not "find it in my heart" to initiate conversation when Flo had "been talking and talking from ten to four."[34] Doctors, nurses, orderlies, officers, everyone wanted to discuss hospital matters important to them. When Florence could snatch a moment, she and Mai trudged through the mud to the General hospital. At least that gave Flo the chance to be outdoors and to "walk. She never" went "out except there"[35] and only to her house on business.

—∞—

"The interest of her 50,000 children" kept "Flo alive through the rugged and dirty paths she" had "been called to traverse."[36] Florence felt a unique, a maternal bond with them, those men who crowded the Balaclava quay to greet her, who gave her Three Times Three on Sevastopol's heights, who carried her stretcher so carefully over the steep, rutted track to the Castle hospital and from the Scutari pier to her small house on the Bosphorus with its view of the cypress-shadowed cemetery where thousands of her children lay.

Victorians raised their daughters to believe a woman's raison d'être consisted of marriage and children. Florence Nightingale rejected marriage the better to serve God and humanity. But she did not reject her upbringing. Nightingale's "children" were her raison d'être. God put her on this earth because the common soldiers needed her. If He let her live, He must intend that she devote her life to them.

15

Victory

I have done my duty. I have identified my fate with that of the heroic dead, & whatever lies these sordid exploiteurs of human misery spread about us these officials, there is a right & a God to fight for & our fight has been worth fighting. I do not despair — nor complain. It has been a great cause.[1]— Florence Nightingale

Great Britain's Constantinople embassy gave a gala for Christmas (1855). Florence Nightingale got an invitation. Mai Smith convinced her reluctant niece to go.

"The drawing-room doors" were "thrown open, and the ambassadress" entered, "smiling a kind welcome." Beside her stood "a tall, fashionable, haughty beauty. I could not help thinking how lovely a person; but the next instant my eyes wandered from her cold unamiable face to a lady," modestly "standing on the other side of" the ambassadress.

[It] was Florence Nightingale, greatest of all now in name and honor among women. [...] I looked at her wasted figure and the short brown hair combed over her forehead like a child's, cut so when fever recently threatened her life. Her dress was black, made high to the throat, its only ornament being a large enameled brooch [Queen Victoria's gift.] Miss Nightingale is by no means striking in appearance. Only her plain black dress, quiet manner, and great renown, told so powerfully altogether in that assembly of brilliant dress and uniforms. She is very slight, rather above the middle height; her face is long and thin, but this may be from recent illness and great fatigue. She has a very prominent nose, slightly Roman; and small, dark eyes, kind, yet penetrating; but her face does not give you at all the idea of great talent. She looks a quiet, persevering, orderly, lady-like woman.[2]

After the festive Christmas dinner, midshipmen arrived from warships anchored off the Golden Horn and everyone "played like so many children; the admiral the life and spirit of every game." Still frail, Nightingale "could not join in the games, but she sat on a sofa, and looked on, laughing until the tears came into her eyes."[3]

The new year saluted Florence with earache, laryngitis, and insomnia.*
She could "have no fire in the stove because it smokes and a pan of charcoal,
the only other resource, affects her head, and the windows shutting badly her
room is very cold. She still loves her 50,000 children" so "much that she would
work with satisfaction if it had not been for those wretched women who have
worn and torn her."[4]

Reverend Mother Bridgeman reigned rebellious at Balaclava hospital.
Mary Stanley and Charlotte Salisbury spread spite throughout London. Chief
medical officer Dr. John Hall continued his anti–Nightingale campaign in
the Crimea.

—⁂—

Early in the new year (1856), medical and military officers of the land
transport corps asked Nightingale to send nurses to its Crimean hospitals.
These bore the dubious distinction of being "the worst in the camp."[5]

Florence asked her friend sanitary commissioner Dr. John Sutherland,
then working at Balaclava, whether she should comply.

"Not until you have stated the case fully to the" war office and asked
"them to place you on a proper footing with the authorities here," Sutherland
advised. "No official intimation as to your having any charge of the hospital
nursing in the Crimea has been sent to dr. Hall," and "the *responsibility* hence
rests officially with him."[6]

"My usefulness is destroyed, my work prevented or hindered and precious
time wasted by the uncertainty of the relations to which I am left with the
Crimean authorities," Florence appealed to her politically influential friend
Sidney Herbert. To be effective, she must have officially confirmed control
over all hospitals "in and north of the Bosporus,"[7] with power to place nurses
in them and stop military and medical officials from hiring any female
Nightingale dismissed, or who voluntarily left her service. For corroboration,
Florence referred Sidney to Colonel Sir John Lefroy.

Deep in war secretary Lord Panmure's confidence, Lefroy had been sent
to the combat zone ostensibly as Panmure's hush-hush advisor on scientific
concerns but actually to ascertain how medical matters stood. Lefroy could
certainly enlighten Herbert on "the attempts which are being made to root
us out of the Crimea."[8]

—⁂—

As part of his due diligence, Lefroy had asked the Crimea's chief purveyor
for a confidential report on nursing. Having already allied himself with Hall

---

*Typical symptoms of recurrent brucellosis.

by denying Nightingale supplies on her last trip to the Crimea, not to mention refusing to accept her checks in payment for nursing supplies, David Fitzgerald now went further. Weaving a web of lies and innuendo, he accused Nightingale of dismissing her devotee and friend Jane Shaw Stewart as superintendent of Balaclava hospital. Actually, officialdom promoted Stewart to the position of matron at the new, larger Castle hospital. Stigmatizing Nightingale's nurses as rowdy, defiant, and drunk, Fitzgerald named several sent home for serious offenses. He lauded Reverend Mother Bridgeman and her nuns as able, orderly, and obedient. Last, Fitzgerald echoed Hall by disputing Nightingale's claim to control in the Crimea. Hall sent copies of the report to anti-reform cronies at the war office.

The war office asked Nightingale to reply, but although the report circulated freely in the Crimea, officials refused to let her see it. Except Florence's new friend Lefroy.

Sitting at her large table covered with papers, the scratching of her quill pen the only sound to break the silence, Florence summoned the exacting standards her father had taught her twenty years ago to demolish Fitzgerald's "tissue of unfounded assertions, willful perversions &, in some instances, malicious & scandalous libels" with precision and logic.

"No fixed appointment appeared to have been" given "the nurses, each attending at pleasure thro' the wards." False. "I have ... before me my first superintendent's report from Balaclava," containing "the no. of each ward, the name of the nurse assigned to it — including even the hours of the *watches*" as "fixed by the medical officers themselves."

"'Discontent prevailed,' is an unsupported assertion."

"Malicious & scandalous libel against the good name of five (not only innocent & respectable but) most excellent & devoted women," three "invalided home by the advice of dr. Hall himself." All "medical officers under whom they have served" testified "to their high merits" in "very remarkable terms." Another, named as having been sent home in disgrace, "is *not 'gone home'* at all, but is with me at this present time & is a woman of faultless character." And Fitzgerald told Nightingale before witnesses, and Hall confirmed, that the fifth nurse should, "for her *unparalleled* service," receive "a pension from the government."

As for "the passage 'it should be the duty of a superintendent to obey the instructions of the hospital authorities & not to criticize or contravene them,'" all Nightingale's "local superintendents have had strict written rules from me, which they have as strictly carried out, to issue no article of food or of clothing whatever to patients, excepting in answer to" the "written requisitions of the medical officer in charge."

"The system at Koulali, whence" Reverend Mother Bridgeman "came to

Balaclava, & her own at Balaclava, have been to issue extras, etc. at their own discretion to patients, *without* requisition from the medical officers."

Subordination to the doctors that Fitzgerald *"so justly* admires, is found among the nuns & ladies under my charge, *& not among … Bridgeman's nuns."*

"The tables of comparative expenditure I can assert to be false, a number of the requisitions having been verified by myself."

> The pay of the nurses is wrongly stated, mr. Fitzgerald not being cognizant of the facts. I have already stated them in my report sent home to the war office. [...] If the war department desire me to continue to exercise these functions entrusted to me by themselves, I must request that they will support me in doing so, by notifying [dr. Hall] that he is to second & not to oppose me in the performance of my duties. The incessant difficulties arising from the want of such support consume my time & strength to the impediment of the work properly belonging to me.[9]

—⁂—

Colonel Lefroy favored central control of female military nursing and judged Nightingale the only woman capable of effecting it. Her claim for sole authority, he told war secretary Panmure, "appears to me indisputable."

> [The] medical men are jealous of it. Dr. Hall would gladly upset it tomorrow, and he knows better than any one, that miss Nightingale is its only anchor. A general order [confirming] her position would save her much annoyance and harassing correspondence, [stop any spirit of] independence among those [females] under her, a spirit encouraged with no friendly intention in more than one quarter.[10]

"Miss Nightingale is recognized by Her Majesty's government as the general superintendent of the female nursing establishment of the military hospitals of the army," Panmure wrote in a general order to the military.

"No lady, or sister, or nurse is to be transferred from one hospital to another, or introduced into any hospital, without previous consultation with her."

"The principal medical officer" must confer with her on "all subjects connected with the female nursing establishment, and will give his directions through that lady."[11]

She had won.*

However, Hall's campaign, not to mention battles in the Barrack hospital, forced Florence into a distasteful reality. Until Scutari she had lived the

---

*The government may well have forsaken Nightingale in her battle with Hall and Fitzgerald had she not had Lefroy's support. Florence recognized his "extreme kindness, judgment, & tact to which, as I always gratefully acknowledge, I owed my position in the Crimea, which you & no one else, obtained for me" (FN, *Letters from the Crimea*, p. 226, November 25, 1864, to Lefroy).

sheltered life of a wealthy English gentlewoman. The Barrack hospital's physical hardship and demanding work were a challenge, but Florence had zeal and energy enough to meet it. Fierce political infighting, spite and egos, she had never faced, never thought she would need to face, never thought could exist in such a dire circumstance as the Crimean calamity. Fighting on unfamiliar ground, therefore, Nightingale asked Herbert to have Fitzgerald's report and her reply made public so that Britons could see what their heroine must cope with. That, her politically astute friend advised, would serve no useful purpose. Publicly airing quarrels would merely serve to provide Stanley, Salisbury, and their ilk with ammunition in their campaign to vilify Nightingale's nursing methods. Florence took Sidney's wisdom to heart.

— ∾ —

She went to the Crimea for the third and last time, at the end of March (1856). Nightingale intended to introduce her nursing system into the dirty, disease-ridden, disorganized land transport hospitals. After a chilly, windswept passage up the Bosporus and across the Black Sea, Florence landed at Balaclava in blinding snow.

Purveyor Fitzgerald withheld rations. Fortunately, Nightingale had brought "every article for cooking, furnishing, warming the huts, even stoves, & every article of food that would keep." So she could "thank God — my charge [Nurse Roberts, three of Reverend Mother Moore's Bermondsey convent nuns, and Miss Nightingale's Man, messenger Robert Robinson] has felt neither cold nor hunger, & is in efficient working order — having cooked & administered" all "extras for 260 bad cases ever since the first day of their arrival."

> [Nightingale had] never been off my horse till 9 or 10 at night, except when it was too dark to walk him over these crags even with a lantern, when I have gone on foot. During the greater part of the day, I have been without food necessarily, except a little brandy & water (you see I am taking up drinking like my comrades of the army) the snow is deep on the ground, but the object of my coming has been attained.

Nothing must be allowed to jeopardize it. Florence forbore to tell officials about Fitzgerald refusing rations. Indeed, she patiently completed piles of official requisition forms and observed "every formality not only of routine but of politeness." Nightingale even refrained from using her newly conferred official status, let alone "my quality of woman, to avoid hardships or fatigue." She would not give Hall and Fitzgerald the slightest chance to say she caused them difficulty.

But Florence showed no such restraint with Sidney Herbert. "I wish to leave on record some instance of that which nobody in England will believe or can even imagine."[12]

Concomitantly, "would not you like to see me hunting rats like a terrier-dog? Me"! Flo regaled Parthe.

Scene in a Crimean hut. Time midnight.

Dramatic personae: sick nun in fever perfectly deaf, me the only other occupant of the hut except, rat sitting on rafter over sick nun's head & rats scrambling about.

Enter me, with a lantern in one hand & broom-stick in the other (in the Crimea, terrier dogs hunt with lanterns in one paw & broom-sticks).

Me, commonly called "pope" by the nuns, makes ye furious Balaclava charge, i. e. the light cavalry come on & I am the Russian gun.

Light cavalry ensconces itself among my beloved boots & squeaks — desperate papal aggression.

Broom-stick descends — enemy dead — "pope" executes savage war dance in triumph, to the unspeakable terror of nun.

Slain cast out of hut — unburied.[13]

—w—

There remained Reverend Mother Bridgeman. War secretary Panmure's general order putting Dr. Hall to rout made Bridgeman's refusal to work under Nightingale problematic. Hall and Fitzgerald advised resignation. Florence urged her to stay, for she thought Bridgeman meant well. So Nightingale suggested the nun adopt only a few aspects of her regime, like keeping wards clean, boiling linens to kill lice, and assigning extras only at a doctor's written request. But Bridgeman resisted these rudimentary reforms; furthermore, she insisted on continuing to give spiritual comfort to the men — which flouted Nightingale and the government's rules. Hence, Bridgeman resigned. She submitted her official resignation to Hall rather than to Nightingale and left bearing Hall's paeans of praise.

Florence arrived at Balaclava hospital in gathering dusk on the day of Bridgeman's departure. Deep snow covered the ground and swirled dizzily down from a slate-gray sky.

NIGHTINGALE: Please give me keys to the nurses' storerooms, kitchens, and quarters.

HOSPITAL PURVEYOR AND FITZGERALD'S HENCHMAN: The keys are unavailable. And in any case, Dr. Hall has already assigned the nurses' huts to my clerks.

NIGHTINGALE: I shall sit outside until the keys are available.

"In about two hours they were produced. Every day for the last week it has been a repetition of the same thing — a contest for the stores for the patients, for food, lodgings,"[14] and no help given.

"Your pig sty is cleaner" than Balaclava hospital, Flo wrote Uncle Sam. "Patients were grimed with dirt, infested with vermin, and bed sores like

Lazarus." (Bridgeman probably "thought it holy.)" After "two days hard white washing & cleaning — after three days washing & dressing the patients," Hall materialized. "Disgusted with the state of the hospital," he wrote the head doctor, who showed Florence the letter, Hall "ordered it all to be put back into the admirable order it was in previously."

"This is the man on whom the lives & healths of the army in great measure, depend. (For he is clever & this is all temper.)"[15]

Nightingale's "last tug of war," the "worst, these last four weeks in the Crimea," utterly enervated her. "And if I could think that the tug of war would continue, that would be the best hearing for me, for that alone would bring reform."[16]

—m—

Meanwhile, Britain, France, and Russia signed the Peace of Paris.[17] So with her position secure and the seven hospitals (five in the Crimea, two at Scutari) under her care in perfect order, Nightingale returned to headquarters at the Barrack hospital.

Convalescents were going home, so she reduced the number of nurses. Florence got the government to help several, dipped into her pocket for the needy, asked Fanny to give worn-out nurses a holiday at Embley, find good positions for others. And Florence convinced Scutari's military commander, General Storks, to pay homebound fare for soldiers' wives employed at the hospitals.

Nightingale wrote a report for each nurse. Without the Castle hospital's Jane Shaw Stewart "our Crimean work would have come to grief— without her judgment, her devotion, her unselfish consistent looking to the one great end, viz. the carrying out the work as a whole — without her untiring zeal, her watchful care of the nurses, her accuracy in all trusts and accounts, her truth, her faithfulness."[18]

"23 years sister in St. Thomas's hospital," Elizabeth Roberts had "infinitely superior" qualifications.

> [A] surgical nurse of the first order, [her] valuable services have been recognized even and most of all by the surgeons (of Scutari, where she has principally been and where, after Inkerman, her exertions were unremitting). Her total superiority to all the vices of a hospital nurse, her faithfulness to the work, her disinterested love of duty and vigilant care of her patients, her power of work equal to that of *ten*, have made her one of the most important persons of the expedition.[19]

Health had forced Reverend Mother Mary Clare Moore's early departure —"the greatest blow I have had yet." But "God's blessing & my love & gratitude go with you, as you well know.

"You were far above me in fitness" to be superintendent, "both in worldly talent of administration, & far more in the spiritual qualifications which God values in a superior."

"I shall do everything I can for the sisters, whom you have left me. I trust you will not with-draw" them "till the work of the hospital ceases to require their presence, & that I may be authorized to be the judge of this." Florence promised to "care for them as if they were my own children. But that you know, and now it is a sacred trust from you."[20]

Climbing up to Balaclava heights, some visitors came upon the Castle "hospital huts built of long planks, and adorned with neatly bordering flowers. The sea" sparkled "before us, and as we lingered to admire the fine view," a "kind, motherly-looking woman came into the little porch, and invited us to enter and rest." Another nun offered a wooden stool. On the large wood table stood "a simple pot of wild flowers, so beautifully arranged, they instantly struck the eye. How charming the little" hut, with "its perfect cleanliness, its glorious view, and the health, contentment, and usefulness of its inmates!" these "brave, quiet women, who had" helped "relieve so much suffering!"[21]

Nightingale found it "impossible to estimate too highly the unwearied devotion, patience & cheerfulness, the judgment and activity, & the single-heartedness with which" the Bermondsey nuns "have labored in the service of the sick."[22]

England anticipated its heroine's return with huge excitement. Public entities planned to welcome Nightingale with ceremonial arches, parades, speeches, even regimental receptions complete with military bands. Lea Hurst locals wanted to draw her carriage from railway station to house. The Nightingale family eagerly looked forward to having their Flo at home, where, they hoped, she would be content to rest on her laurels.

> FANNY NIGHTINGALE: What type of official reception would Flo prefer? Or should we meet her privately?
> MAI SMITH: "I cannot tell you the dread she has of the receptions with which she is threatened."[23]

Florence would not let anyone know when she intended to leave. She looked well, Mai's letter continued, and outwardly seemed in excellent spirits, but her health had suffered. Flo had become heart-wrenchingly thin, and when she was alone her spirits often sank. Rather than enjoying her fame, Florence felt afraid of it. She thought that whatever she did would surely disappoint.

Fear of failure would always haunt Flo. Years of having to face her mother's disapproval had left its mark.

Mai warned the Nightingales not to expect Florence to stay at home for long. Indeed, she preferred, "after a short visit at home," to "go to some foreign hospital where my name has never been heard of & discharging myself of all responsibility, anxiety, writing & administration, work there as a nurse for a year," Flo confided to the Bracebridges, who, of those closest to her, best understood what she had gone through.

"At home I should go distraught with admiring friends & detracting enemies." At a foreign spa "I should go mad with inaction."

"My health is too much broken for a position of responsibility & power. With the story I have to tell I never would enter the world again, not on account of the sickness & suffering, but of the corruption & incapacity I have to tell."[24]

—ᴍ—

Twenty months after she first landed at Scutari in cold autumn rain, Nightingale set out for home as summer sunshine bathed the Bosporus. She had declined the British government's offer of passage to England in a battleship. Rather, Florence traveled as Miss Smith with her aunt Mai and Nurse Roberts and further cloaked her anonymity by sailing to Marseille on a French mail steamer.

From Marseille the three women made their way north to Paris, where they parted. Surprising Julius Mohl at the rue du Bac apartment (Clarkey had, as usual, gone to England for the summer), Florence spent the night. Once across the Channel, she kept her promise to go straight to London's Bermondsey slum. Its stinking, rowdy streets contrasted with the cleanliness and peace inside the Convent of Mercy, where the reunited nuns were preparing for their annual retreat.

Thus, Nightingale again joined a Catholic retreat, spending her first hours in England at prayer and meditation with her dear Crimean colleague, Reverend Mother Moore. Eight years ago in Rome, Nightingale had knelt beside Madre Santa Colomba, beseeching God to teach her to do His will without care for reputation. He had answered.

Still alone, Great Britain's only heroic figure to emerge from the Crimean War caught the train north to Derbyshire, disembarking at the small country station near Lea Hurst. Discreetly veiled, she climbed the steep incline leading to her "hilltop home." Shadows of summer twilight lengthened as Florence opened Lea Hurst's plain wooden gate, walked between the simple stone pillars, up the drive past the circular lawn, the flower beds filled with red and white snapdragons and dark pink delphiniums, to "surprise her dear people sitting in the drawing-room."[25]

16

"I can never forget"

"Florence ... is a great artist. She has a strong creative individuality.... Only since she has burst out like a thunderbolt in her own way" has she "done anything worth while. What folly and cruelty to have made her for years give up her individuality."[1]— Mary Clarke Mohl

I stand at the altar of the murdered men, and, while I live, I fight their cause.[2]— Florence Nightingale

Pacing, pacing, pacing, all night long her family heard Florence pacing the plain wooden floor of her little Lea Hurst bedroom. She must be reliving the horrors she had seen — that splintered army of pest-ridden skeletons who died before her eyes in the Barrack hospital. True, but not quite in the way Flo's "dear people" thought.

Their Flo faced a dilemma that August (1856): how best to continue serving God and humanity. She had sacrificed everything in a great cause, had become an icon at age thirty-six. It might now be time to take an easier path. Florence could resume the plans she made before Scutari, become matron of a large public hospital and train other women to nurse. Indeed, the Nightingale Fund stood ready at hand to enable Florence to realize her dream of creating nurse education.

But what about her "children"? Nightingale had unique knowledge of the action needed to protect soldiers from future Crimean calamities. Nonetheless, reform of the army medical system would mean years of extremely demanding political infighting.

God "entered thee at Scutari ... to be a savior."[3] God also let Florence survive the Crimean catastrophe. Why?

Because He meant Nightingale to eschew the easy path. Scutari gave her exclusive understanding. Scutari gave her singular credibility. Scutari gave her exceptional eminence. Scutari showed her ability. Florence must use these advantages to improve the conditions under which her country's soldiers served. And she must do so while fickle public attention still focused on the Crimea.

175

—⚏—

Flo looked well and seemed well for a few hours in the morning, her concerned family noted, but by lunchtime she had sunk into exhaustion. Utterly spent, Florence sought only peace and quiet. The Nightingales wanted to give her this breathing space, which they judged to be the sole factor that could restore their Flo to the possibility of returning to her precious work.

With Uncle Sam's help, not to mention the excellent records kept by the Bermondsey nuns, Flo finished her accounting of free gift disbursements. As well, she answered congratulations from family and friends and dealt with a mountain of miscellaneous mail. Parthe handled the begging letters. She hated "the sight of the post with its long official envelopes," for Flo would "go on as long as she has strength doing" all that "cannot be left without detriment to" her work. Her mood "so calm, so cheerful, so simple," the "physical hardships one does not wonder at her forgetting to speak of; but the marvel to me is how the mental ones, — the indifference, the ignorance, the cruelty, the" falsehood "never seem to ruffle her."

And despite nausea, palpitations, and insomnia (which Florence's doctor ascribed to excessive fatigue but actually typified lingering brucellosis), she remained "as merry about little things as ever." Flo showed "as much interest about the little things of home as if she had not been wielding the management and organization of the material and spiritual comfort of 50,000 men."

"As for her indifference to praise, it is" extraordinary. She "does not heed it, as it comes in every morning in its flood — papers, music, poetry, friends, letters, addresses."[4]

Florence shunned fame. She felt unworthy of it. Flo had, after all, merely obeyed the will of God. Celebrity would, moreover, harm her cause. A female must avoid attention lest she play into the hands of her enemies. They waited to pounce, particularly if a woman fell short of her goals.

So Nightingale rejected interviews, portraits, and public appearances. She even, to her mother's intense disappointment, refused a gala garden party that the Duke of Devonshire, Derbyshire's most distinguished denizen, proposed to give in her honor.

—⚏—

Florence jumped at an invitation from family friend Sir James Clark. He lived at Birk Hall, in the scenic valley of Scotland's river Dee. As Queen Victoria's physician, Clark knew the royal family would be vacationing at nearby Balmoral Castle. The Queen intended to grant Nightingale an official audience, but Birk Hall provided the perfect venue for private talk. Only Florence could tell Victoria exactly what had befallen her troops. Only Florence could convey how similar calamities could be averted in the future, how the survivors of Sevastopol's trenches, those gates "of the infernal regions,"[5] could be saved.

"With the buzz-fuzz which is above my name at present," Nightingale wrote Crimean ally Colonel Lefroy, senior war-office factotum and war secretary Lord Panmure's confidant, were she to work at a London public hospital "I should succeed in nothing else but in collecting about me much of the vain & needy & frivolous elements of England." Florence would consider working in peacetime army hospitals for an "*indirect*" reason: to have "legitimate means of information by which I could suggest reforms." Would Lefroy, therefore, advise Nightingale to "ask humbly & directly for a female nursing dep't in the army hospitals, which I have little doubt the Queen would grant, without making myself more obnoxious than I am — or should I state boldly the whole case [for reform] at first?"

If Lefroy counseled "telling the truth & the whole truth to" Panmure (scheduled to visit Balmoral) and "the Queen about their war-hospitals, viz. that not one step has been made in reform or to prevent the scene of '54 from being acted all over again in any future war," Nightingale wished to consult with Lefroy. His opinion would be "so far better than mine, as to what reforms are desirable & what are practicable."[6]

Lefroy replied instantly. Florence must join the reformers. They needed her popularity, prestige, and social position to fight the army's deep-rooted diehards. "We have almost a right to ask" for your "account of the trials you have" endured, "difficulties you have" met, and "evils you have" seen "not only because no other person ever was or can be in such a position to give it, but" because "no one else is so gifted."[7]

After telling the Queen and Panmure everything, Nightingale should ask for "a commission to enquire into the existing regulations for hospital administration." She must then officially disclose her story in either "a confidential report addressed" to Panmure "*upon a formal request*, or evidence before such a commission."[8]

Agreed. Florence would tell all. If encouraged, she would propose solutions. If apt, she would offer to consign her comments to paper. If they were approved, she would ask that a royal commission fully examine army barracks, hospitals, and medical department. She would request nothing for herself.

Florence Nightingale had committed herself to reform.

—ᚗᚗ—

En route to Birk Hall, Florence arranged to meet with the two men who had most effectively exposed Crimean flaws. Personally and professionally she liked Dr. John McNeill "best of all who came" to the war zone; he had "done wonders."[9] McNeill lived at Edinburgh. His co-commissioner, Colonel

Alexander Tulloch, traveled from his home in the south of England to confer with them.

Unlike her previous journey to Sir James Clark's home four years ago, this time Florence went not as an unknown miss, dragged away from hard-won hospital visiting in Ireland to rescue her hysterical sister. She went as Great Britain's heroine, summoned to see her sovereign on a subject of national significance.

Scotland's capital sparkled in September sunshine. To its north, beyond the sapphire Firth of Forth, the Fife hills reclined against a pellucid sky. Dahlias glowed in the municipal gardens lining the city's main street, and the imposing gray bulk of crenellated Edinburgh Castle loomed above. Tall houses, "standing like towers,"[10] twinkled with lights after dark. But Florence focused on collating her notes and statistics with those McNeill and Tulloch had collected. In her few spare moments, she inspected barracks and hospitals.

—m—

Constitutional curbs had, by the mid-nineteenth century, considerably weakened royal authority. But the Queen still had some influence over the army. Victoria and her husband, Prince Albert, first saw Florence informally. Nightingale subsequently had several "most satisfactory interviews with" the royal couple, satisfactory "as far as their *will*, not as their *power* is concerned."[11]

Victoria drove herself to Birk Hall in a pony cart, impromptu and alone, a number of times. As the nineteenth century's two most famous women strolled the scenic woodland paths winding about and through the magnificent Birk Hall estate, bounded by high wooded hills ablaze with bronze and gold, they shared their maternal concern for the troops. Nightingale told the Queen about them as only she could.

Confident that her support would help, Victoria asked Florence to put her reform proposals in a letter. This the queen forwarded to her secretary of state for war. Lord Panmure would "be much gratified and struck with miss Nightingale — her powerful, clear head, and simple, modest manner."[12] His sovereign's introduction notwithstanding, Panmure expected to meet a power-hungry, predatory female. Charming, selfless Florence Nightingale came as a distinctly pleasant surprise.

So much so that it moved Panmure spontaneously to ask Nightingale to critique plans for the army's new hospital to be built at Netley. And he agreed with the Queen and prime minister Lord Palmerston, Nightingale family friend and Embley neighbor, that Florence describe her Crimean experience in a confidential report. It should be addressed to the government and include reform proposals. Further, Panmure consented to Nightingale's request for a royal commission.

The war secretary intended to handle the prickly question of reform by procrastinating. For Panmure hated detail and abhorred system. In his predecessor Sidney Herbert's jaundiced view, Panmure avoided the war secretary's huge workload by "the simple process of never attempting to do it."[13]

War-office anti-reformers got ready to fight. But Florence Nightingale enjoyed royal and popular support. She had credibility and tenacity. And, thanks to her mother's exertions, Nightingale moved naturally in the extremely select circle of high society, still closely interwoven with government. No cabinet minister could ignore her.

—⁂—

Florence plunged into plans for the royal commission. To facilitate communication with fellow reformers, she moved to London. Concerned about Flo's frail health and what they judged as her need of a chaperone, Fanny and Parthe went as well. The three ladies settled into a suite at the Burlington hotel, off centrally located Regent Street.

Daily, the reformers* met in what they called "the little war office," Florence's tiny private parlor off the family suite's spacious sitting room. They agreed to base reforms on Nightingale's Crimean experience. Her mastery of detail and clear picture of the whole, to say nothing of her zeal and energy, made Florence project manager.

How "very pretty," Parthe opined, "to see these wise old men so profoundly convinced of her knowledge as well as of her disinterestedness." They looked "up at her with such a mixture of reverence and tenderness, of desire that she should not overwork herself, and of desire that she should do the work which she alone can do so well."[14]

When gray November skies glowered over London, and a restless wind soughed the bare branches of its trees, Panmure paid an official call at the Burlington. He formally requested a Confidential Report describing Nightingale's Crimean War experience and outlining her reform proposals. The war secretary agreed, in principle, that the royal commission would cover the entire army medical department, as well as army health at home and abroad. And Florence extracted a promise that as long as The Bison† held office her

---

*Calling themselves the Band of Brothers, the reformers included Dr. James Clark; Colonel Lefroy; General Sir Henry Storks, Scutari military commander and Nightingale ally; sanitary commissioner Dr. John Sutherland, Florence's Crimean friend and favorite physician; and her close friend and long time fellow reformer popular parliamentarian Sidney Herbert. Lukewarm on the chances for reform when Florence broached the subject during their recent stay with the Bracebridges at Atherstone Hall, Sidney thought Panmure had no stomach for it. True, but Herbert reckoned without Nightingale's determination.

†Panmure's bulk and large head crowned with clumps of bristling hair, which he slowly swayed from side to side, earned him the nickname Bison.

Crimea nemesis, recently knighted Dr. John Hall,[15] would not replace the soon-to-retire army medical department chief.

With little faith in Panmure and feeling unwell besides, the esteemed, politically astute Sidney Herbert hesitated when Nightingale asked him to chair the commission. "If not you, no one else."[16] Sidney's hunger for reform and Florence's enthusiasm won.

—⁂—

She pushed behind the scenes to give the commission teeth. Herbert pushed in parliament. War-office anti-reformers resisted. The Bison delayed. Fanny and Parthe left London to prepare Embley for Christmas. They pressed Flo to join them.

"My heart was very full at parting with you and my dear loving Parthe," Flo wrote her "dear, dear" mother. She would always remember Fanny's "ceaseless watchfulness to ease and help me." Such "devoted love is a very precious possession; it cheers me even while absent from you; it surrounds me with a genial atmosphere even when clouds look black and heavy. You will live with me, I know, if I faithfully strive to do our Father's work as far as is in me, even more than if I left it to see your dear faces."

Florence would conserve "all of life and health" to serve God and her poor, suffering children. "It is a solace to me to strive that those sufferings" were not "in vain, but be assured that I love their cause too well heedlessly or recklessly to risk any means I may possess to serve it," Flo explained to a mother she still felt had not truly understood, indeed, still did not understand, her. If joining the family for Christmas meant "desertion of my work,"[17] Florence would remain in London.

Discouraged at the glacial advance of her cause, Flo finally yielded to Fanny's plea that she spend her first post–Crimea Christmas at home. But when the extended family sat down to dine on crackling roast goose with aromatic trimmings and flaming brandied Christmas pudding bursting with nutmeats and preserved fruit, Flo's thoughts flew to her "poor men who endured so patiently, I feel I have been such a bad mother to you to come home & leave you lying in your Crimean grave."[18]

"My God, my God why hast thou forsaken me." We "are tired of hearing of the Crimean catastrophe. We don't want to know any more about the trenches cold and damp, the starved and frozen camp. The deficient rations, the stores which might have served the great army of the dead lying unused." Words "were given in plenty to the great Crimean catastrophe, but the real tragedy began when it"[19] ended.

—⁂—

Nightingale, meanwhile, reviewed her statistics, inspected hospitals, and consulted experts to comply with Panmure's Balmoral request that she critique the blueprints for the new hospital at Netley. Great Britain's war office intended it to be the country's main military medical facility. Panmure reeled when he received Florence's thorough report.

Particularly when The Bison realized that in his zeal to include charming, modest Miss Nightingale in Netley's planning process he had forgotten the inconvenient fact of construction having begun before she came back from the Crimea. Building had thus advanced too far to allow for Florence's recommended changes. Panmure procrastinated.

During the Christmas holidays, however, Prime Minister Palmerston's wife invited the neighboring Nightingales to dine at colonnaded Broadlands. When the gentlemen joined the ladies in Emily Palmerston's elegant but comfy drawing room, Florence took advantage of the relaxed atmosphere to button-hole her host. She convinced him, Palmerston wrote Panmure, that Netley's plan had major flaws. "Better to pull it down and rebuild" than "finish it upon the present plan," which would spread disease by grouping the patients without proper provision for fresh air.*

"All consideration of what would best tend to the comfort and recovery of patients has been sacrificed to the vanity of the architect, whose sole object has been to make a building which should cut a dash." But when the government spent money on a major hospital, "the first and main purpose" should "be to make a building" calculated "to the greatest possible degree" to "promote the cure and recovery of patients."

Since Netley must "last for a century, and is to be filled" by "hundreds at a time, any sacrifice of money in correcting" construction errors "would be better than a deliberate perseverance in arrangements" shown "to be bad." Panmure should "stop all further progress in the work till the matter can be duly considered."[20]

Petrified at the prospect of having to justify in parliament the huge expense of tearing down the partially built hospital, let alone ruffling some exceedingly important feathers, The Bison procrastinated. Palmerston persisted. "Many of miss Nightingale's suggestions" can "be carried out by alterations, but the total abandonment of the plan will," Panmure finally replied, "be a most serious affair."[21]

Reluctant to provoke Panmure and thereby risk further delay of her main

---

*Nightingale advocated the French Pavilion Plan of hospital construction. It organized the hospital into separate sections or pavilions, for infectious and non-infectious, seriously ill, and less so patients, and provided ample access to fresh air and light. Britain currently used the Corridor Plan, lumping all patients together in wards off one long corridor and minimal or no access to air and light.

object — official launch of the royal commission — Florence compromised. She endorsed "revised plans for Netley," because they made "very great improvements"[22] in ventilation.

—❦—

Nightingale planned to focus her confidential report for Panmure on wartime observations, plus proposals for reform. In support, she gathered data on every facility — such as barracks, infirmaries, asylums, and prisons — that affected the soldier's quality of life. Fascinated by facts since childhood, later by mathematics, Florence had spent hours tabulating and analyzing hospital information in the pre-dawn privacy of her bedroom. She now embraced a nascent science: statistics.

Statistics could be used to develop sound data as a foundation for reform. Statistics drew notice and could influence opinion. And this new discipline had an important religious subtext: God revealed His plan for the world through facts on the ground. Studying them supplied a crucial guide for human action.

At this point Florence gained an ally. She met him at a dinner party.

Son of a farm laborer who had risen through the ranks of class-conscious Britain to become an authority on vital data and epidemiology, William Farr had identified the importance of statistics twenty years before. Physician and apothecary, the bald and bearded widower impressed Nightingale with his talk of civilian mortality tables. She asked Farr to analyze her Crimean mortality statistics.*

Farr saw medicine as a means to better society. He recognized Florence as sole possessor of the facts, let alone the connections, to effect change. And as the government's senior statistician, he had access to key records and a trained staff. So Nightingale and Farr made a pact. Farr would aid in advancing army medical reform; Nightingale would help in lowering civilian mortality.

—❦—

Her comparison of civilian and military mortality statistics revealed a startling result. Military deaths almost doubled civilian deaths.

The "disgraceful state of our Chatham [military] hospitals, which I have been visiting lately, is" another "symptom of a system which, in the Crimea, put to death 16,000 men — the finest" major experiment in modern history of how many "may be put to death at will by the sole agency of bad food and bad air."[23]

---

*Having found the medical records of Scutari's hospitals in a state of utter confusion, Florence introduced an orderly scheme of recording major sickness and mortality data in the hospitals under her jurisdiction.

Florence went to Chatham with a male colleague and "her good angel," cousin Hilary Bonham-Carter, as chaperone. The three set "off at 9½ o'clock," not "returning until 9½ at night; 30 miles to Chatham by rail, several miles in cabs" and "up to 20 miles walking about 3 hospitals,"[24] Fanny wrote WEN. The next day their daughter toured the wards of a large London hospital where she had been made an honorary life governor, inspected another, then returned to the Burlington to work on statistics far into the night.

Since Fanny and Parthe monopolized the family carriage to drive in Hyde Park at a fashionable hour, shop, or pay social calls, Flo walked, used hansom cabs, or even, in a rather unusual move for a young lady, took one of the public omnibuses that clip-clopped past the busy Burlington. And when the hotel mistakenly gave one of the Nightingale rooms to another guest, Florence slept in an annex.

Still smarting over the liberal allowance WEN gave Flo before she went to Harley Street, Fanny thought if her younger daughter disliked using public transportation or working in a little back parlor, she could well afford otherwise. Indeed, Fanny insisted on Florence sharing all hotel expenses, including for the large family parlor, which she hardly ever used. That caused friction.

So did Fanny and Parthe's failure to recognize the nature and scale of Flo's work. Their constant interruptions over trivial social matters, in which she had no interest, sorely tried Florence's patience. As did reproaches at Flo's refusal to join her mother and sister's society events while finding enough time to see her own friends. After a tiring day collecting information, Flo found this censure hard to bear. Her mother and sister seemed only to value the reflected glory of her fame.

—⁊⁊⁊—

War-office diehards had, in the interim, contrived to whitewash the damning report McNeill and Tulloch wrote about army mismanagement of the war.[25] Outraged, Britain's largest-circulation newspaper championed the McNeill-Tulloch report. Many prominent private citizens reacted as did the *Times*. Nightingale rallied her family and friends to influence important people. Parliament pricked up its ears. So did Panmure — thereby inadvertently exposing his Achilles' Heel: vulnerability to the power of public opinion.

Sidney Herbert asked parliament to petition the Queen to honor McNeill and Tulloch. Prime Minister Palmerston made sure Herbert's motion passed. "I direct my letter to the now right honorable sir John McNeill with"[26] great pleasure, Nightingale exulted.

—⁊⁊⁊—

Tulips and forget-me-nots blossomed under blue skies and trees shimmered in a haze of fresh green when Florence left the dusty Burlington to stay with Mai and Sam Smith at their suburban home. Swathed in Aunt Mai's sympathy, Flo organized and hand-wrote her eight-hundred-page confidential report, interrupting only for the long train journey north to confer with McNeill at Edinburgh.

Notes Affecting the Health, Efficiency, and Hospital Administration of the British Army resulted. Based on Florence's Crimea statistics and comments, plus subsequent inspection of medical institutions and study of blueprints, the report detailed the whole field of army medical and hospital administration during the Crimean War, previous wars, and peacetime.

Nightingale's *Notes* would, the reforming Band of Brothers agreed, be the basis of their royal commission report. But Florence believed The Bison would treat her report as a mere sop; Panmure meant to placate while he procrastinated ad infinitum on an official launch of the royal commission.

So despite showing the world a cheerful face, Florence thought "our cause is lost." Army diehards had by now gathered too many allies in parliament. Sidney Herbert felt extremely unwell. The Bison had "no other rule of conduct than that of staving off every question which will give him trouble, till the public interest in it subsides." Panmure broke "all his promises, defeated all reform by his inertia, for his passive resistance, easiest of all to make, is the most difficult to overcome."[27]

Nonetheless, Nightingale's lobbying on behalf of McNeill and Tulloch had shown her Panmure's Achilles' heel. "Three months from this day I publish my experience of the Crimea campaign and my suggestions for improvement, unless there has been a fair and tangible pledge by that time for reform."[28]

17

The Royal Commission

No one can feel for the army as I do.... People must have seen that long, long dreadful winter to know what it was.[1]—Florence Nightingale

Her gentle manner covers such a depth and strength of mind and thought, that I am afraid of nothing for her, but that her health should fail.[2]—Julius Mohl

When lilacs bloomed in London parks and honeysuckle scented the paths, fashionable ladies and gentlemen flocked to town for the social season (1857). And in the middle of a bright, late spring afternoon war secretary Lord Panmure presented himself at the Burlington hotel. One year after the Crimean War ended, Great Britain's government sought Florence Nightingale's official endorsement of its instructions for a royal commission to examine the state of army health.

She and The Bison negotiated for hours. Consequently, Panmure gave the commission full powers of inquiry. And except for the army medical department chief (Florence thought he deserved a court-martial for dereliction of duty in the Crimea) Nightingale got the commissioners she had personally recruited.[3] Sidney Herbert took the chair. As a woman, Florence could not, of course, sit on the commission.

Regardless, "the mainspring of the" effort centered on Nightingale. "Nobody who has not worked with her daily could know her, could have an idea of her strength and clearness of mind, her extraordinary powers joined with her benevolence of spirit," said sanitary expert and commissioner Dr. John Sutherland. "She is one of the most gifted creatures God ever made."[4]

Keen to capitalize on the public's still vivid Crimea memories, resolved to wring every benefit out of each lesson learned from the Crimean calamity, Florence drove herself, and expected no less of others. Besides working on her particular assignment: evaluating statistics, Nightingale coached all the commissioners. She spent afternoons at Sutherland's suburban home preparing him for the next day's session. Florence admired her colleague's enthusiasm, not to mention his expertise, and relied on his judgment. Nevertheless, she deplored Sutherland's lack of punctuality and laxity with documents; besides, Nightingale grumbled, he showed excessive concern over his health and spent too much time gardening.

Florence expected much of Sutherland, but she demanded more from her closest colleague, commission chairman Sidney Herbert. His parliamentary stature and negotiating skills were vital. "A man of the quickest and most accurate reception," Sidney engaged even reluctant witnesses and never made "an enemy or a quarrel."[5] But Nightingale refused to see Herbert's lethargy and gloom as signs of illness. She defied physical frailty. So must he.

Mornings found Florence coaching Sidney in his study facing the trees in Belgrave Square. She prepared a précis for him on each facet of the inquiry, sent Herbert papers — including some Sutherland had "stolen ... for your benefit, a practice I learnt from the army and taught him."[6] Nightingale proposed and interviewed witnesses, scheduled their appearance, and readied questions for Herbert so that he understood "what each could tell" as "a witness in public."[7]

"You know so much more of human nature than I do," Florence wrote her friend Sir John McNeill. "I have been asked to request you to give some hints as to his [Crimean War chief medical officer John Hall] examination, founded upon what you saw of him while in your hands." Nightingale judged Hall "a much cleverer fellow than they take him" for. He must be examined, but "how is it to be done?

"I would only recall to your memory the long series of proofs of his incredible apathy — beginning with the fatal letter approving of Scutari, October/54." Still, "we do not want to badger the old man," which "would do us no good & harm him."[8]

—⁂—

The star witness posed a dilemma. Nightingale must not, Herbert warned, provoke bad blood by blaming officials for gross negligence. She should appear in person but limit her evidence to the lethal effects of Scutari hospitals' abysmal sanitation and the lessons it taught about future hospital construction.

Florence demurred. Her presence would trigger the buzz-fuzz she dreaded as harmful to her cause but let her say nothing salient to compensate. Certainly "it is inexpedient and even unprincipled to bring up past delinquencies," but it would "be untrue and unconscientious for me to give evidence" on a relatively minor matter like hospital construction while "leaving untouched the great matters which affect (and have affected)" the mortality of "our sick.... It would be treachery to the memory of my dead."[9]

The commissioners insisted that Nightingale testify. Lack of her name on the witness list would diminish their report, to say nothing of leading to allegations that the commissioners had failed to invite Florence because they feared her evidence — or that she feared to air her proposals in public.

Hence, Nightingale's written testimony summarized her confidential report to Panmure (*Notes Affecting the Health, Efficiency, and Hospital Administration of the British Army*). Covering every facet of hospital organization, she connected the condition of military hospitals with the army's health and capability. Florence concluded with reform proposals.

She then cloistered herself in her tiny Burlington parlor to write, with Sidney's help, the commission report. Presenting statistics in dramatic, not to say novel, fashion, Florence's colored pie charts showed army mortality at home, in peacetime, doubling that of the civilian population (including children and seniors). Poor diet and hygiene, enervating mental and physical effects of ennui (euphemism for drinking), were to blame. Statistics further revealed army mortality at Scutari reaching record levels early in the war but plunging after initiation of basic sanitation and support services. These not only saved lives but also proved cost-effective, since more men were combat ready in less time.

Concerned to capitalize on their report while Crimean horrors were still uppermost in the capricious public mind, cognizant that restructure of the army medical department could hardly be expected to rivet popular interest, afraid army bureaucrats would bury the report, Herbert and Nightingale hatched a plan.

They would not release the report immediately. Instead, Herbert gave war secretary Panmure a private preview. The report's ringing statistics, coupled with its graphic exposé of army living conditions, would grip the public, Herbert took pains to point out. The Bison could thus expect extremely unpleasant questions at the next session of parliament.

That could be avoided if Panmure corrected the worst conditions before the report reached parliament. He could appoint four sub-commissions,* each with power to effect the report's recommendations. Hence, concurrent publication of the report and of orders based on it would "give the prestige that promptitude always carries with it."[10]

---

*The four sub-commissions would bring sanitation to barracks, create an army statistics section, start an army medical school, and reorganize the army medical department. Herbert promised to head each.

Caught between loyalty to the government, which would mean committing to instant reform, and postponing reform, which would mean risking public fury that would certainly rock the government, The Bison wavered. But soon saw the wisdom of giving in to Herbert, however grudgingly.

Parliament rose; politics and society fled sultry, grimy London. Panmure went north to shoot grouse on his ancestral Highland acres. Herbert crossed the sea to fish the streams watering his green Irish estate. "I never intend to tell you how much I owe you," he wrote Nightingale, "for all your help," since "I should never be able to make you understand how helpless my ignorance would have been among the medical Philistines. God bless you."[11]

Fearing momentum would fade if she lessened her focus for even a few weeks, terrified The Bison would cave in to the anti-reform barrage of war-office bureaucrats, Florence insisted on staying at the stuffy Burlington to delineate the duties of the four sub-commissions. "Most anxious"[12] to join WEN at Lea Hurst yet reluctant to leave Flo alone in London, Fanny and Parthe urged her to go north with them. Florence refused. So despite fatigue brought on by the Season's social whirl, not to mention minor ailments (Fanny got diarrhea; Parthe had migraine headaches), mother and sister stayed. "It is a scene worthy of Molière," Flo told Clarkey, "where two people in tolerable and even perfect health, lie on a sofa all day, doing absolutely nothing and persuade themselves and others that they" are "victims of their self-devotion for another who is dying of overwork."[13]

Florence had been subsisting on tea — her pet beverage — during weeks of twenty-hour workdays. Early one morning as Flo got ready to leave for Sutherland's suburban house — where she had gotten into the habit of staying late into the evening — Fanny reproached.

MOTHER: You "look more exhausted than ever."
DAUGHTER: "The luxury of sitting there without fear of interruption" is priceless.
MOTHER: Here at the Burlington you have "no interruption but from those coming on business whom" you "must see" and have "generally sent for."[14]
Besides, you shouldn't be working so far into the night.
DAUGHTER: I must meet the deadline of Sidney Herbert's return.

The next day, Florence, feeling "dismally poorly quite fagged out with Sutherland," went to lie down "for 5 minutes when [statistician Dr.] Farr arrived." She instantly reappeared "apparently as fresh as ever, and set to work on statistics of the most abstruse kind."[15]

WEN offered to come and help look after Flo. "I would not inflict" London's "intolerable" heat and dust on "you even if I thought you could do for her what she requests — which I do not," Fanny replied. "On this intense labor, which calls forth every power, she so entirely forgets herself that she would not eat at all unless the food were put before her & she eats so little at a time that she requires it very often, so that you must not only order it & put it by for her but see that she eats it. & no man can do this."[16]

"I never saw anything like her way of doing all herself," Parthe wrote her father. "She will not let one even write a note if she can help it. The irritable edge of desire for perfection grows upon her."[17]

Exhaustion grew upon her, too. So did another attack of brucellosis. Racing heart, hampered breathing, fever, nausea, and extreme weakness made Flo swallow former sarcasm about the water cure as fit only to ease imagined ailments of the bored and idle rich. "She took," her flabbergasted mother wrote WEN, "a sudden resolution to go to" Malvern Spa. "Nothing would induce her to take anyone but"[18] the family footman. He returned to report all hydrotherapy houses full, save one. It sat high up on a hill. There Florence settled.

She felt as "when recovering from the fever at Balaclava."[19] Untreated, brucellosis typically recurs. And since Victorian medical science knew nothing of the disease, Florence got no treatment. Her physicians diagnosed neurasthenia, a Victorian malady that covered baffling symptoms, possibly psychosomatic, which, in Nightingale's case, the doctors ascribed to "entire exhaustion of every organ from overwork."[20] They prescribed complete physical and mental rest. Besides, they pointed out, a female who engaged in excessive mental activity stood in danger of suffering nervous collapse.

—⁂—

Malvern's hedges were a riot of summer foliage, and wild roses starred the banks. But Nightingale kept to her room. And aside from the hydro-therapist who applied two cold-water packs daily to slow her racing pulse, Florence refused to see anyone.

Except her father. WEN found his "precious child" sitting at her open window deep in contemplation of the wooded, humpback Malvern hills. Flo faced another dilemma. She had sacrificed everything — love, marriage, children born of her body, youth and energy, now her health — to serve God and humanity. Perhaps the time had come to follow urgent medical advice: rest, recoup her strength, then resume work at a less frenetic pace. But if she fell "out on the march who would work the question of reform?"[21]

Florence's "breathing betrays her moments of distress, her power to take food fails her if excited, her nights are sleepless," WEN reported to his worried wife. "Her days may be numbered."[22] Everyone expected Flo soon to die. So did she. Before Florence Nightingale met her maker, she resolved to finish His work.

SUTHERLAND: You can't go on without new blood, which isn't made from tea. Sticky, airless London won't improve your health. Much better to remain at Malvern and rest.

NIGHTINGALE: I resent your well-meaning advice. You, of all people, should know I must seize the moment. Would Herbert have used me if I hadn't been in London, would the commission report have been written so quickly had I not been there?

"I have written myself into" palpitation. "I am lying without my head, without my claws and you all peck at me" as you've done "110 times a day during the last 3 months."[23]

SUTHERLAND: I want you to live, to work. "I admire your heroism and" devotion, but "it is all" in "a weak, perishing body." Am "I to encourage you to wear yourself" out in a "vain attempt to beat not only men, but *time*"?[24]

NIGHTINGALE: If "we are permitted to finish the work which He has given us to do, it matters little how much we suffer in doing it. In fact, the suffering is part of the work & contingent upon the time or period of the world at which we were sent into it to do its work."[25] So please join me at Malvern. Instructions for the four sub-commissions must be ready for Herbert's return in September.

Sutherland himself felt far from well, let alone reluctant to go to Malvern. What will Herbert and I "do when you are buried?"[26] he temporized. She insisted. He came.

—◊—

Florence's second serious illness in as many years, an illness that now endangered her lifework, reform of the army medical department, triggered an outburst against those closest to her—a not uncommon reaction. In dire circumstances, one often blindly heaps blame on those whose love is steadfast.

Flo's wave of acrimony washed over her former gratitude to Fanny for consenting to Kaiserswerth, Harley Street, and Scutari; for Fanny's "anxious tender thought for" me; for acquiescence in Flo's giving "my all of life and health to the Father, to serve whom is life." The "loving remembrance of you will go about with me wherever I am and whatever I do."[27]

Now—"what have mother & sister ever done for me? They like my glory—they like my pretty things. Is there anything else they like in me? I was the same person who went to Harley st. & who went to the Crimea."

Convention expected Florence "to be not only the property of my parents, but the property of my sister." Parthe had hated Flo's Harley Street position. She treated Flo "like a criminal for taking it. And I felt like one, *then & all my life* till within the last 4 years."

"Since I was 24 (probably long before)," Flo had clear "plans & ideas as to" God's work. Having "the largest hospital experience man or woman has ever had," Flo failed to perceive "the plan I formed at 24, for learning in hospitals," as "imprudent."

"Upon what principle my 'family' opposed this inexorably, overbearingly — I do not know — other than the 'principle' of following the world's *words*." Yet now, Fanny and Parthe took credit for promoting what "they called me unprincipled for proposing."

While Flo struggled "through the very steps" needed "to accomplish that for which I am now praised" all "men forsook me — & chiefly my own family. Now, because I have succeeded by an accident which never might have happened," they "praise me."

"Let me say whose support *has* been of 'worth.' 1. my spiritual mother's," Mai Smith's, "without whom I could have done nothing — who has always been a Holy Ghost to me & lately has lived the life of a 'porter's wife' for me — who left her own people to come out to Scutari to me." — "2. that one who has been a mother to me too in another way — mrs. Bracebridge — & 3. singularly enough that of mr. & mrs. Herbert" — "who did not wait to send me to the Crimea" to "support me, as far as they could, in doing God's work."[28]

Without the Herberts, there would have been no Lady with the Lamp. Selina Bracebridge gave, would always give, Florence unqualified emotional and practical support. And where Mai Smith understood, sympathized with, Flo's drive to sacrifice everything for her work, Fanny Nightingale persisted in urging her daughter to work less and spend more time with family.

"For every one of my 18,000 children, for every one of those poor tiresome Harley st. creatures, I have expended more motherly feeling & action in a week than my mother has expended for me in 37 years."

"Even this summer, had I had but ordinary peace & quiet, not to say help, I could have waded through."[29] Fanny and Parthe had deprived Florence of the female family support she should have had and, indeed, craved.

—⚉—

Flo "must have someone's care, she says so herself. She is perfectly helpless."[30] Exceedingly concerned about their daughter's self-imposed isolation, to say nothing of her health, WEN and Fanny appealed to the only person Florence might tolerate.

Deeply pious Aunt Mai committed to "the course before us irrespectively of any private feeling." She promised to unite with Flo "to pursue two objects" that "the great spiritual guide has left for you as" for me. "Help the work as much as possible then to die in" peace. "You know my heart too well my child, my friend, my guide & up lifter, my dearest on earth & in heaven," Mai Smith confided in extravagant contemporary style. "It is the first wish of my heart to pursue the first wish of yours."[31]

Helping with Flo's cause, let alone looking after her, constituted a considerable challenge. Illness made Florence irritable. Impending death made her impatient and more than usually driven to finish the work.

—⁗—

Still "in a very precarious state"[32]—feverish, sleepless, feeble, and sick at the sight of food—Flo returned to London. Mai moved her into the Burlington annex, one of three large buildings that made up the hotel. Facing a quiet street, away from hotel bustle, Nightingale's suite consisted of a double drawing room on its first floor, two bedrooms, a dressing room, and a room for her personal maid above.* Mai settled Florence with the help of her son-in-law.

Arthur Hugh Clough, 1819–1861. Poet and scholar. Married to Nightingale's double cousin Blanche Smith. Clough's commitment to Florence's cause as her close friend and unofficial confidential secretary gave meaning to his unsatisfactory professional life (artist: Samuel Rowse [1860]. © National Portrait Gallery, London).

Scholar and poet Arthur Hugh Clough entered Nightingale's orbit when Mai and Sam Smith engaged him to tutor their son, Shore. Handsome, fine-featured Clough and Blanche, eldest of those little Smiths who had adored Flo since babyhood, fell in love. Clough had neither money nor prospects, so Sam forbade the marriage. Eventually, Clough found a humdrum government post. It earned the young man enough money to support a family but engaged neither his time nor his intellect.

Like many of their compatriots, Blanche and Arthur Clough admired Flo's Crimean feats. And as Mai and Sam's children they knew about Florence's fight to do her cho-

*Nightingale used her spare bedroom to invite busy colleagues working with her into the evening, to "dine and sleep." Mai had separate quarters.

sen work, not to mention that the Crimea had broken her health. Avid to share in Florence's practical, dynamic cause based purely on serving God, Arthur Clough volunteered to be her unofficial secretary.

"Two in one and one in God."[33] Clough effortlessly exchanged the esoteric world of Oxford and poetry for hospital construction and barracks organization. He edited, wrote notes, delivered letters, and acted as sounding board. Clough's sensitive, sunny personality, the smile lurking in his eyes, brought Flo warmth and sympathy. She felt "extraordinarily blessed"[34] to have such an ideal friend as Clough.

—✻—

Faced with the bleak reality of ongoing physical weakness, resolved to serve God and humanity by squeezing every benefit out of the Crimea's harsh lessons, Nightingale decided that she had no alternative but to adopt a new lifestyle. Still young at age thirty-seven, the woman who loved music, enjoyed travel and horseback riding, walked the hill paths above Lea Hurst, inspected medical institutions, and led a normal social life gave up everything to focus her extremely limited physical energy, let alone her unimpaired mental power, on the work she had battled so long and hard to do.

Florence's contemporaries accepted the invalid state as a way for women to carve out independent time and place in a society that openly condoned neither. Lying on her sofa to conserve diminished strength provided Nightingale with privacy, not to mention a shield against any distraction. And frail health liberated Florence from life's daily demands.

She could no longer visit colleagues. They must come to her. And in the interest of efficiency, visitors would have to arrive by appointment.

Mai guarded Flo from anyone she chose not to see — which included family. "Breath so hurried" meant "all talking must be spared except" the essential, and all upset, so "she may devote every energy to the work," Mai explained to Fanny. Florence "alone can give facts," for "she knows the bearings of the whole which no one else has followed, has both the smallest details at her fingers' ends and the great general views of the whole." Were Fanny and Parthe to stay with Flo, it would be hard to keep out visitors; they would come to see the Nightingale ladies, then interrupt Florence. The family must trust to Mai's letters.

"Laboring day after day until she is almost fainting," Flo focused on "the most important work of all" — reaping "the fruit of the report in working the reforms which have been its purpose — they have now not only to work but to fight,"[35] Mai reported.

"They are drawing up the new regulations (but this you must not tell"), Parthe, in turn, told Clarkey. "Nervous of being known to have anything to do with it," Flo would let no one "know what she is about," would "not even tell *us*." Parthe failed to see why Flo killed "herself with work" while others got "all the credit."[36]

Florence cared not one whit for credit. The cause came first. Her presence in the vanguard would harm it. Crimean nemesis Hall and his war-office cohorts hated Nightingale as a meddlesome female who had exposed their failings to Queen and country. Far better to let respected and canny parliamentarian Sidney Herbert lead the charge.

So by the time gray skies and gloomy chill descended on London and damp, dead leaves made sidewalks slippery, Nightingale believed "all that is necessary now, is to keep" Herbert "up to the point."[37] Poor health must not stop him from battling war-office bureaucrats. They were pushing Panmure to defang the four sub-commissions, which the war secretary had promised to empower to execute the royal commission reforms forthwith.

"To keep up to my work, I feel the necessity of having *one* person with me to perform offices, which I am sure my dear mother & Parthe would feel, each for the other though not for herself, that health would not permit," Flo explained to Fanny. Since the moral import of her cause mandated full attention, Florence felt justified in putting work before family. "I have no other plan, then, but to ask aunt Mai to stay with me."

"Such power for headwork as I ever had, I have still, & with that remaining power, I feel called upon to do what I can to rescue the children committed to me from death, from disease, from immorality," Florence wrote Fanny as one mother to another.

"The help & the ease then, which I ask from *you*, my dear mother, is not to misinterpret what I am thus compelled either to say or else to give up my" work. "I have seen literally no one but those whom" business needs "have compelled me to see."

"If I could give companionship or receive it, I would beg you to come & share it," Flo insisted, reluctant to wound a mother she loved deeply. Secure in Fanny's love, Florence still yearned for her full sympathy, for Fanny's endorsement of Flo's allegiance to work.

"I enclose a little nasturtium or something else which the good people here give me for nosegays. It makes the prettiest winter vaseful. I do not remember ever seeing it. You ought to have it. Ever my dear mum, your loving child."[38]

Forced to accept her daughter's new priority, Fanny made a virtue of necessity. She opened Embley's doors to Florence's friends and colleagues. Fanny kept Flo liberally supplied with nourishing soups and jellies; homemade preserves and fresh butter from Embley's well-stocked stillroom; game shot on the estate; succulent grapes from its greenhouses; fruits, vegetables, and flowers from Embley's gardens. Thus, Florence's mother participated, if only a little, in her daughter's life. Affectionate letters crisscrossed between them.

"I always like *your* 'letter' (however much I am 'pressed')," Flo wrote her "dearest Mum ... because you are the *only* person who writes" without "requiring an answer. And that is the real secret of writing to the sick." Everyone "else writes to me questions."[39]

—⁂—

Chronic brucellosis can cause depression — scarcely surprising considering the length, severity, and recurrence of symptoms, not to mention the lack of any known cure. Hence, as the year (1857) waned, Nightingale wrote letters to be delivered after her death.

"You have sometimes" said "you were sorry you had employed me," she told her closest colleague, Sidney Herbert. "I assure you that it has kept me alive."

"I am sorry not to stay alive to do the 'nurses.'" (Use the Nightingale Fund, donations that Britons of all social classes made during the Crimean War to enable Florence to create nurse training.) "I must be willing to go now as I was to go to the East."

"I always thought it the greatest of your kindnesses sending me there."

"I have no fears for the army now. You have always been our 'Cid'*— the true chivalrous sort — which is to be the defender of what is weak & ugly & dirty & undefended.... You are so now more than ever for us" — meaning "the troops & me."

"I hope you will have no chivalrous ideas about what is 'due' to my 'memory.' The only thing that can be 'due' to me is what is good for the troops."[40]

Flo asked lawyer uncle Sam to help with her will. She bequeathed the Nightingale Fund to St. Thomas's Hospital to establish a nurse training school. All but five hundred pounds of the substantial sum Florence would inherit from her parents must be used to build a model barrack based on her ideas. Nightingale named Herbert, her Crimean friend, Commissioner John McNeill, and sanitarian Sutherland as best able to put the plan into effect.

The five hundred pounds should go to Blanche and Arthur Clough "*now*—and I had rather they should not say thank you."[41] Cash-strapped Clough could use the money to move his family into a better house. He

*A play on Sidney, Herbert's given name. El Cid, eleventh-century Spanish general and national hero, was the epitome of nobility and chivalry. Spain's peasants adopted El Cid as theirs.

declined Flo's bequest. She rejected Clough's refusal. "If I could give him £10,000 a year, it would be a poor acknowledgment of what he has done for"[42] me.

Nightingale's will included legacies to her closest family, but most meaningful were personal keepsakes for intimates including Selina Bracebridge, Hilary Bonham-Carter, Liz Herbert, Clarkey Mohl, and Reverend Mother Mary Clare Moore. Florence asked to be buried with her "children" at Scutari's British military cemetery.

Concomitantly, war secretary Lord Panmure kept his promise. He created the four sub-commissions.

18

"The welfare and efficiency of the British Army"

Nine thousand of my children are lying, from causes which might have been prevented, in their forgotten graves.[1] — Florence Nightingale.

No woman ever before directed the labors of a government office.[2] — Florence Nightingale

Winter (1858) winds buffeted bare trees under lowering skies. One could scarcely believe the deadened grass in London parks would ever again be carpeted with daffodils. Snug in her Burlington hotel suite amidst "beautiful flowers sent her by all sorts of people," with every available surface covered with papers "and plans of new hospitals,"[3] Florence Nightingale found that hotel life facilitated focus on the four sub-commissions.* Sidney Herbert headed each. Nightingale motivated and directed behind-the-scenes.

Hers the genius for organization. His the genius for politics. Silence prevailed as Florence wrote regulations to introduce sanitation to, and improve efficiency at, the cheerless barracks and dreary military hospitals Sidney traveled the country to inspect. "I supplied the detail, the knowledge of the actual working of an army, in which official men are so deficient; he supplied the political weight."[4] Herbert transposed Nightingale's energy and inspiration, her grasp of wide-ranging principles and command of particulars, into reform of the army medical system.

Constantly in contact, they delighted in each other's company. She liked his charm and sparkling conversation. He liked her mind and sense of humor.

Florence had scant sympathy for Sidney's failing health. She worked at full steam despite illness. So should he.

Herbert's wife agreed. Committed to Flo and Sidney's cause, Liz functioned as Sidney's private secretary. She copied memoranda, made sure Florence got them, advised when her husband would call and what he wanted

---

*Army sanitation, medical statistics, medical school, and medical department restructure.

to discuss. "May we dine with you on Sunday?" Liz asked her "dearest Flo." "Yours ever lovingly."[5]

Nightingale hounded Herbert. He scolded her. Neither praised the other. "We were identified. No other acknowledgment was needed."[6]

—⧿⧿—

The four sub-commissions were well underway when Great Britain's government released the royal commission report. But thanks to war-office diehards, its most telling sections — Nightingale's confidential report to war secretary Panmure,* her testimony before the royal commission — had been omitted. So Florence let fly her most effective weapon: public opinion.

With help from her companion, aunt Mai, and unofficial private secretary Arthur Clough, Nightingale prepared her eight-hundred-page *Notes on Army Health* for publication. And underwrote the expense.

Pioneering the presentation of statistics, *Notes on Army Health* featured colored charts. They proved that preventable disease caused many more Crimean deaths than war — and that barrack mortality in Britain, in peacetime, doubled that of civilian life. The solution: introduce hygiene into military facilities so as to provide a healthy environment, and restructure the army medical department to improve management efficiency.

Nightingale and the Herberts pulled strings to get *Notes on Army Health* publicized. They sent copies to Queen Victoria, cabinet members, war-office officials, and other notables. Florence tantalized leading journalists, like her friend Harriet Martineau,† with tidbits.

Consequently, royal commissioner Dr. Thomas Alexander, one of Nightingale's Crimean cronies, became army medical department chief rather than her Crimean nemesis, Dr. John Hall. Another reform-minded royal commissioner joined the army medical department to create a statistics section. Reformer and engineer Douglas Galton, husband of Florence's beautiful cousin and erstwhile bosom friend, Marianne Nicholson (later estranged over

---

Notes Affecting the Health, Efficiency, and Hospital Administration of the British Army, henceforth referred to as *Notes on Army Health*.

†One of Britain's most famous political journalists, Harriet Martineau came from the same social milieu as Florence. Thus the two women shared a heritage of political liberalism and religious dissent.

Unable to taste and smell, deaf by age twenty, Harriet, like Florence, chose to remain single, yet loved children. Martineau published the first of her *Stories from Political Economy* while Nightingale still struggled against "the prison called family."

Twice severe illness confined Martineau to a couch but failed to stop her literary and philanthropic life. Florence supplied her (anonymously) with public health data, which Harriet disseminated to the public in her capacity as the *Daily News* leader writer. Relying heavily on Nightingale's input, Martineau's collected essays, published as the best-selling *England and Her Soldiers*, further spread her friend's ideas.

Flo's refusal to marry her brother Henry but now reconciled to the point where Florence stood godmother to one of her children), got a senior appointment. Galton became the army's key authority on barrack building, water supply, drainage, heating, and ventilation. And parliament passed laws, based on royal commission report statistics, to improve army conditions. "To you more than to any other man or woman alive will henceforth be due the welfare and efficiency of the British army,"[7] congratulated John McNeill, Florence's friend and support since Crimean days.

—ᴡ—

Spiritual reflection absorbed Nightingale's limited leisure time and wakeful night hours. Revisiting her unpublished *Suggestions for Thought*, written during Florence's struggle to escape "the prison called family," she expanded the three-volume tome from a guide to religion for artisans into one for those who doubted religion altogether.

God willed "only good." He left "evil in the world" solely to "stimulate human faculties by" constant "struggle against every form of it."[8] The true meaning of God, the only possible match with morality, nature, and history, consisted of a universal being. Law formed its essence. God's laws were the laws of life — found via experience, search, and orderly assessment (statistics). These allowed humans to know God's character. God's soul remained eternally a mystery.

Florence consulted a selected few when rewriting *Suggestions for Thought*. Her father stood among them. "I shall always be well enough to see *you* as long as this mortal coil is on me," Flo wrote him. She promised to "keep all Sunday vacant ... I should like to have you twice, please, say at 11½ and 3½."[9]

When Nightingale had finished *Suggestions for Thought*, she asked her father and some trusted others for their critique. Some advised publication with minor changes. Steadfast friend McNeill, former suitor Monckton Milnes, and sanitation expert Sutherland agreed on the need for major revisions. So did a new acquaintance.

> I am the great professor Jowett
> What there is to know, I know it.
> I am the master of Balliol college
> And what I don't know isn't knowledge.[10]

Oxford's living legend received an anonymous copy of *Suggestions for Thought* from Arthur Clough, his close friend and Nightingale's cousin-in-law as well as unofficial private secretary. Clough's action initiated a lively correspondence and lifelong intimacy.

"I do so like"[11] Benjamin Jowett, Florence jotted on one of his first letters.

Because Jowett "had more character than anybody I ever knew." He "spoke as he thought and he did as he spoke." Jowett "mastered life — life that did not master him — *that* was what the spirit of life was in him."[12]

His ability always to find "the better part of us"[13] empowered Jowett to influence young minds. That turned him into a man of action, guaranteed to rouse Nightingale's esteem no less than Jowett's erudition. Respecting her as having "the greatest strength of mind of any woman"[14] he knew, the short, chubby bachelor treated Florence as an equal in intellect and commitment to career.

In the end, she felt neither need nor inclination (nor did Nightingale have the patience) to revise *Suggestions for Thought*. The therapy of self-expression and discipline of writing her first version helped con-

Benjamin Jowett, 1817–1893. Greek scholar, master of Oxford University's Balliol College, and vice-chancellor. The only intimate friend whose chiding Nightingale accepted (artists: Thomas and George Shrimpton, after unknown artist. © National Portrait Gallery, London).

quer despair and clarify what Florence must do. This version defined her mature philosophy and articulated her conversion from Cassandra, who saw evil (women could not control their lives) but lacked the means to correct it, to a national figure with power to reverse the waste of female talent. So Nightingale contented herself with having a limited edition of *Suggestions* privately printed.

—⁂—

Concomitantly, Florence wrote her comprehensive *Subsidiary Notes as to the Introduction of Female Nursing into Military Hospitals in Peace and War*. Besides, Charles Bracebridge helped her prepare and publish *Statement to Subscribers*. It detailed the donations given Nightingale for use in war hospitals and showed precisely how each penny had been spent.

Because, meanwhile, her experience with Netley army hospital had illuminated glaring general ignorance about hospital construction, Florence tackled the subject in between writing sanitary regulations for army facilities. Her friend and early supporter the famous reformer Lord Shaftesbury had Nightingale's papers presented at the Social Science congress. Their positive reception encouraged Florence to develop these ideas into a book.

"It may seem a strange principle to enunciate as the very first requirement of a hospital that it should do the sick no harm." *Notes on Hospitals* condemned British medical institutions as strangers to sanitation. Walls dripped with damp, even grew fungus. Filth covered the floors of close-packed wards. Patients suffered inept nursing, dirty beds, scant and often inedible food. "Mortality in hospitals, especially those of large crowded cities, is very much higher than" death among "the same class of patient treated *out* of hospital."[15]

Solution: a discrete pavilion or wing for each illness to avert infection by confining a particular disease; windows on both sides for cross-ventilation and direct sunlight. Such an arrangement had the added advantage of allowing the head nurse to see every patient in her wing, which would improve nursing efficiency.

Notes on Hospitals transformed the concept of hospital construction and management. Its author became *the* expert despite being an invalid, and female, to boot. Hospital builders throughout Britain and her empire, not to mention Continental crowned heads, consulted Nightingale. And because her ideas caught public attention, so did mayors and philanthropists.

Florence's already ample correspondence multiplied. She responded generously. "It is impossible to understand on what principles he has placed his w.c. in the middle of the length of one side, & his scullery opposite," she replied to one request for comments. "The result would be that the scullery would become a mere gossiping place for patients & orderlies. And, whenever the wind blew against the side, where the w. c. is, the foul air, incident to military hospital w.c's, would be carried directly into the wards."[16]

At the same time Nightingale and her statistician friend and colleague William Farr designed a model form. It would promote uniform and accurate data gathering for assessment of hospital mortality. Several institutions agreed to use the form. And Farr presented it at the London meeting of the international statistical congress.[17] "Delegates from every civilized country come," Florence told her father. "They meet in my rooms a good deal for business (I of course not seeing them) under dr. Farr's presidency — and I am obliged to give them to eat."

"Now I want you to send me all your flowers, all your fruit, all your vegetables, in fact *all* you have got, for this great occasion."[18]

Nightingale had recently been extremely unwell but rallied to invite delegates to a series of breakfasts. Close friend and favorite cousin Hilary Bonham-Carter (temporarily relieving Aunt Mai, absent on a well-deserved rest with her family) acted as hostess. "Take care that the cream for breakfast is not turned," Florence reminded. "Put back dr. X's big book where he can see it when drinking his tea."[19]

The congress adopted her forms, but conversion proved too onerous for general use.

—ɯ—

Nightingale kept out of the public eye, so most people thought she had retired. *Notes on Nursing* proved otherwise.

"This is a work of genius if ever I saw one," newspaper columnist Harriet Martineau enthused after receiving an advance copy from her friend Florence for publicity purposes. *Notes on Nursing* "is so real and so intense." Martineau thought the book would "create an order of nurses before it has finished its work."[20]

An instant best seller, the little book went into many editions in Britain and the United States, besides translations into French, German, Italian, Swedish and, in 1974, Japanese. *Notes on Nursing* kept current because its author spoke to the fundamental art and science of nursing based on her experience as both nurse and patient.

Florence wrote for the majority of nurses who, at that time, worked in private houses. To keep people free of hospitals, the nurse must bear in mind that "five essential points"[21]—pure air, untainted water, efficient drainage, cleanliness, and light—determined her patient's health.

Whether in private houses or public hospitals, sufferings "generally considered to be inevitable and incident to the disease" are "often not symptoms of the disease," but "of something quite different—of the want of fresh air, or of light, or of warmth, or of quiet, or of cleanliness, or of punctuality and care in the administration of diet."[22]

"The very first canon of nursing," the "first essential to the patient," is: "KEEP THE AIR HE BREATHES AS PURE AS THE EXTERNAL AIR, WITHOUT CHILLING HIM."[23]

"Dread of night air" forms an "extraordinary fallacy." What "air can we breathe at night but night air? The choice is between pure night air from without, and foul night air from within. Most people prefer the latter." An "open window" will not "hurt anyone."[24]

"Of the fatal effects" of "effluvia from the excreta it would seem unnecessary to speak, were they not so constantly neglected," Nightingale fearlessly tackled a taboo topic. "Concealing the utensil behind the valance of the beds seems all the precaution" thought "necessary for safety in private nursing. Did you but think for one moment of the atmosphere under that bed, the saturation of the under side of the mattress with the warm evaporations, you would be startled and frightened too"![25]

Notes on Nursing invigorated the Victorian ideal of the nurturing female with a strong vein of practicality.

—⚏—

A handsome and well-above-average-height gentleman had, meanwhile, been haunting the Burlington. Almost twenty years Nightingale's senior, the liberal member of parliament and wealthy widower Sir Harry Verney, owner of historic Claydon House, devoted himself to improving the lot of laborers on his Buckinghamshire estate.

Enough innuendo exists, but no evidence, that Verney wanted to marry Florence. Regardless, by attracting his attention she fulfilled her sisterly duty. For without Verney calling on Florence to consult about reform issues, he would not have met Parthe.

"*She* likes it very much," Flo said of her sister's marriage. That is the main thing—"and my father is very fond of sir Harry Verney, which is the next best thing. He is old and rich, which is a disadvantage. He is active, has a will of his own and 4 children ready-made, which is an advantage. Unmarried life, at least in our class, takes everything & gives nothing back." Hence, "on the whole, I think these reflections tend to approbation."[26]

Thrilled at the prospect of her precious firstborn becoming Lady Verney and mistress of Claydon, Fanny lessened her attempts to dissuade Flo from overworking and focused on Parthe's wedding. Her sister's marriage brought Florence the added advantage of rooting another committed reformer into her closest circle. And since WEN gave Parthe a dowry, he increased Flo's allowance. As well, Florence's father showed his pride and support by promising to pay, without question, all her board and lodging bills. Of greatest benefit to Flo, however, Parthe begin to lead her own life rather than fixating on her sister.

—⚏—

Feeling too ill to attend Parthe's wedding at Embley that June (1858), certain she would soon die, Florence stayed in London to press on with the work she loved and drove herself at a frantic pace to finish. Still, "I must thank you my own self for your grapes," Flo wrote her "dearest" Liz Herbert. Reverend Mother Moore "has been and is dangerously ill. She has had all her food from here, and your grapes have almost kept both her and me."[27]

At the same time Nightingale initiated sanitary reform in her household. The Burlington maids had no clue about household hygiene, so Florence promised them the equivalent of a doctor's fee if they kept open (rather than

tightly shut) the windows in her suite. And when Flo's favorite My Boy Shore
went house-hunting for his bride and himself, Flo extracted from Shore a
signed and witnessed promise to make no purchase until her friend and colleague sanitary expert Sutherland had inspected the drains.

Intimate friend Selina Bracebridge helped Florence brighten her Burlington suite with new carpets and curtains. Other friends sent fresh flowers and
plants. "I should be ashamed if (in the worst of times) I had *ever* given *my*
patients what they give me here."[28] So Fanny enhanced the Burlington's
kitchen with well-hung game, succulent greenhouse peaches, raspberries and
gooseberries from the garden, fresh eggs, and cream.

When golden asters were in glory Nightingale returned to Malvern Spa
for a week of fresh air and cold-water packs. Railway officials cleared space
on the platform, shooed away the curious, and hushed the noisy. Station staff
then doffed their hats as Crimean veterans carried Florence's special invalid
carriage[29] as if she were a celestial being.

Aunt Mai Smith went along as guardian. Mai's son-in-law Arthur Clough
accompanied Flo as courier, even though his wife expected the imminent
birth of their first child. Because Mai's daughter wanted "it to be so."[30]

"It's no small matter to see your handwriting again," WEN wrote after
having kept Flo company, "and to make believe that you are a good deal more
than half alive. But the worst of it is, that there's no depending upon you for
any persistence in curing yourself, while you have so many others to cure."[31]

The next year (1859) Lord Palmerston returned to the premiership. He
asked ailing Sidney Herbert to be war secretary. Chair of the British and
Indian army* commissions, plus the four sub-commissions, Herbert quailed
at the enormous task involved in taking on the war office. "But I know," he
wrote Nightingale, "you will be pleased at my being there."[32]

She spurred the four sub-commissions to make maximum use of Herbert's tenure. They stepped up redesign of barracks and hospitals to improve
sanitation. Florence drafted guidelines for streamlining purveyors' duties. She
restructured collection of army medical statistics and insisted on their annual
publication.

As for Nightingale's pet project, the army medical school, she wrote its
regulations in consultation with the Queen's physician and royal commission
member James Clark. Florence wanted to make sure army doctors got the same
fine medical education as civilians. She nominated the professors and recruited

---

*The government had formed a royal commission to do for its army in India what the first royal
commission did and continued to do for the army in Britain.

Crimean friends to teach — among other vital subjects — military hygiene. The school turned to Nightingale over each administrative, and almost every other, issue. Her meticulous attention guaranteed the school's survival.

Florence insisted that a new premise underlie the radically restructured army medical department: the army bore as much responsibility for the soldier's wellness as for his illness.

And Herbert prodded war-office diehards to admit what Nightingale advocated. The common soldier had a mind. Coffee rooms, reading rooms, workshops, even gyms appeared in barracks and hospitals. Britain's military base at Gibraltar got an exceptionally well-equipped reading room thanks to the generosity of Florence, Harriet Martineau, and their circle of friends.

Army mortality dropped. Nightingale publicized the statistics in colored diagrams for maximum impact. Three years of reform had resulted in a 50 percent decline of deaths at domestic barracks. Total mortality from all diseases decreased to less than mortality from a single disease.[33]

Still, the "very slow" and "enormously expensive" war office could too easily negate the secretary's intentions through its various "sub-departments and those of each of the sub-departments by every other."[34] Reform must be secured.

Hence, Nightingale and Herbert undertook a Herculean task. Reform the war office. With Crimean experience in mind, they constructed a plan. It would streamline process, abolish splintered responsibility, specify the duties of each position, hold every department head accountable for his fiefdom, and give him direct access to the war secretary. Herbert took charge of getting the changes through parliament.

—◊—

Brucellosis returned in full force, meanwhile. Not yet forty, frail and emaciated, Florence again suffered fainting, tachycardia, labored breathing, and severe indigestion as well as flushed face and hands — typical of the disease's recurrence. Death seemed near.

"Lying on her couch, wrapt up in her delicate blanket, her little head resting on the pillow peeping from the blanket,"[35] Florence allowed herself a brief rest.

Fanny came. Feeling unwell herself, she had not seen Flo for several months. Speaking with an effort, Florence greeted her mother "as if we had only just been parted, very affectionately," but nervously, "as if she feared to touch" on fraught subjects. Reclining "on pillows in a blue drifting gown, her hair so picturesquely arranged, her expression most trusting, hardly harmonizing with the trenchant things she sometimes says, her sweet little hands lying there ready for action."[36]

Fanny hazarded the suggestion that Flo renounce work, at least temporarily, to recover at Embley amidst loving family. "My people might give me more credit," Florence retorted. "Never was life & health employed or given up so deliberately as I have mine. I only ask that my people will think themselves & say to others, at least she did deliberately what she thought" right. "No woman ever before directed the labors of a government office. She must be" sole "judge as to the when & the how if a woman chooses to undertake to direct men over whom she can have no legitimate or recognized control."

Florence regretted having "let visitors talk to me to the last moment before a meal, thereby incapacitating me for food & sleep." She regretted receiving "two visits on the same day — after 5 o'clock — things which always bring on my spasm &c. These & such like are the things I regret & not that I have done my work, as long as God would let me."[37]

Her "children" wanted to pray for Nightingale. "I had rather have the men's prayers than a vote of thanks from" parliament. But "I should not like a war office circular to order them to do it," Flo told the war secretary's wife. Because then, Liz Herbert "must have a w. o. circular to almighty God to tell him to listen," and "kill a Queen's messenger to take it." So "the men had better be left to pray willingly, please."[38]

Work mandated London. Health mandated a change. So rather than return to Malvern, Nightingale sought fresh air closer to the capital. A scant few miles from its center, Hampstead suburb, surrounded by the eponymous hilly, wooded, and still wild heath, also had the advantage of proximity to sanitary expert Sutherland's home at Highgate.

Reclining on a couch in the airy, sun-drenched drawing room of the lodging kind Mrs. Sutherland helped Mai Smith find, Florence worked. Sutherland and Clough came daily. Cousin Hilary kept Flo company when Mai took a well-earned, albeit brief, respite with her family. War-office work also chained Sidney Herbert to London; he rode out to Hampstead almost every evening. Liz approved. Fresh air and exercise were good for Sidney. "I wonder," she asked her "dearest Flo," whether "you will give Sidney a bed there some Saturday or Sunday? It saves his life getting out of town to sleep and I am always intriguing to bring it about."[39]

Clarkey and her husband, Julius Mohl (who had connections to Persia through his Oriental studies), presented Flo with a family of pure-bred Persian cats. At least one could usually be found curled up at the foot of her sofa, another crouched on Florence's shoulder while she worked.

[Clough's baby] came in its little flannel coat to see me. No one [prepared] me for its royalty. It sat quite upright but would not say a word. [The cats] jumped up [on it.] It put out its hand with a kind of gracious dignity and caressed them. [They] responded in a humble grateful way, quite cowed by infant majesty. Then it put out its little bare cold feet for me to warm, which when I did, it smiled. [After] twenty minutes, it waved its hand to go away, still without speaking a word.[40]

"A pet or baby is an excellent companion for the convalescent," Nightingale had written in her *Notes on Nursing*.

—m—

Witty Uncle Sam, now a treasury department official, took care of all Flo's accounting and business matters. He also handled her many extraneous letters, a task their shared sense of humor facilitated.

LETTER: from a lady who "loved and honored" Nightingale and looked forward to meeting her someday.

FLO TO SAM: "Please choke off this woman and tell her that I shall *never* be well enough to see her, either here or *hereafter*."

LETTER: from a cleric with a "secret cure." He wanted to share it only with Florence.

FLO TO SAM: "These miserable ecclesiastical quacks! Could you give them a lesson? What would they think of me did I possess such a discovery and keep it secret?"[41]

In ceding his wife to Flo for months on end—without even counting the year at Scutari—Sam had agreed that Mai put her niece, let alone her niece's cause, before claims of husband and children. But now Sam wanted Mai at home. Wary of confronting Florence, Sam made his wishes known by way of his sister Fanny. Flo flared up. Impossible to get her work done without Mai.

Shield, spokesperson, comfort, Mai had become crucial to Flo. The confined world of the sickroom, to say nothing of her niece's looming death, intensified Mai's devotion to Florence personally as well as to her work. Flo likened their relationship to that of two lovers—"two in one and one in God." She felt "extraordinarily blest"[42] to have such an ideal friend and willing coworker in God's service.

Everyone gave in to Florence. But when Mai's daughter Beatrice got engaged to be married, she pleaded that her mother come home. Sam gave his wife an ultimatum: her family or Florence. Mai chose family.

Flo "had looked" on Mai "almost as God ever since I was 6 years old." Now it seemed as if "God himself turned (in her) into a passionate unjust old woman—there are things worse than death."[43] In a fog of brucellosis-induced bitterness and depression, more than ordinarily in need of reassurance, Florence saw Mai's departure as betrayal "on the part of my dearest and nearest."*[44]

Never mind her extreme physical debility, how could Mai leave in the midst of Flo and Sidney's crowning achievement — the achievement that would set the seal on all their other reforms: reform of the war office itself?

—◊—

WEN and Fanny did not want Flo to be alone. Hence, cousin Hilary moved into the Burlington. Clough still came daily despite feeling ill. And ignoring fever, nausea, and migraine headaches, so did war secretary Sidney Herbert despite having to cope with pressing issues other than fighting officials over reform.

Flo pushed him on one side, his wife on the other. Sidney carried on. But told Liz that each day of war-office and House of Commons work took a day off his life.

Herbert's doctors diagnosed a terminal kidney disease. They prescribed the usual panacea — total rest. Liz conferred with Flo. They agreed that the cause must come first. Florence would convince Sidney to keep the war office — which he disliked. Liz would talk her husband into giving up the stuffy, raucous House of Commons — where he excelled as a negotiator. Hence, Prime Minister Palmerston asked the Queen to ennoble Sidney. She created him Lord Herbert of Lea so that he could sit in the sedate House of Lords.

Sidney's shaky health terrified Florence. No one else could so effectively guard her children against another Crimean calamity. Frantic, she drove herself yet harder and, refusing to face facts, drove Herbert, too. "It is *not* true that you cannot (sometimes) absolutely mend a damaged organ, almost always keep it comfortably going for many years, by giving nature fair play." Nothing "in your constitution" makes "it evident that disease is getting the upper hand. On the contrary."[45]

---

*Florence soon overcame her resentment. Aunt and niece remained close.

19

Annus Horribilis

"My idea of a friend is: one who will & can join with you in work the sole purpose of which is to serve God.

"During the five" years "I worked with Sidney Herbert every day and nearly all day, from the moment he came into the room no other idea came in but that of doing the work, with the best of our powers, in the service of God." That "is heaven! and is what makes me say: I have had my heaven."[1]— Florence Nightingale

Frantic over Herbert's failing health, dejected at the sluggish pace of war-office reform, debilitated by the "grasping action" of her heart, unable to work if she gave in to the temptation of getting up (the effort to dress drained her), Nightingale, at midyear (1861), saw the worst of illness as "the morbid mind of a person who has *no* variety, *no* amusement, *no* gratification or change of any kind." Ingrained insecurities blended with brucellosis-induced depression to make Florence forever think she "might do more or I had better not have done what I did do."[2]

Bereft of the spiritual mother who best knew how to put her in a good mood, Florence faced a dilemma with Mai Smith's replacement.

Flo thought it wrong, she told close friend, cousin, and now companion Hilary Bonham-Carter, to "absorb your life in letter writing and house-keeping."[3]

Sincerely devout Hilary, however, felt it an honor to help Flo in her great work for God and humanity. Besides, Hilary protested, she loved being with Flo.

Still, Florence felt at fault. How could she, who had to fight so hard to do her chosen work, be selfish enough to keep her cousin from using her artistic talent? Flo thought she should encourage Hilary to pursue a career in art, not take her away from it.

But Hilary averred that her cousin should not, must not, live alone.

Hilary's leaving would be like amputating a limb, said Florence. Nevertheless, she must go.

"If she is as useful to you as a limb," why "amputate her"? close friend Clarkey wrote from Paris. "Keep her." Hilary "loves you better than anyone else does and it would be balm to her poor worn-out spirit" to be "useful to you." If "she is a limb to you, you are the very person for her, for she dotes on you."[4]

God gave Hilary talent, Flo replied. She, of all people, must not stop Hilary from using it.

—◆—

Three losses within a year (1860–1861): Mai, Hilary, and the reformist army medical department chief Dr. Thomas Alexander, who died suddenly. Next, Nightingale's informal secretary, cousin-in-law and close friend, Arthur Clough, fell ill. Only complete rest in a warm climate would cure him. Florence's "hard earned savings"[5] helped fund Arthur's travel to southern Europe. "A man of rare mind and temper," his absence created a chasm in her inner circle. Clough "helped me immensely, tho' not officially — by his sound judgment, & constant sympathy."[6]

Petrified, meanwhile, at the prospect of losing her premier ally, loath to accept Sidney Herbert's dire medical prognosis, Flo urged his wife and her friend to get a second opinion. "You do not know how strong a temptation it is to a" diligent doctor "to give such a" diagnosis. It would relieve him of "terrible responsibility, if he could persuade" Sidney "into giving up all work," Florence wrote Liz. Anyway, "leaving political life or any life-interest *altogether* is more likely to kill than cure — always."[7]

All doctors agreed that Herbert had acute nephritis. Unable any further to carry out the duties of war secretary, he resigned.

A few weeks later, Sidney died of kidney failure. "Poor Florence! Our joint work unfinished,"[8] he lamented on his deathbed.

Herbert's death dealt Nightingale the most cruel possible blow. She lost not only a cherished and supportive friend of fourteen years but also her essential partner in the battle for army medical reform. "Without him I could do nothing."[9]

At this, the nadir of her life, Florence turned to Fanny. "I have lost all," Flo wrote her mother. "All the others have children or some high and inspiring interest to live for — while I have lost husband* and children and all."[10] Yes, Flo had defied her mother by rejecting marriage and insisting on a nursing career, had kept Fanny at arm's length after breaking down with brucellosis

---

*No whiff of evidence exists to suggest anything remotely romantic or sexual in Florence and Sidney's relationship despite both being attractive to the opposite sex. Their union rested on the common purpose of serving God and humanity, which Herbert's wife fully supported.

at the Burlington. But Flo, nonetheless, felt deeply connected to Fanny, still craved her support, her approval. Now that Florence faced the "dreary hopeless struggle"[11] alone, she cried out for her mother.

Yet, Flo scarcely knew "what to say about your coming tomorrow. Even ten minutes talk with those I love best secures me a night of agony and a week of feverish exhaustion.... If you could" just "come in and kiss me, that would be a great delight. But there must be no talk, specially not about anything agitating."*[12]

—m—

Guilt consumed Nightingale. Her physician friend and sanitarian colleague John Sutherland assured Florence that "work in this last 6 months had not in any way increased"[13] Sidney Herbert's illness. Still, Nightingale felt she had used her debility and imminent death to force him into overwork. When Sidney resigned from the war office, she even told her dying friend that no man "in my day has thrown away so noble a game with all the winning cards in his hands." And "his angelic temper with" me "I shall never forget."[14] Nightingale "did not know till the last how the failure of his energy to carry out the finishing stroke," the "re-organization of the war office, had broken his heart — & how it hastened his death."[15]

"I know of no widow more desolate that I."[16]

Herbert's actual widow leaned on his spiritual widow. "You know all I have to bear more than anyone else,"[17] Liz confided to Flo. Liz's "chief comfort" consisted of "a little Chinese dog of his" that came to "kiss her eyelids & lick the tears from her cheeks. My cat does just the same to me."[18]

WEN's words found the most direct path to his favorite daughter's heart. "Your sympathy is very dear to me," Flo replied. "So few people know in the least what I have lost in my dear master.[†] Indeed I know no one but myself who had it to lose. For no two people pursue together the same object as I did with him." He took "my life with him. My work, the object of my life, the means to do it, all in one, depart with him."

"Grief fills the room up of my absent" master. I cannot say "it walks up & down" with me. For I don't walk up & down. But it "eats & sleeps & wakes with me."

"Parthe has found time & strength to write me 8 closely written pages of worry, worry, worry." This "is the *third* time this fatal year" she chose "my time of deepest misery & distress to give me a scold 8 pages long."[19]

---

*Fanny persisted to try to persuade Florence to work less and see more of her family and friends.

†Although theirs had been a partnership of equals, Nightingale honored Herbert's memory by referring to him as her "master."

—m—

Rather than recalling Herbert as "the first war minister who ever seriously" troubled "to master a difficult subject so wisely and so well as to be able to husband the resources of this country" to "preserve the efficiency of its defenders,"[20] the tepid press obituaries focused on problems that had bedeviled Herbert's Crimean War tenure. Furious, his family and friends turned to Florence. Casting aside sorrow, anger at the newspapers, and despair at war-office bureaucrats beginning to unravel Herbert's reforms, Nightingale abandoned the desolate beauty of airy, healthy Hampstead heath for the grimy streets of scorching London where her papers were stacked in the Burlington suite. Two weeks of maniacal work produced *Private and Confidential. Sidney Herbert— on His Services to the Army*.[21]

Florence had the pamphlet printed (anonymously), distributed, and publicized. People should know what "a man struggling with death" did, know "he thought so much more of what he had not done than of what he had done … know that all his latter suffering years were filled not by selfish desire for his own salvation" but by "exertion for our benefit,"[22] Nightingale impressed on her friend the political economist and popular newspaper columnist Harriet Martineau.

Feeling extremely ill, Florence then holed up at Hampstead. She forbade Uncle Sam to give anyone her address. All letters must go through him. Nightingale meant to nurse her sorrow in solitude.

—m—

"Desperate guerilla warfare ending in so" little made Florence "impatient of life." She, "who could once do so much," felt "glad to end a" day, "gladder to end a night, gladder still to end a month."[23] Beset by another bout of brucellosis, dejected at what she saw as the end of reform and the pointless sacrifice of her health, besides groping her way though a fog of grief over Herbert, Nightingale had to bear another blow.

Arthur Clough died. Florence had always felt herself "a great drag on" his "health and spirits, a much greater one than I should have chosen to be, if I had not promised him to die sooner."[24] Considering "the inanities and blundering harasses" that Clough willingly undertook, he seemed "like a racehorse harnessed to a coal truck.... 'Oh Jonathan my brother Jonathan, my love to thee was very great, passing the love of women.'"[25]

He had been told, Arthur's close friend wrote Blanche Clough, that Arthur died from a "fatal weakness of the brain" due to "overwork in the cause of Florence Nightingale."[26]

Blanche had wanted Arthur to "give up all the money-making and working for F. Nightingale which had worn him out," she replied. But "it would have been utterly vain to attempt to persuade him."[27]

Troubled by gossip about having taken advantage of Clough, lonely and grieving, Florence hungered for sympathy. Oxford scholar and theologian Benjamin Jowett, the correspondent Nightingale had met through his friendship with Clough, seemed a practical clergyman; Jowett thought Christian conduct more important than doctrine. So Florence invited him to give her the sacrament. Thereafter, Jowett gave Florence Holy Communion every month. Flo often invited others to join her — intimate friends like Selina Bracebridge or family members: cousin Hilary; Clough's widow, cousin Blanche; Aunt Mai; and if in town, WEN, Fanny, or Parthe and her husband, Harry Verney.

Nightingale and Jowett's frequent and wide-ranging letters developed a warm friendship. "I hope you cultivate peace of mind." No "one has more right to do so."[28] Troubled at "your solitary sufferings — you to whom others owe so much," Jowett thought Florence's desire for death "natural & not" a "subject of self-reproach." God had let her "do great things for your fellow creatures. But far more may be done in the next ten years." Do "not desert your post."[29]

When autumn mists crept over Hampstead heath, brucellosis struck with particular cruelty. Besides the usual tachycardia, nausea, insomnia, and depression, acute spinal pain now assailed Nightingale. She could not walk.

Britain's leading spinal specialist agreed with Florence's doctors that anxiety and sorrow caused "congestion of the spine, which leads straight to paralysis. And they say I must not write letters — wherefore I do it all the more,"[30] Flo told close friend Clarkey.

Not yet forty-two, bedridden, alone in lodgings, Florence mourned her failure, the wreck of her work. Your "imagination is so great a part of" your life, Clarkey said, "that if a crack is come to some of the images" you have "stood up there, all of fine china," you see "the crack for ever and can't look at anything else."[31]

Sidney Herbert's death did destroy Nightingale's dream of war-office reform. But not before army mortality had fallen precipitously. Barracks were sanitary and had recreation facilities. An army medical school gave military doctors the same fine training as civilians. And an army cooks training school, started in consultation with Florence's Crimean colleague chef Alexis Soyer, assured the troops decent food. Through Herbert, Nightingale had brought Britons to acknowledge their stake in army health. Yes, lives had been needlessly lost even in peacetime, but by proving they could be saved Sidney and Florence drove an indelible dent in public apathy.

Submerged in pain and sorrow, Nightingale also failed to realize the impact of her Crimean work on public opinion. Every conceivable kind of charitable group aiding the injured and working for army welfare solicited her counsel. When civil war broke out in America (1861), the U.S. government sought Florence's advice on establishing army hospitals. And a women's relief organization prodded the U.S. government to send a sanitary commission to inspect army camps, as well as place female nurses in military hospitals.

True, "the reign of intelligence at the war office is over. The reign of muffs has begun."[32] But Florence's ally Douglas Galton (cousin Marianne Nicholson's husband) controlled building and upkeep of army facilities, colleague Sutherland sat stalwart on the war office's now permanent sanitary commission, and Prime Minister Palmerston appointed Herbert's disciple under secretary of state for war. "You will find ld. de Grey willing to do all in his power to forward your great and wise designs,"[33] erstwhile suitor and loyal support of her causes Richard Monckton Milnes assured Nightingale.

Bearded, bushy-browed de Grey managed to overcome bureaucratic resistance to some reforms, including construction of a new military hospital named after Herbert at Florence's suggestion. And de Grey personally consulted her when America's Civil War caused the British government to send military reinforcements to its Canadian colony.

Through a haze of illness and grief, Nightingale meticulously revised sanitation orders. She ascertained the average speed of sled haulage to calculate the time needed to move patients over Canada's expanses. She devised plans for transport relays and creation of storage depots. And proposed that troops get buffalo robes instead of blankets.

"I have been working just as I did in the times of Sidney Herbert," Flo wrote Clarkey. "Alas! He left no organization," but military leaders "were so terrified at the idea" of "national indignation if they lost another army, that they have" agreed "to everything."[34]

War did not break out. But the Canadian expedition marked a watershed. At rock bottom, laid up and lonely, Nightingale's bond with her "children" proved stronger than sickness and sorrow.

—⁂—

In obeying the "*Divine Command*" Florence "almost lost the consciousness of self" in "anxiety to attain the" end. "All this I can truly say of my public life — and nothing else would have carried me through it's weary sufferings, during which I have wondered every day how I should have patience to live till morning."[35]

In forty-eight hours she had "40 continuous hours without sleep & during the last 24 of those 40 I can neither read nor write or hardly bear anybody in the room." No one "can know" the "state which this waste of sleep brings one into."[36]

Nonetheless, Nightingale managed to revise her popular *Notes on Nursing*. As well, she wrote a smaller, cheaper version, *Notes on Nursing for the Laboring Classes*. It not only publicized the novel idea that all could enjoy good health by obeying basic rules but also included a new chapter. "Minding Baby" emphasized keeping "every spot of baby's body always clean." Never letting "any pore of its tender skin be stopped up by dirt or unwashed perspiration is the only way to keep baby happy and well."[37]

Florence whiled away some of those sleepless nights in reading Clarkey's book about her friend and mentor, the famed Parisian salon hostess Madame Recamier.[38] Clarkey praised Recamier's influence on women; this Nightingale took as an aspersion cast on her close working relations with men.

"You say 'women are more sympathetic than men.' Now if I were to write a book out of my experience, I should begin, *women have no sympathy.*"

To Florence, sympathy meant mutual feeling for and dedication to, the work — which she and her fellow reformers (all men) shared.

> Yours is the tradition. Mine is the conviction of experience. I have never found one woman who has altered her life one iota for me or my opinions. Now look at my experience of men. [Herbert,] a statesman, past middle age, absorbed in politics for a quarter of a century, out of "sympathy" with me, remodels his whole life and policy — learns a science, the driest, the most technical, the most difficult, that of administration as far as it concerns the lives of men, not, as I learned, in the field, from stirring experience, but by writing dry regulations in a London room by my sofa with me.

"This is what I call real sympathy."

"Clough, a poet born," takes "to nursing-administration in the same way for" me. "I could mention very many others — Farr, McNeill, Tulloch, Storks," all "elderly men" who, "in a lesser degree have altered their work by my opinions."

> Now just look as the degree in which women have sympathy. [And] my experience of women is almost as large as Europe. [So] intimate too. I have lived in the same bed with English countesses and Prussian [peasants, have] had charge of women of different creeds. [Yet,] my doctrines have taken no hold among women. Not one of my Crimean following learnt anything from me — or gave herself for one moment after she came home to carry out the lesson of that war or of those hospitals.

"I attribute this to want of sympathy."

"A woman once told me that my character would be more sympathized with by men than by women.... I do believe it is true. I do believe I am 'like a man'" But how? "*In having sympathy.* I am sure I have nothing else. I am sure I have no genius. I am sure that my contemporaries, Parthe, Hilary, Marianne," were "all cleverer than" me, "and several of them more unselfish. But not one had a bit of sympathy."

"What follows perhaps I may draw too much from observations in my own family."

"Women crave *for being loved, not* for loving. They scream out at you for sympathy all day long, and they are incapable of giving *any* in return, for they cannot remember your affairs long enough to do so."

"I am sick with indignation at" what "mothers will do, the most egregious selfishness. And people call it all maternal ... affection and think it pretty to say so."[39]

—∞—

By now the Burlington hotel proved a less than ideal home. After a flood in her dressingroom, which Nightingale likened to reenaction of her Scutari experiences "on a small scale," she "extorted from mr. X. a weekly inspection of the cistern." He convinced brother-in-law "Harry Verney, Papa, uncle Sam," that "the frost had been at fault and he could do no more. Then *I* had up mr. X., and he admitted at once that" frost had nothing to do with the leak. "The workmen had not changed the waste-pipe." He "came off with an excuse. And I came off with a 'severe internal congestion.'"[40]

Florence tactfully declined Queen Victoria's gracious offer of an apartment in Kensington Palace. Needing to "see a great many people on a great variety of subjects," Florence explained to her father, "*no residence* would be any use to me which was not near enough the business center of London to allow me to see these people *at a moment's notice.*"[41]

Hence, as habitual murk left London in semi-darkness all day long, Florence gave in to her family's urging. At year (1861) end, she accepted an offer from her "good brother-in-law," Harry Verney, "one of the best and kindest of men."[42] He proposed to lend Flo his house in London's elegant and centrally located Mayfair.

"I have been so very ill & even the little change of moving here knocks me down for a month,"[43] Nightingale wrote her cherished Crimean friend and colleague Reverend Mother Mary Clare Moore. "Your dear letters are almost the only earthly encouragement I have."

"I have felt so horribly ungrateful for never having thanked you for your" books. "I am quite ashamed to keep ste. Thérèse so long. But there is a good deal of reading in her. And I am only able to read at night and then not always a large, close-printed book."[44]

Friends like Moore and Jowett supplied sympathy. "Clarkey dear" provided an outlet for Florence's pent-up feelings. But Flo clung to her mother.

"Thank you very much for the weekly box," she wrote her "dearest Mum." "And tell Burton that I ate a piece of her rabbit pie," the "first real meat I have eaten for 3 months. The smallest contribution is thankfully received — even a sausage, when you kill a pig."

The "purple lama dressing-gown arrived resplendent in beauty and now I lie *out*side the bed, in order to hide *none* of its loveliness. Indeed, were it not that I am afraid" it "spots with clean water and does not wash well, I would never go back to poor 'creature' flannel. I think the color quite as pretty as lilac."[45]

"If you could send me up some snowdrops, primroses, anemones & other wild spring flowers with roots, I have a fine balcony here."[46]

—⚑—

God "entered thee with Sidney Herbert ... to be a savior."[47] Guilt and grief engulfed Nightingale. Guilt and grief also galvanized her. She must carry on Sidney's and her cause. "You are destined to do a great work," Crimea friend John McNeill encouraged. "You cannot die till it is" done. "Go on."[48]

Spring (1862) brought Nightingale her first happiness since Herbert's death. It was triggered by the unexpected demise of a key barrier to reform, the war office's powerful permanent under-secretary.* That gave Nightingale and Herbert's protégé, war-office parliamentary under-secretary de Grey, the opportunity to urge abolition of the permanent position. Consequently, Prime Minister Palmerston "forced" his war secretary to effect "Herbert's and my plan for" war-office restructure "*in some measure*," Flo told her father. "And it may seem some compensation to you for the enormous expense I cause you, that, if I had not been here, it would not have been done."[49]

Florence then personally convinced family friend Palmerston to have her ally Douglas Galton promoted within the war office. Galton and de Grey failed to make major headway in reform despite Nightingale's coaching. But when the war secretary died suddenly, she got de Grey appointed in his place. This time Florence won over Lord Palmerston via a letter to her brother-in-law, which she asked Verney to read to the prime minister. And "agitate, agitate," Nightingale urged her political journalist friend Harriet Martineau, "for lord de Grey."[50]

De Grey's war office consulted a bedridden female on almost every administrative matter. Whether equipment for army hospitals; establishing hospitals for soldiers' wives; revising army rations; directions for staff surgeons, for apothecaries, for treatment of yellow fever and cholera, for adjusting

---

*A lifetime appointee, the permanent under-secretary did not answer to parliament, which meant he had virtually unlimited power within the war office.

purveyor and commissariat functions; diet on troop transports; or assignments at military hospitals — all received Florence's meticulous attention. She loaned documents and statistics; shared knowledge; gave the benefit of practical experience; drafted warrants and regulations; wrote official memoranda and summaries for ministers. And Nightingale created a cost-accounting system for the army medical services that a select finance committee reapproved in 1947.

No detail escaped Florence's notice. When soldiers deployed, they could not "make any provision for" support of wives and children until reaching "their destination, say China or Calcutta (after a four months' voyage, round the Cape.)" For sailors "leaving a port in England or Ireland, the admiralty provides power to leave a standing order that a certain amount of pay is to be sent regularly to their families."

But, war-office bureaucrats loudly protested, an arrangement like that would mean a change in bookkeeping.

"It would involve no 'change.' It would involve a small addition. I am willing to go to the length of six-pence to" buy an account book for the war office allowing "them to keep these additional accounts."

"The w. o. would not be the w. o., if such things as these were not."[51]

Florence managed all this in addition to her main work: securing hygiene and efficiency for army facilities and advancing reform of the army medical department. "If you never wish to live for your own sake, yet bear to live, dearest, for a time," Liz Herbert encouraged, "to carry out his work, and to keep his memory fresh."[52]

—⁓—

The war office now concerned itself with venereal disease; too many soldiers got syphilis. Bureaucrats wanted Britain to copy the continental method of prevention: license prostitutes and, if needed, force them into treatment. Nightingale opposed — not only on moral grounds but also because statistics proved that this system failed to provide a solution.

She knew prostitution — from Scutari and Balaclava, not to mention London slums. "Filthy crowded dwellings. 2. Drunkenness. 3. Ignorance and want of occupation"[53] caused army prostitution. Florence urged better opportunities for learning and recreation, more physical exercise, and additional housing for married men.

The government invited her to submit a paper. Consequently, the war office created a committee to inquire into police inspection of prostitutes at designated bases. Nightingale wrote the committee's instructions and named its members.

Still smarting from Florence's Crimean War activities and bent on revenge, reform-resistant war-office denizens fought back. One proposed assigning a specific number of prostitutes to each regiment and giving them religious instruction. "The prostitutes who survive five years of this life should have good service pensions,"[54] Nightingale noted.

Public opinion favored the Continental method. Parliament enacted it into law.

—⁂—

At this all-time low, depressed and frail, lonely and grieving, at work nonstop with no distraction, Florence judged her life a failure. But "I will tell you," she wrote her dear Reverend Mother Moore, "how I spent" the weekend: at war secretary de Grey's request "preparing a scheme"[55] for teaching soldiers some trades.

News of Nightingale's latest enthusiasm spread. Commanding officers throughout the empire applied to her. Florence got them war-office grants, which she supplemented with private means and donations solicited from friends. "We may not hope to make 'saints' of all, but we can make men of them instead of brutes."[56]

20

"How People May Live and Not Die in India"

To preach to a man to do right and send him back to the pigsty, where he cannot do but wrong, is nonsense. We must set about improving the pigsty.[1]— Florence Nightingale

"Flo ... sends me every morning a message if I can see her or not between four and six o'clock.... It is a comfort to her to talk to me about everything she likes, as she never sees anybody but the sanitary doctors and the people of the council of India. She is always in bed and very weak." How "wonderful to see" her "working to organize the sanitary condition of India."[2]—Julius Mohl

"It is 10 years to the day since Inkerman," Florence reflected through a miasma of pain as 1864 drew to its dreary close. "It is 10 years yesterday since we landed at Scutari. It seems to me like 3 lives — tho' I have spent 7 of those 10 years in bed."[3]

One year after Nightingale returned from Scutari, mutiny gripped the crown jewel of Great Britain's empire.* Consequently, the government took over direct rule of its Indian colony (Bangladesh, India, and Pakistan today) from the British East India Company. Lord Stanley became Britain's first secretary of state for India.

Florence knew him well. Soon after she had come back to England, friend and socialite Richard Monckton Milnes, thinking Nightingale ought to get acquainted with some potentially useful politicians, invited her to a dinner party to meet the wealthy, liberal-leaning member of parliament. Stanley and Nightingale hit it off immediately.

*In 1857 Britain's East India Company had, under the aegis of the British government, direct responsibility for administering the colony. Indians made up most of the army. These troops mutinied. A rumor that new gun cartridges were greased with the fat of (sacred) cows outraged Hindus; Muslim troops heard that (prohibited) pig fat greased their gun cartridges. Indian soldiers committed terrible atrocities against British women and children. Only after a year of hard fighting did Britain regain control.

Whether "we shall hold or lose India will depend very much on the steps taken to protect" the large British troop contingent there "from disease."[4] Florence convinced Stanley to form a royal commission for India. It should do for the army there what the first, post–Crimean, royal commission and its subsequent four sub-commissions were doing for the army at home: streamline the army medical department, sanitize barracks, create a statistics section and a medical school.

The government had asked ailing Sidney Herbert to head this new commission. Daunted by the challenge, in any case extremely busy as chairman of the four sub-commissions, Herbert hesitated. Dismissing her own debility, determined to "'scrat on' as well as I can, as long as I can work at all,"[5] Nightingale promised to help. Herbert thus agreed to take on the added responsibility. His death reenergized her purpose.

India lacked statistics. So after consulting trusted friends and colleagues — statistician William Farr, Crimea commissioner John McNeill, and sanitarian John Sutherland — Nightingale designed a *Circular of Enquiry*. It went to every military station on the subcontinent. And Florence asked each of the two hundred larger stations for copies of their health and sanitary codes. To assure compliance, she wrote to every senior army and medical officer in India.

A flood of data cascaded over Florence's quarters. She, Farr, and Sutherland spent several weeks evaluating it. Their conclusion: three times more soldiers died annually in India than at home *before* Nightingale and Herbert's reforms.

This dramatic disclosure must, the India commission concluded, form the core of its report. But the person responsible did not, could not, as a woman, sit on the commission; nor did she meet the criteria for witnesses. So the commission formally asked Nightingale to submit a paper. It would be included in the report under her name. Bedridden, deluged with army medical department and sanitation work, sunk in sorrow over Herbert and Clough, Florence wrote *Observations by Miss Nightingale*.

It featured graphic illustrations. Replies to Florence's *Circular of Enquiry* had included unsolicited sketches of congested barracks built of plank and plaster, of earthen floors smoothed with cow dung, and of extremely primitive privies. Florence got her talented artist cousin, Hilary Bonham-Carter, to touch up these drawings, then used them to emphasize salient points in her report.

Each year death claimed seven in every hundred soldiers. And that staggering statistic excluded "the amount of inefficiency from sickness — of invaliding."[6] Moreover, tropical diseases did not kill troops. Camp diseases did.

Britons took "plentiful and pure water" for granted. An Indian barrack got its water "either from tanks, into which" rain washed "all the filth of the neighboring surface; or from shallow wells, dug" in "doubtful soil. So simple" a "mechanism as a pump is unknown." When "men drink water, they drink cholera with it."[7]

One major station featured "filth from the latrines" collecting a mere "100 yards from the barracks"; dead animals "accumulated in the same places." "Abominable cesspools" poisoned the air. Of course neglect "of the commonest principles of sanitary science" caused cholera. And to crown all, sheep got fed "from the native latrines"![8]

Confined to barracks all day in the Indian heat, men had no means of recreation, no exercise, nothing to do. At midday they got their main meal, plus a generous alcohol ration, which army medical wisdom — if, indeed, it merited such a label — claimed protected against disease. "What with overeating, over-drinking, total idleness, and vice springing directly from these, the" soldier had "small chance indeed of coping with the climate, so-called."[9]

Climate: a convenient scapegoat. "The cause of ill health in India lies, *not* in the climate, but in the absence of"[10] hygiene.

Moderate eating and drinking, lightweight clothing, plenty of exercise, smaller barrack rooms housing fewer soldiers and, above all, basic sanitation would radically reduce the death rate. And that would mean significant savings of public money.

—⟋⟍⟍—

"After four years heavy work (how much those four years have done!) the Indian sanitary commission signed their report, begun by *him*," Flo wrote her "dearest" Liz Herbert. "There were three days" of "sharp fighting ... to carry" a vital clause. "To have a 'working' commission at home, after the fashion of *his*, to carry out" reforms; for people failed to see that work began "when the report is finished." It "was *his* glory to have introduced this new fashion of working reports. And upon *his* name we carried it."[11]

Squirming under the report's disclosures, the war and India offices prepared a Précis of Evidence. It ignored the most damning data. Besides, bureaucrats curtailed distribution.

Nightingale fought back. Farr and Sutherland got *Observations by Miss Nightingale* published. It circulated widely to positive press reviews.[12] Florence sent an advance copy to her friend the political economist and newspaper columnist Harriet Martineau. Florence also lobbied members of parliament. She emphasized the subject nearest their hearts: expenditure of public money.

"Unless the death rate & invaliding rate of the Indian army can be reduced," British troops would fail to hold India, Nightingale impressed on her brother-in-law, liberal member of parliament Sir Harry Verney. Seeking twenty-five thousand recruits for next year, the army saw its only recourse as a raise in pay "to extend re-enlistment." A "better method than this, would be to improve the sanitary condition of India."[13]

Florence next convinced her friend and ally war secretary Lord de Grey to let her rewrite the Précis. And by offering to open her private purse for printing and distribution costs, Nightingale thwarted the government's predictable protest about expense.

Once the commission's report had become official, she proceeded to impress on India secretary Stanley that its recommendations must be put into effect.

"Do not fear that lord Herbert's work will be left unfinished: sanitary ideas have taken root in the public mind, and they cannot be treated as visionary," Stanley replied. "We must give them time to read the report." There "is ample time to consider all this."[14]

Florence disagreed. She pulled strings. Other cabinet ministers spoke to Stanley.

"The report of the commissioners will be acted upon," he promised.[15]

Stanley asked Nightingale to outline a basic all–India sanitary code. She persuaded him to ask each Indian presidency (administrative unit) to form a sanitary commission. Two members representing India joined the war office's barrack and hospital improvement commission, headed by Florence's ally engineer Douglas Galton.

"It is a great exertion to me to get up & dress & sit up to see these gentlemen," Florence confided to her "dear, dearest friend" and Crimean colleague, Reverend Mother Mary Clare Moore. "But I feel as if I never could be thankful enough to almighty God. I feel always a kind of wonder that He should employ so miserable an instrument as I — to give me such chances."[16]

—⚬⚬⚬—

"I have suffered so very much." Nightingale felt "well nigh done" for. Prescribed massages did little to alleviate her "rheumatism of the spine." Nothing did "any good but a curious new-fangled little operation of putting opium in under the skin, which relieves one for 34 hours, but does not improve the vivacity or serenity of one's intellect."[17]

Intellect. It meant everything. Without brainpower, Florence would fail to improve conditions for her "children." So rather than put her mind at risk, Nightingale stopped the opium treatment.

Internal tumors, meanwhile, caused beloved cousin Hilary to suffer cruelly. Cursing her inability to nurse Hilary, Flo, nonetheless, kept closely involved. "God bless you for what you have done for Hilary," she thanked her friend Oxford professor Benjamin Jowett. "It is the greatest comfort to her. She was so pleased with your letter."

"You do me good," Nightingale confided to Jowett. "I wish I did you credit. I hope no one ... will ever be so near despair as I have been.

"I have not spoken to a hero of your caliber since Sidney Herbert's death." And "it is that which does me good to know that you are in this world."[18]

Florence saw forty-four-year-old Hilary's death as particularly tragic because the Bonham-Carter family had battened on her sweet nature, instead of allowing Hilary freedom to develop her artistic abilities. What shameful sacrifice of female capability on the altar of convention, what heartbreaking waste of a woman's competence. Grieving anew, but angry as well, Flo compared her cousin to pure but unprocessed gold.*

Concomitantly, the onset of menopause (a taboo subject to Victorian women, Florence included), with its physical changes and emotional fragility, exacerbated brucellosis symptoms. Depressed and in unremitting pain, Florence entrusted her "dearest Selina Bracebridge" with a solemn charge. "When this call" God "made upon me for other work stops, and I am no longer able to work, I should wish to be taken to St. Thomas's hospital, and to be placed in a bed *in a 'general' ward* ... I beg you" to "see that this" is done "as a true friend, which you always have been, are, and will be."[19]

If, however, Flo "should have an acute illness, such as a fever, in which removal would be probable death, good nursing at home would give a possibility of return to work," Selina should have Florence's competent and faithful Crimean War nurse, "Roberts, who, I know would come to me at once," take care of her at home. However, if "removal would no longer frustrate my chance of return to work," then Selina's "grateful affectionate"[20] Flo wanted to die at St. Thomas's.

Clarkey blamed Flo's depression on her lonely life. "Darling," Florence replied, "my solitary life" is "entirely the effect of calculation. I cannot live to work unless I give up all that makes life pleasant. People say, 'Oh see the doctors have said these 8 years she could not live 6 months — therefore it is all a mistake.' They *never* say: she has lived 8 years when the doctors said she could

---

*Florence had, in her will, left Hilary "£1000 in the earnest hope that, though not in possession, it may enable you ... to provide yourself with an atelier, or other means of pursuing your art" (BL ADD. 45794, f. 174, January, 1863, FN to Hilary).

not live 6 months by adopting the kind of life, of sacrificing everything else in order" to work. "I NEVER said it was 'best for me.'" Flo said "it was the only" way "work could be done."[21]

Nightingale did, indeed, rue her "horrible loneliness." Yet, "maids of all work and poor governesses, have been more lonely than I — and have done much better than I."[22] Haunted by fear of failure, Florence questioned whether sacrifice of love and marriage, of health, of a conventional and easier life, had been worthwhile.

"What hast thou to do with rest and ease?" she heard God asking in the wakeful wee hours. "I thought thou hadst given these up long since."[23] Nightingale reflected constantly on God having called her to the perfection of His service, to be a savior. "How hast thou answered? What opportunities have I not given thee?"[24]

Jowett's sympathy, his devotion to her ideals, reassured Florence. She confided in him and, although in general prickly at suggestions that she amend her lifestyle, accepted supportive critique from Jowett.

> HE: "You ought seriously to consider how your work may be carried on, not with less energy, but in a calmer spirit."[25]
>
> SHE: "Quite right ... I mar the work of God by my impatience & discontent.... It has never been in my power to arrange my work. No more than I could help having to receive & provide for 4000 patients in 17 days (in the Crimean war) and how easy that was compared with what has happened since"! My entire life has been "in a hurry: if the thing were not done to the day, it would not be done at all."[26]
>
> HE: "It is hard to say to" one "ill & alone, 'Get another attitude of mind.'" So keep "your plans & proposals but wait & trust to time & have faith in God, and don't seek to move the world by main force, but give the world a push when it is going your way."[27]
>
> SHE: "I will try to take your advice."*[28]

—⁂—

India's viceroy, meanwhile, died unexpectedly. The British government replaced him with a national hero. Sir John Lawrence, former governor of Punjab presidency, had promoted infrastructure building, striven to ease the plight of heavily taxed peasants, and tried to end the egregious practice of suttee.[29] Having stopped the Mutiny from spreading to the Punjab, he led British troops to ultimate victory. "Among the multitude of affairs and congratulations which will be pouring in" there "is no more fervent joy," no "stronger good wishes, than those of one of the humblest of your servants,"

---

*Some evidence suggests that, at one point in their relationship, Jowett proposed marriage to Nightingale. She begged him not to let her refusal interfere with their friendship. Nor did it.

Nightingale wrote. "There is no greater position for usefulness under heaven than" governing "the vast empire you saved for us. And you are the only man to fill" it. "Pray think" of "our sanitary things on which such millions of lives and health depend."[30]

India secretary and sanitary commission chairman Lord Stanley thought Lawrence should learn about the subcontinent's sanitation from a sickly single female who had never been there. "The plans are in the main yours; no one can explain them" better. "Advice from you will come with greater weight than from anyone else."[31]

Lawrence spent several hours with Nightingale. Inside of a month after arriving in India, he established a sanitary commission for each presidency.

And as dense fog cloaked London in darkness during daylight hours, Florence, with help from statistician Farr and sanitarian Sutherland, wrote India's first sanitary code (1864). Following protocol, she sent *Suggestions in Regard to Sanitary Works Required for the Improvement of Indian Stations* to the war office for dispatch to the India office. Months passed. Where, Lawrence prodded, were the promised instructions? Nightingale probed. The war and India offices were at odds, so the former filed, and promptly forgot, *Suggestions*. Impatient with petty politics, Nightingale paid to have *Suggestions* printed and shipped to Lawrence.

She had respected Dr. John Sutherland's expertise and relied on his advice since their first meeting at the Barrack hospital. Now Sutherland functioned as Nightingale's right hand. Combining common sense with practical public health experience and proficiency in sanitation, Sutherland knew how to get things done, particularly within realistic limits. Florence had more ideas and faster insight, greater drive and willpower; besides, her writing skills cloaked Sutherland's prosaic prose in eloquence; and her fame guaranteed attention. Together, they made a terrific team.

Sutherland's professional and official connections as a leading sanitary expert, plus his seat on several important committees, especially the army's permanent sanitary commission, brought him information barred to bedridden Nightingale. As well, Sutherland helped with both work-related correspondence and social obligations.

Nightingale acknowledged her debt to him, but that did not stop her from driving Sutherland as hard as ever. "I am sorry you are ill," but "I suppose, as I have not heard again, that you intend me to believe you are either well or dead. I am so busy that I have not time to die. Here are three things."[32] She still deplored Sutherland's lack of organization — a cardinal sin — his slipshod attitude towards papers, his sporadic petulance. And physical frailty aggravated Florence's irritation at having to raise her voice in order to penetrate Sutherland's growing deafness.

"I am so weak, no one knows how weak I am. Yesterday because I saw dr. Sutherland for a few minutes in the afternoon, after the morning's work, with my good mrs. Sutherland for a few minutes after him, I was with a spasm of the heart till 7 o'clock this morning and nearly unfit for work all to-day."[33]

Lively and urbane, "kindest, dearest" Sarah Sutherland once viewed forty houses before deciding on summer lodgings for Florence. Sarah mediated sticky logistical issues between her spouse and his demanding colleague. And if Selina Bracebridge, Mai Smith, or Fanny Nightingale could not provide Flo with a good maid (she preferred servants her mother had trained), Sarah Sutherland found one. "I think of our thirty years of friendship and thank God for having given me such a friend,"[34] Florence would later write.

Her father disliked having his cherished child shunt between lodgings at Hampstead, various London locations, and her brother-in-law's borrowed house. Flo should have her own home. So WEN bought a long-term lease on Mayfair's 35 South Street (later renumbered 10). Central, convenient, and close to Parthe's house, Florence's home until her death abutted a large, private garden. It provided ample fresh air, light, and trees. "I am *very much* obliged to Papa for buying the house for me. It is on the whole a great relief, though I am afraid it is mainly for the relief it will give to my dear and unwearied friend mrs. Sutherland, (in looking for houses for me) that it is a pleasure to me. I am so weary."[35]

"Impatient for death," bedridden, and in such pain "that I wonder how anybody can dread an operation," Florence found it took great "faith to make God's will mine." And no comfort lay in thinking, "*I* shall soon be past my sufferings. For" that would not make the army better off.

"I have felt this much more in setting up, (for the first time in my life) a fashionable old maid's house in a fashionable quarter" because "it is as it were deciding upon a new & independent course in my broken old age." Florence had not yet arrived at fifty! Always before "my path was so clear to me, what I ought to do, tho' often not how to do it."

"Oh! if I were now able to do what I could do" ten years ago, how "little my griefs would be to me, except to inspire me to do more," Flo confessed to her mother.

"People say that time heals the deepest griefs." Not true. "Time makes us feel what *are* the deepest griefs every day only the more by showing of the blank."[36]

"Saw Florence for half an hour this morning, over-fatigued certainly, but speaking with a voice only too loud and strong,"[37] WEN told Fanny after one of his frequent visits. Since Clarkey and Julius Mohl also gave the Nightingales some pure-bred Persian cats, talk of these absorbing creatures often interrupted WEN and Flo's metaphysical musings. "I take no end of pains to marry them well. But they won't have the husbands I choose, while they take up with low toms, of recent extraction, out of the mews,"[38] Florence lamented.

She expected Clarkey "the first day you can come — to stay as long as you can bear the dullness." Flo had "no time to write but" Clarkey's letter gave her "much to say."[39] Besides, "you will be doing me a favor," for "August 2 is a terrible anniversary"* (Herbert's death). "And I shall not have my usual solace, for mrs. Bracebridge has always" spent "that day with me" and "would have come this year," but Flo felt unsure about getting "Lawrence's things off by that time. It does me good to be with you."[40]

—⁂—

"It is not for the soldier alone that we speak." Ten years after the Mutiny, Florence Nightingale's *How People May Live and Not Die in India* made its debut at the annual (1867) social science congress, which she and WEN used to attend regularly before Florence went to Harley Street.

"The time has gone past" to consider India "a mere appanage of British commerce. In holding India, we must be able to show the moral right of our tenure." People all over the land suffered "epidemic diseases; constant high death rates." Pestilence could easily "sweep over large tracts, gathering strength" to "pass over gigantic mountain ranges and to spread their ravages over western Asia and Europe. And all this might be saved."

No Indian metropolis had drainage. "Domestic filth round the people's houses" defied description. Water came from "wells, or tanks, in ground saturated with filth. No domestic conveniences." No "sanitary administration. No sanitary police."

Certainly railway and canal construction were advancing and education improving. But what good is a school "if the people are left prey to epidemics"?

"The next great work" consisted of sanitary reform. "The work is urgent." The "real, the main point in" the "royal commission report is": "look to the state of your stations first." They and your "cities are in a condition which, in the finest temperate climate in Europe, would be — have been, the cause of the Great Plague." No "climate in the world, certainly not" of "India, could kill us, if we did not kill ourselves by our neglects."

*Soon after Sidney's death, Liz Herbert went to live in the south of France, then Italy. There she converted to Catholicism. Liz and Flo's correspondence shows that the two women remained close all their lives. No matter how ill, how overworked, Florence always found time for Liz.

Nightingale proposed forming "a public health department for India." What "a noble task for a government." It "would be creating India anew. For God places His own power, His own life-giving laws in the hands of man. He permits man to create mankind by those laws — even as He permits man to destroy mankind by neglect of those laws."[41]

—m—

INDIA VICEROY LAWRENCE: "I am doing what I can to put things in order out here; but it is very uphill work."

NIGHTINGALE: "Your Bengal sanitary commission is doing its work, like men — like martyrs, in fact, — and what a work it is"![42]

India must have the means to effect modern sanitation, Florence decided, before the end of Lawrence's term as viceroy. She also resolved that India must have an executive sanitary authority with clout in London. And the system had to be subject to public scrutiny via publication of an annual report on work accomplished.

In this venture Nightingale attracted a vital new ally.

Recently returned from the governorship of Mumbai presidency, tall, slim, blond Sir Bartle Frere thought Great Britain had a duty to govern India only until the Indians could take over. He therefore promoted economic and municipal development — modern Karachi and Mumbai owe their existence to him. And unlike those who wanted India Christianized and Anglicized, Frere sought to preserve the country's indigenous culture, particularly through education. Now a member of the British government's India council, fascinated at the thought of meeting the famous and noble-minded Nightingale, Frere asked if he might call at 35 South Street.

A trim parlor maid in spotless starched uniform opened the polished, oak-paneled front door. After relieving Frere of his caped coat, kid gloves, tall tapered hat, and Malacca cane, she showed him into Florence's neat, light-filled drawing room. Since this chanced to be one of her better days, Nightingale awaited her visitor downstairs.

Reclining on a couch near the window, she wore a simple but modish black silk dress; a light woolen shawl covered Florence's feet. Frere sat facing her, the tea table laden with thinly cut cucumber and cress sandwiches, cakes, and the tea service between them. Abundant fresh flowers softened the room's severe white walls and plain blue curtains. Tall, built-in bookcases bulging with government blue books lined the walls, except for framed engravings of Michelangelo's much-admired Sistine Chapel ceiling; Florence had bought them in Rome. A print of Raphael's Madonna, which had made a profound impression when Nightingale visited Dresden with the Bracebridges en route to her first stay at Kaiserswerth, took pride of place. The openwork "frame is beautiful," Florence thanked Fanny, "just what that kind of print wants to lighten it."[43]

Nightingale and Frere took to each other at once. Florence asked her mother to invite Frere and his wife to Embley. A fearless horseman and champion shot, not to mention distinguished India official, the charming and courteous Frere appealed to Fanny. WEN shared his academic interests. The two families quickly became friends.

Frere educated Nightingale on India administration. She educated him on sanitation. A personal and professional friendship flourished.

—∽∽—

Famine, meanwhile, startled India's government into chaos and flung British bureaucrats "into a great fright." They thought "'something must be done' (about Indian administration) which gives a favorable" chance for "simplicity & direct action."[44] How, Nightingale therefore asked war-office ally Galton, did he advise that she time a letter to the new secretary of state for India, bewhiskered, bushy-bearded Sir Stafford Northcote?

"We have a decision of a r. [royal] commission, presided over by ld Herbert & ld Stanley, which points out what the administrative principle ought to be."

"Health questions in India comprise two classes:

"1. those of military stations & the populations about them

"2. those groups of population where there are no military stations.

"Both require inspection. Both require funds."

"Now is the time to begin."

We want "to organize a health service once and for all." It is not difficult "to do."

"There is a member of council [Frere] just come home from India & of ye largest Indian experience — who thoroughly understands the whole subject."

"It will require a very large measure of your indulgence to enable you to pardon" this letter. "I should esteem it the greatest favor to be allowed to communicate with you on the subject, at any time or in any way least inconvenient to yourself."[45]

Mild-mannered Northcote asked to visit Nightingale. "I don't know that he saw how afraid I was of him. For he kept his eyes tight shut all the time. [Northcote's long lashes may have given this illusion.] And I kept mine wide open."[46]

The India secretary promised a sanitary commission at the India office with Frere as chairman. It would have paramount power in India. Nightingale failed to win a public health department, but she did get public health officers for each presidency.

"We will make 35 South street the India office till this is done,"[47] Frere vowed, unconsciously echoing the Band of Brothers who made up the first royal commission.* "Our Indian affairs which have been looking as black as thunder for the last year, are likely to be restored by sir Bartle Frere who has taken up my things almost as Sidney Herbert did,"[48] Flo joyfully informed her father.

Because "I do the work in 3 hours I used to do in one,"[49] Florence slaved that fall (1867). Northcote called again. He asked Nightingale to sum up India sanitation from creation of the royal commission to date. Done — within weeks. As well, Florence outlined instructions for the new India office sanitary commission. Spontaneously, she drafted a dispatch asking stations to report on their sanitary progress. Northcote's office sent the dispatch and printed the reports. The *India Office Sanitary Annual* appeared each year, thus realizing Nightingale's goal that India's sanitary situation come under public scrutiny.

When her brucellosis periodically abated, Florence toyed with the idea of visiting India but never felt well enough for long enough to travel so far. Still, work for the subcontinent's sanitation gave her exceptional wisdom. Years spent poring over copious statistics empowered Nightingale to bring salient facts to bear on every issue. Her Crimean experience and iconic status brought singular credibility. Florence's sheer comprehension, her fortitude, not to mention her fame, intimidated some senior India officials. Others harbored hostility against a mere female for presuming to meddle in their male fiefdom. Nevertheless, no high-ranking India appointee would dream of taking up his post without first calling on Florence Nightingale.

*See p. 179.

Nursing

"A commonly received idea among men, and even among women," is that "disappointment in love, the want of an object," or "incapacity in other things" will "turn a woman into a good nurse." "No *man*, not even a doctor," defines "what a nurse should be" other than: "'devoted and obedient.' This definition would do just as well for a porter. It might even do for a horse. It would not do for a policeman."[1]— Florence Nightingale

Nursing is an art, and an art requiring an organized practical and scientific training.[2]— Florence Nightingale

One of Nightingale's many correspondents, the philosopher and economist John Stuart Mill, invited her to join the board of the newly formed (1867) Women's Suffrage Society.

"That women should have the suffrage, I think no one can be more deeply convinced than I," Florence replied. "But it will probably be years before you obtain" it.

"In the mean time, are there not evils which press more hardly on women than not having a vote?" For instance, until "a married woman can be in possession of her own property, there can be no love or justice."

Today, Britain's all-male parliament could grant females this right.

Florence had been "too busy ... to wish for a vote," she continued. Besides, during her years working with the war and India offices, she had wielded "more administrative influence than if I had been" in parliament, and that "notwithstanding the terrible loss I have had of him who placed me there."

"If I draw your attention to myself, it is only because I have not time to serve on the society you" mention. "I could not give my name without my work."

Mill persisted. The Society needed the prestige of Nightingale's name.

She agreed "that women's 'political power' should be 'direct and open,'" Florence replied. "But I have thought that *I* could work better for others, even for other women, off the stage than on it."[3]

—⚏—

Roses were in full bloom, Florence buried in army medical reform and fighting brucellosis, when her pioneering Nightingale School for Nurse Training opened (1860) at London's St. Thomas's Hospital.* The Crimean War had popularized nursing and sparked a desire to increase nurse numbers. Concomitantly, medical science improved, prompting a need for more and better-trained nurses. Experience and personality led Florence to insist that her school be secular. (Several religious sisterhoods already gave informal, on-the-job training.) And her school must initiate organized, scientific nurse education.

Nightingale aimed to produce nurses able to teach others. Her graduate nurses would enter hospitals as model professionals, nursing missionaries who spread The Nightingale System.

It rested on three principles. Observation at Kaiserswerth and experience at Scutari, let alone knowledge of nursing reform at home and abroad, caused Florence to insist that *"one female trained head"*[4] (the matron or superintendent) have full power over, and full responsibility for, the entire nursing staff.

A nurse must be sober and honest. She should obey hospital rules, doctors, the matron, and the sister or head nurse in whose ward she worked.

A nurse's character must be on the same superior level as her technical skills.

Nightingale worked closely with St. Thomas's matron, "the only one of any existing hospital" that she "would recommend to form a school for nurses." It would start "in a very humble way" (fifteen probationers) but not with failure — "the possibility of upsetting a large hospital — for she is a *tried* matron."[5]

Widow and mother, gently born and well-educated, Sarah Wardroper had impressed Nightingale as "a real hospital genius"[6] when she visited St. Thomas's to recruit nurses for the Crimean War. (Wardroper sent the invaluable Roberts.) With definite ideas on the qualities she wanted in a nurse and resolved to develop her through training, Wardroper had already begun to reform by hiring better types of women and asserting control over them.

---

*Great Britain's formal expression of gratitude for Nightingale's war work burdened her conscience. Crimean responsibilities prevented immediate use of the Nightingale Fund to create nurse training. After the war Florence pitched into army medical reform; then brucellosis hit. So she asked Fund council chairman Sidney Herbert to release her from implementing nurse education. He refused. She symbolized nursing, and the public expected her to lead. So they agreed that Nightingale sponsor and direct a nursing school. The Fund council would engage a paid secretary (Arthur Clough, then Florence's first cousin businessman and lawyer Henry Bonham-Carter) to manage daily business.

—⚌—

Florence sought as probationers upper domestic servants or farmers' daughters in their late twenties. Since these women were expected to raise nursing to a respected profession and because one false step could endanger Nightingale's entire nursing experiment, each candidate must give references proving not only her ability but also her probity. She must also provide a health certificate. After a month, the probationer could leave or the matron dismiss her. If accepted, the woman must agree to complete an unprecedented full year of rigorous training. "We train her in habits of punctuality, quietness, trustworthiness, personal neatness. We teach her how to manage large wards. We train her in dressing wounds and other injuries; and in performing all those minor operations which nurses are called upon day and night to undertake."[7] Students must attend lectures, submit their notes to inspection, pass examinations, and act as assistant nurses in the wards where surgeons and sisters gave practical training.

Because probationers must bring strong morals to an occupation notorious for depravity, Wardroper tightly controlled conduct. She completed a detailed monthly report — which Nightingale devised — for each student. Florence read them regularly.

Every month, probationers had to record a day in the wards for Nightingale. Coming "off duty" at "8 pm fagged, footsore, and weary," a student heard that "my report must be written immediately (we never knew beforehand when this sword of Damocles would fall upon us). So after a hurried supper, I" started to jot "down the day's work." All "we had done in the wards must be entered. A combination of truthfulness and temper resulted" in: "8.15 am. Tooth-combed seven heads, had grand sport; mixed bag, measured one teaspoonful; cleanliness is next to godliness!"[8] This takeoff on a shooting party tickled Florence's sense of humor.

A probationer who passed the school's stiff examinations must agree to serve under the Nightingale Fund at St. Thomas's, or another Fund-approved hospital, for three to five years. In return the Fund paid all teaching expenses, St. Thomas's room and board, plus an allowance for personal expenses. As well, the Fund provided the students' "neat, pretty style"[9] uniforms — gray dresses with white aprons and caps.

Nightingale developed the novel idea that probationers live in a nurses residence, or home. It had a bedroom for each woman, plus common sitting room containing comfortable chairs, books, maps, prints, and flowers refreshed weekly from Embley's generous gardens. The sister in charge occupied a two-room suite. Illness kept Florence from inspecting the facility, but Selina Bracebridge acted as her eyes and ears.

Flirting meant instant discharge. Nor could any student leave the school by herself. "We always parted as soon as we got to the corner,"[10] reminisced one graduate.

—⚏—

A liberal member of parliament, scion of shipping magnates from England's major manufacturing port of Liverpool, meanwhile, initiated a district nursing service for the city's sick poor, in their homes, with one trained nurse. He wanted to expand, but there were no more skilled nurses. William Rathbone turned to Florence Nightingale.

Why not train nurses in Liverpool's main hospital? she suggested. So Rathbone put together a plan. Florence gave it "as much consideration as if she herself were going to be the superintendent."[11] The success of Rathbone's newly built nurse training school and nurses' home inspired him to propose trained nurses for Liverpool's workhouse infirmary,[12] but the infirmary's board of governors balked at the cost. Confident his plan would prove viable enough for the governors eventually to assume expenses, Rathbone promised funding for a three-year trial period. But he made one proviso: Nightingale must give guidance and find a superintendent.

Despite illness, to say nothing of heavy war-office and India work, she agreed instantly. For "to set poor people going again with" a "sound body and mind is about as great a benefit as can be given them — worth acres of relief. This is depauperizing them."[13]

Rathbone next asked Nightingale to draft a formal letter for him to send to the board of governors. "There has been as much diplomacy and as many treaties and as much of people working against each other, as if we had been going to occupy a kingdom instead of a workhouse,"[14] Florence told her interested Crimean war friend, Reverend Mother Mary Clare Moore, whose nuns nursed the indigent sick in London's Bermondsey slum.

Five years after founding her school, Nightingale selected twelve graduate nurses for the Liverpool workhouse infirmary. As matron she chose genteel, young, "rich and witty" Agnes Jones, "ideal in her beauty as a Louis XIV shepherdess."[15] Inspired by Florence's Crimea work, Jones had trained at Kaiserswerth, then at the Nightingale school.

Since grimy, industrial Liverpool would come as a nasty shock to Agnes, used to gracious living in the green Irish countryside, Rathbone financed the cheerful décor of her suite and filled it with fragrant white and purple lilac. But nothing could ease Jones's horror at the vast, crammed, filthy wards or the drunk and depraved patients.

Since Jones's powers lacked clarity, serious conflicts soon cropped up. With a flurry of letters Florence calmed, cajoled, and brought all sides to compromise. Jones proved a stellar matron. Within two years, dramatically decreased costs convinced the City of Liverpool to assume all expenses.

To celebrate, Rathbone asked Nightingale if she would let him be her "gardener to the extent of doing what I have long wished — providing a flowerstand for your room and keeping it supplied with plants."[16] So Florence's simple, airy bedroom got a jardinière. Until his death forty years later, Rathbone kept it filled with fresh foliage.

—⁂—

A pauper died at a workhouse infirmary. Official inquiry faulted dirt due to palpable neglect. The press pounced. Public outrage escalated. "I was so much obliged to that poor man for dying,"[17] Nightingale confided to her friend Crimea commissioner John McNeill.

Did not the current furor prove the need for better nursing in workhouse infirmaries? Florence asked the president of Britain's poor-law board. Might he be interested in the Liverpool workhouse infirmary's experience?

Yes.

Nightingale then convinced him that workhouse nursing reform would fail without workhouse administrative reform. It must start in London. But first, facts. She designed a Form of Enquiry to be sent to each workhouse infirmary and sick ward in the city.

Statistics revealed the disgraceful state of pauper medical institutions. So Florence designed a pilot program for London — the ABC of workhouse reform.

A. "The sick, insane, incurable and children must be dealt with separately in proper institutions and not mixed up in infirmaries and sick wards as at present. The care and government of the sick poor" is "totally different from the government of paupers. Why do we have hospitals to cure and workhouse infirmaries in order not to cure? Taken solely from the point of view of preventing pauperism what a stupid anomaly this is!"[18]
B. Create one central administration answerable to parliament.
C. Impose a uniform and consolidated tax. Local taxes now paid for workhouses and infirmaries; local officials appointed staff. This invited graft. "I don't believe it to be at all certain that an improved & efficient system of hospitals for the sick would cost more than the present disgraceful no-system of betraying the sick."[19]

The government fell. Consequently, Nightingale's ABC plan got shelved.

—⁂—

Her mother had, meanwhile, been injured in a carriage accident (1866). Alarmed, Florence demanded daily reports from Parthe, staying at Embley with her husband, Harry Verney. "You have such beautiful weather at Embley (and here it is a bitter blighting east [wind]) that I hope, as I hear from" Harry, "you get out in the garden, it will do you good," Flo wrote Fanny. "It *ought*, by the beautiful azaleas I have had from Embley."[20]

Still feeling unwell at midsummer, Fanny let WEN travel to Lea Hurst alone. Social obligations recalled the Verneys to their Claydon country estate.

Florence's concern about her aging mother and confidence in her decision to put work before family, and Oxford friend Benjamin Jowett's gentle prodding to visit her parents and get some country air rather than constantly stay indoors and overwork, convinced Florence to keep Fanny company. "At whichever place you are, when I am able to leave London, I shall go *there* my dearest Mum." Flo certainly would not consider traveling for her own health, "but to see my dearest Mum — and, if it were possible, Papa too."[21]

Neither Embley nor Lea Hurst had seen Florence for nine years.

"I mean to come ... *for the two months* immediately following the breaking up of parliament."[22] Because as long as parliament sat and ministers were in town, Nightingale had be there to confer with her chiefs at the war and India offices.

Florence had not traveled since Clough's death. Now, aside from her work, she must do what he had done — make arrangements, including hire of an invalid carriage. WEN and Fanny little knew "what my life is, without husband, brother, housekeeper," how difficult "for me to work at all."[23] "It is a misfortune that none of my" family "have ever known"[24] illness.

Nonetheless, Flo did "not dread the journey whether to Embley or Lea Hurst so much as you think with you at the end of it," she told Fanny. "I don't believe it will do me as much" damage "as moving to Hampstead (house, furniture & maids,) without a man to" help. "I have always lost the whole three months at Hampstead in recovering the move. 7 weeks at home without a household — even with two journeys — will do me less harm."[25] Note: Nightingale's use of the word "home."

—⚭—

Concern for Florence's frailty and aloneness caused Jowett, two years later, to urge exchanging hot, chaotic London for the clear, fresh breezes of her "hilltop home." Only if her mother were at Lea Hurst, said Flo. Jowett wrote Fanny. She begged Florence to come.

Flo found her mother "so much gentler, calmer, more thoughtful."[26] Fanny had gained "in truth of view, in real memory of the phases of the past, in appreciation of her great blessings, in happiness, real content & cheerfulness — and in lovingness."[27]

Shocked, nonetheless, at how Fanny's fading health had put a dent in her perfect housekeeping, let alone that both aging parents were proving unfit to manage their affairs, Flo took over. "People who have carriages and butlers and housekeepers and who drive out every day for their pleasure" ask "me, who have none of these things and am always in bed — and am chained to the oar — ask ME to pay their [parents'] bills and do their business,"[28] Flo fulminated against Parthe.

As late summer sun filtered through the chintz blinds of Fanny's bedroom, its chest of drawers, mantelpiece, and small tables covered with framed family likenesses and other memorabilia, Flo and her mother spoke frankly of past disputes. "*This* sort of conversation only arises when she is lying quite quietly in bed & I am sitting close to her quite quietly. *Never* when she is walking about the room, or when she makes me walk about the room looking at things." Flo had never seen Fanny "anything like so good, so happy, so wise or so really true as she is now." With "regard to me, her views are so clear," so "generous." Flo felt them "not deserved."[29]

Fanny admitted much blame. Florence admitted the truth of her mother's words: "you would have done nothing in life, if you had not resisted me."[30]

—⟋⟍—

Once back in London, Nightingale pulled strings to prod the new poor-law secretary. Consequently, he convened a committee to ascertain the space needs of workhouses and their infirmaries including provision for nurses. But the secretary excluded Florence.

Swallowing her pride, she asked to be heard. The committee agreed. Nightingale's paper promoted the importance of ABC for workhouse nursing.[31] To her utter surprise, the secretary based the bill he introduced into parliament, on Florence's paper. She lobbied influential friends and got brother-in-law Harry Verney to persuade fellow members of parliament. The bill passed.*

"We have been so busy with the metropolitan poor bill," Flo apologized to her mother, that "it has been quite impossible to me to write." And "I have had such an attack on my chest [racking cough] that for 17 nights I could not lie down. It could not have happened at a worse time. For it has made me in arrears with my work."[32]

Concomitantly, tragedy struck the Liverpool workhouse infirmary. Its

---

*Within ten years trained and salaried nurses were tending the sick poor classified and housed in separate medical institutions according to Nightingale's ABC plan.

outstanding matron died of typhoid fever. Florence used the eulogy she wrote for Agnes Jones to endorse nursing.[33] WEN disliked "let her not merely rest in peace. But let hers be the life to stir us up to fight the good fight." That "sentence I would repeat," Flo declared, "if I could, like a street preacher, to all those lazy, selfish women in carriages whom" she saw from her bedroom window "blocking up the park at this moment."

"As for myself, I am so weary & heavy-laden that, if the next existence for me were that of an owl, so that I could live for 100 years at rest, without any men throwing their business upon me which they ought to do themselves, I should be glad."[34]

The task of finding Agnes's successor fell, of course, to Florence. And "they expect me to manage the" Liverpool workhouse infirmary "from my bedroom."[35] "Days & weeks in arrear,"[36] Nightingale nonetheless made sure Agnes Jones's death did not mean failure of the Liverpool workhouse experiment.*

—◊◊◊—

Florence now received a welcome request. The army wanted female nurses. To head the venture, Nightingale recommended the only woman with experience and ability to superintend army nurses. But Florence's friend and Crimean colleague Jane Shaw Stewart did not see herself as a pioneer. Extremely reluctant to become superintendent of the military's female nursing service and matron at the army's major hospital, Shaw Stewart, in the end, succumbed to Nightingale's urging. Stewart insisted on Florence's Crimean model: all nurses directly responsible to her and she to the war secretary. This sidestepped hospital governor Colonel Wilbraham. Conflicts, naturally, came up.

"A lawyer seeing this letter," plus the fact that Stewart never "breathed a word against col. W., while he has filled the air with his complaints & to people who had as little to do with it as the Queen of the Sandwich islands — would at once" say "he & not she" should resign, Nightingale said.

She advised her ally senior war-office functionary Douglas Galton that the war office should order Stewart "to bed for a week. Order col. Wilbraham" and "all those who made the 'row' in the ward, to bed for a week — Then order them to kiss & shake hands."[37]

Instead, Wilbraham accused "Stewart of manslaughter — *because* she

---

*At the same time uncle Sam Smith, who took care of Florence's money matters, fell ill. She offered to relieve him. Sam refused. So Flo apologetically asked him to take care of a question about taxes on her house. Ill and drowning in work due to Agnes Jones's death, Florence felt unable to deal with such small business details — and rued the fact that her father and brother-in-law did not offer to relieve her of them.

interfered to prevent every patient from choosing his own orderly to sit up with him" and said orderly "forbidding the ward night-orderly to enter his ward!!! Half an hour after this insane proceeding had been" stopped, a patient died. Wilbraham blamed Stewart. To Nightingale, "the worst of it" was not the "too absurd" accusations against her protégée — "but how can her post be of any use to the service after such a scene as this?"[38]

Shaw Stewart resigned. Florence "had to do the most painful" thing "I have ever had to do in my most painful life."[39] Admit to failure. Twelve years after the Crimean War, her attempt to create a permanent army nursing service fell short. Nightingale insisted on the matron's supremacy in all matters of nursing discipline. The war office wanted female nurses to conform to the military hierarchy.*

Pleurisy, meanwhile, brought Nightingale's dear Mother Moore close to death. Careful nursing saved her, but the nun's failure to "recover her strength or appetite" worried Florence. Moore "liked some orange jelly" that Fanny sent her daughter "from Embley two or three weeks ago better than anything else. And, since then, I have been supplying her with orange jelly & other things from Gunter's.[40] If, by Tuesday's box, mrs. Watson could send some more *orange* jelly for her — & also, are there not nourishing things like *arrowroot blancmange* or *rice blancmange*? — we should be very much obliged."[41]

Nightingale provided her friend with ample portions of "Gunter's turtle soup. She understands that I shall never forgive her, unless she becomes as fat as a lord mayor with time & soup."[42] And keeping in mind the beneficial effect on convalescents "of beautiful objects," especially "brilliancy of color,"[43] Florence made sure Moore's modest room had fresh flowers. "I see the reign of azaleas is beginning," Flo wrote her "dearest Mum." I "shall be quite furious if Hill does not send me *twice* a week ... a *sheet* of azaleas, yellow, white & red, scarlet & pink & not mulct me as he did last year. But I don't complain of your scarlet rhododendrons — they have been splendid this year — but hardly any lilies of the valley have I had."[44]

Affection deepened Moore and Nightingale's mutual esteem, born at Scutari. Florence treasured the nun's rare visits, appreciated her loan of religious books, and could "never forget your kindness." To "think of your being willing to leave your most important post to come & nurse only me, or to send me one of my dear sisters. I feel as if I never could, God only can, tell you how grateful I am. But I must not take advantage ... I shall struggle on

*Four years after Nightingale's death World War I broke out (1914). Britain created a military nursing service on her model. The matron-in-chief reported directly to the war office.

until I can work no longer." Nevertheless, "mind you write to me, dearest reverend mother, for your letters are nearly the only earthly comforts I have."[45]

In turn, Moore "never felt restraint in speaking with you, or rather, you are almost the only one, dearest miss Nightingale, to whom I can speak freely on religious subjects — I mean my own feelings on them."[46]

Seeking God's will with a pure heart, the two women strove to lead honest, selfless lives. They believed in religious truth as a guide and reason for active service. Genuine devotion to the will of God showed itself in work for the needy, not in talking about faith. "The most religious mind I ever knew was that of a R. Catholic revd. mother, who was so good as to go out with me to the Crimea. After we came home I found her one day cleaning out a gutter with her own hands. I know she did it on no theory. I think she had much better have employed a man to do it, but that is what I mean by a true idea of religious life, and she the only R. Catholic too I have ever known who never tried to convert me."[47]

"I am trying to break a daily intermittent fever" and "am totally unable to sit up or to talk." For "the next fortnight at least, I" could not "see even you," Flo wrote her dearest Liz Herbert. "I saw my mother on Sunday, & have scarcely been able to breathe since."[48] The insomnia, headaches, mood swings, even depression of menopause now exacerbated similar brucellosis symptoms. To conserve her energy, Florence received visitors one at a time only. And in reply to discreet inquiries, she said her health precluded seeing any royal lady who had no practical interest in hospitals or nursing. She certainly would never be well enough to see royalty attended by its usual entourage of ladies-in-waiting.

Consequently, Nightingale got "a fresh neophyte"[49] in the person of Prussia's crown princess (Queen Victoria's daughter). "I liked her — much better than I expected* ... (I received her in bed.)"[50] She "has a quick intelligence, and is cultivating herself in knowledge of sanitary (and female) administration for her future great career [building a hospital and nurse training school in Berlin]. She comes alone like a girl, pulls off her hat and jacket like a five-year-old, drags about a great portfolio of plans, and kneels by my bedside correcting them. She gives a great deal of trouble. But I believe it will bear fruit."[51]

Concomitantly, Florence launched a new project. Medical advances like chloroform caused women to demand painless childbirth. Having a baby

---

*True to her liberal upbringing, Nightingale disapproved of Prussia's autocratic government.

changed from a natural, female-dominated, at-home event attended by lay midwives to a hospital-based medical specialty.

Judging childbearing "*not* a disease or an accident" but "*naturally* a *natural process* of health,"[52] Nightingale thought trained midwives could handle village deliveries. So she crafted a midwifery training course and, with the Nightingale Fund council, arranged its placement in London's well-known King's College hospital. Graduates would offer expert childbirth services to women who had none — the rural poor. Florence intended this program to be the nucleus of a national, government-run plan.

County parishes were asked to choose candidates in their late twenties and "of good health & good character, to follow a course of *not* less than 6 months practical training." The parish paid for room and board. In return, a graduate agreed to serve her parish for four years. The Fund gave each trainee a stipend, paid for training expenses, bought and kept up "the lying-in beds. In fact, we establish this branch of the hospital which did not exist before," Nightingale wrote her friend the influential journalist Harriet Martineau when she accepted Harriet's offer to publicize this new venture.

Obstetricians "generously entered heart & soul into the plan." They undertook to teach the women who were "entirely under the lady sup't of the hospital — certainly the best moral trainer of women I know. They will be lodged *in* the hospital, close to her."[53]

Mary Jones, head of Anglican St. John's House, and Florence Nightingale had been friends and colleagues since the latter recruited nurses for Scutari. Jones and some of her nurses already worked at King's as an autonomous unit. They had improved cleanliness and food and eliminated patient inebriation. Now put in charge of the midwife training program as well, Jones wanted to install The Nightingale System. That caused a clash with the hospital's all-male clerical and medical council, who challenged Jones's power to hire and fire nurses. "One female trained head" must be responsible for all nursing management and discipline, Florence encouraged. "Don't let the doctor make himself the head nurse, and there is no worse matron than the chaplain."[54]

Jones, however, decided her staff would function more effectively if she were chaplain. She had an altar put in her room the better to minister to nurses' spiritual needs. Other sects, not to mention the hospital governors, objected. Nightingale advised Jones to compromise. Jones refused. Hospital authorities stood firm. Without telling Florence, Jones resigned and removed her nurses. To Nightingale the affair proved that "*sisterhoods are from henceforth impossible.*"[55]

—ɯ—

Mary Jones's defection* and King's College hospital's high rate of death from puerperal fever (actually no higher than in any other large metropolitan hospital) ended the Nightingale midwife training program. Nonetheless, Florence wanted to know why so many women died in childbed.

Statistics must contain a clue to the answer. But no data existed for childbirth mortality. Shocked, Nightingale began to gather facts despite being "so overwhelmed with business that I know not what it is to do anything but choose *which* is most urgent to do first."[56] Staunch friend and sanitation colleague Sutherland helped. Doctors were doubtful, institutions disobliging. Still, her contacts gave Nightingale enough information for an initial deduction. Regardless of poverty and dirt, home deliveries had a much lower mortality rate than those in hospital maternity wards.

Thunderstruck, Florence corresponded with doctors, matrons, sanitarians, and engineers around the world. *Introductory Notes on Lying-in Institutions* resulted.

The little book used statistics to prove how maternity wards harbored disease. Student doctors attended deliveries directly after dissecting cadavers and without washing their hands or changing their aprons; indeed, many proudly pointed to the amount of blood and pus splashed across their protective clothing. Hence, hospitals must ban medical students from delivery rooms and lying-in wards. Further, hospitals must be organized to house mothers in small rooms separate and far from medical and surgical cases. And lying-in sections should have more sinks to facilitate frequent hand-washing. Nightingale also provided detailed instructions for mother and baby baths, cleaning of bed linen, beds, ward furniture, and rooms. "Risks in lying-in institutions may" be "materially diminished by providing proper hospital accommodation, and by care, common sense, and good management."[57]

Florence did not invent these notions.[58] But her small, readable book and the prestige associated with her name brought them to public attention.

—⚹—

Introductory Notes on Lying-in Institutions also promoted midwifery as a career for educated women. Instead of agitating to enter medical school, they should use current opportunities, such as "attending as physicians their own sex — especially in lyings-in." Nightingale thought females should "begin by that branch of the profession (midwifery) which is undoubtedly theirs," do "it as well as possible," and the "rest will follow."[59]

---

*The debacle at King's failed to interrupt Nightingale and Jones's friendship. Immediately after a serious illness, for instance, Jones stayed with Florence at South Street; afterwards, Nightingale got her mother to invite Jones to convalesce at Embley. And Nightingale continued to consult Jones on nursing matters.

"It is a good thing you are at Lea Hurst," said Sutherland, "or your 'dear sisters' would infallibly break your head."[60]

Her "dear sisters" had good cause to thank Florence Nightingale despite her refusal to be co-opted into the formal women's liberation movement. Experience had shown Nightingale a need — for trained hospital nurses. She saw women — the Victorian model of the nurturing female — as uniquely qualified to fill that need.

Through personal example and assiduous attention to her school, Florence led the way in changing the concept of hospital nurse from drunken menial to medical professional. And by insisting that nursing be a secular vocation she gave it credibility.

Nightingale's resolve, moreover, that the matron rule in nursing matters not only popularized the pyramid arrangement of matron, sister, nurse but also, by locking it into The Nightingale System, established a career structure. Within a generation the Nightingale nurse training school created an accepted, respectable, well-paid occupation for women at a time when they had few, if any, options to earn their way to independence.

As a young woman, Florence Nightingale identified an evil in the world: a woman's lack of power over her life. Because she perceived the evil others did not yet see, Florence described herself, in *Cassandra*, as having "awakened too early." And lamented her lack of "power to discover the remedy for"[61] that evil.

Now Nightingale could take comfort in having empowered females to take control of their lives. She had succeeded in providing women like herself, women who sought a profession, what Florence described as a "necessary occupation," something to satisfy and make full use of their faculties, with the opportunity to fulfill their dreams.

22

Family Matters

Florence the first
Empress of scavengers
Queen of nurses
Maîtresse of drôlesses[1]
Governess of the governors of India
Reverend mother superior
Mother of the British army
&c. &c. &c.[2] — Benjamin Jowett

Deep-red dahlias and pink-petalled echinacea adorned Nightingale's elegant South Street home when close friends Clarkey and Julius Mohl came to stay (1868). "The nicest little house in London"[3] had four floors besides cellar and attics. Upper rooms gazed across the gardens of a grandiose private house to Hyde Park.

"Maids and little dinners perfect,"[4] said WEN, whose wife had long ago given him good cause to judge. Five maids, cook, and footman, an army veteran known as Miss Nightingale's Messenger, made up the flawlessly run household. Florence managed every detail including each day's menu, which she returned to her cook the next morning with comments. These tended to be positive, but sometimes "grilled chicken like wood, all nourishment out of it. Irish stew the same — & in a puddle of potato purée — not potatoes properly broken over it."[5]

Flo conversed "with all her old animation. On the whole" she seemed "rather better than six or seven years ago, when" Clarkey turned "at the door to look at her, thinking I would never see her again."

Nonetheless, Clarkey thought Flo's work "too much for her. Not only has she that huge business of sanitary organization in India, but to keep up the war office to the new sanitary regulations and the incessant correspondence about nurses she has sent" to "towns in England and the colonies." Then she "must inspire other nurses to fight with towns and counties about infirmaries, workhouses, water-supply." What "an endless, ever-renewed, almost hopeless fight with indifference, ignorance and waste."[6]

245

—*m*—

Two years after the Mohls' visit, a "dreaded letter" arrived. Since war had broken out between Prussia and France,[7] Nightingale's Fresh Neophyte, the Prussian crown princess, sought advice on several hospital issues having to do with war wounded. "What *am* I to answer; how to express sympathy to Prussia without alienating France"?[8]

Florence harbored the liberal's distaste for Napoléon III's despotism, but it trumped her intrinsic dislike of Prussia's autocracy and militarism. Still, war victims mandated strict neutrality. So she sent a Nightingale nurse to help Prussia's crown princess with hospital war work, and nurses to tend the wounded of both sides. With help from longtime friend Lady Ashburton,* moreover, Florence raised money among her circle of friends and family for relief of all injured, ill, or imprisoned soldiers.

Great Britain's recently formed Red Cross society asked Nightingale to drop all work and take charge. She declined on grounds of poor health. Actually, Florence thought sanitation for India, which affected the lives of millions, must take priority.

Nevertheless, "all that *can* be done, how little, *must* be done for the sufferers by one already" overloaded with work and "incurable illness."[9] When the Red Cross sent Nightingale's close friend and colleague sanitarian John Sutherland and her cousin and Nightingale Fund secretary, Henry Bonham-Carter, to visit combatant hospitals, Florence helped write their report. She also vetted volunteers for Red Cross service and advised the executive committee, whose members included war-office ally and senior factotum Douglas Galton, as well as brother-in-law, Fund chairman, and member of parliament Harry Verney. "It would be little use to the wounded" were we "to send hospital supplies to the seat of war" and they "be seized by the enemy. They must be neutralized" and "placed under the 'Red Cross.' O that I could go out myself to the" battlefield "to work, instead of all this writing, writing, writing"![10]

The French awarded Nightingale their Société de Secours aux Blessés[11] medal. Germany bestowed the Prussian Cross of Merit. And when the Swiss founder of the international Red Cross visited London, he opened his address to the British Red Cross with: "Though I am known as the founder of the Red Cross and the originator of the" Geneva convention, "it is to an Englishwoman that all the honor of that convention is due." The "work of miss Florence Nightingale in the" Crimea "inspired me."[12]

---

*Louisa Baring, Lady Ashburton, member of Clarkey and Selina Bracebridge's circle. Friend, comfort, and support to Florence during her early struggles between duty to family and desire to nurse.

—w—

At about the same time, St. Thomas's Hospital, home of Florence's eponymous, pioneering school for nurse training, moved to new quarters (1871). Located in Lambeth, on the bank of the busy river Thames opposite the houses of parliament and Big Ben, the enlarged hospital consisted of seven airy, light-filled pavilions. More beds meant a need for more nurses. Sadly, the school could not provide them.

Florence summoned sisters, nurses, and students. With mounting horror she heard how technical and moral training failed to meet her standards. Ward sisters gave no practical instruction. Overworked students had no time for classes, while regular nurses were underused. Sloppy bookkeeping prevailed. Pressures of the larger facility made hospital matron and school superintendent Sarah Wardroper alarmingly cantankerous. And "for 7 years" chief medical instructor Whitfield did "nothing — absolutely nothing — in instruction to our probationers." He "has not even said one word to them to show them *how to keep cases,*" has "given them no assistance as to their notes of lectures."

Even worse, Whitfield "*for 7 years*" had "habits of intoxication."

"For 5 years or more he has been in habits of intercourse with our women to the verge (& beyond) of impropriety." Were Nightingale "to pursue the enquiry, I believe it would be found to the verge of immorality."[13]

Florence aimed to lift nursing out of drunkenness and depravity. Her school admitted only women of proven moral character. She created a system to protect them from sexual harassment. Centered in the nurses home where matron and sisters supervised closely and disciplined strictly (flirting meant immediate dismissal), students were taught to wrap themselves in a cloak of ladylike conduct. It had proved beneficial to Nightingale in the Crimea. Emulation would shield her nurses from unwanted attentions. Whitfield's egregious conduct threatened the very fabric of the school, to say nothing of the nascent nursing profession.

—w—

Nightingale blamed herself. Focus on her children in the army, at home and in India had led to laxity over her school. But since a recent change in government meant the departure from office of ministers sympathetic to Florence's interests, she could, indeed must, concentrate on her other children — her daughters. The best way would be to enter St. Thomas's as a patient in a general ward.

"Do not do this; 1. because it is eccentric & we cannot straighten our lives by eccentricity: 2. because you will not be a patient, but a kind of directress to the institution viewed with great alarm by the doctors," begged

Nightingale's Oxford intimate, the classics professor and theologian Benjamin Jowett. Besides, becoming a patient in a general ward "will kill you — I do not add the annoyance to your father of a step which he can never be made to understand."[14]

As she often did, Florence listened to Jowett. But decided to move next door to the hospital and asked loyal friend Sarah Sutherland to find housing. Matron Wardroper balked; everyone would see Nightingale as her superior and apply to her as such. So to the relief of all, Florence stayed at number 10 South Street.

After much delicate diplomacy, she and Fund secretary Bonham-Carter got Whitfield to resign. They then engaged a new medical director. He and Nightingale organized a rigorous course of instruction, raised examination standards, and instituted required reading.

Dispensing dollops of tact, Florence then got Wardroper's agreement to engage an assistant who would relieve her of responsibility for the students' home. This home sister took charge of befriending the girls, encouraging their interest in literature, music, and art, as well as regular church attendance. For Florence believed character development to be as important to a nurse as her technical training.

Finally, Nightingale made sure to see Wardroper more often. They unraveled the mystery of a pyaemia (blood poisoning with fever) outbreak. "*All the refuse of the hospital*" and "officers' houses, had been" brought "to a dusthole between *No. 7* block & the *steward's* house — & only emptied twice a week."

"A few weeks ago the *steward* (not liking the smell) transferred the dusthole to the *basement under* no. 3 block — & close under the windows of our probationers' home."

"A fatal case of pyaemia appeared immediately in *no. 3 block* — & several cases of illness among the prob'rs."

No pyaemia appeared "in no. 7 block since" removal of "the dust-hole."

"All this time no" man made "the least enquiry" despite "appalling" smells. Two females "(one a sick woman in her bed ½ an hour's distance off)"[15] solved the problem.

—〰—

A sick woman had maximum impact on each student's education and personal growth. Used "to influence people" by "leading in *work*," having to "influence them by talking and writing is hard." Worse "than being cut short by death is being cut short by life in a paralyzed state."[16] Nonetheless, Florence saw her probationers regularly, invited their appraisal of practical training and medical lectures, and wrote a character evaluation for each.

"Carefully dressed in my best garments," a student stood ready for her first visit to South Street. A nurse ran up. "'Miss Nightingale always gives a cake to the probationer who has tea with her, and the size of the cake varies according to the poverty or otherwise of'" her visitor's dress, said the nurse. Our student "hurried upstairs, exchanged my best coat" for an old one, "and came home from my tea-party the proud possessor of a cake so large" it "went the round of" all "thirty-six probationers."[17]

This story vastly amused Florence.

Whether her graduates served in London or a faraway colony, Nightingale planned for, and advised, each. And she made sure they took holidays, often helping with expense, inviting them to stay at South Street, or asking her mother to do the honors at Embley. "I am immersed in such a torrent of my trained matrons and nurses, going and coming," to "and from watering-places for their health, dining, tea-ing, sleeping — sleeping by day as well as by night."[18] This "not only compels me to give up" much "of my Indian & war office work, but takes out of me" more "than any thing did before."[19]

Like her mother an excellent hostess, Florence made the nurse's "visit not only restful and restoring by all manner of material comfort," such as morning tea in bed, but "interesting and brightening as well." If "the Verneys were in residence at no. 4" South Street, "Nightingale laid them under contribution for our entertainment, and right kindly did they respond." Parthe might take her sister's guest for a drive in the park at a fashionable hour or Sir Harry secure entry to parliament's visitors gallery to hear a debate. And dinner at the Verneys' guaranteed interesting conversation.

Nonetheless, meeting The Chief took pride of place. If Florence felt well enough, she came down to the drawing room. How "cheerful to find her on the couch, relieved from the imprisonment of bed, dressed in soft black silk with a shawl over her feet; always the transparent white kerchief [of fine hand-made lace] laid over her hair and tied under the chin," letters and papers piled high beside her, a sharp-pointed pencil ready at hand.

The discussion usually started "at half past four and often lasted through several hours; sometimes with a short interval." Hostess and guest talked business, but "naturally you gave her an account of the day's doings; she entered into them with zest," which "led on to other subjects. Sometimes she would speak of India," or Egypt, but rarely of the Crimea and, if she did, always "with affectionate remembrance of mrs. Bracebridge."

Florence "listened to all one said with an open mind and made much of" points "she approved. But now and again she flashed out a dissent, in a tone of maternal authority."[20]

Indeed, Nightingale's attitude "to her lieutenants in the field" represented that "of a mother to daughters."[21]

"You are all my children," Florence wrote one of her nurses, "& I only wish God gave me a mother's duties. He has given me a mother's heart towards you."[22]

She loved her nurses' company, especially the bright and beautiful, and they reciprocated. In exaggerated Victorian epistolary style, she nicknamed tall, lovely Rachel Williams "Goddess Baby." Rachel's doctor prescribed a seaside holiday. Florence urged her not to cut it short, contributed towards the cost, and invited Rachel to South Street on her return. "Dishes for miss Williams," Florence instructed her cook, "rissoles, or fillets of sole à la maître d'hôtel, or oyster patties, or omelette aux fines herbes, or chicken à la mayonnaise with aspic jelly, or cutlets a la 'béchamelle.'"[23]

—⁊⁊⁊—

"My father and mother are well, but they age very much," Flo confided to Selina Bracebridge. "They are unfit to be left. I spent two thirds of last year with them, to the destruction of my work, and twenty-two hours out of every twenty-four in the room next my mother's. And still felt I could not do enough for them."[24]

Fanny varied "so exceedingly that I can form no settled judgment about her. Yesterday she rushed into my room and" said "she "was 'a dying woman.' And indeed I thought so. Three hours afterward she was walking, like a girl of 15, briskly on the terrace — calling cheerfully to me in bed ... to come & admire the view. N. B. It was quite dark."[25]

Arriving at Embley in rhododendron time (1872), Flo found her mother's longtime personal maid locking increasingly blind and confused Fanny in her room for hours on end. Reluctant to upset her mother by summarily sacking a familiar servant, Florence thought it best to let the maid stay until she found a suitable replacement. Although losing her memory, Fanny Nightingale still had her wits; infirm rather than ill, she had no need of a sick nurse. Rather, Flo sought "a confidential attendant, a maid to an invalid aged lady — a person of some education."[26] With faithful Sarah Sutherland's help, Florence found her.

Installing the new maid in a household staffed with well-established servants called for consummate tact. So did firing the old personal maid. And all that paled in comparison to accustoming confused, almost blind Fanny to a stranger's care. Florence's mother refused to let the new maid do anything for her. "Twice I was summoned to my mother's bedside" to "find her livid & as far as my knowledge goes on the brink of convulsions."[27] Over several fraught weeks, interrupted by urgent business demanding her presence in London, Florence successfully negotiated the transition her mother had sworn would kill her.

—⟋∭⟍—

"Every day ... I" do "what my doctor calls: absolute self-destruction." Even "worse, I am destroying my work by my visits of attendance to my mother. I cannot do more."[28]

Jowett advised taking advantage of this exceedingly difficult situation by writing some essays on the idea of God.

Unhappy, frustrated at being away from the work she loved, Florence again found solace in metaphysical speculation. Two of her essays were published.

JOWETT: Will you help with my translation of Plato's *Dialogues*?

NIGHTINGALE: I'm so pleased you've decided to use my comments.

JOWETT: I'd like you to choose some Bible stories for a children's edition. You might also enjoy collecting and translating extracts from medieval mystics[29] and showing how mysticism applies to contemporary life.

JOWETT: I liked your extracts. Why not write a preface expressing your idea of mysticism and explaining how to use mystical books?

This project comforted Nightingale during months (1873) at Lea Hurst, as she struggled to learn how to "love & forgive & *not* to care for people or their opinions nor to live in thoughts of them but of God. O God teach me"![30] Mysticism also brought a "taste of heaven in daily life," since managing her parents' households meant coping with dreary domestic details. "To be turned back to this petty stagnant stifling" life. "I should hate myself (I *do* hate myself) but I should LOATHE myself, oh my God, if I could *like* it."[31] Lately Flo had felt herself to be "so broken up & broken down: nothing solaces me so much as to write upon the laws of the moral world: especially as exemplifying, if possible, the character of the perfect God, in bringing us to perfection thro' them in eternity."[32]

"Jowett spent three days here," Clarkey wrote husband Julius Mohl from Lea Hurst. "He is a man of mind; I think he would suit you. He is very fond of Flo, which would also suit you. She is here," her conversation "most nourishing," truly "eloquent." She "quite surprised me."[33]

"I am the most unfortunate Tantalus in your hands," Flo wrote her dear Julius Mohl. "What! You wrote to me on the very subject of all others I care most about, viz. the 'principle of morals' & your 'speculations' about it, & 'on its difference or agreement with the Stoics & others.' And you did not send it to me."

"'Fiend! thou torment'st me ere I come to hell!' Send it me this minute."[34]

—⟋∭⟍—

To her disgust, meanwhile, Florence had to deny her friend William Rathbone, pioneer in bringing trained nurses to workhouse infirmaries. He wanted help in creating a district nursing plan for London. Nightingale could not do the work from Lea Hurst. But she could — and did — write *Suggestions for Improving the Nursing Service for the Sick Poor*. Rathbone based the metropolitan nursing association on it, and a Nightingale protégé became London's first district nursing superintendent.

Florence chose another protégé, Franco-Prussian War veteran Elizabeth Barclay, as matron for the eminent Royal Edinburgh Infirmary. She liked Barclay's "simplicity, straight-forwardness, uncompromising duty-ideas, strong will & courage & I think sense."

The Nightingale Fund council should insist on basic conditions for Barclay, "easier for us to do for her." For example, "the fever house now to be converted into nurses' house shall be lime washed so as almost to be turned into lime — floors thoroughly saturated with beeswax & turpentine or such mixture — drainage thoroughly seen to &c &c."

"There are some things which she will much better obtain by her own personal influence when *there*" — "e.g. the persuading the doctors to evacuate the compartments appropriated to their use & their clerks in nearly every ward — (a most horrible invention — how *can* you answer for nurses' behavior with such a trap in the ward.)"[35]

Whether Edinburgh proved too much for Barclay or her weaknesses were slow to surface, she became addicted to drink and drugs. Nightingale summoned Barclay to Lea Hurst. "But when she drove up to the door, I felt as if all my senses were forsaking me: & I could not think what I had to say to her. However, I suppose God" helped. "*I* could speak to her as a woman to another woman's *higher self* in the presence of God: & not in the presence of authority: since I am only her chief by courtesy."

After extremely painful yet astoundingly frank talks the two women agreed that Barclay return to Edinburgh for a month, then request six months' leave, ostensibly to recover her health. During that time a Nightingale favorite, Angélique Pringle, whom she nicknamed The Pearl beyond Price, would take over.

Barclay's "confessions were" pitiful. "I never saw a face such a tragedy of woe," such "a wreck of a woman," Flo told her trusted cousin and Fund secretary Henry Bonham-Carter. For that reason Nightingale insisted on Barclay taking six months' leave. But afterwards, Flo and Henry agreed, Barclay could not return to Edinburgh because "to go back & fail would be: worst of all."[36]

—⁂—

Having moved her parents from Lea Hurst to Embley in the autumn (1873), Florence supervised their households from London. Concomitantly, she and Aunt Mai prevailed on Parthe to look after Fanny for a while. Suffering severe rheumatoid arthritis, responsible for a husband and two households — historic Claydon and 4 South Street — Parthe had, besides, created a writing career for herself. She traveled for research, as well as for pleasure and her health.* Parthe felt that Flo had always been the privileged sister — spending months in Rome and Egypt, allowed to follow her grail to Kaiserswerth and Harley Street, having become a national heroine and darling of the reformers — while dutiful Parthe tended the domestic hearth. Now Parthe's turn had come. Her unmarried younger sister personified nursing. Parthe felt fully justified in leaving their frail mother to Florence.

The extended family gathered at Embley that Christmas. Feeling extremely unwell and, thus, particularly relieved to relinquish her mother's care to Parthe, even if for a short time, Flo left to attend to pressing matters in London. Barely had she settled in South Street when shattering news arrived.

Eighty-year-old WEN had gone for his daily ride along Hampshire's frost-bitten lanes. He then carved the dinner roast for his guests. The next morning, WEN came down to breakfast but, having forgotten his watch, left the table to get it. He slipped on the stairs and died instantly (January 5, 1874).

"No one knows what a break up it is to us; and to have had no last word," Flo lamented. Still, she could take comfort in the thought of her father's death not being "awful for *him*. His was the purest mind" and "the most simple heart I have ever known." WEN "always wished to go out of the world" quietly. "I never saw anyone who hated the smallest 'demonstration' or show so much."[37] No wonder WEN's daughter traveled home from the Crimea incognito.

Bound to bed by illness, she did not attend her father's funeral. Flo and her sister agreed that with Embley full of guests, Flo should come when Parthe left.

Two weeks after WEN's death Florence arrived to find Embley "'all withered when my father died.' For me it is different from what it is for anyone else." Although "I lie in the same rooms," "I did not ... hear the same laughing."[38] Worst of all, Fanny wandered "much and painfully."[39] Flo's mother cried in confusion. She could not comprehend why she must move out of her home.

---

*Marriage removed Parthe's need to contend with Flo. Household management, not to mention her husband's insistence on full attention to all his interests, filled a confident and happy Parthe's time. She hosted a small salon in her London house where Verney's parliamentary and philanthropic associates mixed with family and friends. Proud of Parthe's books on dreams, female education in France, the dignity of labor, and decline of honesty in commerce, Florence bought many as gifts and for military libraries.

The Nightingale entail left WEN's landed property — Embley and Lea Hurst — to his only sibling, Mai Smith. Mai would, Flo knew, "be very much overcome" by WEN's death. "She did so love him."[40] Mai insisted that WEN's widow not "be moved" from Embley "or disturbed in any way." But Mai's masterful daughter Beatrice sent Flo an "exceedingly painful communication." Its strong objection to Mai's kindness "almost killed"[41] Florence.

Daily, family members came up with another plan for Fanny. "We Smiths," Flo thought, "all exaggerate." We "are a great many too many strong characters" and very unlike, "all pulling different ways."[42] In the end, Florence prevailed on the Verneys to ease Fanny's transition by inviting her to Claydon for three months.

Meanwhile, Flo returned to a role of her youth: shouldering responsibility for the dismal details of death. And she took on responsibility for clearing Embley of fifty years of Nightingale life.*

Parthe went to Embley to collect her mother. "Though this day robs me of the last vestige of an earthly home," Florence wrote her sister from London, "I do not forget what this day must be to you in speeding her departure from the home of 50 years. I cannot speak about it."[43]

Home. To Florence home meant Embley. She relied on it, not to mention her mother, for creature comforts like fresh country food, flowers, domestics, even laundry when Flo had no washerwoman. Fanny's personal maid sewed clothes for Flo, or her mother bought them — "the splendid coat enables me to get out of bed & see workmen without having to dress." Thanks, Flo wrote, "for all you did for me in London. It saved me immensely. No one does anything for me but you."[44]

Despite setting parents at a distance while battling to fulfill her dream, to establish her own identity, Florence wanted WEN and Fanny to be, indeed, took for granted that they always would be, a steady, reliable presence in her life. "It was quite a new idea to me that I should survive *her*. The idea that *I* should survive *him* never once (really) crossed my mind. I thought he had 10 years of life: I not one."[45] WEN's death deprived Florence of her father; it also took away her home, her sheet anchor. Death comes in many forms.

Flo had a heart-to-heart talk with Mai's son, My Boy Shore. His family had no immediate need for Lea Hurst, so after three months Florence escorted her mother from Claydon to Derbyshire.

"*Of course*, personally, it would be such a task for me who ought to have

---

*WEN husbanded his personal fortune well. Despite the entail on his landed property, his women were comfortably endowed. Florence's allowance increased and she got a lifetime lease on her South Street house. Fanny inherited a sizeable sum that allowed her to keep a retinue of servants and her carriage. At her death, Fanny left each daughter a respectable amount of money, as well as some shares.

some one to take charge of me to take charge of my dear mum at Lea Hurst," Flo told Parthe. "I should not think of going there *for myself.*"[46] Flo had "not been so ill" since "Herbert's & Clough's deaths, 13 years ago." Yet, Fanny "enjoyed this place" beyond "all I could have anticipated."[47] Sometimes "a gleam of divine happiness" came to "her face worth living to see."[48] Flo's mother found peace among familiar objects and voices, giving "*her* the greatest pleasure that remains to her to be at what she calls 'home.'"[49]

—⚹—

Miserable during those months (1874) at Lea Hurst, suffering the insomnia, headaches, muscle pain, and depression of mutually aggravating brucellosis and menopause, Flo ignored Parthe's and Clarkey's urging to return to London and her beloved work. Florence would not leave her mother to the care of strangers.

She rose before dawn broke over the Derbyshire hills clearly visible from her balcony. The Derwent River rushed below as Florence spent these few precious private hours on essential work issues before tedious household details claimed her.

Flo grieved for her father, her intellectual alter ego who taught her all she ever knew, gave her all the ideas she ever had. WEN's "reverent love for" his daughter had been "inexpressibly touching."[50] He had come round to supporting Kaiserswerth; his commitment, let alone his liberal allowance, made Harley Street possible and gave Flo her freedom. Proud and pleased about her "work — though he did not understand" why she gave up all that makes life pleasant to do it — diffident WEN proved his love, his esteem and loyalty, by giving Florence the means to live in an elite, centrally located London neighborhood. Jowett told "him once that to have a daughter who would keep alive his name was better than to have many sons. He was greatly taken by this."[51]

No matter how ill she felt, how burdened with work, Florence always welcomed her father. She would keep faith with him by lavishing her Incredible Bonté on Fanny.

—⚹—

"Everything has gone from my life except pain,"[52] Flo lamented. "My friends drop off one by one."[53]

Reverend Mother Mary Clare Moore lost a battle with typhoid fever.

Selina Bracebridge, "the angel of my life,"[54] died "a dreary end," a long and painful illness "for her who had been all warmth and radiance." More "than mother to me: and oh that I could not be a daughter to her in her latter times; what should I have been without her?" What "would many have been without her?" "To one living with her as I have, she was unlike any other being here below: hers *was* faith: real sympathy with God…. Excepting my dear Father, I never knew any so really humble: and with hers the most active heart & mind & buoyant soul that could well be conceived."[55] Without Selina "life is indeed" dreary. "She was to me wings, the pure heroic soul who lifted me out of the baser perplexities of life, or gave me strength to do and dare everything."[56]

Charles had died two years before.* "He and she have been the creators of my life." They shared such happy times in Rome, "and when I think of him at Scutari, the only man in all England who would have lived with willingness such a pigging life, without the interest and responsibility which it had to me, I think that we shall never look upon his like again."[57]

Julius Mohl died. "Dearest friend, ever dearest," Florence wrote her devastated Clarkey, leaning on Flochen† for sympathy. She thought daily and "nightly of him and of you: the world is darker"[58] without him. Why "distress yourself (your loss is great" enough, "irreparable, for this world) with saying such things about not having made the most of him while you had him? *He* would not have said so. You found him a melancholy man: you made him a happy one. You gave zest to his life: all" it wanted. "He could not bear to be without you." God "be with us all. Your old Flo."[59]

—⟋⟍⟍—

When early frost descended on Derbyshire, Florence conferred with her sister. Parthe wanted to install Fanny in a rented London house, with Flo in charge.

That "is & must be the merest farce," Florence replied. "I am a prisoner not only of my house but my" floor. "I *can* be of no use to my mother, not only except I be in the same house with her, but except I be on the same floor."[60]

Flo thus arranged that her mother live in London with Shore. His love for Fanny "was like God's," and Shore's wife heaped "devotion and care, beautiful, beautiful care"[61] on her. Nonetheless, the new venue agitated Fanny.

So Florence informed Clarkey that "I am 'out of humanity's reach' in a red [suburban] villa like a monster lobster, in charge of my mother by doctor's orders, as her only chance of recovering her strength enough to see her old home (Lea Hurst) after which she cruelly craved."[62]

Once Fanny no longer blocked the path to her daughter's freedom, Flo-

---

*Selina's sorrow made Flo "glad that when I go there will be no such heart rending grief felt for me as when two are parted, who had lived for nearly half a century with each other and for each other — or as I felt when Sidney Herbert died and feel every day more and more" (Woodham-Smith, *FN*, p. 332, private note, FN).

†German use of "chen" at the end of a name connotes affection.

rence felt the power of her bond with her mother. Certainly Flo realized that she had succeeded in serving God and humanity; equally, she believed there remained much for her to do. Regardless, Florence's link to her mother proved so strong that she now put Fanny before the cause. In making this conscious choice Flo resolved the central conflict in her life: how to reconcile her drive to please Fanny, prove her love, with just as strong a desire to fulfill her dream.

For the first time in twenty-two years Florence Nightingale accepted a salient fact: her work did not decide "where I should live and how I should live."[63]

23

"The People of India"

You initiated the reform which initiated public opinion which made things possible, and now there is not a station in India where there is not something doing.[1]— John Lawrence

We have three compacts: First, that you are to give an hour a day to writing or some unprofessional occupation (and not to overwork) in return for which I will observe hours and days.... Secondly, we have a minor compact ... not to speak evil of others ... this, however, may be occasionally broken when human nature can endure no longer.... Thirdly, we will have a great compact that every year is to be calmer, happier, and more efficient and productive of results than the one which has preceded.[2]— Benjamin Jowett

Lush layers of green covered Derbyshire hills and dales when Nightingale took her mother to Lea Hurst (1879). "My own Flo," her Clarkey dearest wrote, you know I "love you truly"; thus, "you will bear what I say," also you know I "have common sense: you can't help" knowing "it, I defy you"! "If you don't leave that absurd place" instantly, "you must be a little insane — partially, not entirely; and if you saw another person knowingly risking a life that might be useful *dans les grands choses d'ensemble*[3] to potter after sick" persons, "and if you were in a lucid moment you would say 'That person is not quite sane or she has not the strength of will to follow her judgment.'"[4]

"Why do you abuse me for being here?" Flo replied. "Do you think I am here for my own pleasure? Do you think any part of my life is *as I please*? Do you know what have been the hardest years of my life? Not the Crimean war. Not the 5 years with Sidney Herbert at the war office when I sometimes worked 22 hours a day. But the last 5 years and three quarters since my father's death."[5]

Florence's head agreed with Clarkey, but her heart did not. Fanny felt better in her daughter's presence. Flo's wit cheered a mind like "the ceiling of the Sistine chapel — darkened, blotted, effaced, and with great gaps; but if you looked and looked and accustomed your eye to the dimness and broken lights, there were the noble forms transparent through the darkness."[6]

Florence devoted three hours of each afternoon to her mother. "Music to the sick, who *cannot* be active, gives the enjoyment and takes away the nervous irritation of their incapacity,"[7] Flo's popular *Notes on Nursing* advised. She sang to partially blind Fanny, read entertaining novels and cheerful letters aloud. Mother and daughter spoke of religion. Fanny voiced regret for their earlier, fraught relationship. Proud and pleased about her daughter's fame, Fanny Nightingale felt "you have a right to laugh so few of us have. You are so good—so much better than the rest of us. You do me so much good."[8]

Her mother's affirmation that Florence had gladdened Fanny's loving heart by following the commands of her inner spirit certainly gratified Flo. Yet, the coveted blessing she had sought from Kaiserswerth so long ago failed fully to dispel familiar insecurities. Tormented by fear that sacrifice might make her smug, Florence asked, "God what would Thou have me do? (going back to London so ill.) Sin is not the most sinful part of ourselves. *Before* we come to the sin & when we are well content with ourselves, we are often the worst. To have let you (me) go on with the Indian or army work successfully was simply like to letting you go on building beautiful houses. And now you may become complacent in what you are doing here (Lea Hurst.)"[9]

"O God, the slavery I have bound myself to. It has shut me down.... O God take off this yoke," Florence jotted in her diary.

"O God. I do not know" whether "I am thy servant or even whether I wish to be thy servant.

"O God, how canst Thou take one as Thy servant who is bed-ridden and unnoble?

"O take me as Thy hired servant."[10]

Flo spent summer and fall with her mother and the Shore Smiths at Lea Hurst. When My Boy Shore and his family moved back to London, Flo settled Fanny with them. "My mother is like a resurrection under Shore's care and love."[11] Florence also prevailed on Parthe to invite Fanny to Claydon. She usually accompanied her mother, but if urgent business recalled Flo to London she continued to oversee Fanny's care, writing her brother-in-law, Harry Verney, for instance, how happy he made Fanny by visiting her every morning for prayers.

Regardless of location, work absorbed Nightingale. Popular demand plus her enthusiasm made Florence *the* central information source on hospitals. Daily, the postman stopped at 10 South Street to deliver fat envelopes, many bearing exotic stamps. They contained blueprints for every sort of medical institution. Each got a careful critique. These plans "are all very well, as far as they go; but your hospital will never be efficient without adequate provision for a supply of properly trained nurses," read a typical reply if the question referred only to a building. "By all means," Nightingale answered when asked to supply nurses, "but you must satisfy me first that your buildings are sanitary."[12]

Friend, ally, and India viceroy John Lawrence requested a plan to put female nurses in the subcontinent's military hospitals. "From the voluminous Indian documents" she received, Florence knew female nursing in India's general hospitals, so far tried "under very unfavorable circumstances," proved to be "of inestimable advantage to the patients."[13]

But the abysmal state of India's medical service caused her to suggest "a tentative measure"— placement of a select few nurses in one hospital only, to "obtain the experience & knowledge required for future guidance in a new" country. "An extended scheme would" be "not only inexpedient but absolutely impracticable."[14]

Lawrence passed Nightingale's modest proposal to India's medical service. Without "requisite practical knowledge or experience — (not being matrons),"[15] medical officers proposed placing a large number of female nurses into several hospitals simultaneously. This extravagant plan, to say nothing of its cost, scared India's government into scrapping the whole idea.

"There is really no connection between the humble proposal I made" and the plan "condemned without even having been referred to me." Had she seen it Florence would "without doubt or hesitation have condemned it," not only on the basis of expense, "but because I never could have lent my aid or sanction" to "any such system which the experience of my whole life tells me contains proposals which would swamp every principle of good nursing." The "course I ventured to suggest, in obedience to the gov't desire, as the best, has never been considered at all by the gov't on its own merits,"[16] an outraged, not to mention disappointed, Nightingale pointed out to Lawrence.

This incident proved particularly galling as the world saw her as the ultimate authority on nursing. Nor did the episode enhance Florence's ingrained feeling of low self-worth.

Nonetheless, she had the last word. Twenty years later the Indian government decided to put female nurses in its army hospitals. Nightingale personally selected each matron, met with her before she left, and corresponded with them all.

—⚜—

"I remember Scutari and I am one of the few original faithful left, and I think I am attached to you irrespective of sanitation."[17] Robert Napier, former secretary at Great Britain's Constantinople embassy, had, three weeks after Nightingale's arrival at the Barrack hospital, reported on its marked improvement. Later governor of Madras presidency, "truly happy to find that I can do something to please you," Napier built irrigation and drainage systems as well as roads and schools. He urged Florence to "count me as a humble but devoted member of the sanitary band, of *your* band."[18]

To her intense joy the government now appointed Napier commander in chief of the army in India. He spent his last morning in London at number 10 South Street.

Its plain, neat drawing room had acquired some additions since WEN's death forced evacuation of Embley. An upright piano stood against one wall. A vitrine displaying delicate china figures hung in a corner. Tulips and daffodils that Aunt Mai sent from Flo's "dear Embley" filled crystal vases, and the heady scent of hyacinths suffused the room. Nightingale greeted her visitor from a couch near the glowing hearth. She and Napier "were like a brace of lovers on our Indian objects or rather passions & even our rages"[19] about viceroy Lord Mayo.

Mayo had requested a guide for sanitary administration. After consulting her friend former India administrator Sir Bartle Frere and her closest colleague, sanitarian Dr. John Sutherland, Florence summarized the entire subject with an ancillary emphasis on irrigation and agricultural development. Mayo improved sanitation and furthered irrigation; he initiated a census and statistical survey — both basic to sanitary advance — but not fast enough for Nightingale. "He writes & writes — and we write & write — and our letters are masterly. And nothing is done." Napier's "quite extraordinary" practical "knowledge of & love for the native races" would change that.

Since the new commander in chief went straight from South Street to his ship, Florence sent Napier "to India without anything to eat! He said he had too much to talk about to waste"[20] time on a meal.

They designed a plan to reform Indian army health. It ranged from barrack and hospital improvement to education and physical training. But Napier needed Nightingale's help. "A letter from you" would prepare Viceroy Mayo and "have great weight as it was you who raised public opinion in England on these subjects."[21]

"Too much to do, they say, bars progress as much as too little." Florence thought the former fitted her. "I don't feel my work advance. Yet I feel more & more how much it takes out of me" — a "woman overwhelmed with business & illness."[22]

—⁂—

How Some People Have Lived, and Not Died in India[23] summarized sanitary advances on and around British military stations ten years after Nightingale popularized the royal commission report and presented her vision for the subcontinent in *How People May Live and Not Die in India*. Sanitary rules now governed such centers of disease as fairs and pilgrimages. Hospitals, jails, and asylums had better hygiene. Calcutta pointed proudly to its pure water supply.

Florence's experience proved the value of fresh air, so she promoted it for India despite the subcontinent's torrid temperatures, which made shuttered windows in daytime more apt. Her insistence fed ammunition to those who doubted Nightingale in any case — how could she order rules for a place she had never seen? Worse followed.

Thanks to Herbert and Nightingale, high sanitary standards were now the norm at domestic barracks. The India sanitary commission recommended the same for the subcontinent. So Florence and her war-office ally, engineer Douglas Galton, together with sanitarian Sutherland and India expert Frere, planned a model barrack. It delineated the basics but left details to local officials.

Since military defense made up the major part of government expense, "the truest economy" consisted of advancing the improvement of "military stations and their surroundings until every station in India has been put in the most healthy state practicable,"[24] Nightingale introduced her model barrack plan. The India secretary forwarded it to the viceroy. "On seeing your letter," a well-placed friend told Nightingale, the viceroy first fully exonerated "himself to the secretary." His second action, "I have no doubt, will be to call for his officials and hurry on the work."[25] The viceroy did.

But the construction engineers decided to build barracks without civilian meddling — and meddling from a female, to boot. The result: pretentious European-style buildings that totally ignored Indian needs. And soon after the men moved in, cholera struck. A public outcry ensued. Sanitary reform got linked to senseless extravagance.

"I don't let these things corrode me" now. "I am becoming quite a tame beast,"[26] Florence confided to Clarkey. Mellowing with age, Nightingale also absorbed the advice of Oxford luminary Benjamin Jowett, the one close friend whose chiding she could bring herself to accept. "When you think" to "have done nothing, that may be in some degree true, as a fact, amid the difficulties and hindrances of human beings. But is not the greater part a certain state of nerves or a certain attitude of character, like the way which good people have of declaring that they are miserable sinners?"[27]

Delhi held the dubious distinction of being India's least healthy major metropolis. Florence blamed its rising mortality on the disgusting state of the drains. Officials implored her to galvanize their superiors into action. She did but in doing so realized the crucial connection between irrigation and land-ownership. That, in turn, raised issues of representation, education, and usury. So in characteristic fashion Nightingale determined to understand them. Correspondence with senior officials in Britain and India gave her unique access to information. She also consulted retired Anglo-Indians and sought expert tutoring. How, Parthe pressed, could Flo ever know enough about the labyrinthine complexities of India's land questions to be useful? Much better to sever her tie to India. Jowett agreed. Florence refused. After all, in her youth she had known next to nothing about hospitals.

Silvery moonbeams slipped across the leafless trees outside Nightingale's bare bedroom window, open to the brisk night air. She heard God (The Voice) ask if she would willingly cede her *name* for India. Yes — without hesitation.

"Oh God, they are Thy ryots [peasants]." Florence suffered agonies of frustration over the famine in Madras presidency. She prayed that God grant the irrigation she advocated, because "if we had given them water we should not now have to be giving them bread."[28] Ruing her impotence — "the day has been when I might have had a commission on this famine"[29] — Nightingale blamed herself for not having done enough to relieve the sorry lot of the Madras ryots.

Ryots paid a tax (known as a cess) for specific local needs. Nightingale proposed that if a village lacked clean water and drainage, had cholera or typhoid, its cesses first be used to correct these conditions. She drew up a detailed plan. Sanitation experts endorsed it. But the government decided to put its money into railroads, which would turn a quick profit; besides, trains would facilitate grain delivery to drought-stricken areas.

"I have been doing sanitary work for India for 18 years, but for the last four have been continually struck by this dreadful fact: what is the good of trying to keep people in health if you can't keep them in life?" Florence wrote friend and former suitor Richard Monckton Milnes. "Ryots are being done to death by floods, by drought, by zemindars [landowners], and usurers. You must live in order to be well."[30]

—⁂—

Pervasive poverty throughout India, not to mention danger of drought and famine, mandated government action. Florence decided to focus her efforts on irrigation, a field where her sanitary expertise gave credibility. "Your willingness, some months ago, to take steps for securing accurate irrigation statistics from India: & your just complaints that there were none: seem to show you as thinking" there "is ample scope for asking for enquiry," she wrote the India secretary, "& make the prayer of me (who have been up to my neck in Indian 'returns' for 16 years) less audacious." Florence begged pardon, not for urging execution of irrigation plans based on sound statistics, but for "the length of these notes meant to help show the direction inquiry should take, if it is desired to have real results."[31]

They failed to materialize. The India secretary agreed with Nightingale, but his colleagues had different priorities. And budgets were tight.

"The Indian ryot" represents the "most industrious peasantry on the face of the earth," Florence persisted in "The People of India."[32] When famine in Mumbai and Madras presidencies killed one in four people, eight and one-half million in all, the Madras farmer showed "extraordinary self-control." He kept secret "his hoarded pits of grain, hoarded for seed-corn but also for another year of famine — a secret which" many villagers must have known — and "not selling at the time of highest prices — reveals to us a thrift, a self-denial, a political economy" unknown "to any Western nation." This alone would justify "giving the ryots, especially in southern India, every legal help against the money-lender, into whose hands the ancestral lands seem to be passing." Could England "reconquer India by enabling the indebted country ryot to redeem his lands & pay off his debts? What a glorious conquest that would be."[33]

Britain had a duty to those in her empire, but did the public care about Indians dying from needless causes? Reliable statistics were the requisite first step in relieving this tragedy. Then must "better agriculture be taught," to show ryots "how to raise better & more produce" and "give them a market" via "cheap water communication & roads."[34]

The India secretary asked the viceroy to act. But that particular viceroy had his sights set on adding neighboring Afghanistan to Britain's empire.

Nightingale then lobbied the leader of the parliamentary opposition. No success.

Meanwhile, she worked on a book about Indian irrigation and land tenure. Jowett made several revisions but thought the style "too jerky and impulsive, though I think it is logical and effective."[35] Impatient and discouraged, Florence tabled the book.

—⟡—

"My mother is ninety-one and infirm, though she still drives out every day, enjoys a great deal of reading aloud (by a lady companion) and dines with the family."[36] A year later, "after much weariness and" pain, Fanny Nightingale "fell asleep just after midnight" at Shore's London house (early February 1880). "The last three hours were in beautiful peace and all through she had been able to listen to and to repeat her favorite hymns and prayers, and to smile a smile as if she said, 'I am dying: it's all right.'"[37]

Too ill to attend her mother's burial next to WEN in Embley's Wellow village churchyard, Florence, as executor of her mother's will, dove into the bleak duties of death. "Heart and hand and mind have been fuller than I could bear."[38] After "twenty-three years of overwork and illness, of which the last six have been without one day's rest of body or mind,"[39] she felt utterly spent. The doctors prescribed bracing ocean breezes.

Nightingale worked nonstop during her three weeks at the seaside. She thought the hotel, which Parthe recommended, too society oriented to suit her. But Florence did like sitting at her window to watch the wind-whipped waves pounding the shore, a sight not seen since Balaclava. The sea air seemed to make little, if any, difference in her health.

She "must be 'free' for at least a year 'from the responsibilities which have been forced upon me' and 'from letters,'" Nightingale's doctors warned. "But when is that year to come?" Florence decided to leave London again, if only "to work up the arrears of my Indian work, which weigh heavily on my mind."[40]

Faithful old friend and fund-raising helper Louisa Ashburton loaned Nightingale a small country house where she could focus on work in peace and mourn her mother in private. From there, Florence went straight to Claydon. Parthe, suffering from acute rheumatic arthritis, cherished her sister's cheering visits. The Verneys begged Flo to treat Claydon as her country home. Miss Nightingale's Rooms (bedroom, maid's room, and parlor) became a fixture.

Before going for an extended stay, Nightingale provided for her cats. The Persian tom, Mister White, "never made dirt in his life: but he has been brought up to go *to a pan* with sand in it," she told the caretaker.

"He has always been used to have his meals by himself like a gentleman on a plate put upon a 'table-cloth' (on old newspaper) spread on the floor.

"He is not greedy: has never stolen anything: & never drags his bones off his newspaper. But I am sorry to say he has always lived well: he has bones, & milk, in the morning: after 7 o'clock dinner he has any remains of fish not fish bones or chicken — or — game-bones: which he eats like a gentleman off a plate in my room."

"The most affectionate & intelligent" of Florence's feline pets, Mister White "likes of all things to be above in a room with me" and "when his own little sister cat died, he refused food & almost broke his heart. He washes & dresses two little kits we have here (of his) himself. I never saw a tom-cat do this before."[41]

—⚏—

Now almost sixty and free of menopause, Florence felt better physically despite the spinal pain that too often troubled her. Settling cheerfully to the work she found so fulfilling, living in cozy number 10 South Street with her maids, cook, messenger, and cats, not to mention the welcome attentions of affectionate family and friends, Flo derived comfort from having proved to be a true daughter to Fanny.

Her mother's death freed Florence from daily responsibility for an aging and infirm parent. It failed to free her from feelings of inadequacy rooted in earlier conflict with Fanny. "Night of misery.... Pull my soul out of the pit.... *Send me thy love,*"[42] Nightingale implored God. She chastised herself for lack of faith, for not fully listening to God, for not having enough sensitivity about people with whom she dealt. Above all, Florence begged "God forgive me, Oh God save me Christ. I have *never* been thy servant. Make me *thy servant altogether*, not the servant of many seeking their sympathy."[43]

24

"The love that is so broad"

"Thousands of girls" are "named after you." Everyone "has heard of you and has a sweet association with your" name. "May the later years of your life be clearer and happier and more useful than the earlier! If you will believe it, this may be so."[1]— Benjamin Jowett

I want to do a little work, a little better, before I die.[2]— Florence Nightingale

On a glorious spring day in 1881, the Nightingale nurse training school probationers assembled on the smooth green lawn of St. Thomas's Hospital to hear Sir Harry Verney, chairman of the Nightingale Fund council, read his sister-in-law's annual address. "To be a good nurse one must be a good woman," Florence Nightingale advised her daughters.

"What makes a good woman is the better or higher or holier nature: quietness — gentleness — patient endurance — forbearance — forbearance with her patients — her fellow workers — her superiors — her equals. We need to remember that we come to learn, to be taught. Hence we come to obey. No one ever" could "govern who" could not "obey. No one" ever could "teach who" could not learn.

"A good woman should be *thorough*; thoroughness in a nurse is a matter of life & death to the patient," especially "thoroughness in the *unseen* work. Do that well & the other will be done well too." "What does 'like a woman' mean when it is said in contempt"? It means pettiness, envy: "foolish talking: unkind gossip: love of praise." While "we try to be 'like women' in the noble sense of the word let us fight as bravely against all such 'womanly weaknesses.' Let us be anxious to do well, not for selfish praise but to honor & advance the" cause. "Let us value our training not as it makes us cleverer or superior to others, but inasmuch as it enables us to be more useful" to "our fellow" creatures. "Let it be our ambition to be thorough good women, good nurses."

"You are here to be trained for *nurses — attendants* on the wants of the sick — *helpers*, in carrying out doctors' orders." Never "let us be ashamed of the name 'nurse.'"

267

"Let us" stand "shoulder to shoulder" in "the good cause. But let us be" quiet. "Women's influence ever has been ever should be quiet & gentle in its working."[3]

—⁓—

The next year Nightingale felt well enough to visit her school for the first time. She inspected the facilities as minutely as she read each probationer's diary "from month to month." "*As* this was the first day in a new ward, she learnt nothing," Florence noted. "One would think it would be just the contrary."

"Another remark I would make almost universally. No one gives" the "*progress* of the *cases*. One cannot make out from any one's diary whether the case is going well or ill. Surely for one interested in her cases, this is of the first interest."

"In 'taking the temperatures,' she does not tell us *what* they are." Useless "for instance to tell us that she has 'taken the temperatures.' She should at least give us those 'temperatures' which are abnormally high."[4]

Florence had added to her school's curriculum the novelty of probationers attending the national cookery training school. So it scarcely came as a surprise when they complained of "want of variety, want of sufficient *supper*, and want of milk." The students were "tired of cold mutton," they told Nightingale, and would "like cold ham (a thirsty thing methinks) & (more) eggs for breakfast."[5]

—⁓—

Florence Nightingale, 1820–1910. In later life (artist: Sir William Richmond [1887], Photographic Survey, The Courtauld Institute of Art, London, private collection).

Requests for matrons and nurses flooded the school. So much so that Nightingale felt "like a mother, all of whose children are crying for food, & she is agonized at having little or none to give them."[6] Still, Florence managed to send nurses for the army's Egyptian campaign.* Serious flaws soon surfaced. In close touch with her daughters, Nightingale discovered the cause for this reprehensible Crimea Redux: war-office abolition of the purveyor's department, which she and Sidney Herbert had restructured.

The government formed a special committee to make improvements. Florence proposed and prepared witnesses, advised about data gathering, helped identify and solve problems. "Many of the best suggestions come from you,"[7] the chairman acknowledged.

Troops trickled home. Verney persuaded Nightingale "for the first time for 25 years" to go "out to see a sight — to Victoria railway station to" greet the returning Foot Guards. "A more deeply felt and less showy scene could not have been imagined."[8]

Prime Minister Gladstone then invited Florence to a royal review of all returning troops. She sat between him and his wife. Mrs. Gladstone noted "tears in miss Nightingale's dear eyes as the poor ragged fellows marched past."[9] Pleased to see her "looking well,"[10] the Queen asked Florence to the opening ceremony for a new building.

The government requested female nurses for its expeditionary force to the Sudan.† So Nightingale sent a typically "decisive yet kindly" note to one of her daughters.

Would I leave in three days' time for service in the Sudan? If so, I must be at her house for instructions on Monday at 8.30 A.M., at Marlborough house to be interviewed by [the] princess of Wales at 11 A.M.; and immediately [after] fitted for my war uniform. Would I also breakfast with her on Wednesday, so that she "might check the fit of my uniform, and wish me God-speed." [Sister Philippa felt] in a fever of excitement, not so much at the thought of going to the front, as at the fact I had been chosen by her to follow in her footsteps.

Ten minutes with Florence gave Philippa "unbounded admiration" and

"affection for the warm-hearted old lady who counseled me as a nurse, mothered me as an output" of her School, "and urged me to spare no point — myself especially — where the soldiers were concerned. 'Remember,' she said, 'when you are far away up-country, possibly the only English woman there, that those men will note and remember our every action, not only as a nurse, but as a woman.'" Be sure "'your every word and act is worthy of your profession and your womanhood.'" Then she asked me to accept" a "rubber traveling bath as 'her parting gift to a one-time probationer who had once reminded her that cleanliness was next to godliness,'‡ and in spite of the merry twinkle in her eye" there "were tears of anxious kindness."

---

*1882. During a time of alarming civil and military strife in Egypt, Great Britain sent troops to protect its investments, particularly its majority holding in the Suez Canal.

†August 1884 to relieve the besieged General Gordon at Khartoum.

‡See page 234.

The ship left at eleven on Wednesday morning. Florence invited Philippa to breakfast at half past seven. "Propped up in bed, the pillows framing her kindly face with its lace-covered silvery hair, and twinkling eyes," Philippa thought "her sense of humor must have been as strong a bond between her and the soldiers as her sympathy."

"Coffee, toast, eggs, and honey, a real English breakfast, dear child. It is good to know that you will have honestly earned the next one you eat in England."

"Suppose I don't return to eat one at all?" Philippa asked.

"Well! You will have earned that too, dear heart," came the quiet reply.

"Who can be surprised that we worshipped our chief?"

When the nurses "entered our cabins we found a bouquet of flowers for each of us," with a note attached. "God-speed from Florence Nightingale."

Philippa did return. Florence invited her to Claydon, the Verneys' estate that Parthe and Harry urged Flo to treat as hers. "During a month's rest in one of" England's loveliest "country homes, I learned to know and understand miss Nightingale, to realize what the friendship of a character like hers means. 'The essence of friendship,' says Emerson, 'is tenderness and trust.' No words better describe our chief than these."[11]

—⁀ℳ⁀—

Another daughter, matron at a London hospital, ran into trouble with her medical superiors. Florence sympathized with her stubborn Goddess Baby, Rachel Williams, over a salary spat. But when Rachel threatened to resign over a technical issue "everything, I believe I may say *every*thing was done that could be done either on earth or under the earth to make me resign during the Crimean war," Nightingale wrote. Nonetheless,

> I never felt a moment's doubt on the question:
> I would not resign
> I might not be driven from my post
> I would not run away.[12]

Williams resigned.

The army subsequently invited her to lead a group of nurses intended for its hospital at Suez. Nightingale disapproved. Willful Rachel could not manage a military hospital; she would fight every qualified female and harass each military man. Still, Florence helped Rachel select staff and wrote her supportive letters.

"I think so much of your Egyptian expedition," Florence told a different daughter. "You must not, please, say, 'I may fail, & then I shall come back in a year.' But screw your courage to the sticking point, and you'll not fail."

"To clothe *loosely*, to have *nothing tight* about one, is a sine qua non in a hot climate," Nightingale advised, remembering her Nile cruise with the Bracebridges.

"You know the *Sirene Stays* (to be had at any Indian outfitters) made of a cross-stitch material like canvass? These are *so* recommend by those who wear them, as combining the utmost comfort with the necessity of having good stays for nursing in. I am sure you will agree with me that half the soul & health are squeezed out of a woman who wears tight stays. In a hot climate it is destructive, simply."

"High heeled shoes/boots are the same."

"A very loose dressing-gown to throw on at night, if you *should* have to get up."[13]

—⁂—

Insomnia and acute spinal pain interrupted Florence's nights. "My doctor entirely repudiates the idea of any possibility of my doing any work 'under pressure,' such as writing & reading within a given time, for the present. I should not mind what he said, or what any doctor said, but that I feel so ill & suffering that it 'points' his moral."[14]

Self-doubt filled these wakeful hours. With bedroom windows open a crack to admit frigid fresh air "it is *you* who have brought St Thomas's to this 'terrible pass,'" Nightingale scribbled on a scrap of paper. "You have never been it's 'mother-chief.'"[15]

For years frustrated by the old-fashioned ways of hospital matron and school superintendent Sarah Wardroper, Florence wanted a young, energetic, forward-looking woman to succeed the soon-to-retire superintendent. Nightingale pinned her aspirations on a favorite daughter, her Pearl beyond Price, Angélique Pringle.

Angélique got off to an excellent start. But before long, she involved Florence in months of agonized soul-searching. After a year as superintendent, Pringle then converted to Roman Catholicism.

The strictly secular Nightingale nurse training school should not have a Catholic superintendent, and a leading Protestant voluntary hospital could not accept a Catholic as matron. Florence beat back intense disappointment, let alone strong personal preference that Angélique Pringle stay. The good of the school took priority. "My illness has so much increased that I am scarcely equal to the work constantly" growing "upon me. I hardly see any one not closely connected to"[16] work, Nightingale answered long-time friend Liz Herbert. Herself a convert to Catholicism, Liz wanted to plead for Pringle. Flo, as usual, managed to find time for Liz. The two friends spoke long and earnestly, but Liz's eloquence failed in its purpose.

Nevertheless, she and Florence agreed that "you & I can never misunderstand one another."[17]

—⁓⁓—

To Nightingale's delight, her personal friend and former war-office ally Lord de Grey, now Lord Ripon, became viceroy of India.[18] Florence saw him as true successor to the eminent India reformers with whom she had worked — Bartle Frere, John Lawrence, and Robert Napier. They agreed with Nightingale that Indians held the key to the subcontinent's future.

She had been studying Indian land tenure for years. For even longer, Florence had been convinced that man could perfect himself by following God's laws. She now encouraged Ripon to make major and positive changes, such as teaching the ryot better agriculture; and the village headman, sanitation. Ripon increased the ryot's right to land, secured him against tyranny, advanced primary education, introduced local elections, and strove to extend freedom of the press to Indians.

Hearing "with delight of your measure, so very much needed," to create "a native army hospital corps," Florence reminded her friend that under the old system

> ward coolies or nurses may be children of 10, old men of 80, cripples, blind: in short any one who will come for 4 rupees a month. No other inducement is given: no promotion: no reward: no good conduct pay: no increase of pay for long service: no camp equipage. [Nurses] lie for shelter under the walls [of] hospital tents during the bitter cold nights.
>
> The nursing is *the worst nursing* in *any* existing army & threatens often to become no nursing at all. The cooking is as bad. But all this will now be altered by your beneficent arrangements. And might I [ask] you to be so very good as to send [further] arrangements & particulars of your new army hospital corps — I mean the details of the system.

"May I remind you of the recommendations 26, 27, 28: of the r. [royal] commission on the sanitary state of the army in India," headed first by Sidney Herbert, next by Lord Stanley. (Despite having conceived, motivated, and managed both royal commissions, Nightingale credited others because — to be most effective — a woman must be quiet, gentle, and stay in the background.)

Recommendation 26: "*Trained* hospital attendants be introduced into all [military] hospitals in India, female nurses at large station hospitals, European hospital orderlies 'to provide personal attendance for the sick.' Hospitals to" have "properly *trained* cooks."

"It seems like a God-send that you should have taken up this mean though large & important & difficult question."[19]

Ripon then introduced the Ilbert bill.[20] It gave officially qualified Indian judges limited power to try Europeans, including Britons, for criminal offenses.

Still smarting from twenty-year memories of the Mutiny, when Indian soldiers savagely murdered their women and children, Britons reacted with a storm of outrage. Encouraging Ripon to stand firm, Nightingale lobbied high-ranking friends at the India office. She galvanized sympathizers to act, proposed publicity, wrote articles, and helped others write. The bill passed with modifications.

Thereupon, Ripon resigned. Because, he explained to his reproachful friend Florence, he wanted to seize the moment — a propitious time to promote appointment of a like-minded successor. The new viceroy visited number 10 South Street. Confessing complete ignorance of sanitation, he asked Nightingale for instructions and promised to obey them.

She, meanwhile, met with Indians and impressed on each how he could advance hygiene. And to focus attention on it, Florence arranged that the international congress of hygiene and demography, meeting in London, include an India section. As well, she got the Verneys to entertain Indian delegates at Claydon.

—⁂—

By this time (late 1880s), Nightingale's constant colleague and faithful friend since Crimean days, octogenarian John Sutherland, wanted to retire. Too infirm any longer to help Florence personally, he still played a pivotal role. Sutherland functioned as sole salaried member, not to mention inspiration, of the army sanitary commission. It ran army sanitation at home and in India — the system Nightingale had built. If, on Sutherland's retirement, the government failed to appoint a successor, that system would crumble.

Further disturbing news then jolted Florence. Because annexation of Burma added a burden to India's budget, the subcontinent's sanitary commissions stood on the brink of abolition. She wrote the viceroy. He reassured her. She pressured the war office. It advanced Herbert and Nightingale's work by building more and better barracks.

In the midst of this flurry, Sutherland resigned. The government failed to appoint a successor. Florence invited the war secretary to tea. Consequently, he re-formed the sanitary commission to include a salaried member and an India expert. They and the new commission chairman were Nightingale allies.

—⁂—

"I shall be ready for the carriage at '3.30' if that is the hour proposed," Flo wrote her sister. "And I don't know, after all, that it would hurt me, *if I don't talk* to go with you. And it would be a great pleasure."[21] Formerly rare, drives in the park with Parthe became more frequent. Brother-in-law Harry Verney coaxed Florence to take a stroll in fine weather. She felt well enough to walk in Claydon's daffodil-carpeted gardens, go out to enjoy pine and bracken while staying at a friend's country house. But palpitations, headaches, insomnia, and joint pain lingered.

And deaths in Flo's inner circle made encroaching age a reality. Supportive, jovial uncle Sam died.

> Dearest aunt Mai — thinking of you always, grieved for your sufferings.
>
> In this month 34 years ago you lodged me in Harley street (Aug. 12) and in this month 31 years ago you returned me to England from Scutari (Aug. 7th). And in this month 30 years ago the first royal" commission "finished (Aug. 7). And since then 30 years of work often cut to pieces but never destroyed, God bless you! In this month 26 years ago Sidney Herbert died, after five years of work for us (Aug. 2). And in this month 24 years ago [we finished] the work of the second royal commission (India).
>
> In this month, this year, my powers seem all to have failed and old age set in.[22]

Flo had reached age sixty-seven. Three years later ninety-one-year-old Mai died. Her niece mourned a beloved aunt as the "dearest friend ... loving, loving soul; humble mind of high and holy thought."[23]

Nightingale lost William Farr, personal friend and colleague in statistics, then John McNeill, trusted counselor and steadfast friend since the Crimea. And her "Clarkey dearest," intimate, confidante, and support for over forty years.

Friend and favorite India expert Bartle Frere passed away, then Richard Monckton Milnes, now Lord Houghton, erstwhile suitor, eternal supporter.

"My dear friend," Florence had written Richard not long before, "I *will* give you joy, I *do* give you joy, and I condole with you too as you desire on your boy's marriage. On the other hand, there is something very inspiring in the faithful love, the early and the late, when two always say 'we.' Two in one through a life together, God in both and both in one; but then the wife must help the husband in work." She never regretted her refusal to make that commitment. Nonetheless, Nightingale wished that "such a life be given to your young pair; may all the true blessings be theirs, and may it be theirs to be a blessing to many."[24]

Loss of close friends made family more precious. Even during the bitter days of her fight for freedom, later acute illness, Florence had not cut herself off from family. And throughout the Crimean War Flo wore, concealed under her sleeve, the trim snakeskin bracelet containing woven strands of hair from those she loved most — parents and sister.

Each sister had realized her ambition: Parthe, a happy marriage; Flo, fulfillment in the service of God and humanity. Parthe's clinging to Flo, and Flo's resentment at Parthe's attitude, faded. As well, the serenity that comes with aging calmed the intense sibling rivalry of younger years.

After her sister survived a serious illness, Flo braved winter cold "every day that is fine to see whether Parthe's windows are open." They "are *always* shut: & the blinds are generally drawn. And the drawing room windows also always shut," she wrote Harry. Parthe's windows should "be *always* open: open at the top (as far as they will go) every fine day — and a chink open at the top every bad day & all night."

"*Will you write your orders to her?*" Please "add that you authorize me to throw stones & break the upper panes every time I see the windows shut — but as the bill will be a large one, *she* must pay it. It breaks one's heart to see all sun & air excluded."[25]

Flo's Incredible Bonté responded to Parthe's worsening health. Cancer complicated her crippling arthritis, causing clouds to cover Parthe's sunny personality. Flo sustained her sister through seven years of acute suffering. And for Harry Verney and his children Florence became the "family solicitor to whom we all turn when we get into a scrape."[26]

Harry's daughter-in-law Margaret, "a sort of heavenly young woman," as "lovely as Fra Angelico's virgins and saints," lived at Claydon with her husband and children. Margaret Verney's wit and sense of humor endeared her to Nightingale as much as her "administrative power, that power of detail which makes work succeed and is called capacity for business."[27]

Margaret cherished "dearest aunt Florence" as "the presence which to all of us brings such balm of sympathy and peace."[28] Flo persuaded Parthe to apologize for being "outrageously discourteous" to Margaret. Consequently, Parthe grew "so kind and gentle" that Margaret felt "as if the echoes of" Flo's calming effect, her "loving words and thoughts and prayers still linger here."[29]

A large group of young cousins also treasured their "aunt Florence." Visiting singly and by appointment only, they usually found her upstairs in the simple, white-walled sitting room with a bed, rather than bedroom per se. French windows and flower-filled balconies, free of blinds or curtains, opened onto a vista of trees, garden, and lawns belonging to the grand private house next door.

These younger members of Nightingale's extended family liked the frank, witty old lady who exuded strength and integrity, who followed their enthusiasms with her nimble mind open to modern ideas. And they valued her undivided attention. Cousin Blanche Clough's boys (Mai and Sam Smith's grandsons) confided concerns about their loves; My Boy Shore's daughters (especially favorite Rosamund) discussed their studies. "My only dearest Rosie, aunt Florence's heart is filled with you and your going to Girton [Cambridge university's college for females],"[30] wrote the woman who had, in her youth, yearned to be A College Man.

Nightingale supported a new vegetarian by sending eggs and lentils, helped fund a would-be traveler's foreign tour, tucked a check into birthday letters, and provided invalids with beneficial soups. Harry Verney received a special lampshade to relieve strain on his weakening eyes. An overworked cousin got concert tickets; Margaret Verney, sandwiches, coffee, and a comfortable cushion when traveling on the night train. "Your sympathy and love for us all is counted of great" value. "We all know that we come in for a share of the love that is so broad,"[31] wrote one of Parthe's stepchildren.

Flo could do little for Parthe, fully in possession of mental faculties but sleepless despite heavy sedation. "I am with you in the weary nights,"[32] Flo comforted. "I am always thinking of you and longing to hear how you are and longing still more to think that you are somewhat better, and taking care of your dear self."[33] "How I mourn, dearest Pop, for your great suffering." Florence admired her sister for bearing pain so heroically. "To the Father whose love is tenderer even than ours I commend you almost hourly. I shall hope to be with you soon, dearest."[34]

Florence spent weeks at Claydon with Parthe. "I expect to be home in about 10 days: but it will depend upon lady Verney who is very ill," Nightingale wrote her housekeeper. "I am no better: & little able to write."[35] When Parthe came to London, Flo spent all of Sundays with her. On other days, Parthe would have herself carried the short distance to Florence's house.

"I learn at your courage." "Hail to thee, happy soul the soul of sweetness and faith,"[36] Florence wrote a few weeks before Parthe's death — May 12, 1890, Florence's seventieth birthday.

Harry and Margaret's "dear daily letters" were "the comfort of my life."[37] Margaret must keep Parthe's jewelry for herself and her children, since Parthe had told Flo "with tears of pleasure that" Margaret made "the dear children think of her as their real grandmamma."[38]

—⟶⟵—

"You contributed more than anyone to what enjoyment of life" she had, Harry wrote a few days after his wife's death. "I have no comfort so great as to hold intercourse with you. You and I were the objects of her tender love, and her love for you was intense. It was delightful" to "hear her speak of you and to see her face, perhaps distorted with pain, look happy when she thought of you."[39]

Still alert and handsome at almost ninety, Harry Verney held an important place in Florence's life. Having first entered the Nightingale orbit via his interest in reform, Verney took over chairmanship of the Nightingale Fund council when Sidney Herbert died. Florence and her brother-in-law communicated closely on Fund and school matters. And in her mother's last years Florence yielded to Harry's insistence that he help her with correspondence related to them.

They now wrote each other daily. When in London Harry called on his sister-in-law each morning. She got interested in Claydon matters. Improvements were a challenge, as Harry disliked change and Parthe had been careless over money. So Florence and Margaret Verney restored order to the household and instituted new drains.

Claydon village hygiene also needed improving. Nightingale, together with Margaret's husband, got local taxes allocated for training in Health at Home. This Florence expanded into a plan that the work of district nurses be supported by health missioners, women who would learn to teach village mothers basic domestic hygiene. In England as in India, sanitary education must start in the village and must be personal.

For health missioners and nurses alike, Florence Nightingale had the same advice: "The work that tells is the work of the skilful hand, directed by the cool head, and inspired by the loving heart."[40]

25

"A blessed life"

"How many lives are saved by your nurses in hospitals," how "many thousand soldiers who would have fallen victims to bad air, bad water, bad drainage and ventilation, are now alive owing to your forethought and diligence; how many natives of India" in "this generation and in generations to come have been preserved from famine and oppression" by "the energy of a sick lady who can scarcely rise from her bed. The world does not know all this or think about it. But I" want "you to, so ... you may see" what "a blessed life yours is and has been."[1]— Benjamin Jowett

Festivities for Queen Victoria's diamond jubilee (1897) featured an exhibition. Its nursing section focused on Florence Nightingale. Organizers requested Crimean keepsakes. "The absurdity of people and the vulgarity! The 'relics,' the 'representations' of the Crimean war! What are they? They are, first, the tremendous lessons we have had to learn from its tremendous blunders and" ignorance. "They are trained nurses and the progress of" hygiene. "I will not give my foolish portrait (which I have not got) or anything else as 'relics' ... I won't be made a *sign* at an exhibition."[2]

Instead, Florence urged recognition for "*Sidney Herbert's* r. [royal] commission & 4 sub-commissions which laid the imperishable seed of" great "improvements in the solder's daily life"; "*training of nurses* both in character & technical skill"; progress in "*hygiene & sanitation* the want of which in the military & medical authorities caused" needless death for "thousands of our men from disease."[3]

Consequently, the nursing section's pretty, "so gracious" and charming chairperson, "such a very good woman,"[4] asked if she might call at number 10 South Street.

Like all visitors, Lady Wantage* arrived alone and by appointment. She found her septuagenarian hostess sitting up in bed, her back bolstered by sev-

---

*Wife and helpmate of decorated Crimean War veteran, prominent public servant, and distinguished philanthropist Lord Wantage, a founder of the British Red Cross and Nightingale's longtime friend.

eral snow-white, cotton-covered pillows. A dark brown quilt overlaid Nightingale's lower body.

At her bedside stood a small, round pedestal table with white linen cloth and a jug of the fresh country flowers sent weekly by faithful friend Louisa, Lady Ashburton. Another table, within easy reach, held books, papers, pen, and a bowl of fruit. A comfortable chair rested between two windows. The jardinière kept full of fresh greenery year round by longtime friend and colleague William Rathbone, workhouse and district nursing pioneer, stood at another window. India viceroy John Lawrence's likeness, a lithograph of the area around Sevastopol, and a watercolor of an Egyptian sunset hung on the walls. The mantelpiece facing Florence's bed held a framed text: "It is I. Be not afraid."

Forty years of illness, not to mention overwork, had kept Nightingale from vigorous exercise, like the horseback riding and walks she used to enjoy. That and spending most days lying in bed or on a couch took a toll despite Florence being "a small but *delicate* eater."[5] So a stout senior lady with keen eyes and cordial mien welcomed Lady Wantage — and met her match in perseverance.

Immediately after the Crimean War Florence had yielded to soldiers' insistence that she sit for a bust that they wanted to give her. "It is left in my will back to the soldiers." Nightingale knew not who told Wantage "of this bust — it was not I." When she "came to me she knew about it. And it was impossible for me to decline *lending* it to them for the" exhibition. "I have such a respect for lady Wantage."[6]

And "that wretched" covered Crimean mule cart, "all dismantled, *hangs* round my *neck*." It was found in pieces at "an Embley farmhouse when" Nightingale's beloved cousin My Boy Shore sold the property, and she "never cared *what* became of it."[7] Wantage did.

Throngs of people crowded the exhibition. Old soldiers kissed the cart that carried Florence Nightingale safely over the snowcapped Crimean heights to her hospitals.

> Now I must ask you about my bust. (Here I stop to utter a great many bad words not fit to put on paper. I also utter a pious wish that the bust may be smashed.) I should not have remembered it [but] am told somebody came every day to dress it with fresh flowers. I utter a pious wish that that person may be saved, [Florence wrote Shore's son.] You (for I know not what sins), it appears, are "my man of business." What *is* to be done about the bust?[8]

—⁓—

Now part of the global dialogue, nursing held a prominent place at the Chicago exhibition. To mark the exhibition's groundbreaking section on women's work, Nightingale contributed *Sick-Nursing and Health-Nursing.*[9] "A new art and a new science has been created since and within the last forty" years. "One would think this had been created or discovered for some new" want. "Not so. The want is nearly as old as the world, nearly as large as the work, as pressing as life or death. It is that of sickness. And the art is that of *nursing the sick; not* nursing sickness. We will call the art nursing proper."[10]

Sick-Nursing and Health-Nursing featured the experiment Florence, together with her late sister Parthe's stepson, had recently initiated near the Verney family's Claydon estate. Because Nightingale believed sanitary schooling must start in the village, trained health missioners taught hygiene to country women in their cottages.

Florence underlined her personal approach to health missioner training in *Health Teaching in Towns and Villages Rural Hygiene.*[11] Medical officers must select tactful women of good character and health, able to teach, understand, and like cottage mothers. "You cannot know" rural women "by just seeing them in class"; they "cannot be managed or influenced in a lump — rather less than anybody else. You must know each and her individuality" if "you are to do any good."[12]

Anticipating criticism like "'you are describing a process that will'" take "'months and years. Life is not long enough for this,'" Florence countered that "for centuries there have been superstitions, for centuries the habits of dirt and neglect have been steadily and perseveringly learnt." If "we can transform by a few years' quiet persistent work the habits of centuries, the process will not have been slow, but amazingly rapid."[13]

—⟋ᴍ—

The Nightingale nurse training system now served as a model for nursing schools at most of Great Britain's hospitals. Every major British medical institution had a Nightingale school graduate matron. And Nightingale matrons led nursing cadres in Australia, Canada, Ceylon, Germany, India, Sweden, and the United States.

Nonetheless, Florence looked askance at nursing having become "a fashion, an amusement, a talk, or a literature — a dress."[14] And she deplored the dearth of disciplined women for training. Few probationers had "any life purpose & many are not purpose-like at all." There is no "*staying* power even among *young matrons.*"

Troubling modern trends seemed to blame. They "let out nurses like plumbers — for so many hours a day to the wards — sisters or head nurses included — & then to let them live for the remaining hours quite apart from the hospital — wanting the motherly element altogether — essential to a nurse who is not a plumber — but has the care of soul & body in her patients, & in her assistant nurses."[15]

Ongoing nurse training must include discipline, Nightingale wrote in her contribution to *A Dictionary of Medicine*.

> Discipline embraces order, method, and, as we gain some knowledge of the laws of nature ("God's laws"), we not only see order, method, a place for everything, [but] we find no waste, [no] hurry; and we learn to have patience with our circumstances and ourselves; and so, as we go on learning, we become more disciplined, more content to work where we are placed, more anxious to fill our appointed work; and so God [gives] us the required patience and steadfastness to continue in our "blessed drudgery" which is the discipline He sees best for most of us.[16]

—⚶—

Advances in medical science made hospital stays beneficial for middle- and upper-class patients. But not enough nurses existed to meet the demand. Because, some said, Nightingale's standards were too high. These critics proposed a solution: train more students for a longer period. No, Florence said. That would merely provide the hospital with additional time to exploit its probationers' free labor; if the powerful Nightingale Fund council could not stop this practice, how would nursing schools without a Fund fare?

Calls for training extra nurses grew strident. The hospitals association stepped in. It created an independent organization, unaffiliated with any of the nurse training schools. This organization evolved into the British nursing association (BNA). Queen Victoria's popular daughter, Princess Christian, accepted the office of president. The BNA proposed to prepare an examination. Nurses who passed it would be put on an official register.

Nightingale opposed BNA registration. It ignored character training, with which she had "raised nursing from the sink."[17] The crucial need for moral credentials precluded selecting "the good from the inferior by any test or system of examination."[18] One "might as well register mothers"[19] as quantify the qualities making a first-class nurse.

"While you have a ward, it must be your *home* & the inmates your" children. "Don't be like water turned on from a" tap "& turned off again."[20] The vocation and profession of nursing meant tending to "living bodies and spirits. It cannot be formulated like engineering. It cannot be numbered and registered like arithmetic or population. It cannot be tested by public examination, though it may be tested by current supervision."[21]

The BNA menaced this crucial principle by promoting a test of three-year training via a standardized examination administered by an outside board. That, Florence argued, would put tests at a premium, deflect focus from nurse training homes, breed a "want of earnestness; mere money-getting" and "a mechanical view of nursing."[22] Moreover, an official register would encourage nurses "to flock to the institutions which gave the easiest certificate at the least trouble of training."[23]

Nor would a nurses' register protect the public. The register meant only that the nurse had passed a certain test at a certain time. A hospital register, on the other hand, should be kept current for each graduate nurse and include character evaluation.

"What is the moral & technical discipline" that the nurse "will receive when armed with her certificate, of which the public does not know the value, she leaves her inf'y or hosp'l," Nightingale asked. A nurse must recognize "the need of what no cert'e can certify, no exam'n can touch," the need "of attaching herself to some home with motherly & trained supervision, so that she *may* have some 'esprit de corps' to guide & support her."[24]

Florence had "a terror, lest the BNA's and anti–BNA's should form two hostile camps, judging one another by that test chiefly or alone. That would be disastrous."[25]

—∞—

The BNA formally applied to parliament for a charter (permission to form a public company) to structure a nurses register and set its criteria. Nightingale agonized for days and nights over what to do — so intensely that she heard the divine call to work. "God is the commander. He lays out the plan of battle. (Do not know how to cope with the many new engagements.)"[26] The fault lay with her; she had misused her God-given chances, been an ineffective servant to Him, and had failed to impress her ideal on others.

Florence decided to fight. Against a charter incorporating the BNA and allowing a registry. And against a registry of nurses who had passed only a standardized examination.

She rallied the nurse training schools into formally declaring their opposition to the BNA's charter application. Prominent physicians familiar with nurse training backed Nightingale. With her blessing, non–BNA nursing groups created a directory. Any nurse who had worked for one year in an infirmary or hospital, who had trained in nursing duties, and who had a testimonial of good character could enter her name.

Florence recruited her brother-in-law and longtime Fund council chairman, Harry Verney, to lead the charge in parliament. The Nightingale method, she coached, strove to raise the nurse's character, to nurture and protect her moral qualities. A nurses' home let good women live in comfort, with decent food and realistic hours under the regulation of an educated matron. The

Nightingale school and its ilk chose healthy students, gentle and tactful, with common sense and similar qualities basic to good nursing. To this the school added precise practical and scientific training, carried out in the wards by head nurses and specially appointed medical staff for a minimum one to maximum three years, so that probationers learned to obey doctors' orders intelligently.

The proposed BNA register ignored many of these essentials.

Parliament agreed.

The BNA fought back. It applied for a royal charter.

Nightingale and her cohorts countered with two petitions against the granting of a royal charter. The Nightingale Fund council, pioneer in nurse training, signed one petition. Thousands of senior nursing professionals signed the other. Florence Nightingale's signature headed the list.

Thanks to the patronage of its royal president, the BNA got its royal charter.

Thanks to the efforts of Florence Nightingale, the BNA did not get its register.

"It is time this unseemly, not to say disgraceful squabbling should be at an end,"[27] Florence said. She set about mending fences within the nursing community.

—⁂—

Chronic brucellosis symptoms abated, meanwhile. But advancing age made inroads. The loss of more intimates brought this home with painful clarity.

"Give her my love and blessing,"[28] sanitarian Dr. John Sutherland, close friend and colleague since Scutari, said on his deathbed.

Oxford luminary Benjamin Jowett, friend, confidant, and supporter for thirty years, had a heart attack. Nightingale went to see him. "I am always thankful for having known you,"[29] Jowett told her, "you are the best & kindest [of] friends to me."[30] After suffering a second heart attack, Jowett struggled to London to visit Florence. "Fare you well!" he dictated shortly before death. "How greatly am I indebted to you for all your affection. How large a part has your life been of my life."[31]

Flo grieved at the loss of her dear brother-in-law. How she missed Harry Verney's "courage, his courtesy, his kindness."[32] That year (1893) she also lost My Boy Shore, Mai and Sam Smith's son, who had inherited the Nightingale properties. Flo counted Shore's kindness to Fanny in her last years as one of life's greatest rewards.

Four of Florence's closest gone within a year. Still, on her seventy-fifth birthday she felt "there is so much to live for." She had "lost so much in failures and disappointments, as well as in grief but, do you know, life is more precious to me now in my old age."[33]

—⟋⟍—

"The immense blessings I have had — the longings of my heart accomplished — and now drawn to Thee by difficulties and disappointments." "Homeward bound." "I have entered in."[34]

Sacrifice of love, marriage, health, and "all that makes life pleasant" vindicated. As Nightingale reflected on the change she had wrought in treatment of illness and concept of public health, she could feel satisfied. No less a marvel were all those who built hospitals and improved hygiene who still sought her advice. The war secretary consulted constantly. When Nightingale heard of bubonic plague at the Hong Kong colony, she badgered him and his colonial office counterpart for better barracks. Done.

The India office sent everything relevant to sanitation. Viceroys continued to call at South Street. "Painfully aware how difficult, how almost impossible, it is for any one at a great distance to do anything to help forward a movement requiring unremitting labor and supervision on the spot," Nightingale, nonetheless, seized every chance "of urging a practical" start, "however small." And "from time to time" she saw "Indian friends who are heartily desirous of obtaining for their poorer fellow-countrymen the benefits which, through sanitary science, are gradually being extended to the masses here," doing "so much to promote their health and happiness."[35]

"I am soaked in work,"[36] although "people naturally think … I have gone to sleep or am dead."[37] Florence kept in close touch with every daughter. And each of them cherished her maternal consideration, be it fresh country produce, convalescing at the seaside courtesy of The Chief, or getting special dishes when ill. Nightingale insisted that the butcher send "a fore quarter of your best mutton. I prefer four year old mutton."[38] She monitored all menus. "Roast leg mutton perfectly good. Cherry meringue. Rice with apricots very nice. Irish stew *not* made of good mutton — stringy."[39] "Sauces and gravies are not to be thickened with flour. The bones of the meat are simmered down with vegetables to make the stock, which is then reduced to make the sauces. Use plenty of herbs for flavoring."[40] Fanny Nightingale had proved a good teacher, Crimean colleague Alexis Soyer (when Florence had the time to attend to him) as well. "Roast pheasant must be hung not too near a good fire and basted every minute or two with good butter for an hour."[41]

During sleepless nights Florence filled many scraps of paper with penciled notes. Prayers predominated, both formal and profoundly personal. Her reflections on religion, mostly Christianity but also Buddhism and Judaism, covered many pages. Other jottings revealed Nightingale's continued preoccupation with the nature of God, as well as the prophets and saints.

At the same time she noticed her memory starting to fray at the edges, a normal part of aging but in Florence triggering deep-seated feelings of inadequacy. "Let me omit nothing to help these poor rural mothers and girls all over England," let "me omit nothing to help the Bombay rural poor. O God *don't let* me omit anything to help those who are nearest to me or who are dependent on me. I who have sinned so in all this."[42]

—ɷ—

The debility of old age — deteriorating eyesight, like Fanny, and declining energy — kept Florence at South Street. She might move around or walk, still gracefully, in her house, but mostly Nightingale sat up in bed or her armchair to receive chosen visitors — a favorite family member, or former probationer.

"My heart *is* full of you; but immersed in very sour business, I find nothing to *say* worthy of your sweetness," Florence's now enlarged handwriting wobbled across the paper to congratulate her beloved Rosamund (Shore's daughter) on her engagement. "I do give you joy for having found a man whom you can so thoroughly love & esteem & work with." And

> I, of course, give him joy at having found you. And I give us all joy. But please look to the shillings. [The fiancé had everything to commend him but money.] We cannot live on sweets. And we must live in order to work together. I know you think me very worldly. But, you see, unfortunately, we live in the world.[43]

Parthe's step-daughter-in-law and Flo's favorite, Margaret Verney, welcomed a granddaughter into the world. Aunt Florence's lively letter suggested one of the prettiest names for the infant: Balaclava.

"No 'hockey,' no games will equal" horseback riding "for improving the circulation all over and exercising the muscles and animal courage," aunt Florence told Margaret's younger daughter. "A live horse and the sympathy of 'the horse and its rider' is worth all the bats and (deaf and dumb) balls put together. So 'drat' hockey and long live the horse! Them's my sentiments."[44]

—ɷ—

Blindness descended as the twentieth century dawned. To fight mental frailty, Nightingale asked her companion to read the *Times* aloud every morning; as well, she liked listening to biographies and articles about people of action. Florence recited poetry to herself, sometimes sang arias from the operas she had loved as a debutante. And she liked visitors who brought energetic conversation.

At age eighty-seven Nightingale became the first woman awarded the Order of Merit, "in recognition of invaluable services to the country and to humanity."[45] A year later, she received the Freedom of the City of London. Congratulations cascaded over 10 South Street. The mayor of Florence sent an official accolade. The Florence Nightingale Society of America and the Tokyo ladies of the Red Cross Society sent tributes. Thousands of women named Florence in Nightingale's honor sent a joint message. So did Crimean War veterans.

The Freedom of London certificate came in a gold box valued at one hundred guineas. Florence asked that rather than spending money on the box, the City of London should give the guineas to the Harley Street institution for the care of sick gentlewomen in distressed circumstances, where she had started her nursing career fifty-five years ago. The institution got its hundred guineas. Nightingale's certificate arrived in its gold box.

A little time later, her companion asked that the India office stop sending papers. Florence could no longer understand them. Still, she received many visitors — singly and by appointment — but had to be prepared in advance. Three months before Nightingale's ninetieth birthday a cherished daughter found The Chief "sitting up by the fire in the familiar room, her mind evidently busy with happy thoughts, and once or twice she spoke in a tone of satisfaction."[46]

Honors and good wishes swamped number 10 South Street on Nightingale's ninetieth birthday, but she could no longer acknowledge them. Without suffering, all her powers gradually had failed. She dozed most of the time. Three months after her ninetieth birthday, Florence Nightingale died peacefully in her sleep (August 13, 1910).

Afterword

The Son of God goes forth to war
A kingly crown to gain,
His blood-red banner streams afar
Who follows in his train?
Who best can drink His cup of woe,
Triumphant over pain,
Who patient bears His cross below—
He follows in His train.[1]

A fine English drizzle descended as two dark-colored horses drew the glass-paneled funeral carriage slowly along winding country roads to Embley's Wellow village. Great Britain had respected Florence Nightingale's wish for a plain, private burial—up to a point.

Her country offered Nightingale interment among its glorious dead in Westminster Abbey. But in death as in life, she eschewed the limelight. Florence left instructions that she be laid to rest beside her parents in the Nightingale family plot.

Given Florence's fame, however, a completely private and simple funeral proved impossible. Hence, that morning a splendid memorial service took place in St. Paul's Cathedral, London's premier house of worship. Nightingale's compatriots wanted to express appreciation for her efforts on their behalf, as well as admiration for her service to humanity.

The immense cathedral might have been filled several times over had it been possible to fill every ticket request to attend the simple, solemn tribute paid Florence Nightingale's memory. Royalty, government, and armed forces were present, as were almost a thousand nurses dressed in the distinctive uniforms of their discrete training schools. Many gnarled, gray-haired army veterans came despite some being ill able to afford the expense of a train journey to London. Each man wore his uniform and Crimean medal.

—⚞⚟—

Wellow village lies in peace and seclusion about four miles from Hampshire's old market town of Romsey. The railway station stood empty of people when Nightingale's special funeral train steamed in from London. Out of respect for her wishes, Romsey's inhabitants had curbed their natural inclination to assemble at the station.

Nine men in full dress uniform, who had been chosen from three Guards regiments that served in the Crimean War, transferred Nightingale's coffin from train to hearse. Its windows showed the coffin covered with a white cashmere shawl Florence often wore, as well as magnificent wreaths, one a cross of mauve orchids bordered by white roses and lilies sent by the Queen.[2]

Five black coaches containing family and close friends followed. As the funeral procession passed through Romsey at walking pace, people interrupted their activities to come into the streets and stand bareheaded. The nine-hundred-year-old abbey's tolling bells could be heard for miles around; its Union Jack hung at half-mast.

The cortege continued its slow, somber progress along sodden, hedgerow-lined country roads. Not a soul came to sight. Everyone had gone to the churchyard. Three and four deep, under dripping umbrellas, this unexpected throng watched in silence as soldiers carried Nightingale's coffin up the steep path leading to the thirteenth-century church.

The coffin rested in the chancel on a high black trestle. Beyond it, placed on the otherwise unadorned altar, a large floral cross, tribute from the Nightingale nurses at St. Thomas's Hospital, supplied the only color. On the floor at the coffin's foot stood one other wreath. It came from Sidney Herbert, Earl of Pembroke.[3]

Wellow village's church organist and choir opened the plain funeral service with one of Florence's favorite hymns, "The Son of God Goes Forth to War." She had often recited its lines to her children — soldiers and nurses — and, even in extreme age, astounded her audience with the passion she put into the words.

By the time her bareheaded military bearers carried Nightingale's coffin to the churchyard, a heavy downpour soaked the numerous floral tributes. Wreaths included those from several veterans associations, the Red Cross society, and the twenty-five-thousand member International Council of Nurses. Thirty-five professional nursing associations representing British and overseas nurses sent separate wreaths. None of these nursing groups existed when Florence Nightingale set out to "raise nursing from the sink."

Flowers lined the open grave. At its head, mounted on a pedestal, stood a large cross of white blossoms from the matrons and nursing staffs of all London hospitals.

After a brief committal service, the coffin carriers lowered their burden

into the vault. In accordance with Nightingale's wishes, only a small cross
with: "F. N. Born 1820. Died 1910" marks her grave.

—⁓—

A modern apartment block now occupies the space where "the nicest
little house in London"[4] once stood. But from the front of number 10 South
Street one can still see the treetops in Hyde Park. And one can read the blue
London county council plaque.

In a house
On this site
FLORENCE NIGHTINGALE
1820—1910
Lived and died.

Unlike other official plaques identifying homes of famous bygone Lon-
doners, this one does not say "Statesman," "Soldier," "Inventor," or the like.
It simply states: "Florence Nightingale."

Chapter Notes

Epigraph

BL ADD. 45845, f. 268, Jan. 3, 1895, private note, Florence Nightingale.

Introduction

1. Anna Sticker, *Florence Nightingale: Curriculum Vitae*, pp. 3–4, July 24, 1852. FN wrote this autobiographical précis as an introduction to her stay at Germany's Kaiserswerth institute.

2. Florence Nightingale, *Ever Yours, Florence Nightingale: Selected Letters*, M. Vicinus and B. Nergaard, eds., p. 47, 1851, private note, Florence Nightingale (henceforth referred to as FN).

3. Peter Pincoffs, M.D., *Experiences of a Physician in Eastern Military Hospitals*, pp. 75–80. From a speech by Sir John McNeill, M.D., chief of a parliamentary commission sent to the Crimea, given at the Oct. 31, 1856, Crimean banquet and published in *The Times* on Nov. 3.

4. FN, *Ever Yours*, p. 138, Jan. 31, 1856, to close friend Charles Bracebridge (hereafter referred to as Bracebridge).

5. Frances Margaret Taylor, *Eastern Hospitals and English Nurses — a Narrative of Twelve Months' Experience in the Hospitals of Koulali and Scutari by a Lady Volunteer*, vol. 1, pp. 69–71.

6. Cecil Woodham-Smith, *Florence Nightingale*, p. 180, multiple private notes, FN. The author saw Nightingale family papers plus those of friends, unavailable to FN's official biographer (Edward T. Cook) and subsequently lost or destroyed. Woodham-Smith often omits particulars of the quote she is citing.

7. Edward T. Cook, *The Life of Florence Nightingale*, vol. 2, p. 160, April 3, 1869, Sir John Lawrence, viceroy of India, to FN. Written at the request of FN's family shortly after her death, Cook's comprehensive work is the basis for every subsequent biography. The first to have unfettered access to FN's papers, Cook quoted extensively from them but sometimes omitted particulars. He also had the advantage of being able to interview people who knew Nightingale.

8. Monica Baly, *As Miss Nightingale Said*, p. 53, 1867, FN to J. P. Walker, M.D.

Chapter 1

1. FN, *Cassandra* and other selections from *Suggestions for Thought*, M. Poovey, ed., p. 170.

2. Sticker, *FN: Curriculum Vitae*, pp. 3–4, July 24, 1852.

3. Cook, *Life of FN*, vol. 1, pp. 151–154, Oct. 15, 1854, secretary-at-war and FN's close friend Sidney Herbert (henceforth referred to as SH) to FN.

4. Sidney Gololphin Osborne, *Scutari and Its Hospitals*, pp. 25–26. Osborne's observations during six weeks at Scutari as a volunteer auxiliary military chaplain in the hospitals. He arrived a few days after FN.

5. Protestants who rejected the Church of England. Also known as Dissenters.

6. Cook, *FN*, vol. 2, p. 235, Julius Mohl, close friend of the Nightingale family.

7. FN, *Ever Yours*, p. 46, 1851, private note.

8. Wellcome Library, Claydon copy, MS 8991/f. 44, Feb. 24, 1830, FN to her sister (henceforth referred to as Parthe).

9. Claydon House Trust N7, no. 14, probably 1826, Fanny Nightingale (henceforth referred to as Fanny) to governess Miss Christie.

10. FN, *Ever Yours*, p. 14, 1828, to Fanny.

11. Wellcome, Claydon copy, MS 8991/f. 15, Dec. 18, 1827, FN to her father (henceforth referred to as WEN).

12. Elizabeth Gaskell, *The Letters of Mrs. Gaskell*, J. Chapple & A. Shelston, eds., pp. 317–318, Oct. 27, 1854, Gaskell to E. Shaen. Well-known author Gaskell often stayed with the Nightingales.

13. Wellcome, Claydon copy, MS 8992/f. 41, 1840s, note on Parthe, FN.

14. Ida B. O'Malley, *Florence Nightingale 1820–1856: A Study of Her Life Down to the End of the Crimean War*, p. 17, Aug. 26, 1827, diary, FN. Although this biography stops in 1856, it has value because O'Malley relied on FN diaries

later destroyed. The author sometimes omits particulars of the quote she is citing.

15. Parthenope, Lady Verney, *Recollection*, undated but written soon after her marriage (1858) when Parthe still hoped for "a little Flo," Claydon House Trust N39.

16. O'Malley, *FN*, p. 24, Nov. 15, 1829, diary, FN.

17. Claydon House Trust N39, Parthe's recollection.

18. O'Malley, *FN*, p. 24, Nov. 15, 1829, diary, FN.

19. Sticker, *FN: Curriculum Vitae*, p. 3, July 24, 1851.

20. Cook, *Life of FN*, vol. 1, p. 12, private note, FN.

21. Wellcome, Claydon copy, MS 8991/f.34, Dec. 21, 1829, Mai Smith (henceforth referred to as Mai) to Fanny.

22. Florence Nightingale, *The Collected Works of Florence Nightingale*, Lynn McDonald, ed., vol. 1, p. 109, Jan. 7,1830, FN to Fanny. This comprehensive collection is indispensable to any study of FN.

23. Cook, *Life of FN*, vol. 1, p. 11, 1851, private note, FN.

24. FN, *Ever Yours*, p. 14, Feb. 1830, to her parents.

25. Wellcome, Claydon copy, MS 8991/f. 34, Dec. 21, 1829, Mai to Fanny.

26. O'Malley, *FN*, p. 26, 1830, FN to Parthe.

27. Gaskell, *Letters*, pp. 317–318, Oct. 27, 1854, Gaskell to Shaen.

28. Sticker, *FN: Curriculum Vitae*, p. 3, July 24, 1851, FN.

29. Claydon House Trust N39, Parthe's recollection.

30. O'Malley, *FN*, p. 35, March 24, 1832, FN to her cousin Hilary Bonham-Carter (henceforth referred to as Hilary).

31. FN, *Ever Yours*, p. 15, March 28, 1830, to Parthe.

32. FN, *Collected Works*, vol. 5, pp. 331–333, 1834, to Fanny.

33. Wellcome, Claydon copy, MS 8991/f. 83, Feb. 2,1837, FN to Parthe.

34. © The British Library Board, ADD. 45844, f. 64, May 3, 1867, private note, FN.

Chapter 2

1. Baly, *As FN Said*, p. 16, private note, FN.

2. Wellcome, Claydon copy, MS 8991/f. 93, Dec. 20, 1837, FN to her cousin Marianne Nicholson.

3. Woodham-Smith, *FN*, p. 15, Jan. 1838, diary, FN.

4. Woodham-Smith, *FN*, p. 15, Jan. 17, 1838, FN to Hilary.

5. O'Malley, *FN*, p. 50, journal, FN.

6. Wellcome, Claydon copy, MS 8991/f. 97, Oct. 6, 1837, FN to Grandmother Shore.

7. Kathleen O'Meara, *Madame Mohl: Her Salon and Friends*, p. 33, quote from a contemporary.

8. O'Meara, *Madame Mohl*, pp. 36–37, quote from a contemporary.

9. O'Meara, *Madame Mohl*, pp. 46–47, Mary Clarke Mohl (henceforth referred to as Clarkey).

10. Woodham-Smith, *FN*, p. 20, Clarkey to a friend.

11. O'Malley, *FN*, p. 63, Clarkey.

12. Julia Ward Howe, *Reminiscences 1819–1899*, pp. 136–137, 1844.

13. Cook, *Life of FN*, vol. 1, p. 39, Gaskell to C. Winkworth, 1854.

14. Cook, *Life of FN*, vol. 1, p. 39, Parthe to Fanny.

15. Sticker, *FN: Curriculum Vitae*, p. 3, July 24, 1851.

16. Cook, *Life of FN*, vol. 1, pp. 24–26, June 1, 1839, FN to Clarkey.

17. Margaret Lesser, *A Portrait in Letters of Mary Clarke Mohl*, pp. 102–103, Parthe. Lesser relies on extracts from the FN-Clarkey correspondence; Woodham-Smith saw the originals before they were destroyed and chose the extracts.

18. Woodham-Smith, *FN*, p. 25, Clarkey.

19. Sticker, *FN: Curriculum Vitae*, p. 6, July 24, 1851.

20. Woodham-Smith, *FN*, p. 26, March 1840, Mai to Fanny.

21. FN, *Ever Yours*, p. 19, to Hilary.

22. Howe, *Reminiscences*, pp. 136–137, 1844.

23. FN, *Ever Yours*, p. 21, 1844 or 1845, to Hannah Nicholson.

24. Ray Strachey, *The Cause*, p. 410, excerpt from FN's *Cassandra*.

25. O'Malley, *FN*, p. 104, fragment of letter, FN to Hilary.

26. O'Malley, *FN*, pp. 124–125, FN.

27. I understand nothing.

28. O'Malley, *FN*, pp. 104–105, Summer 1845, FN to Hilary.

Chapter 3

1. Lesser, *Clarkey*, p. 146, Aug. 21, 1856, Clarkey to Hilary.

2. Howe, *Reminiscences*, p. 138.

3. Howe, *Reminiscences*, p. 138.

4. Woodham-Smith, *FN*, p. 34, private note FN.

5. FN, *Ever Yours*, p. 25, probably 1844, to Parthe.

6. Baroness Frances Bunsen, *A Memoir of Baron Bunsen*, vol. 2, p. 22.

7. Woodham-Smith, *FN*, p. 31, Autumn 1842.

8. Deaconesses were a Protestant order devoted to religious and charitable work. Kaiserswerth's nurses formed a sisterhood not bound by vows. After six months' training, they pledged to observe the rules of the order for five years; thereafter, they could return to private life or renew their contract.

9. Lesser, *Clarkey*, p. 131, Feb. 5, 1852, Clarkey to Hilary.

10. Sticker, *FN: Curriculum Vitae*, p. 6, July 24, 1851.

11. O'Malley, p. 99, March 1845, FN to Clarkey.

12. O'Malley, p. 106, Autumn 1845, FN to Hilary.

13. O'Malley, p. 109, Winter 1845, FN to Hilary.

14. Cook, *FN*, vol. 1, pp. 44–45, Dec. 11, 1845, FN to Hilary.

15. Cook, *FN*, vol. 1, pp. 44–45, Dec. 11, 1845, FN to Hilary.

16. Cook, *FN,* vol. 1, pp. 44–45, Dec. 11, 1845, FN to Hilary.

17. Strachey, *The Cause*, p. 396, excerpt from *Cassandra,* FN.

18. BL ADD. 43402, ff. 178–187, 1857, private note, FN.

19. Woodham-Smith, *FN*, p. 38, 1865, private note FN.

20. FN, *Ever Yours*, p. 28, Dec. 5, 1845, to Hilary.

21. Howe, *Reminiscences*, p. 136.

22. Florence Nightingale, *Letters from Egypt: A Journey on the Nile 1849–1850*, A. Sattin, ed., p. 213.

23. FN, *Letters from Egypt*, p. 213, Clarkey.

24. Howe, *Reminiscences*, pp. 136–137.

25. FN, *Ever Yours*, p. 35, July 10, 1847, to Clarkey.

26. O'Malley, *FN*, p. 116, diary FN.

27. FN, *Ever Yours*, p. 33, April 1846, to Hilary.

28. FN, *Ever Yours*, p. 33, Oct. 1846, FN.

29. O'Malley, *FN*, pp. 119–120, July 16–18, 1846, notebook, FN.

30. BL ADD. 43402, ff. 178–87, 1857, private note, FN.

31. FN, *Ever Yours,* p. 24, Feb. 1, 1846, to Hannah Nicholson.

32. O'Malley, *FN*, p. 130, 1847, FN notebook.

Chapter 4

1. Cook, *FN*, vol. 1, p. 100, excerpt from *Suggestions for Thought*, FN.

2. Strachey, *The Cause*, p. 396, excerpt from *Cassandra*, FN.

3. O'Malley, *FN*, p. 126, 1846, private note, imaginary conversation with Selina Bracebridge, FN.

4. Cook, *FN*, vol. 1, p. 28, FN.

5. Thomas Carlyle, *The Collected Letters of Thomas Carlyle and Jane Welsh Carlyle*, vol. 12, pp. 9–10, Jan. 6, 1840.

6. T. Wemyss Reid, *The Life, Letters and Friendships of Richard Monckton Milnes, First Lord Houghto*, vol. I, pp. 337–338, quoted from Benjamin Disraeli's *Tancred*, 1847.

7. Reid, *Houghton*, vol. 1, pp. 337–338, quoted from Disraeli's *Tancred*, 1847.

8. Woodham-Smith, *FN*, p. 30, FN.

9. Strachey, *The Cause*, p. 410, excerpt from *Cassandra*, FN.

10. FN, *Cassandra*, Myra Stark, ed., p. 44.

11. J. Pope-Hennessy, *Monckton-Milnes, — the Years of Promise 1809–1850, the Flight of Youth 1851–1855*, vol. 1, p. 306.

12. O'Malley, *FN*, p. 152, 1849, FN.

13. BL ADD. 43397, ff. 296–300, Oct. 13, 1847, FN to Clarkey.

14. FN, *Ever Yours*, pp. 37–38, Oct. 13, 1847, to Clarkey.

15. Strachey, *The Cause*, p. 397, excerpt from *Cassandra*, FN.

Chapter 5

1. Woodham-Smith, *FN*, p. 47, FN.

2. FN, *Collected Works*, vol. 1, p. 445, Oct. 20, 1847, to Hilary.

3. O'Malley, *FN*, p. 133, Oct./Nov.1847, Parthe to Hilary.

4. *The Friendship of Florence Nightingale and Mary Clare Moore*, Mary Sullivan, ed., p. 178, Dec. 30, 1874, FN to Rachel Williams.

5. *Florence Nightingale in Rome. Letters Written in the Winter of 1847–1848*, Mary Keele, ed. (Memoirs of the American Philosophical Society, vol. 143), p. xiii, Jan. 22, 1848, Selina Bracebridge (hereafter referred to as Selina) to Fanny. Florence entertained her family with a lively, detailed, and enthusiastic account of her experiences.

6. FN, *Letters from Rome*, p. 3, Oct. 28, 1847, to immediate family.

7. FN, *Letters from Rome*, pp. 4–5, Oct. 29, 1847, to immediate family.

8. FN, *Letters from Rome*, p. 6, Nov. 1, 1847, to immediate family.

9. FN, *Letters from Rome*, p. 15, Nov. 2, 1847, to immediate family.

10. FN, *Letters from Rome*, p. 21, Nov. 5, 1847, to immediate family.

11. FN, *Letters from Rome*, p. 35, Nov. 11, 1847, to immediate family.

12. FN, *Letters from Rome*, pp. 40–41, Nov. 12, 1847, to immediate family.

13. FN, *Letters from Rome*, pp. 27–28, Nov. 11, 1847, to immediate family.

14. FN, *Letters from Rome*, p. 42, Nov. 12, 1847, to immediate family.

15. Wellcome, Claydon copy, MS 9045/f. 15, Nov./Dec. 1847, Selina to WEN.

16. FN, *Letters from Rome*, p. 42, Nov. 14, 1847, to immediate family.

17. FN, *Letters from Rome*, p. 30, Nov. 11, 1847, to immediate family.

18. FN, *Letters from Rome*, p. 104, Dec. 12, 1847, to immediate family.

19. Cook, *FN*, vol. 2, p. 236, Feb. 3, 1874, FN to Mohls.

20. FN, *Letters from Rome*, pp. 107–108, Dec. 13, 1847, to Parthe.

21. FN, *Letters from Rome*, pp. 83–84, Dec. 2, 1847, to immediate family.

22. FN, *Letters from Rome*, pp. 107–108, Dec. 13, 1847, to Parthe.

23. FN, *Letters from Rome*, p. 93, Dec. 9, 1847, to Fanny.

24. Wellcome, Claydon copy, MS 9045/f. 15, Nov./Dec. 1847, Selina to WEN.

25. Lord Stanmore, *Sidney Herbert, Lord Herbert of Lea*, vol. 1, p. 97, Liz Herbert.

26. FN, *Letters from Rome*, pp. 172–173, Jan. 17, 1848, to immediate family.

27. FN, *Letters from Rome*, pp. 203–206, Jan. 26, 1848, to immediate family.

28. Cook, *FN*, vol. 1, p. 77, Winter, 1847–1848, private note, FN.

29. O'Malley, *FN*, p. 144, 1848, notebook, FN.

30. FN, *Letters from Rome*, p. 146, Dec. 27, 1847, to Parthe.

31. Cook, *FN*, vol. 1, pp. 71–74, Dec. 17, 1847, FN to Parthe.

32. FN, *Letters from Rome*, pp. 239–244, Feb. 17, 1848, to immediate family.

33. FN, *Letters from Rome*, pp. 181–184, Jan. 21, 1848, to immediate family.

34. FN, *Letters from Rome*, pp. 276–77, Mar. 16, 1848, to immediate family.

35. Cook, *FN*, vol. 1, p. 65, FN.

Chapter 6

1. FN, *Ever Yours*, p. 47, 1851, private note.

2. O'Malley, *FN*, p. 132, private note, FN.

3. Sticker, *FN; Curriculum Vitae*, pp. 4–5, July 24, 1851, FN.

4. Cook, *FN*, vol. 1, p. 100, autobiographical note, FN.

5. Strachey, *The Cause*, p. 407, excerpt from *Cassandra*, FN.

6. FN, *Ever Yours*, pp. 37–38, Oct. 13, 1847, to Clarkey.

7. Cook, *FN*, vol. 1, p. 100, autobiographical note, FN.

8. BL ADD. 43402, ff. 53–54, Dec. 24, 1850, private note, FN.

9. BL ADD. 45844, f. 64, Feb. 7, 1892, private note, FN.

10. O'Malley, *FN*, p. 126, 1846, private note,

possible imaginary conversation with Selina, FN.

11. BL ADD. 43402 ff. 53–54, Dec. 24, 1850, private note, FN.

12. Strachey, *The Cause*, p. 405, excerpt from *Cassandra*, FN.

13. Cook, *FN*, vol. 1, p. 43, notebook, FN.

14. Wellcome, Claydon copy, MS 8993/f. 12, 1848, FN to Fanny.

15. Wellcome, Claydon copy, MS 8993/f. 13, 1848, FN to Fanny.

16. Wellcome, Claydon copy, MS 8992/f. 9, May 15, 1843, FN to Fanny.

17. O'Malley., *FN*, p. 125, 1846, private note, FN.

18. FN, *Ever Yours*, p. 36, July 10, 1847, to Clarkey.

19. BL ADD. 43396, f. 223, Feb. 3, 1874, FN to Elizabeth (Liz) Herbert.

20. Cook, *FN*, vol. 1, p. 39, 1854, Gaskell to Winkworth.

21. Wellcome, Claydon copy, MS 8993/f. 26, Nov. 2, 1849, FN to immediate family.

22. FN, *Letters from Egypt*, pp. 22–23, Nov. 19, 1849, to immediate family.

23. A Roman Catholic charitable order.

24. FN, *Letters from Egypt*, pp. 39–40, Nov. 29, 1849, to immediate family.

25. Cook, *FN*, vol. 1, p. 85, Dec. 1849, FN to Parthe.

26. FN, *Letters from Egypt*, pp. 68–69, Dec. 26, 1849, to immediate family.

27. FN, *Letters from Egypt*, p. 42, Dec. 9, 1849, to immediate family.

28. FN, *Letters from Egypt*, pp. 53–56, Dec. 14, 1849, to immediate family.

29. FN, *Letters from Egypt*, pp. 95–105, Jan. 17, 1850, FN to immediate family.

30. Florence Nightingale, *Florence Nightingale in Egypt and Greece: Her Diary and "Visions,"* M. D. Calabria, ed., pp. 30–31, Jan. 22, 1850, diary.

31. FN, *Letters from Egypt*, pp. 113–115, Jan. 28, 1850, to immediate family.

32. FN, *Egypt Diary*, Jan. 26, 1850.

33. FN, *Letters from Egypt*, pp. 137–139, Feb. 11, 1850, to immediate family.

34. O'Malley, *FN*, p. 156, Feb. 22 and Feb. 28, 1850, diary, FN.

35. Woodham-Smith, *FN*, pp. 52–53, March 7, 1850, diary, FN.

36. O'Malley, *FN*, pp. 156–157, Mar. 1850, diary, FN.

37. FN, *Egypt Diary*, p. 46, March 12, 1850.

38. FN, *Letters from Egypt*, pp. 137–139, Feb. 11, 1850, to immediate family.

39. BL ADD. 45844, f. 64, Feb. 7, 1892, private note, FN.

40. FN, *Letters from Egypt*, p. 189, March 1850, FN to immediate family.

41. FN, *Letters from Egypt*, p. 19.

42. A British fleet patrolled the eastern Mediterranean and blockaded Piraeus, the port of Athens, over a dispute with Greece (the Don Pacifico affair). This forced the ship carrying Florence and her friends to crisscross the ocean.

43. FN, *Collected Works*, vol. 7, pp. 377–379, April 29, 1850, to Parthe.

44. FN, *Ever Yours*, p. 42, diary, FN.

45. FN, *Collected Works*, vol. 7, p. 397, May 12, 1850, to Fanny.

46. FN, *Egypt Diary*, pp. 67–68, June 18, 1850.

47. O'Malley, *FN*, p. 132, private note, FN.

48. FN, *Collected Works*, vol. 8, p. 541, April 18, 1874, to Compton, relative and close friend of Selina.

49. FN, *Egypt Diary*, p. 69, July 9–11, 1850.

50. FN, *Collected Works*, vol. 7, pp. 461–464, July 10–17, 1850, to immediate family.

51. FN, *Collected Works*, vol. 7, pp. 461–464, July 10–17, 1850, to immediate family.

52. FN, *Ever Yours, FN*, p. 43, July 31, 1850, diary.

53. Sticker, *FN; Curriculum Vitae*, p. 4, July 24, 1851, FN.

54. FN, *Egypt Diary*, p. 79, Aug. 17, 1850.

55. FN, *Egypt Diary*, p. 80, Aug. 13, 1850.

56. Parthenope Verney, *Life and Death of Athena. An Owlet from the Parthenon*, p. 6.

57. FN, *Egypt Diary*, p. 80, Aug. 13, 1850.

Chapter 7

1. O'Malley, *FN*, p. 186, Autumn 1851, Hilary to Clarkey.

2. FN, *Cassandra and Other Selections* from *Suggestions for Thought*, Poovey, ed., pp. 119–121.

3. Wellcome, Claydon copy, MS 8993/f. 37, end of 1850, FN to Fanny.

4. FN, *Ever Yours*, p. 46, 1851, private note.

5. Wellcome, Claydon copy, MS 9006/ f. 66, Jan. 8, 1874, FN to Parthe.

6. FN, *Ever Yours*, p. 46, 1851, private note.

7. BL ADD. 43402, f. 66, Dec. 7, 1851, private note, FN.

8. BL ADD. 43402, ff. 178–87, 1857, private note, FN.

9. FN, *Ever Yours*, pp. 177–182, 1857, private note.

10. BL ADD. 45845, f. 136, 1868 or 1869, private note, FN.

11. BL ADD. 43402, ff. 178–87, 1857, private note, FN.

12. FN, *Ever Yours*, pp. 177–182, 1857, private note.

13. FN, *Ever Yours*, p. 46, 1851, private note.

14. Wellcome, Claydon copy, MS 8992/f. 141, 1840s, private note, FN.

15. FN, *Ever Yours*, pp. 46–47, 1851, private note.

16. FN, *Ever Yours, FN*, pp. 50–51, June 15, 1851, private note.

17. FN, *Ever Yours, FN*, p. 45, Jan. 7, 1851, private note.

18. FN, *Ever Yours*, pp 56–57, Nov. 1852, Parthe to Clarkey.

19. BL ADD. 43402, f. 55, Dec. 30, 1850, private note, FN.

20. FN, *Suggestions for Thought*, Poovey, ed., p. 180.

21. Strachey, *The Cause*, excerpt from *Cassandra*, p. 415, FN.

22. Strachey, *The Cause*, excerpt from *Cassandra*, pp. 395–396, FN.

23. Dr. Elizabeth Blackwell, *Pioneer Work in Opening the Medical Profession to Women*, p. 176, 1850.

24. Cook, *Life of FN*, vol. 1, p. 29, 1851, FN.

25. O'Malley, *FN*, p. 174, March 16, 1851, FN, journal.

26. FN, *Ever Yours*, p. 48, June 8, 1851, private note.

27. FN, *Ever Yours*, pp. 49–50, June 8, 1851, private note.

28. FN, *Ever Yours*, p. 179, 1857, private note.

29. Cook, *Life of FN*, vol. 1, p. 112, July 16, 1851, FN to Fanny.

30. Wellcome MS 9025/ff. 70–72 passim, Aug. 1851, Kaiserswerth Notes, FN.

31. FN, *Ever Yours*, p. 54, Aug. 31, 1851, to Fanny.

32. Claydon N69, Aug. 10, 1851, WEN to Fanny.

33. Claydon N274, Sept. 7, 1851, Fanny (unsigned) to FN. Written while FN at Kaiserswerth, Fanny and Parthe at German spas.

34. Baly, *As Miss Nightingale Said*, p. 13, notebook, FN.

35. FN, *Collected Works*, vol. 7, p. 676, Oct. 22, 1848, to Parthe.

36. Woodham-Smith, *FN*, p. 62, 1851, private note, FN.

37. FN, *Collected Works*, vol. 7, p. 680, Jan. 8, 1852, to Fanny.

38. FN, *Ever Yours*, p. 57, May 12, 1852, to WEN

39. O'Malley, *FN*, pp. 192–193, 1852, FN to Henry Manning.

40. FN, *Cassandra and Other Selections*, Poovey, ed., excerpt from *Suggestions for Thought*, p. 5.

41. JoAnn Widerquist, *Florence Nightingale's Calling*, p. 113, excerpt from *Suggestions for Thought*, FN.

42. FN, *Cassandra and Other Selections*, Poovey, ed., excerpt from *Suggestions for Thought*, pp. 57–59.

43. FN, *Suggestions for Thought*, Poovey, ed., pp. 57–59.

44. Nightingale did not seek publication at this time. Busy with plans for more nurse training, she postponed final editing but did solicit critique of the manuscript from several trusted friends, including Richard Monckton Milnes.

45. FN, *Ever Yours,*, pp. 60–61, 1852, FN to Manning.

46. Wellcome, Claydon copy, MS 8993/f. 105, Sept. 21, 1852, FN to Fanny.

47. Wellcome, Claydon copy, MS 8993/f. 106, Sept. 1852, FN to Fanny.

48. The Sisters cared for two hundred poor orphans and had a lying-in facility in their main house. The attached hospital tended aged and sick women. The Sisters also ran a general and a children's hospital. At Flo's request, Manning arranged that she conform to House rules as a postulant; as a non–Catholic, she could not use the Sisters' dormitory and refectory; hence, Florence must eat and sleep in her room. She could join sisters in visiting the poor, serve the sick under their direction, and help take care of the orphans.

49. BL ADD. 45844 f. 6, May 7, 1867, private note, FN.

50. O'Malley, *FN*, p. 198, Dec. 31, 1852, diary, FN.

51. Lesser, *Clarkey*, p. 132, Oct. 30, 1852, Clarkey to Hilary.

52. Claydon N123, February 1853, FN to Fanny.

53. Cook, *Life of FN*, vol. 1, p. 128, Spring 1853, FN to Hilary.

Chapter 8

1. FN, *Ever Yours*, p. 76, Jan. 11, 1854, to Hannah Nicholson.

2. FN, *Ever Yours*, pp. 66–68, June 5, 1853, to Lady Charlotte Canning, chairwoman of the Harley Street institution's ladies' committee.

3. FN, *Ever Yours, FN*, p. 54, Aug. 31, 1851, to Fanny.

4. Lesser, *Clarkey*, pp. 138–139, April 8, 1853, FN to Clarkey.

5. Cook, *Life of FN*, vol. 1, pp. 134–135, Aug. 20, 1853, FN to Clarkey.

6. FN, *Ever Yours*, pp. 69–70, June 28, 1853, to Clarkey.

7. Lesser, *Clarkey*, pp. 138–139, June 8, 1853, FN to Clarkey.

8. Cook, *Life of FN*, vol. 1, pp. 137–139, Aug. 27, 1853, FN to Clarkey.

9. FN, *Florence Nightingale: Her Wit and Wisdom*, E. R. Barritt, ed., p. 21, from *Notes on Nursing*.

10. FN, *Florence Nightingale at Harley Street; Her Reports to the Governors of Her Nursing Home*, p. 2.

11. FN, *FN at Harley Street*, p. 4.

12. FN, *Ever Yours, FN*, p. 73, Sept. 13, 1853, to Canning.

13. FN, *Wit and Wisdom*, p. 26, excerpt from *Notes on Nursing*.

14. FN, *Ever Yours*, pp. 71–72, Oct. 29, 1853, to Fanny.

15. Gaskell, *Letters*, pp. 319–320, Oct. 27, 1854, to Shaen.

16. FN, *FN at Harley Street*, p. 26.

17. Baly, *As Miss Nightingale Said*, p. 20, 1854, FN to WEN.

18. Baly, *As Miss Nightingale Said*, p. 19, 1853, FN to Fanny.

19. FN, *Ever Yours*, p. 75, Dec. 3, 1853, to WEN.

20. O'Malley, *FN*, pp. 208–209, Oct. 20, 1854, Gaskell to Winkworth.

21. Elizabeth Gaskell, *Further Letters of Mrs. Gaskell*, p. 114, Oct. 27, 1854, to Shaen.

22. Gaskell, *Letters*, pp. 317–318, Oct. 27, 1854, to Shaen.

23. O'Malley, *FN*, pp. 208–209, Oct. 20, 1854, Gaskell to Winkworth.

24. FN, *Ever Yours*, pp. 71–72, Oct. 29, 1853, to Fanny.

25. Wellcome, Claydon copy, MS 8994/f. 99, April 12, 1854, FN to Fanny.

26. O'Malley, *FN*, pp. 208–209, Oct. 20, 1854, Gaskell to Winkworth.

27. Sticker, *FN: Curriculum Vitae*, p. 15, Autumn 1853, FN to Caroline Fliedner.

28. FN, *Florence Nightingale at Harley Street*, pp. 34–36, Aug. 7, 1854.

Chapter 9

1. Pincoffs, *A Physician in Eastern Military Hospitals*, pp. 75–80, excerpt from J. McNeill speech at the Oct. 31, 1856, Crimean banquet and published in *The Times* on Nov. 3.

2. Elizabeth Grey, *The Noise of Drums and Trumpets; W. H. Russell Reports from the Crimea*, pp. 102–103, Oct. 1854, *The Times*, article by special Constantinople correspondent Thomas Chenery.

3. Cook, *Life of FN*, vol. 1, p. 147, *The Times*, Oct. 1854, article by William Russell, special correspondent accompanying the army.

4. FN, *Florence Nightingale; Letters from the Crimea*, Sue M. Goldie, ed., p. 18, the *Times*, Oct. 13, 1854.

5. FN, *Letters from the Crimea*, p. 23, Oct. 15, 1854, Sidney Herbert (henceforth SH) to FN.

6. Cook, *Life of FN*, vol. 1, pp. 151–154, Oct. 15, 1854, SH to FN.

7. Cook, *Life of FN*, vol. 1, pp. 151–154, Oct. 15, 1854, SH to FN.

8. FN, *Letters from the Crimea*, p. 25, Oct. 15, 1854, EH to FN.

9. FN, *Letters from the Crimea*, pp. 26–27,

Oct. 20, 1854, Secretary-at-War to Miss Nightingale.

10. Besides lively controversy among several sects within the established Church, let alone Protestant groups outside it, there existed strong anti–Catholic sentiment compounded by fear of proselytizing.

11. FN, *Letters from the Crimea*, pp. 26–27, Oct. 20, 1854, Secretary-at-War to Miss Nightingale.

12. FN, *Letters from the Crimea*, pp. 28–29, Oct. 24, 1854, the *Morning Chronicle* p. 4, SH.

13. FN, *Ever Yours*, pp. 79–80, Oct. 14, 1854, to EH.

14. Stanmore, *Sidney Herbert*, vol. 1, pp. 341–342, Mary Stanley.

15. Bermondsey nuns visited the sick poor at home and in London's two major hospitals, ran schools for toddlers and girls, taught converts and lapsed Catholics, and helped the poor materially and spiritually.

16. Sarah Anne Terrot, *Nurse Sarah Anne; with Florence Nightingale at Scutari*, R. G. Richardson, ed., p. 66, Oct. 21, 1854.

17. Cook, *Life of FN*, vol. 1, pp. 183–184, Nov. 14, 1854, FN to William Bowman, M.D., distinguished ophthalmic surgeon and FN's colleague at Harley Street.

18. Cook, *Life of FN*, vol. 1, pp. 164–165, Oct. 28, 1854, excerpt from article in the *Examiner*.

19. FN, *Ever Yours*, pp. 135–136, Nov. 14, 1855, to immediate family.

20. Cook, *Life of FN*, vol. 1, p. 155, Oct. 19, 1854, Parthe to a friend.

21. Cook, *Life of FN*, vol. 1, p. 161, Fanny to FN.

22. FN, *Ever Yours*, p. 54, Aug. 31, 1851, to Fanny.

23. Roman god of wine.

24. Cook, *Life of FN*, vol. 1, p. 162, Oct. 26, 1854, Sam Smith (hereafter referred to as Smith) to Nightingales.

25. Cook, *Life of FN*, vol. 1, p. 163, Smith to Nightingales.

26. Terrot, *Nurse Sarah Anne*, p. 76, Oct. 31, 1854.

27. Cook, *Life of FN*, vol. 1, p. 171, Nov. 4, 1854, FN to immediate family.

Chapter 10

1. FN, *Ever Yours*, pp. 114–115, May 5, 1855, to immediate family.

2. Reid, *Life of Houghton*, vol. 1, p. 505, Jan. 1855, Augustus Stafford to Milnes.

3. Pincoffs, *A Civilian in Eastern Military Hospitals*, p. 1.

4. Trevor Royle, *Crimea*, pp. 253–254, Dr. Menzies to Lord Stratford de Redcliffe, Oct. 26, 1854.

5. Osborne, *Scutari and Its Hospitals*, p. 7.

6. Grey, *Noise of Drums and Trumpets*, pp. 44–45, W. Russell.

7. Alexis Soyer, *A Culinary Campaign: Being Historical Reminiscences of the Late War*, pp. 93–94.

8. Terrot, *Nurse Sarah Anne*, pp. 80–81, Nov. 4, 1854.

9. Osborne, *Scutari and Its Hospitals*, p. 19.

10. FN, *Florence Nightingale: Her Wit and Wisdom*, p. 21, from *Notes on Nursing*.

11. A. W. Kinglake, *The Invasion of the Crimea*, vol. 7, pp. 371–372. Kinglake consulted FN in writing his history; this is a quote from her letter.

12. FN, *Letters from the Crimea*, pp. 81–82, Feb. 1, 1855, to Fanny.

13. Stanmore, *Sidney Herbert*, vol. 1, p. 344, Nov. 8, 1854, Charles Bracebridge (hereafter referred to as Bracebridge) to SH.

14. FN, *Letters from the Crimea*, pp. 39–40, Nov. 25, 1854, to SH.

15. FN, *Ever Yours*, pp. 83–85, Nov. 14, 1854, to Bowman.

16. William H. Russell, *The War, from the Landing at Gallipoli to the Death of Lord Raglan*, pp. 279–80, Nov. 25, 1854.

17. Russell, *The War*, pp. 279–80, Nov. 25, 1854

18. Stanmore, *Sidney Herbert*, vol. 1, p. 347, Nov. 14, 1854, FN to SH.

19. William H. Russell, *The British Expedition to the Crimea*, p. 250.

20. Osborne, *Scutari and Its Hospitals*, pp. 34–35.

21. Margaret Goodman, *Experiences of an English Sister of Mercy*, p. 128.

22. Stanmore, *Sidney Herbert*, vol. 1, p. 347, Nov. 14, 1854, FN to SH.

23. FN, *Ever Yours*, pp. 83–85, Nov. 14, 1854, to Bowman.

24. Terrot, *Nurse Sarah Anne*, pp. 87–88, Nov. 9, 1854.

25. Terrot, *Nurse Sarah Anne*, pp. 88–89, Nov. 9, 1854.

26. Terrot, *Nurse Sarah Anne*, pp. 88–89, Nov. 9, 1854.

27. FN, *Letters from the Crimea*, pp. 42–43, Dec. 5, 1854, to Ms. Gipps, St. John's House.

28. Taylor, *Eastern Hospitals*, vol. 1, p. 71.

29. FN, *Letters from the Crimea*, p. 37, Nov. 14, 1854, to SH.

30. Osborne, *Scutari and Its Hospitals*, p. 29.

31. Osborne, *Scutari and Its Hospitals*, p. 3.

32. Goodman, *Experiences of an English Sister of Mercy*, pp. 111–113.

33. Woodham-Smith, *FN*, p. 115. Excerpt from Augustus Stafford's testimony to the parliamentary Roebuck committee, inquiring into the state of the army before Sevastopol.

34. Cook, *Life of FN*, vol. 1, p. 180, Jan. 29, 1855, excerpt from Augustus Stafford's parliamentary speech.

35. Stanmore, *Sidney Herbert*, vol. 1, p. 349, Nov. 1854, Osborne to SH.

36. Cook, *Life of FN*, vol. 1, p. 183, Nov. 20, 1854, Bracebridge to Nightingales.

37. Goodman, *Experiences of an English Sister of Mercy*, pp. 105–106.

38. Cook, *Life of FN*, vol. 1, p. 237, excerpt from the parliamentary report of sanitary commission proceedings.

Chapter 11

1. FN, *Ever Yours,* pp. 92–93, Dec. 5, 1854, to immediate family.

2. Osborne, *Scutari and Its Hospitals*, p. 27.

3. Terrot, *Nurse Sarah Anne*, p. 80, Nov. 4, 1854.

4. Cook, *Life of FN*, vol. 1, p. 207, Dec. 21, 1854, FN to SH.

5. O'Malley, *FN*, p. 246. Overhearing his men say this while in the trenches, an officer wrote home about it.

6. Woodham-Smith, *FN*, p. 118, excerpt from a soldier's letter home.

7. Cook, *Life of FN*, vol. 1, p. 237, excerpt from a soldier's letter home.

8. Osborne, *Scutari and Its Hospitals*, pp. 19–20.

9. Stanmore, *Sidney Herbert*, vol. 1, p. 349, Osborne to SH, Nov. 1854.

10. Darwin, *A Century of Family Letters*, vol. 2, p. 156, Dec. 15, 1854, F. Allen to E. Wedgwood.

11. James H. Skene, *With Lord Stratford in the Crimean War*, pp. 38–39.

12. Nancy Mitford, *The Stanleys of Alderly*, p. 116, Dec. 30, 1854.

13. Lady Alicia Blackwood, *A Narrative of Personal Experiences and Impressions during a Residence on the Bosphorus throughout the Crimean War*, pp. 49–50.

14. Taylor, *Eastern Hospitals*, vol. 1, pp. 69–71.

15. Osborne, *Scutari and Its Hospitals*, p. 26.

16. Goodman, *Experiences of an English Sister of Mercy*, pp. 105–106.

17. Cook, *Life of FN*, vol. 1, p. 218, FN to SH.

18. FN, *Ever Yours,* pp. 92–93, Dec. 5, 1854, to immediate family.

19. FN, *Ever Yours*, p. 92, probably Dec. 1854, to Parthe.

20. Cook, *Life of FN*, vol. 1, p. 239, FN.

21. Cook, *Life of FN*, vol. 1, p. 240.

22. Osborne, *Scutari and Its Hospitals*, p. 23.

23. Taylor, *Eastern Hospitals*, vol. I, p. 68.

24. Osborne, *Scutari and Its Hospitals*, p. '23.

25. Cook, *Life of FN*, vol. 1, p. 216, Dec. 14, 1854, Queen Victoria to FN.

26. FN, *Letters from the Crimea*, pp. 57–59, Dec. 25, 1854, to SH.

27. O'Malley, *FN*, pp. 300–301, April 1855, FN.

28. FN, *Ever Yours*, pp. 93–96, Dec. 10, 1854, to SH.

29. December 8, 1854.

30. FN, *Letters from the Crimea*, pp. 28–29, Oct. 24, 1854, the *Morning Chronicle* p. 4, SH.

31. O'Malley, *FN*, p. 252, Henry Manning.

32. FN, *Letters from the Crimea*, p. 49, Dec. 2, 1854, Mrs. Stanley to Parthe.

33. FN, *Letters from the Crimea*, p. 49, Nov. 27, 1854, Mrs. Stanley to Parthe.

34. Mitford, *The Stanleys*, p. 112, Nov. 30, 1854.

35. Cook, *Life of FN*, vol. 1, p. 191, Dec. 18, 1854, Bracebridge to Smith,

36. John Beddoe, M.D., *Memories of Eighty Years*, p. 65. A civilian physician, he volunteered to work in the Scutari hospitals so as to free army doctors for fieldwork.

37. FN, *Letters from the Crimea*, p. 50, Dec. 15, 1854, to SH.

38. FN, *Ever Yours*, pp. 93–96, Dec. 10, 1854, to SH.

39. Blackwood, *A Lady on the Bosphorus during the Crimean War*, p. 64.

40. Woodham-Smith, *FN*, p. 122, Dec. 15, 1854, FN to SH.

41. Cook, *Life of FN*, vol. I, p. 253, FN to SH.

42. FN, *Ever Yours*, p. 97, Jan. 4, 1855, to SH.

43. FN, *Ever Yours*, p. 97, Jan. 4, 1855, to SH.

44. FN, *Letters from the Crimea*, p. 57, Dec. 25, 1854, to SH.

Chapter 12

1. O'Malley, *FN*, pp. 266–269, Jan. 4, 1855, FN to SH.

2. Claydon N290, Jan. 11, 1855, Selina to Parthe.

3. Russell, *The War*, pp. 213–215, Jan. 19, 1855.

4. Terrot, *Nurse Sarah Anne*, p. 112, end 1854.

5. Terrot, *Nurse Sarah Anne*, p. 112, end 1854.

6. Woodham-Smith, *FN*, p. 127, Dec. 14, 1854, Bracebridge to SH.

7. FN, *Letters from the Crimea*, pp. 57–59, Dec. 25, 1854, to SH.

8. Stanmore, *Sidney Herbert*, vol. 1, p. 397, Jan. 19, 1855, FN to SH.

9. FN, *Ever Yours,* pp. 102–107, Jan. 28, 1855, to SH.

10. FN, *Letters from the Crimea*, pp. 70–75, Jan. 8, 1855, to SH.

11. Stanmore, *Sidney Herbert*, vol. 1, p. 397, Jan. 19, 1855, SH to FN.

12. Osborne, *Scutari and Its Hospitals*, p. 26.

13. FN, *Ever Yours,* pp. 109–110, Feb. 22, 1855, to SH.

14. O'Malley, *FN*, pp. 266–269, Jan. 4, 1855, FN to SH.

15. An army internal affairs investigator, Tulloch had studied law and interested himself in statistics on troop sickness and mortality.

16. Florence Macalister, *Memoir of the Right Hon. Sir John McNeill*, p. 403, Feb. 1856, McNeill.

17. FN, *Ever Yours,* pp. 115–117, May 10, 1855, to Parthe.

18. Blackwood, *A Lady on the Bosphorus during the Crimean War*, p. 78.

19. Osborne, *Scutari and Its Hospitals*, pp. 25–26.

20. Soyer, *A Culinary Campaign*, p. 82.

21. Woodham-Smith, *FN*, p. 165, FN.

22. Claydon N274, undated, Sutherland.

23. Cook, *Life of FN*, vol. 1, p. 281, Nov. 16, 1855, Parthe to FN.

24. FN, *Ever Yours,* pp. 148–149, March 6, 1856, to colonel Sir John Lefroy, war secretary lord Panmure's confidential advisor.

25. Taylor, *Eastern Hospitals*, p. 260.

26. FN, *Letters from the Crimea*, pp. 81–82, Feb. 1, 1855, to Fanny.

27. Woodham-Smith, *FN*, p. 131, Feb. 12, 1855, FN to SH.

28. FN, *Ever Yours,* pp. 108–109, Jan. 14, 1855, to Lady Cranworth, member of the committee vetting nurses.

29. Woodham-Smith, *FN*, p. 131, Feb. 12, 1855, FN to SH.

30. John Shepherd, *The Crimean Doctors*, p. 351.

31. O'Malley, *FN*, p. 288, excerpt from an official complaint made by the medical men.

32. O'Malley, *FN*, pp. 327–328, Oct. 1855, Mary Stanley to FN.

33. O'Malley, *FN*, p. 328, Dec. 19, 1855, FN to Stanley.

34. Two Brothers (A. & G. Money), *Sevastopol. Our Tent in the Crimea; and Wandering in Sevastopol*, pp. 35–36. Contemporary account by two visitors on leave from India.

35. Pincoffs, *Eastern Military Hospitals*, pp. 30–31.

36. BL ADD. 45844 f. 6, May 7, 1867, private note, FN.

Chapter 13

1. FN, *Ever Yours,* p. 136, Nov. 29, 1855, to Fanny.

2. Royle, *Crimea*, p. 254.

3. Woodham-Smith, *FN*, p. 145, Oct. 20, 1854, John Hall to Andrew Smith, head of the army medical department.

4. Soyer, *A Culinary Campaign*, p. 90.

5. FN, *Ever Yours,* pp. 114–115, May 5, 1855, to immediate family.

6. Soyer, *A Culinary Campaign*, pp. 93–94.

7. Soyer, *A Culinary Campaign*, p. 99.

8. Soyer, *A Culinary Campaign*, pp. 99–100.

9. FN, *Letters from the Crimea*, p. 123, Oct. 28, 1855, to immediate family.

10. Soyer, *A Culinary Campaign*, p. 101.

11. Soyer, *A Culinary Campaign*, p. 101.

12. Soyer, *A Culinary Campaign*, p. 102.

13. FN, *Ever Yours,* pp. 115–117, May 10, 1855, to Parthe.

14. FN, *Letters from the Crimea*, p. 130, May 10, 1855, to Parthe.

15. FN, *Ever Yours,* pp. 115–117, May 10, 1855, to Parthe.

16. FN, *Ever Yours,* pp. 115–117, May 10, 1855, to Parthe.

17. Regimental hospitals were not under FN's authority. A lone, headstrong female nursed in one. Martha Clough came to Scutari with Mary Stanley; her officer fiancé had died of cholera in the Crimea, and Clough wanted to nurse his colleagues. The fiancé's brother was war secretary Lord Panmure. FN's rules excluded nursing individual officers, so Clough went to Balaclava hospital with seven other Stanley nurses despite FN's reluctance to let them go to a facility with a well-earned reputation for filth, inefficiency, and rowdy orderlies, one, moreover, where she had not yet established control. Then the commander of Clough's fiancé's regiment invited her to work at his hospital. Viewing herself independent of FN, Clough agreed. Hall backed her. The singular sight of an unmarried lady working alone among men, sans chaperone, caused considerable gossip, especially as Clough often got drunk and seemed to have no income. FN thought her conduct sullied the name of nurse; many agreed, including Mary Stanley. Some saw Clough as FN's rival. With more important matters on her mind than a probably vain and certainly messy attempt to dislodge Clough — rival or not — FN ignored her. In the summer (1855) Clough fell ill. Shaw Stewart nursed her at the Castle hospital. A frail Clough set sail for England. She died on the Black Sea. When Clough's body arrived at Scutari, FN made sure she had a decent burial, notified her loved ones, and herself paid for Clough's effects to be sent home.

18. Christopher Hibbert, *The Destruction of Lord Raglan*, p. 265, letters from Dr. Ethelbert Blake, manuscript source.

19. Claydon N290, Jan. 11, 1855, Selina to Parthe.

20. BL ADD. 45797, f. 88, Robert Robinson's diary.

21. BL ADD. 45797, f. 88, Robinson diary.

22. FN, *Collected Works*, vol. 8, p. 538, Feb. 8, 1873, to Selina.

23. Cook, *The Life of FN*, vol. 1, pp. 265–266, Dec. 8, 1855, Parthe to FN.

24. BL ADD. 45797, f. 90, Robinson diary.

25. FN, *Letters from the Crimea*, p. 166, Oct. 19, 1855, to Mai Smith (henceforth referred to as Mai).

26. Soyer, *A Culinary Campaign*, p. 180.

27. Soyer, *A Culinary Campaign*, p. 181.

28. FN, *Ever Yours,* pp. 111–112, March 8, 1855, to Parthe.

29. FN, *Letters from the Crimea*, p. 133, July 9, 1855, to immediate family.

30. Verney, *Life of Athena*, p. ix.

31. Cook, *The Life of FN*, vol. 1, p. 266, chorus from the most popular of many songs about FN.

32. FN, *Letters from the Crimea*, p. 131, June 18, 1855, to immediate family.

33. Cook, *The Life of FN*, vol. 1, p. 260, July 9, 1855, Fanny to FN.

34. FN, *Letters from the Crimea*, p. 208, Feb. 11, 1856, to Fanny.

35. FN, *Letters from the Crimea*, p. 137, July 28, 1955, to immediate family.

36. FN, *Letters from the Crimea*, p. 132, July 5, 1855, to immediate family.

37. BL ADD. 45793, f. 104, July 18, 1855, FN to Mai.

38. O'Malley, *FN*, p. 331, Oct. 1855, Mai to Nightingales.

Chapter 14

1. FN, *Letters from the Crimea*, p. 147, Nov. 30, 1855.

2. Cook, *Life of FN*, vol. 1, pp. 295–296, Jan. 25, 1856, Mai.

3. FN, *Letters from the Crimea*, p. 157, Sept. 2, 1855, Bridgeman to Hall.

4. FN, *Letters from the Crimea*, p. 163, mid-end Oct. 1855, to Mai.

5. Oct. 16, 1855.

6. Woodham-Smith, *FN*, p. 160, Nov. 5, 1855, FN to Bracebridge.

7. Soyer, *A Culinary Campaign*, pp. 257–258.

8. FN, *Letters from the Crimea*, p. 167, Oct. 24, 1855, to Fanny.

9. FN, *Ever Yours*, pp. 132–135, Nov. 17, 1855, to EH.

10. Cook, *Life of FN*, vol. 1, p. 274, Nov. 1855.

11. Cook, *Life of FN*, vol. 1, p. 274, Dec. 27, 1855, Parthe to FN.

12. Woodham-Smith, *FN*, pp. 163–164, Nov. 29, 1855, from the official announcement of the meeting.

13. Cook, *Life of FN*, vol. 1, p. 306, Nov. 29, 1855, SH speech at inaugural meeting of the Nightingale Fund.

14. Cook, *Life of FN*, vol. 1, p. 238, Jan. 1855, Stafford (parliamentary observer at Scutari hospitals) to Milnes.

15. Cook, *Life of FN*, vol. 1, p. 270, Nov. 29, 1855, Parthe to FN.

16. Cook, *Life of FN*, vol. 1, p. 269, Nov. 29, 1855, Fanny to FN.

17. FN, *Ever Yours*, p. 54, Aug. 31, 1851, to Fanny.

18. Cook, *Life of FN*, vol. 1, pp. 270–271, Dec. 1855, FN to her parents.

19. Lucy Seymer, *Florence Nightingale's Nurses: The Nightingale Nurse Training School, 1860–1890*, p. 3. Written to coincide with the school's one hundredth birthday, this account is based on Nightingale Fund council minutes and FN correspondence.

20. Gaskell, *Letters*, pp. 382–383, Jan. 18, 1856, Gaskell to Parthe.

21. Cook, *Life of FN*, vol. 1, p. 271, Jan. 6, 1856, FN to SH.

22. FN, *Letters from the Crimea*, p. 184, Jan. 6, 1856, to SH.

23. Cook, *Life of FN*, vol. 1, p. 271, Jan. 6, 1856, FN to SH.

24. Council members included Sidney Herbert and Charles Bracebridge; Sir James Clark, physician and family friend; Drs. Henry Bence Jones and William Bowman, whom Nightingale knew from Harley Street; parliamentary commissioners Dr. John McNeill and Colonel Alexander Tulloch, friends and colleagues from the Crimea; and the dean of Hereford, and prison reformer Sir Joshua Jebb, longtime and trusted family friends.

25. O'Malley, *FN*, p. 356, Jan. 24, 1856, Mai to Nightingales.

26. Cook, *Life of FN*, vol. 1, p. 295, Dec. 31, 1855, Mai.

27. FN, *Ever Yours,* pp. 121–127, Sept. 9, 1855, to Canning, who, with EH interviewed and hired nurses for the Crimean War hospitals.

28. FN, *Ever Yours,* pp. 121–127, Sept. 9, 1855, FN to Canning.

29. FN, *Ever Yours, FN,* pp. 128–132, Oct. 1, 1855, FN to Canning.

30. O'Malley, *FN*, p. 346, Dec. 20, 1855, Mai to Nightingales.

31. O'Malley, *FN*, pp. 344–345, Dec. 9, 1855, Mai to Nightingales or Smith.

32. O'Malley, *FN*, p. 349, Dec. 25, 1855, FN to Panmure.

33. O'Malley, *FN*, p. 346, Dec. 22, 1855, Mai to Nightingales.

34. O'Malley, *FN*, p. 346, Dec. 11, 1855, Mai to Nightingales.

35. O'Malley, *FN*, p. 346, Dec. 22, 1855, Mai to Nightingales.

36. O'Malley, *FN*, p. 354, Jan. 27, 1856, Mai to Nightingales.

Chapter 15

1. FN, *Ever Yours,* pp. 111–112, March 8, 1855, to Parthe.

2. Lady Hornby, *Constantinople during the Crimean War,* pp. 150–151, Jan. 5, 1856.

3. Hornby, *Crimean War,* p. 152, Jan. 5, 1856.

4. O'Malley, *FN,* p. 346, Dec. 22, 1855, Mai to Nightingales.

5. FN, *Ever Yours,* pp. 142–143, Feb. 20, 1856, to SH.

6. FN, *Ever Yours,* pp. 143–144, Feb. 20, 1856, FN quoting Sutherland verbatim in her letter to SH.

7. FN, *Ever Yours,* pp. 142–144, Feb. 20, 1856, to SH.

8. FN, *Ever Yours,* pp. 142–144, Feb. 20, 1856, to SH.

9. FN, *Letters from the Crimea,* pp. 192–194, Jan. 11, 1856, to Lefroy.

10. FN, *Letters from the Crimea,* p. 214, Feb. 1856, Lefroy to Panmure.

11. FN, *Letters from the Crimea,* p. 229, March 16, excerpt from Panmure's General Order.

12. FN, *Ever Yours,* pp. 149–153, April 3, 1856, to SH.

13. FN, *Ever Yours,* p. 155, April 22, 1856, to Parthe.

14. FN, *Letters from the Crimea,* p. 253, Apr. 17, 1856, to Smith.

15. FN, *Letters from the Crimea,* p. 253, Apr. 17, 1856, to Smith.

16. FN, *Letters from the Crimea,* p. 255, Apr. 19, 1856, to Parthe.

17. March 30, 1856.

18. Cook, *Life of FN,* vol. 1, p. 300, FN to Cranworth, now an official government nursing recruiter.

19. FN, *Letters from the Crimea,* pp. 64–65, note 14, June 26, 1856, FN.

20. FN, *Ever Yours,* pp. 156–157, April 26, 1856, to the Reverend Mother Mary Clare Moore (henceforth referred to as Moore).

21. Lady Hornby, *In and around Stamboul,* May 1856, vol. 2, pp. 68–69.

22. FN, *Ever Yours,* p. 156, June 16, 1856.

23. Cook, vol. 1, p. 303, Early Summer 1856, Mai to Nightingales.

24. FN, *Letters from the Crimea,* pp. 267–268, May 30, 1856, to Bracebridges.

25. FN, *Egypt Diary,* p. 80, Aug. 13, 1850.

Chapter 16

1. Lesser, *Clarkey,* p. 146, Aug. 21, 1856, Clarkey to Hilary.

2. Cook, *Life of FN,* vol. 1, p. 318, Aug. 1856, FN, private note.

3. BL ADD. 45844, f.6, May 7, 1867, private note, FN

4. Cook, *Life of FN,* vol. 1, p. 320, Aug. 1856, Parthe to E. Tollet.

5. Cook, *Life of FN,* vol. 1, p. 317, FN.

6. FN, *Ever Yours,* pp. 160–162, Aug. 25, 1856, to Lefroy.

7. FN, *Letters from the Crimea,* pp. 285–286, Aug. 28, 1856, Lefroy to FN.

8. Cook, *Life of FN,* vol. 1, pp. 322–323, Aug. 28, 1856, Lefroy to FN.

9. FN, *Ever Yours,* pp. 115–117, May 10, 1855, to Parthe.

10. Wellcome, Claydon copy, MS 8993/f.104, Sept. 20,1852, FN to parents.

11. Cook, *Life of FN,* vol. 1, p. 324, Sept. 25, 1856, FN to Smith.

12. *The Panmure Papers,* Douglas and Ramsey, eds., vol. 2, pp. 305–306, Oct. 4, 1856, Queen Victoria to Lord Panmure.

13. Woodham-Smith, *FN,* p. 186, SH.

14. Cook, *Life of FN,* vol. 1, p. 353, May 2, 1857, Parthe to Clarkey.

15. To FN's fury, knighted for his services as chief medical officer in the Crimean War.

16. Woodham-Smith, *FN,* p. 190, Nov. 16, 1856, FN to SH.

17. FN, *Collected Works,* vol. 1, p. 144, Dec. 14, 1856, to Fanny.

18. FN, *Ever Yours,* pp. 172–173, end 1856, private note, FN.

19. Woodham-Smith, *FN,* p. 191, Dec. 25, 1856, private note, FN.

20. *Panmure Papers,* vol. 2, pp. 332–334, Jan. 17, 1857, Palmerston to Panmure.

21. *Panmure Papers,* vol. 2, pp. 337–338, Jan. 19, 1857, Panmure to Palmerston.

22. *Panmure Papers,* vol. 2, p. 401, July 1, 1857, FN to Panmure. Nonetheless, FN had the last word. The royal commission recommended that all new hospitals be built "in separate pavilions" to "prevent a large number of sick from being agglomerated under one roof" (Cook, *Life of FN,* vol. 1, p. 342).

23. Cook, *Life of FN,* vol. 1, p. 316, March 28, 1857, FN to McNeill.

24. Woodham-Smith, *FN,* p. 196, Nov. 1856, Fanny to WEN.

25. The war office sent McNeill and Tulloch to the Crimea (1855) to ascertain transport and commissariat arrangements. Their report named officers responsible for the mess. These men raised an uproar. The war office appointed a panel (the Chelsea board) of officers to look into the McNeill-Tulloch report. The Chelsea board fully absolved the named officers, which, in effect, killed the report.

26. Cook, *Life of FN,* vol. 1, p. 338, May 12, 1857, FN to McNeill.

27. FN, *Ever Yours,* pp. 173–174, March 1, 1857, to McNeill.

28. Woodham-Smith, *FN*, p. 194, late Feb. 1857, FN to SH.

Chapter 17

1. Cook, *Life of FN*, vol. 1, p. 314, Feb. 9, 1857, FN.
2. Cook, *Life of FN*, vol. 1, p. 133, Jul. 25, 1854, Mohl to WEN.
3. Commissioners included: able, fearless surgeon Thomas Alexander; ("a gentle giant of a Scotchman" described by the *Times* special correspondent as "sitting on the beach with a man's leg in his lap" [Woodham-Smith, *FN*, p. 188] cursing Hall for landing the army without medical supplies; the army got rid of Alexander by posting him to Canada, but FN convinced Panmure to recall him to serve on the commission); distinguished doctor James Clark; statistician William Farr; General Henry Storks, Scutari commander; sanitarian John Sutherland; and because the war office could not spare Colonel Lefroy, Augustus Stafford, M.P., who had visited the Barrack hospital early in the war.
4. Woodham-Smith, *FN*, p. 199, Sutherland to Mai.
5. Woodham-Smith, *FN*, pp. 201–202, private note, FN.
6. FN, *Collected Works,* vol. 1, p. 46, June 5, 1856, to SH.
7. Woodham-Smith, *FN*, p. 199, 1867, FN to Clarkey.
8. FN, *Ever Yours,* pp. 183–184, June 4 and 12, 1857, to McNeill.
9. BL ADD. 43394, f. 95, July 7, 1857, FN to SH.
10. Cook, *Life of FN*, vol. 1, p. 363.
11. Cook, *Life of FN*, vol. 1, p. 312, Aug. 7, 1857, SH to FN.
12. Claydon N308, Aug. 17, 1857, Fanny to WEN.
13. Woodham-Smith, *FN*, p. 199, Summer 1857, FN to Clarkey.
14. Claydon N308, Aug. 17, 1857, Fanny to WEN.
15. Claydon N308, Aug. 17, 1857, Parthe to WEN.
16. Claydon N308, Aug. 17, 1857, Fanny to WEN.
17. Claydon N308, Aug. 17, 1857, Parthe to WEN.
18. Claydon N308, soon after Aug. 17, 1857, Fanny to WEN.
19. Cook, *Life of FN*, vol. 1, pp. 371–372, Sept. 1857, Parthe to Clarkey.
20. Cook, *Life of FN*, vol. 1, pp. 371–372, Sept. 1857, Parthe to Clarkey.
21. FN, *Ever Yours,* p. 170, end of 1856.
22. Woodham-Smith, *FN*, p. 208, Sept. 1857, WEN to Fanny.

23. Woodham-Smith, *FN*, p. 207, late August 1857, FN to Sutherland.
24. Cook, *Life of FN*, vol. 1, p. 370, Sept. 7, 1857, Sutherland to FN.
25. FN, *Ever Yours,* pp. 177–182, 1857, private note.
26. Woodham-Smith, *FN*, p. 208, Sept. 11, 1857, Sutherland to FN.
27. FN, *Collected Works*, vol. 1, p. 144, Dec. 14, 1856, to Fanny.
28. FN, *Ever Yours,* pp. 177–182, 1857, private note.
29. FN, *Ever Yours,* pp. 177–182, 1857, private note.
30. Claydon N308, soon after August 17, 1857, Parthe to WEN.
31. BL ADD. 45793, f. 133, Sept. 1857, Mai to FN.
32. Cook, *Life of FN*, vol. 1, pp. 371–372, Sept. 1857, Parthe to Clarkey.
33. BL ADD. 45783, ff. 222–223, July 1870, FN to her close friend Oxford luminary Benjamin Jowett (hereafter referred to as BJ).
34. BL ADD. 45783, ff. 222–223, July 1870, FN to BJ.
35. Woodham-Smith, *FN*, pp. 212–213, Nov. 1857, Mai to Nightingales.
36. Cook, *Life of FN*, vol. 1, p. 372, Dec. 5, 1857, Parthe to Clarkey.
37. FN, *Ever Yours,* p. 193, Nov. 16, 1857, to McNeill.
38. FN, *Ever Yours,* pp. 195–196, Jan. 6, 1858, to Fanny
39. Wellcome, Claydon copy, MS 9002/f. 9, April 6, 1866, FN to Fanny.
40. FN, *Ever Yours,* pp. 191–192, Nov. 26, 1857, to SH.
41. BL ADD. 45792, ff. 77–78, Jan. 20, 1858, FN to Smith.
42. BL ADD. 45792, f. 80, July or Aug. 1858, FN to Smith.

Chapter 18

1. Woodham-Smith, *FN*, p. 193, Feb. 9, 1857, FN, private note.
2. FN, *Ever Yours, FN*, p. 240, Sept. 6, 1862, to Fanny.
3. Cook, *Life of FN*, vol. 1, p. 499, Feb. 1861, Parthe to Clarkey.
4. Cook, *Life of FN*, vol. 1, p. 412, 1861, FN to Harriet Martineau.
5. BL ADD. 43396, f. 77, Sept. 16, 1859, EH to FN.
6. Woodham-Smith, *FN*, p. 220, 1861, FN to Clarkey.
7. Cook, *Life of FN*, vol. 1, p. 375, May 13, 1858, McNeill to FN.
8. Cook, *Life of FN*, vol. 1, p. 481, FN to WEN.

9. Cook, *Life of FN*, vol. 1, p. 503, June 13, 1860, FN to WEN.

10. Geoffrey Faber, *Jowett*, p. 22, commonly recited at Oxford.

11. Woodham-Smith, *FN*, p. 237, FN.

12. BL ADD. 45785, ff. 224–225, circa Jan. 1894, FN.

13. BL ADD. 45785, f. 222, Jan. 7, 1894, FN.

14. Jowett, *Dear Miss Nightingale*, p. 105, Sept. 1866, BJ to FN.

15. Cook, *Life of FN*, vol. 1, p. 215, 1863, FN.

16. FN, *Ever Yours*, p. 212, Sept. 27, 1860, to engineer R. Rawlinson, member of Sutherland's Crimean sanitation commission.

17. FN was the first woman elected a member of the international statistical congress.

18. FN, *Ever Yours*, p. 208, July 12, 1860, to WEN.

19. Cook, *Life of FN*, vol. 1, p. 431, July 1860, FN to Hilary.

20. Cook, *Life of FN*, vol. 1, p. 448, Harriet Martineau.

21. Florence Nightingale, *Notes on Nursing: What It Is and What It Is Not*, V. Stretkowicz, ed., p. 35.

22. FN, *Notes on Nursing*, p. 5.

23. FN, *Notes on Nursing*, p. 21.

24. FN, *Notes on Nursing*, pp. 30–31.

25. FN, *Notes on Nursing*, pp. 32–33.

26. FN, *Ever Yours*, p. 198, July 1858, to Lady McNeill.

27. BL ADD. 43396, f. 59, May 13, 1858, FN to EH.

28. FN, *Collected Works*, vol. 1, p. 732, Feb. 20, 1861, to Fanny.

29. A lined, cushioned, wickerwork armchair with head- and footrest hung between two large wheels. In back, the carriage had handles for pushing, in front could be harnessed to a pony.

30. Arthur Clough, *The Correspondence of Arthur Hugh Clough*, F. L. Mulhauser, ed., vol. 2, p. 542, Feb. 5, 1858, Clough to FN.

31. Cook, *Life of FN*, vol. 1, p. 380, Sept. 25, 1858, WEN to FN.

32. Woodham-Smith, *FN*, p. 222, June 13, 1859, SH to FN.

33. When FN and SH initiated reform, seventeen of every hundred men died in the army at home; forty years later three of every hundred men died.

34. Woodham-Smith, *FN*, p. 222, Nov. 1859, FN.

35. Woodham-Smith, *FN*, p. 223, Hilary to Nightingales.

36. Woodham-Smith, *FN*, p. 223, Sept. 1859, Fanny to Parthe.

37. FN, *Ever Yours*, p. 240, Sept. 6, 1862, to Fanny.

38. FN, *Ever Yours*, p. 205, March 20, 1860, to EH.

39. BL ADD. 43396, ff. 67–68, Aug. 3, 1859, EH to FN.

40. Woodham-Smith, *FN*, p. 240, Sept. 1, 1860, FN to her cousin Blanche Clough.

41. Cook, *Life of FN*, vol. 1, p. 495, FN to Smith.

42. BL ADD. 45783, ff. 222–223, July 1870, FN to BJ.

43. BL ADD. 45783, ff. 222–223, July 1870, FN to BJ.

44. Cook, *Life of FN*, vol. 2, p. 15, Dec. 13, 1861, FN to Clarkey.

45. Woodham-Smith, *FN*, p. 242, Dec. 1860, FN to SH.

Chapter 19

1. BL ADD. 45783, ff. 222–223, July 1870, FN to BJ.

2. Woodham-Smith, *FN*, p. 243, June 2, 1861, FN to Smith.

3. Woodham-Smith, *FN*, p. 244, March 1861 or 1862, FN to Hilary.

4. Lesser, *Clarkey*, pp. 165–166, Feb. 5, 1862, Clarkey to FN.

5. Woodham-Smith, *FN*, p. 260, Dec. 13, 1861, FN to Clarkey.

6. FN, *Ever Yours*, p. 228, Nov. 18, 1861, to McNeill.

7. FN, *Ever Yours*, pp. 215–216, Dec. 5, 1860, to EH.

8. BL ADD. 43396, f. 153, Aug. 12, 1861, EH to FN.

9. Woodham-Smith, *FN*, p. 219, Nov. 1857, FN to McNeill.

10. *Between Ourselves: Letters between Mothers and Daughters*, Karen Payne, ed., March 7, 1862, FN to Fanny.

11. *Between Ourselves*, March 7, 1862, FN to Fanny.

12. FN, *Collected Works*, vol. 1, p. 177, July 28, 1865, to Fanny.

13. *Clough Correspondence*, vol. 2, pp. 595–596, Aug. 4, 1861, Blanche Clough to Arthur Clough.

14. Cook, *Life of FN*, vol. 1, p. 407, Sept. 24, 1861, FN to Martineau

15. FN, *Ever Yours*, pp. 224–226, Sept. 10, 1861, to Farr.

16. Woodham-Smith, *FN*, p. 249, Aug. 14, 1861, FN to Smith.

17. Woodham-Smith, *FN*, p. 250, Nov. 1861, EH to FN.

18. FN, *Ever Yours*, pp. 235–238, March 7, 1862, to Fanny.

19. FN, *Ever Yours*, pp. 223–224, Aug. 21, 1861, to WEN.

20. Cook, *Life of FN*, vol. 1, p. 399, FN.

21. Later expanded and published as *Army Sanitary Administration and Its Reform under the late Lord Herbert.*

22. Cook, *Life of FN*, vol. 1, p. 407, Sept. 24, 1861, FN to Martineau.

23. *Between Ourselves*, March 7, 1862, FN to Fanny.

24. Cook, *Life of FN*, vol. 2, p. 11, Dec. 11, 1860, FN to Smith.

25. FN, *Ever Yours*, p. 228, Nov. 18, 1861, to McNeill.

26. *Clough Correspondence*, vol. 2, p. 606, Nov. 23, 1861, F. W. Newman to B. Clough.

27. *Clough Correspondence*, vol. 2, p. 608, Nov. 29, 1861, B. Clough to C. E. Norton.

28. *The Life and Letters of Benjamin Jowett,* E. Abbott and L. Campbell, eds., vol. 1, p. 370, Oct., 1864, BJ to FN.

29. Jowett, *Dear Miss Nightingale*, pp. 28–29, Summer 1863, BJ to FN.

30. FN, *Ever Yours*, p. 233, Dec. 21, 1861, to Clarkey.

31. Lessser, *Clarkey*, p. 169, March 1862, Clarkey to Hilary.

32. Cook, *Life of FN*, vol. 2, p. 4, Sept. 10, 1861, FN to Farr.

33. Cook, *Life of FN*, vol. 2, p. 5, Oct. 21, 1861, Milnes to FN.

34. Cook, *Life of FN*, vol. 2, pp. 9–10, Dec. 13, 1861, FN to Clarkey.

35. BL ADD. 45844, f. 3, May 7, 1867, private note, FN.

36. BL ADD. 45790, f. 243, Jan. 6, 1862, FN to WEN.

37. FN, *Notes on Nursing*, p. 194.

38. The wit and charm of beautiful Recamier, hostess of a prominent Parisian salon, attracted early nineteenth-century France's most prominent political and literary figures, including many opponents of Napoléon. He exiled her in 1805. After Napoléon's defeat (1815), Recamier returned to Paris and resumed her salon.

39. FN, *Ever Yours*, pp. 229–233, Dec. 13, 1861, to Clarkey

40. Cook, *Life of FN*, vol. 1, p. 506, 1861, FN to Hilary.

41. Woodham-Smith, *FN*, p. 243, April 20, 1861, FN to WEN.

42. Cook, *Life of FN*, vol. 2, pp. 81–82, Dec. 15, 1863, FN to Moore.

43. Cook, *Life of FN*, vol. 2, pp. 81–82, Dec. 15, 1863, FN to Moore.

44. *FN-Moore Friendship,* pp. 110–111, Dec. 15, 1863, FN to Moore.

45. Wellcome, Claydon copy, MS 9001/51, Aug. 20, 1864, FN to Fanny.

46. FN, *Ever Yours*, pp. 235–238, March 7, 1862, to Fanny.

47. BL ADD. 45844, f. 6, May 7, 1867, private note, FN.

48. FN, *Ever Yours*, p. 229, Nov. 19, 1861, McNeill to FN.

49. Woodham-Smith, *FN*, p. 264, May 24, 1862, FN to WEN.

50. Cook, *Life of FN*, vol. 2, p. 30, FN to Martineau.

51. FN, *Ever Yours*, p. 245, Sept. 21, 1863, to Galton.

52. Cook, *Life of FN*, vol. 2, p. 60, March 7, 1862, EH to FN.

53. Woodham-Smith, *FN*, pp. 267–268, 1862, FN to Edwin Chadwick, sanitary reformer.

54. Woodham-Smith, *FN*, p. 268, 1863, FN.

55. Cook, *Life of FN*, vol. 2, p. 76, Jan. 3, 1864, FN to Moore.

56. Cook, *Life of FN*, 2, vol. 2, p. 78, FN.

Chapter 20

1. FN, *Wit and Wisdom*, p. 38.

2. Lesser, *Clarkey*, p. 160, Sept. 27, 1861, Mohl to Martin.

3. FN, *Ever Yours*, p. 261, Nov. 5, 1864, private note.

4. FN, *How People May Live and Not Die in India*, p. 4, 1863.

5. *FN-Moore Friendship*, pp. 125–126, Oct. 31, 1864, FN to Moore.

6. FN, *India*, p. 4.

7. FN, *India*, p. 6.

8. FN, *India*, p. 11.

9. FN, *India*, p. 5.

10. FN, *Ever Yours*, pp. 242–244, Sept. 19, 1863, to Sir Harry Verney (referred to as HV).

11. BL ADD. 43396, f. 190, May 26, 1863, FN to EH.

12. Known as the Red Book, *Observations by Miss Nightingale* became a bible for politicians and India administrators.

13. FN, *Ever Yours*, pp. 242–244, Sept. 19, 1863, to HV.

14. Cook, *Life of FN*, vol. 2, p. 41, July 10, 1863, Stanley to FN.

15. Cook, *Life of FN*, vol. 2, p. 42, July 24, 1863, Stanley to FN.

16. *FN-Moore Friendship*, pp. 125–126, Oct. 31, 1864, FN to Moore.

17. Cook, *Life of FN*, vol. 2, pp. 105–106, July 12, 1866, FN to Mohl.

18. BL ADD. MS 45783, ff. 27–28, May 24, 1865, FN to BJ.

19. Cook, *Life of FN*, vol. 2, p. 103, Jan. 1864, FN to Selina.

20. BL ADD. 43397, ff. 195–196, Jan. 1864, FN to Selina.

21. FN, *Ever Yours*, p. 262, 1865, to Clarkey.

22. FN, *Ever Yours*, p. 263–264, July 12, 1865, to BJ.

23. BL ADD. 45844, f. 4, Aug. 1866, private note, FN.

24. BL ADD. 45844 f. 6, May 7, 1867, private note, FN.

25. Cook, *Life of FN*, vol. 2, July 9, 1865, BJ to FN.

26. FN, *Ever Yours*, pp. 263–264, July 12, 1865, to BJ.

27. FN, *Ever Yours*, p. 274, Feb. 1867, BJ to FN.

28. FN, *Ever Yours*, pp. 263–264, July 12, 1865, to BJ.

29. Suttee (also spelled "sati") called for a widow to immolate herself on her husband's funeral pyre.

30. Cook, *Life of FN*, vol. 2, p. 44, FN to Lawrence.

31. Cook, *Life of FN*, vol. 2, p. 44, Dec. 1, 1863, Stanley to FN.

32. FN, *Ever Yours*, p. 268, Sept. 12, 1870, to Sutherland.

33. Cook, *Life of FN*, vol. 2, p. 89, Oct. 4, 1865, FN to Clarkey.

34. FN, *Collected Works,* vol. 8, p. 604, March 9, 1887, to Sarah Sutherland.

35. FN, *Collected Works*, vol. 1, p. 193, 1868, to Fanny.

36. FN, *Ever Yours*, pp. 235–238, March 7, 1862, to Fanny.

37. Cook, *Life of FN*, vol. 2, p. 116, June 1866, WEN to Fanny.

38. FN, *Ever Yours*, p. 360, July 30, 1864, to Mohls.

39. BL ADD. 43397, f. 326, Aug. 23, 1864, FN to Clarkey.

40. Cook, *Life of FN*, vol. 2, p. 89, July 30, 1864, FN to Clarkey.

41. FN, *India*, pp. 8–10.

42. Cook, *Life of FN*, vol. 2, p. 50, June 12, 1864, Lawrence to FN and FN to Lawrence.

43. FN, *Ever Yours,* pp. 235–238, March 7, 1862, to Fanny.

44. FN, *Ever Yours*, p. 283, July 30, 1865, to Galton.

45. FN, *Ever Yours*, pp. 284–287, July 31, 1867, to Sir Stafford Northcote.

46. Cook, *Life of FN*, vol. 2, p. 152, Aug. 20, 1867, FN to Sutherland.

47. Woodham-Smith, *FN*, p. 292, Aug. 20, 1867, FN to Sutherland.

48. Wellcome, Claydon copy, MS 9002/f. 176, Sept. 8, 1867, FN to WEN.

49. Woodham-Smith, *FN*, p. 293, July 1867, FN to Clarkey.

Chapter 21

1. FN, *Notes on Nursing*, pp. 164 and 172, respectively.

2. FN, *Wit and Wisdom*, p. 20.

3. FN, *Ever Yours,* pp. 287–289, and *Florence Nightingale: Letters and Reflections*, Rosemary Hartill, ed., p. 52, Aug. 11, 1867, to John Stuart Mill. He eventually convinced FN to join the society's general committee, but she never played an active part.

4. Seymer, *FN's Nurses*, pp. 32–33, 1867, FN to Mary Jones, superintendent of Anglican St. John's House, which gave some on-the-job nurse training. Jones and FN became friends over Jones's decision to send nurses to the Crimea to serve under FN. She respected Jones's judgment and consulted her closely on nursing issues.

5. Baly, *FN and the Nursing Legacy*, p. 35, May 24, 1859, FN to SH.

6. Seymer, *FN's Nurses*, p. 25, FN.

7. Rosalind Nash, *A Short Life of Florence Nightingale*, p. 34, FN. Daughter of Nightingale's double cousin My Boy Shore, Nash was very close to her "aunt Florence."

8. Cook, *Life of FN*, vol. 2, pp. 351–352, Philippa Hicks, later matron at a major London hospital.

9. Margaret Tabor, *Pioneer Women*, p. 108.

10. Woodham-Smith, *FN*, p. 235.

11. Cook, *Life of FN*, vol. 2, p. 125, William Rathbone.

12. Mid-Victorian workhouse infirmaries (large public hospitals supported by local taxation to accommodate the sick poor) rivaled Scutari's pre-FN Barrack hospital. But inmates were mentally as well as physically ill. A policeman usually patrolled the wards at night; ignorant old female paupers, often thieves, drunks, or prostitutes, did the nursing, if such one could call it, "supervised" by inexpert parish officers. Mainly concerned to protect their hands, these officials wore gloves in the wards.

13. Baly, *As Miss Nightingale Said*, p. 9, 1867, FN to Rathbone.

14. Cook, *Life of FN*, vol. 2, pp. 125–126, Sept. 3, 1864, FN to Moore.

15. Cook, *Life of FN*, vol. 2, p. 126, June 13, 1868, FN to Clarkey.

16. Cook, *Life of FN*, vol. 2, p. 127, May 12, 1865, Rathbone to FN.

17. Woodham-Smith, *FN*, p. 297, Feb. 7, 1865, FN to McNeill.

18. Baly, *As Miss Nightingale Said*, p. 49, 1865, FN to Charles Villiers, president of Britain's poor-law board.

19. FN, *Ever Yours,* pp. 270–274, July 6, 1866, to Chadwick.

20. Wellcome. Claydon copy, MS 9002/f. 16, May 30, 1866, FN to Fanny.

21. Wellcome, Claydon copy, MS 9002/f. 49, Aug. 11, 1866, FN to Fanny.

22. Wellcome, Claydon copy, MS 9002/f. 69, July 9, 1867, FN to Fanny.

23. Wellcome, Claydon copy, MS 9001/f. 44, July 28, 1865, FN to parents.

24. Wellcome, Claydon copy, MS 9002/f. 52, Aug. 13, 1866 FN to WEN.

25. Wellcome. Claydon copy, MS 9002/f. 33 June 23, 1866, FN to Fanny.

26. Cook, *Life of FN*, vol. 2, p. 119, Aug. 21, 1866, FN to Clarkey.

27. FN, *Ever Yours, FN*, pp. 311–312, probably 1870, to WEN.

28. Woodham-Smith, *FN*, p. 326, Summer 1868, FN to Clarkey.

29. FN, *Ever Yours*, pp. 311–312, probably 1870, to WEN

30. Cook, *Life of FN*, vol. 2, p. 163, private note, FN.

31. *Suggestions on the Subject of Providing, Training, and Organizing Nurses for the Sick Poor in Workhouse Infirmaries.*

32. Wellcome, Claydon copy, MS 9002/f. 105, Feb. 26, 1867, FN to Fanny.

33. "Una and the Lion" appeared in *Good Words* (June 1868.)

34. FN, *Ever Yours, FN*, p. 295–297, June 13, 1868, to WEN.

35. Cook, *Life of FN*, vol. 2, p. 141, March 20 and April 30, 1867, FN to Clarkey.

36. FN, *Ever Yours, FN*, p. 295–297, June 13, 1868, to WEN.

37. FN, *Ever Yours*, pp. 297–298, May 1, 1868, to Galton.

38. FN, *Ever Yours*, pp. 248–250, undated confidential letter to Mary Jones.

39. FN, *Ever Yours*, pp. 248–250, undated confidential letter to Mary Jones.

40. London's premier food emporium.

41. BL ADD. 45790, f.365, April 25, 1868, FN to Fanny.

42. *FN-Moore Friendship*, p. 156, April 30, 1868, FN to Parthe.

43. FN, *Notes on Nursing*, p. 81.

44. Wellcome, Claydon copy, MS 9002/f. 150, May 7,1867, FN to Fanny.

45. *FN-Moore Friendship*, pp. 125–126, Oct. 31, 1864, FN to Moore.

46. *FN-Moore Friendship*, p. 16, Moore to FN.

47. BL ADD. 45783, ff. 11–12, July 1862, FN to BJ.

48. BL ADD. 43396, ff. 193–194, July 19, 1865, FN to EH.

49. Cook, *Life of FN*, vol. 2, p. 188, Dec. 25, 1868, FN to McNeill.

50. Wellcome, Claydon copy, MS 9002/f. 69, July 9, 1867, FN to Fanny.

51. Cook, *Life of FN*, vol. 2, p. 188, Dec. 25, 1868, FN to McNeill.

52. FN, *Ever Yours*, pp. 362–363, April 19, 1876, to H. Acland, physician and sanitarian.

53. FN, *Ever Yours*, pp. 226–227, Sept. 24, 1861, to Martineau.

54. Baly, *FN and the Nursing Legacy*, p. 73, May 1, 1867, FN to Mary Jones.

55. Baly, *FN and the Nursing Legacy*, p. 74, Dec. 22, 1867, FN to Bowman.

56. Wellcome, Claydon copy, MS 9002/f. 171, Aug. 6, 1867, FN to Fanny.

57. FN, *Introductory Notes on Lying-in Institutions*, p. 67.

58. American physician Oliver Wendell Holmes and Hungarian obstetrician Ignaz Semmelweiss had already recommended (1843 and 1861, respectively) that medical students change their aprons and wash their hands in chloride of lime before each obstetric examination, but their ideas were not widely accepted.

59. FN, *Ever Yours*, pp. 277–282, April 16, 1867, to HV.

60. Woodham-Smith, *FN*, p. 305, July 1871, Sutherland to FN.

61. Strachey, *The Cause*, excerpt from *Cassandra*, pp. 395–396, FN

Chapter 22

1. Mistress of witticisms.

2. Jowett, *Dear Miss Nightingale*, p. 153, Nov. 9, 1868, BJ to FN.

3. Cook, *Life of FN*, vol. 2, p. 301, Parthe.

4. Woodham-Smith, *FN*, p. 356, 1867, WEN.

5. BL ADD. 45849, f.40, Nov. 13, 1888, FN.

6. Lesser, *Clarkey*, p. 183, Oct. 8, 1868, Clarkey to Martin.

7. The Franco-Prussian War arose from Prussian chancellor Bismarck's ploy to use war with France to prod the South German states to join a pan–German union under Prussia, and French emperor Napoléon III's drive to regain public approval through military victory.

8. Cook, *Life of FN*, vol. 2, p. 200, Dec. 20, 1870, FN to Sutherland.

9. FN, *Ever Yours*, pp. 308–310, Aug. 7, 1870, to Mrs. Colonel Cox, a war relief organizer working in northern France.

10. FN, *Ever Yours*, pp. 308–310, Aug. 7, 1870, to Cox.

11. Society to Help the Wounded.

12. Woodham-Smith, *FN*, p. 322, 1872, Jean Henry Dunant.

13. FN, *Ever Yours*, pp. 330–337, Oct. 15, 1872, to Henry Bonham-Carter (hereafter referred to as HBC).

14. Jowett, *Dear Miss Nightingale*, p. 229, June 22, 1872, BJ to FN.

15. FN, *Ever Yours, FN*, pp. 326–327, July 8, 1872, to Sutherland.

16. Cook, *Life of FN*, vol. 2, p. 251, FN to a friend.

17. Cook, *Life of FN*, vol. 2, p. 252, Philippa Hicks.

18. Cook, *Life of FN*, vol. 2, p. 257, June 21, 1873, FN to Mohl.

19. FN, *Ever Yours*, pp. 344–345, May 9, 1873, to Mary Jones.

20. Cook, *Life of FN*, vol. 2, pp. 303–305, account by one of the Nightingale school's pupils and frequent visitor to 10 South Street.

21. Cook, *Life of FN*, vol. 2, p. 257, one of FN's matrons in a hospital outside London.

22. FN, *Ever Yours*, pp. 342–343, May 23, 1873, to Rachel Williams.

23. Woodham-Smith, *FN*, p. 337, 1879, FN to her cook.

24. FN, *Collected Works*, vol. 8, p. 538, Feb. 8, 1873, to Selina.

25. Wellcome, Claydon copy, MS 9002/f. 69 Nov. 5, 1866, FN to HV.

26. Wellcome, Claydon copy, MS 9006/f. 1, Jan. 10, 1873, FN to HV.

27. Wellcome, Claydon copy. MS 9006/f. 18, Mar 3, 1873, FN to HV.

28. Wellcome, Claydon copy, MS 9006/f. 14, Feb. 23, 1873, FN to HV.

29. Mystics combined an active life with religious practice

30. BL ADD. 45847, Aug. 20, 1877, diary, FN.

31. Woodham-Smith, *FN*, p. 327, private note, FN.

32. FN, *Ever Yours*, p. 351, Dec. 19 and 30, 1873, to Mohl.

33. Cook, *Life of FN*, vol. 2, p. 307, 1873, Clarkey to Mohl.

34. FN, *Ever Yours*, p. 351, Dec. 19 and 30, 1873, to Mohl.

35. FN, *Ever Yours*, pp. 330–337, Oct. 15, 1872, to HBC.

36. FN, *Ever Yours*, pp. 346–350, Oct. 1, 1873, to HBC.

37. Wellcome, Claydon copy, MS 9006/f. 66, Jan. 8, 1874, FN to Parthe.

38. Wellcome, Claydon copy, MS 9006/f. 70, Feb. 4, 1874, FN to Verneys.

39. BL ADD. 43396, f. 223, Feb. 3, 1874, FN to EH.

40. Wellcome, Claydon copy, MS 9006/f. 64, Jan. 6, 1874, FN to Parthe.

41. Wellcome, Claydon copy, MS 9006/f. 68, Jan. 16, 1874, FN to HV.

42. Cook, *Life of FN*, vol. 2, p. 238, Feb. 3, 1874, FN.

43. Wellcome, Claydon copy, MS 9006/f. 99, May 26, 1874, FN to Parthe.

44. Wellcome, Claydon copy, MS 9001/f. 83, Nov. 23, 1864, FN to Fanny.

45. Wellcome, Claydon copy, MS 9006/f. 64, Jan. 6, 1874, FN to Parthe.

46. FN, *Ever Yours*, p. 353, June 25, 1874, to Parthe.

47. Wellcome, Claydon copy, MS 9006/f. 131, Nov. 2, 1874, FN to Verneys.

48. BL ADD. 43396, f.223, Feb. 3, 1874, FN to EH.

49. FN, *Ever Yours*, p. 353, June 25, 1874, to Parthe.

50. Cook, *Life of FN*, vol. 2, p. 235, Jan. 13, 1874, Milnes to FN.

51. Jowett, *Dear Miss Nightingale*, p. 251, Jan. 8, 1874, BJ to FN.

52. Woodham-Smith, *FN*, p. 331, June 8, 1874, FN to Clarkey.

53. Woodham-Smith, *FN*, p. 332, May, 1873, FN to Mohl.

54. *FN-Moore Friendship*, p. 178, Dec. 30, 1874, FN to Williams.

55. BL ADD. 43396, f.223, Feb. 3, 1874, FN to EH.

56. FN, *Collected Works*, vol. 8, p. 541, April 18, 1874, to Mrs. Compton, Selina's relative and close friend.

57. Cook, *Life of FN*, vol. 2, p. 236, Feb. 3, 1874, FN to Mohls.

58. Cook, *Life of FN*, vol. 2, p. 319, Feb. 7, 1878, FN to Clarkey.

59. Cook, *Life of FN*, vol. 2, p. 319, Aug. 6, 1876, FN to Clarkey.

60. FN, *Ever Yours*, pp. 353–354, Aug. 22, 1874, to Verneys.

61. BL ADD. 45795 ff.149–150, Feb. 6, 1880, FN to Shore's daughter Rosamund.

62. Woodham-Smith, *FN*, p. 333, June 8, 1875, FN to Clarkey.

63. Woodham-Smith, *FN*, p. 333, June 8, 1875, FN to Clarkey.

Chapter 23

1. Cook, *Life of FN*, vol. 2, p. 160, April 3, 1869, Lawrence to FN.

2. *Life and Letters of Benjamin Jowett*, E. Abbott and L. Campbell, eds., vol. 1, pp. 431–432, May 28, 1867, BJ to FN.

3. In great matters in general

4. Cook, *Life of FN*, vol. 2, pp. 212–213, Oct. 16, 1879, Clarkey to FN.

5. Woodham-Smith, *FN*, p. 339, Sept. 13, 1879, FN to Clarkey.

6. Cook, *Life of FN*, vol. 2, p. 313, Feb. 5, 1880, FN to Mai.

7. FN, *Notes on Nursing*, p. 79.

8. Cook, *Life of FN*, vol. 2, pp. 313–314.

9. BL ADD. 45847, f. 47 Nov. 20–21, 187, diary, FN.

10. BL ADD. 45847, Dec. 12–13, 1877, diary, FN.

11. FN, *Collected Works*, vol. 8, p. 589, Dec. 6, 1875, to Clarkey.

12. Cook, *Life of FN*, vol. 2, p. 186, FN.

13. FN, *Ever Yours*, pp. 292–294, Sept. 18, 1867, to Lawrence.

14. FN, *Ever Yours*, pp. 292–294, Sept. 18, 1867, to Lawrence.

15. FN, *Ever Yours*, pp. 292–294, Sept. 18, 1867, to Lawrence.

16. FN, *Ever Yours,* pp. 292–294, Sept. 18, 1867, to Lawrence.

17. Cook, *Life of FN,* vol. 2, p. 169, June 24, 1868, Napier to FN.

18. Cook, *Life of FN,* vol. 2, p. 170, Sept. 3, 1868, Napier to FN.

19. FN, *Ever Yours,* pp. 306–308, April 1, 1870, to Mohl.

20. FN, *Ever Yours,* pp. 306–308, April 1, 1870, to Mohl.

21. Woodham-Smith, p. 316, Napier to FN.

22. FN, *Ever Yours,* pp. 306–308, April 1, 1870, to Mohl.

23. Prepared at the social science association's request, Nightingale's paper was presented by a proxy to the annual meeting.

24. Cook, *Life of FN,* vol. 2, p. 277, Oct. 28, 1874, FN to Salisbury.

25. Cook, *Life of FN,* vol. 2, p. 281.

26. Woodham-Smith, p. 319, Sept. 1868, FN to Mohls.

27. *Jowett Letters,* vol. 1, p. 423, June 1867, BJ to FN.

28. BL ADD. 45847 f. 2, Oct. 1877, diary, FN.

29. BL ADD. 45847, Sept. and Nov. 1877 et passim, diary, FN.

30. Cook, *Life of FN,* vol. 2, p. 284, Nov. 27, 1877, FN to Milnes.

31. FN, *Ever Yours,* pp. 357–359, Oct. 5, 1875, to Salisbury.

32. October 1878 issue of *Nineteenth Century* magazine.

33. FN, *Ever Yours,* pp. 369–375, Feb. 1878, FN to Sir Louis Mallet. Permanent under-secretary of state for India, he sympathized with FN.

34. FN, *Ever Yours,* pp. 369–375, Feb. 1878, to Mallet.

35. Cook, *Life of FN,* vol. 2, p. 296, Aug. 11, 1874, BJ to FN.

36. FN, *Collected Works,* vol. 8, p. 542, March 3, 1879, to Compton.

37. Cook, *Life of FN,* vol. 2, p. 323, Feb. 2, 1880, FN to Pringle.

38. FN, *Collected Works,* vol. 1, p. 209, Feb. 4, 1880, to Parthe.

39. Reid, *Life of Houghton,* vol. 2, pp. 389–391, May 18, 1880, FN to Milnes.

40. Cook, *Life of FN,* vol. 2, p. 324, March 28, 1880, FN to Pringle.

41. FN, *Ever Yours,* pp. 360–361, Dec. 13, 1875, to Frost.

42. BL ADD. 45844, f.59, Nov. 26–27, 1891, private note, FN.

43. BL ADD. 45844, f. 50, Jan. 9, 1891, private note, FN.

Chapter 24

1. Cook, *Life of FN,* vol. 2, pp. 321–322, Dec. 31, 1879, BJ to FN.

2. Woodham-Smith, p. 341, June 30, 1881, FN to Clarkey

3. FN, *Ever Yours,* pp. 385–387, May 6, 1881, *To the Nurses and Probationers of St. Thomas's Hospital.*

4. FN, *Ever Yours,* pp. 380–381, Aug. 1881, to Home Sister Mary Crossland.

5. FN, *Ever Yours,* pp. 201–403, May 7, 1887, to John Croft, M.D.

6. FN, *Ever Yours,* pp. 387–388, Aug. 1, 1881, to Williams.

7. Cook, *Life of FN,* vol. 2, p. 337, May 5, 1883, Lord Wantage to FN.

8. Cook, *Life of FN,* vol. 2, p. 335, Nov. 13, 1882, FN.

9. Cook, *Life of FN,* vol. 2, p. 236, Nov. 18, 1882, Mrs. Gladstone.

10. Cook, *Life of FN,* vol. 2, p. 336.

11. Cook, *Life of FN,* vol. 2, pp. 348–350, Hicks.

12. FN, *Ever Yours,* p. 396, Dec. 2, 1884, to Williams.

13. FN, *Ever Yours,* pp. 408–409, May 21, 1888, to Munro.

14. BL ADD. 68883, f. 128, Feb. 13, 1885, FN to Fred Verney.

15. BL ADD. 45844, f. 45, Feb. 1–2, 1890, private note, FN.

16. BL ADD. 43396, Feb. 24, 1890, f.226, FN to EH.

17. BL ADD. 43396, March 15, 1890, f.235, EH to FN.

18. 1880–1884.

19. FN, *Ever Yours,* pp. 382–384, April 14, 1881, to Ripon.

20. 1883. Named for Courtney Ilbert. He had visited FN to discuss his proposed bill before leaving for India to join Ripon's executive council as legal advisor.

21. Wellcome, Claydon copy, MS 9002/f. 152, May 11, 1867, FN to Parthe.

22. Woodham-Smith, p. 348, Aug. 5, 1887, FN to Mai.

23. BL ADD. 45793, f.225, 1890, FN to Shore Smiths.

24. Reid, *Life of Houghton,* vol. 2, pp. 389–391, May 18, 1880, FN to Milnes.

25. FN, *Ever Yours,* p. 391, Feb. 5, 1883, FN to HV.

26. Woodham-Smith, p. 340, Jan. 1881, HV to FN.

27. Woodham-Smith, p. 358, 1896, FN to F. Verney.

28. Woodham-Smith, p. 359, 1888, M. Verney to FN.

29. Woodham-Smith, p. 359, Sept. 8, 1887, M. Verney to FN.

30. BL ADD. 45795, f. 165, Aug. 22, 1881, FN to Rosamund Shore Smith.

31. BL ADD. 68882, f. 83, Sept. 25, 1873, Fred Verney to FN.

32. FN, *Collected Works*, vol. 1, p. 360, Feb. 11, 1883, to Parthe.

33. FN, *Collected Works*, vol. 1, p. 375, June 21, 1886, to Parthe.

34. FN, *Collected Works*, vol. 1, p. 361, Aug. 6, 1883, to Parthe.

35. FN, *Ever Yours*, p. 395, Oct. 1, 1884, to Groundsell.

36. FN, *Collected Works*, vol. 1, p. 395, Feb. 4, 1889, to Parthe.

37. FN, *Collected Works*, vol. 1, p. 602, May 20,1890, to HV.

38. FN, *Collected Works*, vol. 1, p. 663, May 20, 1890, to M. Verney.

39. Cook, *Life of FN*, vol. 2, p. 382, May 15, 1890, HV to FN.

40. Cook, *Life of FN*, vol. 2, p. 384, Nov., 1983, *Rural Hygiene*, FN.

Chapter 25

1. Cook, *Life of FN*, vol. 2, pp. 321–322, Dec. 31, 1879, BJ to FN.

2. Cook, *Life of FN*, vol. 2, p. 409, FN.

3. FN, *Ever Yours*, p. 437, March 10, 1897, to Edmund Verney.

4. Cook, *Life of FN*, vol. 2, p. 409, FN.

5. Woodham-Smith, *FN*, p. 357, 1889, FN.

6. FN, *Ever Yours*, p. 437, March 10, 1897, to E. Verney.

7. Woodham-Smith, *FN*, p. 363, March 1897, FN to HBC.

8. Cook, *Life of FN*, vol. 2, p. 410, Oct. 16, 1897, FN to Louis Shore Nightingale. A bronze bust cast from Steell's original sits at the entrance to the Florence Nightingale Museum in the grounds of St. Thomas's Hospital.

9. Later published as *Woman's Mission*.

10. *Selected Writings of Florence Nightingale*, Lucy Seymer, ed, p. 355, excerpt from *Sick-Nursing and Health-Nursing*.

11. Written for the Leeds conference of women workers.

12. FN, *Selected Writings*, p. 378, excerpt from *Health Teaching in Towns and Villages Rural Hygiene*.

13. FN, *Selected Writings*, pp. 395–396, excerpt from *Health Teaching in Towns and Villages Rural Hygiene*.

14. FN, *Ever Yours*, pp. 427–428, Aug.16, 1893, to F. Spencer, superintendent of Edinburgh royal infirmary.

15. FN, *Ever Yours*, pp. 427–428, Aug. 16, 1893, to Spencer.

16. FN, *Selected Writings*, pp. 333–334, excerpt from *Nursing the Sick*.

17. Woodham-Smith, *FN*, p. 352, FN.

18. Woodham-Smith, *FN*, p. 352, 1890, FN.

19. Seymer, *FN's Nurses*, p. 109, FN.

20. FN, *Ever Yours,* pp. 431–432, Aug. 4, 1896, FN to J. Roundell, author whose books included one on Agnes Jones.

21. Baly, *FN and the Nursing Legacy*, p. 193, FN.

22. Cook, *Life of FN*, vol. 2, p. 365, 1893, FN.

23. Cook, *Life of FN*, vol. 2, p. 360, May 1892, FN to BJ.

24. FN, *Ever Yours,* pp. 425–426, Jan. 18, 1893, to H. Acland, M.D.

25. Cook, *Life of FN*, vol. 2, pp. 356–357, April 20, 1889, FN to HBC.

26. BL ADD. 45844, f.64, Feb. 7, 1892, private note, FN.

27. Seymer, *Florence Nightingale's Nurses*, p. 112, FN.

28. Cook, *Life of FN*, vol. 2, p. 387, July 1891.

29. Cook, *Life of FN*, vol. 2, p. 398, Oct. 16, 1890, BJ to FN.

30. Jowett, *Dear Miss Nightingale*, pp. 208–209, May 16, 1871, BJ to FN.

31. Cook, *Life of FN*, vol. 2, p. 399, Sept. 18, 1893, BJ to FN.

32. Cook, *Life of FN*, vol. 2, p. 399, FN.

33. Woodham-Smith, p. 361, May 12, 1895, FN.

34. Cook, *Life of FN*, vol. 2, p. 415, Nov. 3–4, 1893, FN.

35. Cook, *Life of FN*, vol. 2, pp. 405–406, 1896, FN.

36. Cook, *Life of FN*, vol. 2, p. 404, Jan. 1897, FN to Galton.

37. Cook, *Life of FN*, vol. 2, p. 404, Sept. 1895, FN to HBC.

38. Woodham-Smith, *FN,* p. 357, 1889, FN.

39. BL ADD. 45849, July 18, 1888, FN.

40. Woodham-Smith, *FN,* p. 357, 1889, FN.

41. Woodham-Smith, *FN,* p. 357, 1889, FN.

42. BL ADD. 45844, f. 59, Nov. 26–27, 1891, private note, FN.

43. FN, *Ever Yours*, p. 423, Feb. 8, 1892, to Rosamund Shore Smith.

44. Woodham-Smith, *FN*, p. 364, 1900, FN.

45. Cook, *Life of FN*, vol. 2, p. 418.

46. Cook, *Life of FN*, vol. 2, p. 421, Feb. 1910, Pringle.

Afterword

1. First verse of hymn "The Son of God Goes Forth to War," words by Reginald Heber, music by Henry Cutler.

2. Alexandra, wife of king Edward VII.

3. Second son of Florence's intimates Sidney and Liz Herbert. Their sons inherited the Pembroke title from their uncle, Sidney's elder brother. Liz outlived Flo by three months.

4. Cook, *Life of FN*, vol. 2, p. 301, Parthe.

Select Bibliography

Archives

Nightingale Papers, British Library, London
Nightingale Papers, Wellcome Library, London
Nightingale Papers, Claydon House, Buckinghamshire

Primary Sources

Beddoe, John, M.D. *Memories of Eighty Years*. Bristol: J. W. Arrowsmith, 1910.

Blackwell, Dr. Elizabeth. *Pioneer Work in Opening the Medical Profession to Women*. London: Longmans, Green and Co., 1895.

Blackwood Lady Alicia. *A Narrative of Personal Experiences and Impressions during a Residence on the Bosphorus throughout the Crimean War*. London: Ballantyne Press, 1881.

Bunsen, Baroness Frances. *A Memoir of Baron Bunsen*. London: Longmans, Green and Co., 1868.

Calthorpe, Somerset. *Letters from Headquarters, by an Officer on the Staff*. London: Hamish Hamilton, Ltd., 1979.

Carlyle, Thomas. *The Collected Letters of Thomas Carlyle and Jane Welsh Carlyle*. R. C. Sanders, ed. Durham, NC: Duke University Press, 1985.

Clifford, Henry. *Henry Clifford, V.C.: His Letters and Sketches from the Crimea*. C. Fitzherbert, ed. London: Michael Joseph, 1956.

Darwin, Emma. *A Century of Family Letters, 1792–1896*. Henrietta Litchfield, ed. London: John Murray, 1915.

Davis Elizabeth. *The Autobiography of Elizabeth Davis, a Balaclava Nurse*. Jane Williams, ed. London: Hurst & Blackett, 1857.

Duberly, Frances Isabella. *Mrs. Duberly's War; Journal and Letters from the Crimea, 1854–1856*. Christine Kelly, ed. Oxford: Oxford University Press, 2007.

Eastlake, Lady. *Journals and Correspondence of Lady Eastlake*. John Murray, London: 1895.

Evelyn, George Palmer. *A Diary of the Crimea*. Cyril Falls, ed. London: Duckworth & Co., Ltd., 1954.

Franks, Sergeant-Major Henry. *Leaves from a Soldier's Notebook*. Essex, England: C. W. Poole & Sons Ltd., 1904.

Gaskell, Elizabeth C. *The Letters of Mrs. Gaskell*. J. A. V. Chapple and Arthur Pollard, eds. Manchester: Manchester University Press, 1966.

_____. *Further Letters of Mrs. Gaskell*. John Chapple & Alan Shelston, eds. Manchester: Manchester University Press, 2000.

Goodman, Margaret. *Experiences of an English Sister of Mercy*. London: Smith, Elder and Co., 1862.

Gowing, Timothy. *Voice from the Ranks*. Kenneth Fenwick, ed. London: The Folio Society, 1954.

Higginson, General Sir George. *Seventy-One Years of a Guardsman's Life*. London: Smith, Elder & Co., 1916.

Hornby, Lady. *Constantinople During the Crimean War*. London: Richard Bentley, 1863.

_____. *In and Around Stamboul*. London: Richard Bentley, 1858.

Howe, Julia Ward. *Reminiscences, 1819–1899*. New York: Houghton Mifflin and Company, 1899.

Jowett, Benjamin. *Dear Miss Nightingale*. V. Quinn and J. Prest, eds. Oxford: Clarendon Press, 1987.

Lawson, George. *George Lawson, Surgeon in the Crimea; the Experiences of George Lawson Recorded in Letters to His Family.* Victor Bonham-Carter and Monica Lawson, eds. London: Constable & Co., Ltd., 1968.

Nightingale, Florence. *Cassandra.* Myra Stark, ed. New York: The Feminist Press, 1979.

_____. *Cassandra* and other selections from *Suggestions for Thought.* Mary Poovey, ed. New York: New York University Press, 1992.

_____. *Collected Works of Florence Nightingale.* Lynn McDonald, ed. Waterloo, ON: Wilfred Laurier University Press, 2001.

_____. *Ever Yours, Florence Nightingale: Selected Letters.* Martha Vicinus and Bea Nergaard, eds. London: Virago, 1990.

_____. *Florence Nightingale at Harley Street; Her Reports to the Governors of her Nursing Home.* London: J. M. Dent & Sons, Ltd., 1970.

_____. *Florence Nightingale: Her Wit and Wisdom.* E. R. Barritt, ed. Mount Vernon, NY: Peter Pauper Press, 1975.

_____. *Florence Nightingale in Egypt and Greece: Her Diary and "Visions."* M. D. Calabria, ed. Albany: State University of New York Press, 1997.

_____. *Florence Nightingale in Rome. Letters Written in the Winter of 1847–1848.* Mary Keele, ed. Memoirs of the American Philosophical Society, vol. 143, Philadelphia, 1981.

_____. *Florence Nightingale; Letters from the Crimea.* Sue. M. Goldie, ed. New York: Mandolin, 1997.

_____. *How People May Live and Not Die in India.* London: Emily Faithfull, 1863.

_____. *Introductory Notes on Lying-in Institutions.* London: Longmans, Green, and Co., 1871.

_____. *Letters from Egypt: A Journey on the Nile 1849–1850.* Anthony. Sattin, ed. London: Barrie & Jenkins, 1987.

_____. *Notes on Nursing: What It Is and What It Is Not.* Victor Stretkowicz, ed. London: Scutari Press, 1992.

_____. "People (The) of India." *Nineteenth Century,* no. 4 (1878), pp. 193–221.

_____. *Suggestions for Thought to the Searchers After Truth Among the Artisans of England: Selections.* M. D. Calabria and J. A. Macrae, eds. Philadelphia: University of Pennsylvania Press, 1994.

Osborne, Sidney Godolphin. *Scutari and Its Hospitals.* London: Dickinson Brothers, 1855.

Pincoffs, Peter, M.D. *Experiences of a Civilian in Eastern Military Hospitals.* London: Williams & Norgate, 1857.

Portal, Robert. *Letters from the Crimea.* Winchester: Warren & Son, 1900.

Robinson, Frederick, M.D. *Diary of the Crimean War.* London: Richard Bentley, 1856.

Russell, William H. *The British Expedition to the Crimea, 1858.* London: G. Routledge & Co., 1858.

_____. *The Great War with Russia; the Invasion of the Crimea.* London: G. Routledge & Sons, Limited, 1895.

_____. *Russell's Dispatches from the Crimea 1854–1856.* Nicholas Bentley, ed. London: Trinity Press, 1966.

_____. *The War, from the Landing at Gallipoli to the Death of Lord Raglan.* London: G. Routledge & Co., 1856.

Skene, James H. *With Lord Stratford in the Crimean War.* London: Richard Bentley and Son, 1883.

Soyer, Alexis. *A Culinary Campaign: Being Historical Reminiscences of the Late War.* M. Barthrop & E. Ray, eds. England: Southover Press, 1995.

Sterling, Colonel Sir Anthony. *The Story of the Highland Brigade in the Crimea.* London: John Maqueen, 1897.

Taylor, Frances Margaret. *Eastern Hospitals and English Nurses — a Narrative of Twelve Months' Experience in the Hospitals of Koulali and Scutari by a Lady Volunteer.* London: Hurst & Blackett, 1856.

Terrot, Sarah Anne. *Nurse Sarah Anne; with Florence Nightingale at Scutari.* R.G. Richardson, ed. London: John Murray, 1977.

Two Brothers (A. and G. H. Money). *Sevastopol. Our Tent in the Crimea; and Wandering in Sevastopol.* London: Richard Bentley, 1856.

Verney, Frances Parthenope, Lady. *Life and Death of Athena. An Owlet from the Parthenon.* San Francisco: Grabhorn-Hoyem, 1970.

Secondary Sources

Abbott, Evelyn, and Campbell Lewis. *Life and Letters of Benjamin Jowett*. London: John Murray, 1897.

Allen, Donald R. "Florence Nightingale: Toward a Psychohistorical Interpretation." *Journal of Interdisciplinary History* 6 (1) 1975, pp. 23–45.

Anderson. Olive. *A Liberal State at War : The Crimea*. Great Britain: Macmillan and Company Limited, 1967.

Baly, Monica. *As Miss Nightingale Said*. London: Bailliere Tindall, 1997.

_____. *Florence Nightingale and the Nursing Legacy*. London: Whurr Publishers, 1997.

Barnsley, R. E. "Teeth and Tails in the Crimea." *Medical History*, vol. 7, 1963.

Baylen, J. O. "The Florence Nightingale/Mary Stanley Controversy: Some Unpublished Letters." *Medical History*, vol. 18, 1974.

Beales, Derek. *From Castlereagh to Gladstone, 1815–1855*. New York: Norton & Co., 1969.

Blake, R. L. V. French. *The Crimean War*. London: Leo Cooper, 1971.

Bonham-Carter, Victor. *In a Liberal Tradition: A Social Biography*. London: Constable and Company, Ltd., 1960.

Bostridge, Mark. *Florence Nightingale: The Making of an Icon*. London: Farrar, Straus and Geroux, 2008.

Boyd, Nancy. *Three Victorian Women Who Changed Their World: Josephine Butler, Octavia Hill, Florence Nightingale*. New York: Oxford University Press, 1982.

Briggs, Asa. *Victorian People*. Chicago: University of Chicago Press, 1955.

Bulloch, Vern. *The Care of the Sick: The Emergence of Modern Nursing*. New York: Prodist, 1978.

_____, ed. *Florence Nightingale and Her Era; a Collection of New Scholarship*. New York: Garland Publishing, Inc., 1990.

Chorley, Catherine. *Arthur Hugh Clough: The Uncommitted Mind*. Oxford: Clarendon Press, 1962.

Compton, Piers. *Colonel's Lady and Camp Follower: The Story of Women in the Crimean War*. New York: St. Martin's Press, 1970.

Concannon, Helena. *The Irish Sisters of Mercy in the Crimean War*. Irish Messenger Office, 1950.

Cook, Sir Edward T. *The Life of Florence Nightingale*. London: Macmillan & Co., 1913.

Cope, Zachary. *Florence Nightingale and the Doctors*. London: Museum Press, Ltd., 1958.

Crewe, Robert Offley Ashburton Crewe. "Richard Monckton Milnes, Lord Houghton." *Fortnightly Review,* April, 1929.

Davies, Celia, ed. *Rewriting Nursing History*. London: Croom Helm Ltd., 1980.

Dossey, Barbara. "Florence Nightingale; Her Crimean Fever and Chronic Illness." *Journal of Holistic Nursing* 16, no. 2 (June 1998), American Holistic Nurses' Association.

_____. *Florence Nightingale: Mystic, Visionary, and Healer*. Springhouse, PA: Springhouse Publishing, 2000.

Douglas, G., and G. D. Ramsey, eds. *The Panmure Papers*. London: Hodder and Stoughton, 1908.

Eyler, John M. *Victorian Social Medicine: The Ideas and Methods of William Farr*. Baltimore: Johns Hopkins University Press, 1979.

Faber, Geoffrey. *Jowett*. Cambridge: Harvard University Press, 1957.

French, Yvonne. *Florence Nightingale, 1820–1910*. London: Hamish Hamilton, Ltd., 1954.

Finlayson, Geoffrey. *The Seventh Earl of Shaftesbury*. London: Eyre Methuen, 1981.

Gill, Gillian. *Nightingales: The Extraordinary Upbringing and Curious Life of Miss Florence Nightingale*. New York: Random House, 2004.

Goldsmith, Margaret L. *Florence Nightingale: The Woman and the Legend*. London: Hodder and Stoughton, 1937.

Gorham, Deborah. *The Victorian Girl and the Feminine Ideal*. Bloomington: Indiana University Press, 1982.

Grey, Elizabeth. *The Noise of Drums and Trumpets; W. H. Russell Reports from the Crimea*. London: Longman Group Limited, 1971.

Herbert, R. G. *Florence Nightingale—Saint, Reformer or Rebel*. FL: Robert R. Krieger Publishing Co., 1981.

Hibbert, Christopher. *The Destruction of Lord Raglan*. London: Longmans, 1961.

Hodder, Edwin. *The Life and Work of the Seventh Earl of Shaftesbury.* London: Cassell & Company, Limited, 1887.

Huxley, Elspeth. *Florence Nightingale.* London: Weidenfeld & Nicholson, 1975.

Jenking, Christine. *The Bracebridge Family and Atherstone Hall.* Bracebridge Court, Atherstone, Warwickshire, 2001.

Kinglake, A. W. *The Invasion of the Crimea.* London: William Blackwood and Sons, 1877–1888.

Kirby, P. R. *Sir Andrew Smith.* Cape Town and Amsterdam: Gothic Printing Company Limited, 1965.

Kopf, Edwin W. "Florence Nightingale as Statistician." *Publication of the American Statistical Association,* vol. 15, 1916–1917.

Lambert, Andrew, and Stephen Badsey. *The Crimean War: The War Correspondents.* Dover, NH: Allen Sutton Publishing, 1994.

Lammond, D. *Florence Nightingale.* London: The Camelot Press, Ltd., 1935.

Lane Poole, S. *The Life of Lord Stratford de Redcliffe.* London: Longmans, Green, and Co., 1890.

Leslie, Shane. "Forgotten Passages in the Life of Florence Nightingale." *The Dublin Review* 161, no. 323 (October 1917).

_____. *Henry Edward Manning.* London: Burns Oates & Washbourne Limited, 1921.

Lesser, Margaret. *Clarkey: A Portrait in Letters of Mary Clarke Mohl (1793–1883).* Oxford: Oxford University Press, 1984.

Macalister, Florence Stewart. *Memoir of the Right Hon. Sir John McNeill. G. C. B., and of His Second Wife, Elizabeth Wilson.* London: John Murray, 1910.

Mackerness, E. D. "Frances Parthenope, Lady Verney." *Journal of Modern History,* 20, no. 2, June 1958.

Mitford, Nancy, ed. *The Stanleys of Alderly.* London: Chapman & Hall, Ltd., 1939.

Mitra, S. M. *Life of Sir John Hall.* London: Longmans, Green and Co., 1911.

Mulhauser, Frederick L., ed. *The Correspondence of Arthur Hugh Clough.* Oxford: Clarendon Press, 1957.

Nash, Rosalind. *A Short Life of Florence Nightingale.* New York: The Macmillan Company, 1938.

_____. *A Sketch of the Life of Florence Nightingale.* London: Society for Promoting Christian Knowledge, 1937.

Neff, Wanda Fraiken. *Victorian Working Women.* New York: Columbia University Press, 1929

Nuttall, P. "The Passionate Statistician." *Nursing Times* 79, no. 39, 1983.

O'Malley, I. B. *Florence Nightingale, 1820–1856: A Study of Her Life Down to the End of the Crimean War.* London: Thornton Butterworth, Limited, 1931.

O'Meara, Kathleen. *Madame Mohl: Her Salon and Friends.* Boston: Roberts Brothers, 1886.

Payne, Karen, ed. *Between Ourselves: Letters between Mothers and Daughters, 1750–1982.* Boston: Houghton Mifflin Company, 1983.

Pickering, George, M.D. *Creative Malady.* New York: Oxford University Press, 1974.

Pope-Henessy, J. *Monckton-Milnes — the Years of Promise 1809–1850, the Flight of Youth 1851–1855.* London: Constable and Company, Ltd, 1949–1952.

Quinn, E. V., and J. M. Prest, eds. *Dear Miss Nightingale: A Selection of Benjamin Jowett's Letters.* Oxford: Clarendon Press, 1987.

Quinton, Lord. *Richard Monckton Milnes, Founders and Followers.* London: Sinclair-Stevenson, 1992.

Reid, Sir T. Wemyss. *The Life, Letters and Friendships of Richard Monckton Milnes, First Lord Houghton.* London: Cassell & Company, Limited, 1890.

Rover, Constance. *Love, Morals and the Feminists.* London: Routledge & Kegan Paul, 1970.

Roxburgh, Sir Ronald. "Miss Nightingale and Miss Clough: Letters from the Crimea." *Victorian Studies* 13, no. 1, Sept. 1969, pp. 71–89.

Royle, Trevor. *Crimea.* New York: Palgrave Macmillan, 2000.

St. Aubyn, Giles. *Queen Victoria, A Portrait.* London: Sinclair-Stevenson Limited, 1991.

Seymer, Lucy. *Florence Nightingale's Nurses: The Nightingale Training School, 1860–1890.* London: Pitman Medical Publishing Co., Ltd., 1960.

_____. *Selected Writings of Florence Nightingale.* Lucy Seymer, ed. New York: Macmillan, 1954.

Shepherd, John. *The Crimean Doctors*. Great Britain: Liverpool University Press, 1991.

Shiman, Lilian Lewis. *Woman and Leadership in Nineteenth-Century England*. London: The Macmillan Press Ltd., 1992.

Showalter, Elaine. *The Female Malady: Women, Madness, and English Culture, 1830–1980*. New York: Pantheon Books, 1985.

_____. "Florence Nightingale's Feminist Complaint." *Signs* 6 (1981), pp. 395–412.

Simpson, Mary Charlotte Muir. *Letters & Recollections of Julius & Mary Mohl*. London: Keegan Paul, Trench & Co., 1887.

Small, Hugh. *Florence Nightingale, Avenging Angel*. London: Constable and Company Limited, 1998.

Smith, F. B. *Florence Nightingale: Reputation and Power*. New York: St. Martin's Press, 1982.

Stanmore, Lord. *Sidney Herbert, Lord Herbert of Lea*. London: John Murray, 1906.

Sticker, Anna. *Florence Nightingale: Curriculum Vitae*. Diakoniewerk, Düsseldorf-Kaiserswerth, 1965.

Strachey, Lytton. *Eminent Victorians*. Oxford: Oxford University Press, 2003.

Strachey, Ray. *The Cause*. Bath, Great Britain: Cedric Chivers, Ltd., 1928.

Sullivan, Mary C., ed. *The Friendship of Florence Nightingale and Mary Claire Moore*. Philadelphia: University of Pennsylvania Press, 1999.

Summers, Anne. *Angels and Citizens: British Women as Military Nurses, 1854–1914*. London: Routledge & Keagan Paul, 1988.

_____. "Pride and Prejudice: Ladies and Nurses in the Crimean War." *History Workshop*, Issue 16 (Autumn 1983), The Camelot Press, Great Britain.

Surtees, Virginia. *The Ludovisi Goddess; the Life of Louisa, Lady Ashburton*. Great Britain: Michael Russell, Ltd., 1984.

Tabor, Margaret Emma. *Pioneer Women*. London: The Sheldon Press, 1927.

Temperley, Harold William Vazeille. *England and the Near East: The Crimea*. London: Longmans, Green, 1936.

Thomson, David. *England in the Nineteenth Century*. Baltimore, MD: Penguin Books, 1963.

Tooley, Sarah A. *The Life of Florence Nightingale*. London: Cassell and Co., 1910.

Tresham Lever. *The Letters of Lady Palmerston*. London: John Murray, 1957.

Vicinus, Martha, ed. *Suffer and Be Still: Women in the Victorian Age*. Bloomington: Indiana University Press, 1972.

Watts, Brenda, and Eleanor Winyard. *The History of Atherstone*. North Warwickshire, England: Mercia Publications, 1988.

Widerquist, JoAnn G. "Florence Nightingale's Calling." *Second Opinion* 17, no. 3, January 1992.

Woodham-Smith, C.B.F.G. *Florence Nightingale*. London: Constable, 1950.

Woodward, E. L. *The Age of Reform, 1815–1870*. Oxford: The Clarendon Press, 1962.

Young, D. A. "Florence Nightingale's Fever." *British Medical Journal,* December 1995.

Young, Edward J. "An Overview of Human Brucellosis." *Clinical Infectious Diseases*, 21, no. 2, Aug. 1995, pp. 283–289.

Young, G.M. *Portrait of an Age*. Oxford: Oxford University Press, 1964.

Newspapers and Periodicals

Punch. October–December 1854, January–February 1855, Punch Publications, London.

The Times. October 12, 13, 14, 1854, R. Nutkins, London.

Index

Numbers in **bold italics** indicate pages with photographs.